ARMS TRANSFERS IN THE MODERN WORLD

ARMS TRANSFERS IN THE MODERN WORLD

Edited by
Stephanie G. Neuman
and
Robert E. Harkavy

PRAEGER

PRAEGER SPECIAL STUDIES • PRAEGER SCIENTIFIC

Library of Congress Cataloging in Publication Data
Main entry under title:

Arms transfers in the modern world.

Bibliography: p.
Includes index.
1. Munitions—Addresses, essays, lectures.
2. International relations—Addresses, essays,
lectures. I. Neuman, Stephanie G. II. Harkavy,
Robert E.
HD9743.A2A75   382'.45'6234   78-19778
ISBN 0-03-045361-5

Published in 1979 by Praeger Publishers
A Division of Holt, Rinehart and Winston/CBS, Inc.
383 Madison Avenue, New York, New York 10017 U.S.A.

© 1979 by Praeger Publishers

9 038 987654321
Printed in the United States of America

PREFACE

In recent years, the international trade in arms has become the focus of considerable worldwide attention. Some unofficial estimates place the global value of arms transfers for 1977-78 at over $20 billion—a 100 percent increase (in constant prices) in a decade. Although the transfer of military technology is not a new feature of international relations, some recent trends merit particular attention: first, there has been a rapid extension of arms to the less developed countries, particularly to OPEC states in the Middle East; second, advanced "high technology" weapons systems have been diffusing more rapidly throughout the world; and third, there has been some growth of new indigenous weapons development and production capabilities, which has, in turn, expanded the number of arms suppliers.

The implications of these developments are not fully clear. It is apparent, however, that never before has the supply of arms been as important an instrument of diplomacy as it is today. Prior to World War II, the arms trade was dominated by private suppliers and significantly removed from governmental direction. Arms supply relationships were, therefore, often surprisingly at variance with overall diplomatic alignments. During the early, bipolar cold war years, the situation changed markedly. Both superpowers dominated the arms markets of client states closely tied to them by formal alliances and/or ideological ties. Given the dependence of most recipients on super-power military protection and largess at that time, arms transfers usually further supplemented the diplomatic leverage of the suppliers. Former colonies, many formally or informally still dominated by metropole states, added weight to the bipolar character of the system.

In recent years, arms supply diplomacy has become more complicated. Increasing multipolarity, a growing number of states not formally allied with either major power bloc, a decline in the ideological basis for global alignments, a larger number of arms producers, and the expanding economic power of many developing nations (based on control of oil and other raw materials) all appear to have enlarged the leverage of most nations in the arms market. Many of them are now able to bargain effectively with the major arms suppliers, using raw materials, trade and investment markets, strategic access, and overall diplomatic influence as items of exchange. As a result, arms supplies have become the single most weighty diplomatic instrument in the hands of major powers, and arms supply relationships are now perhaps the most useful indicators of the immediate political orientation of the world's nations.

Numerous other corollary developments suggest the complex role arms transfers play in the modern world. Victory or defeat in regional conflicts may now be determined by third-party supplier states which are not directly involved in the conflict, as recent events in the Horn of Africa demonstrate. Supplier states sometimes involuntarily dragged into regional and internal matters may find themselves escalating local disputes into big power conflicts. Infusions of advanced new weapons technology, and/or major increases in the magnitude of weapons shipments can result in sudden destabilizations of regional balances. Some small states organize lobbyists to directly participate in the political process of large supplier states in order to secure a reliable flow of arms to their countries, and are often remarkably successful in doing so. Arms manufacturers in one state may sell arms to groups in other states without the sanction (or sometimes knowledge) of the legitimate governments. Fear of economic or political reprisals from small states (particularly those which have oil reserves) motivates the superpowers to transfer sophisticated weaponry to countries often unable to absorb them. In the less industrialized world, regional opponents sometimes find themselves fighting with weapons obtained from the same sources. Some nations worried about the denial of arms supplies now threaten to acquire nuclear weapons if their arms requests are not adequately met.

These developments in the diplomacy of arms transfers are accompanied by a paradoxical cross-cutting of East-West and North-South cleavages. Major powers continue to compete strenuously for arms markets and the political and economic returns that go with them, while entering into exploratory talks about controlling the global arms flows. Meanwhile, the less industrialized nations give rhetorical support to arms control efforts in the UN and elsewhere, while continuing to increase their arms purchases. Ironically, talk about controls escalates in lock step with the annual rise in figures measuring the dimensions of the world arms trade.

Events such as these defy the old image of the world of hierarchically ordered, impenetrable, rational, sovereign states. Instead they suggest a complicated, interconnected, global network in which the arms traffic becomes a significant actor—at times seeming to take on an independent life of its own.

In the modern world arms transfers are emerging as a separate actor or system operating on all three levels of political activity—domestic, international, and transnational—creating innumerable linkages among them. Seen from this perspective, arms transfers take on a global significance which reaches far beyond the bilateral and multilateral agreements among states which are generally thought to generate the arms traffic.

STATE OF THE LITERATURE

James Rosenau has pointed out that political science as a discipline has yet to accommodate itself to an interdependent and shrinking world.[1] Like the field of political science, the subfield of arms transfers and controls has yet to adjust to the global significance of these developments. National, international, regional, and transnational linkages have not been subjected to systematic, sustained, and comparative inquiry. For the most part, the arms transfer literature has confined itself to asking and answering descriptive questions about who is buying what from whom for how much and how this affects the U.S.-USSR balance. Only recently has the world's attention been drawn to the consequences of arms transfers for other states and regions of the world, and to the complex interrelationship between arms transfers and developments within and among nations. Yet much of the literature still focuses on the mechanics of the arms trade.[2] Researchers also continue to concentrate on one level of analysis or the other—domestic or international—failing to integrate their insights into a broader conceptual framework. What James Rosenau concluded about the field in general is true for the subfield as well. Students of domestic arms politics tend to take the international environment for granted, as if national systems were immune to external influences and in full control of their policy-making process. Students interested in the international traffic in arms tend to make a series of assumptions about the international behavior of national systems, as if all such states responded only to international strategic balances and weapons counts, ignoring the internal, domestic demands that constrain them. The larger theoretical questions and broader analytical perspective the developments described above imply, remain, for the most part, unexplored. How are they related? Do global arms transfers limit the political and

---

1. James N. Rosenau, *Linkage Politics: Essays on the Convergence of National and International Systems* (New York: The Free Press, 1969), p. 2.

2. There are notable exceptions, for example: United States Senate, Committee on Foreign Relations, *U.S. Military Sales to Iran: A Staff Report to the Subcommittee on Foreign Assistance*, July 1976.

economic behavior of governments? What internal influences within states affect the arms decisions of policy makers? How do transnational weapons transactions affect the arms decisions of policy makers? How do transnational weapons transactions affect the functioning of the international system and the stability of individual states? Does the structure of the international system influence the pattern of arms transfers? And in what way does the global nature of the arms trade affect the structure of the international system as a whole—now and in the future?

As technology shrinks the world, increasing communication between diverse peoples, governments, and organizations, the linkage phenomena of the weapons trade are too plentiful and too influential to be ignored. This volume grew out of our conviction that an understanding of the dynamics of arms transfers—and the factors which influence them and their consequences—depends upon adopting a broader, less parochial approach to the subject.

PURPOSE AND SCOPE

It was the intent of the present editors to bring together in one volume essays which address some of these questions. Our organizational inspiration came from J. D. Singer who wrote, in 1961, about the level of analysis problem in international relations:

In any area of scholarly inquiry, there are always several ways in which the phenomena under study may be sorted and arranged for purposes of systemic analysis.... The observer may choose to focus upon the parts or upon the whole, upon the components or upon the system...and while he may choose as his system any cluster of phenomena from the most minute organism to the universe itself, such choice cannot be merely a function of whim or caprice, habit or familiarity.[3]

By organizing the contributions to this volume into a level of analysis framework, and by selecting authors working on some of the still unexplored theoretical and methodological issues relating to arms transfers, it was the editors' intention to produce a volume that in total might begin to make some conceptual order out of a field in conceptual chaos. This is not to suggest that each of the individual contributors succeeds in sorting out the multiple linkages between arms transfers and the national and international systems. This was not their intent or ours, given the pre-theoretical state of the field. Rather we hope that for some of our readers the whole will represent more than the sum of its parts; that the presentation of many arms transfer issues within a general analytical framework will stimulate others to

---

3. J. D. Singer, "The Level of Analysis Problem in International Relations," in *The International System: Theoretical Essays,* eds. Klaus Knorr and Sidney Verba (Princeton: Princeton University Press, 1961), pp. 77-78.

see new relationships and pursue more sophisticated theoretical work in the future. We envision this volume as only a first step in the direction of conceptual order. The systematic exploration of the flow of arms in an interdependent world—one which establishes causal linkages between the several units of analysis—still remains a task to be accomplished.

Given the state of the field, one of our goals as editors was to present arms transfers from as many different perspectives as possible. We therefore solicited contributions from authors with wide-ranging research interests, orientations, and approaches to the subject. Although the articles in this book are subsumed into two broad levels of analysis—international and national—many of the individual essays focus on other units of analysis as well, that is, regional, transnational, and subnational. Furthermore, cutting across the vertical levels of analysis structure of the book, the essays collectively examine not only the consequences arms transfers have for individual states and the international system, but also those factors which determine the character of the arms trade itself. Domestic political, economic, and social influences are considered by some authors; regional, transnational, or international conditions by others. In some chapters arms transfers are treated as the outcome of these factors. In others the dynamics of the arms trade are seen as a source of foreign policy behavior for both suppliers and recipients. In other words, depending on the research interests of the contributors to this volume, weapons transfers are analyzed as both dependent and independent variables. For example, Chapters 4-8, 10, and 11 treat the arms trade as an independent variable, analyzing the effects weapons have on either the domestic and foreign policies of states, or on regional and international stability; Chapters 13, 14, and 16 explore the consequences arms transfers have on the infrastructure of recipients. On the other hand, Chapters 9, 12, 15, and 17 concentrate on factors influencing the arms transfer policies of suppliers and recipients. In these essays, arms transfers are viewed as a dependent variable.

The approach of most of the authors is conceptual rather than quantitative. Although empirical data to support theoretical generalizations have been included where appropriate and available, the lack of such data has not inhibited the contributors from asking questions or from using anecdotal materials for explanatory purposes. Nor has the existence of quantitative data determined the limits of our investigation. At this primitive, exploratory stage of conceptualization, the primary concern of the editors has been to (1) establish relevant variables, (2) raise theoretically interesting questions, and (3) stimulate further research on the implications and consequences of conventional arms transfers.

The reader will undoubtedly be struck by the widely different normative positions the authors in this book bring to their work. As discussed in the Conclusion, the arms transfer literature has been dominated by the "utopian" school of thought[4] which perceives military technology in largely negative and mischievous terms. Given this bias, the editors tried to present in this volume a more balanced picture of the ideological spectrum of opinions relating to arms transfers by including representatives of various political persuasions. We leave it to the judgment of the reader to decide where "truth" lies.

The group of articles included in the present study are offered as a sampling of new research on arms transfers. With the exception of Chapters 6 and 7 (Burt and Rosen), all essays are published here for the first time. The book is divided into four main sections. Part One provides an overview of some of the conceptual, methodological, and definitional problems facing the field. Chapter 1, by Edward A. Kolodziej, develops a general typology based on the level of analysis framework which examines the various factors influencing the arms transfer policies of states. Designed as an heuristic device, he offers it here as a catalyst for more research and thought on the subject. Richard H. Wilcox, in Chapter 2, explores some of the definitional problems facing arms control advocates and analysts. Chapter 3, by Edward Fei, discusses some of the difficulties associated with compiling data sets and their interpretation. Fei explains why data on arms transfers and military expenditures are not easy to understand, and examines some of the methodological choices which precede data collection.

Part Two describes the international arms system—how it works and its consequences for international and domestic politics. Michael Mihalka, in Chapter 4, draws a picture of the changing pattern of arms acquisitions at the global and regional levels. Using tabular data, he describes the changing nature of weapons transfers between suppliers and recipients, and their trends over time. C. I. Hudson, Jr., in Chapter 5, analyzes the effect of new weapons technology on international stability, and Richard Burt, in Chapter 6, examines the relationship between new conventional weapons and nuclear proliferation. The proliferation of new land-based technologies and their implications for regional balances is the focus of Steven J. Rosen's Chapter 7. The final essay in Part Two, by Robert Harkavy (Chapter 8) investigates the relationship between arms transfers and the major powers' competition for overseas strategic access.

Parts Three and Four focus on the national level of analysis. They are concerned with the individual states, the factors affecting the behavior of suppliers and recipients in arms-transfer decision making, and the consequences of these decisions for their internal development and foreign policies. Jo Husbands, in Chapter 9, attempts to unravel the U.S. foreign

---

4. For a more detailed discussion on the ideological differences between "utopians" and "realists," see Stephanie G. Neuman, "Detente in the Middle East: Appearance or Reality?" *Intellect* 103, no. 2365 (April 1975): 432–38.

military sales decision-making process and the bureaucratic factors that influence it. The economics of the arms trade—balance of payments, domestic employment, amortization of production costs, maintenance of a "warm" arms production base, etc., and the role these variables play in U.S. arms-transfer decisions is the concern of Anne Cahn in Chapter 10. William Lewis investigates the reciprocal influence/leverage relationship between suppliers and recipients of arms in Chapter 11; and Ingemar Dörfer, in Chapter 12, analyzes the role industrial interest groups and the services play in U.S. arms-transfer decisions. His essay deals specifically with the F-16 fighter plane "deal of the century" involving the United States and Norway, Denmark, the Netherlands, and Belgium.

Part Four of this volume discusses arms transfers from the foreign policy perspective of the recipients. In Chapter 13, Stephanie Neuman explores the relationship between arms transfers and economic development. Herbert Wulf, in Chapter 14, discusses the relationship between arms transfers, arms production, and dependency in the Third World. Chapter 15, by Geoffrey Kemp, analyzes the constraints, such as lack of basic skills and infrastructure, operating on the political and military capabilities of less developed countries. Ernest W. Lefever writes about the effects of arms transfers and military training on the internal political development and stability of recipients in Chapter 16. Chapter 17, by Michael Moodie, examines the growing indigenous weapons development and production capabilities of some Third World states.

The final chapter, Chapter 18, is a summing up by the editors. The book concludes with an extensive bibliography, compiled by Nicole Ball, which includes articles and books related to arms transfers published since 1945.

– the editors

ACKNOWLEDGMENTS

The editors of *Arms Transfers in the Modern World* are indebted to a number of persons and institutions whose contribution to this volume was invaluable.

Both Cornell and Columbia Universities gave generously of their facilities and we are especially grateful to them. Robert Harkavy spent a postdoctoral year with the Peace Studies Program, Center for International Studies at Cornell University during the period in which this book was edited. The entire staff of the Program is thanked for their material and moral support. We extend particular thanks to Franklin Long, Director of the Peace Studies Program, George Quester, Sean Killeen, Executive Director, and Deborah Ostrander, who handled a variety of administrative tasks in connection with this project. We are also grateful to the Institute for the Study of World Politics whose generous financial assistance helped support Robert Harkavy during the period this book was being prepared.

The staff of the Center for the Social Sciences at Columbia University is also thanked for their assistance. Stephanie Neuman was a Research Associate at the Center when this book was being edited. Harold Watts, Director, Claudia Iredell, Administrator, and William Glaser, Senior Research Associate, were particularly supportive. We are also grateful to Madeline Simonson for her secretarial expertise at moments of crisis.

Helen Danner provided the main secretarial and coordinating assistance. Her work on the index is gratefully acknowledged. We are indebted to her for her patience and stamina. Without her this volume could not have been produced.

We also extend our gratitude to Colonel James Fluhr, Rob Silverstein, and Louis Nebel who contributed helpful comments on portions of the manuscript.

Finally, this acknowledgment would not be complete without a word of thanks to Bruce Warshavsky, our editor at Praeger, who served as midwife for this volume. His advice and support encouraged the editors at every stage of the project. Thanks to all.

CONTENTS

LIST OF TABLES

LIST OF FIGURES

LIST OF ACRONYMS

ACDA	Arms Control and Disarmament Agency
AECB	Arms Export Control Board
AEW	airborne early warning system
AID	Agency for International Development
APC	armored personnel carrier
ATGM	antitank guided missile
AWACS	Airborne Warning and Control System
CIA	Central Intelligence Agency
CENTO	Central Treaty Organization
DIA	Defense Intelligence Agency
DSAA	Defense Security Assistance Agency
FAA	Foreign Assistance Act
FMS	Foreign Military Sales
GDP	gross domestic product
GNP	gross national product
IISS	International Institute for Strategic Studies
LTV	Ling-Temco-Vought
MAAG	Military Assistance Advisory Group
MPLA	Mouvement Populaire Liberation d'Angola
NASA	National Aeronautics and Space Administration
NATO	North Atlantic Treaty Organization
NPT	Non-Proliferation Treaty
OPEC	Organization of Petroleum Exporting Countries
PGM	precision guided munition(s)
POL	petrol, oil, lubricants
SALT	Strategic Arms Limitation Talks
SAM	surface-to-air missile
SEATO	South East Asia Treaty Organization
SIPRI	Stockholm International Peace Research Institute
RPV	remotely piloted vehicle
WMEAT	World Military Expenditures and Arms Transfers

PART ONE

METHODOLOGICAL AND THEORETICAL PROBLEMS

1 ARMS TRANSFERS AND INTERNATIONAL POLITICS: THE INTERDEPENDENCE OF INDEPENDENCE

Edward A. Kolodziej

This chapter addresses a set of related questions: What factors and conditions explain why arms transfers occur or do not occur? What is the quantity and quality of such exchanges? What is the timing, duration, and circumstances of each transaction? These questions do not admit of ready or easy answers. Serious students differ not only in their explanations for transfers but also on how to pose the question, in the first instance, of the *why* of arms transfers. Many studies focus on nation-state or donor-recipient relations. The most thorough of these, SIPRI's (Stockholm International Peace Research Institute) study of Third World transfers, portrays arms transfers as a product of state objectives. It categorizes donors into three purpose-oriented subgroups: those following policies which are hegemonic (searching for security or partial influence, like the USSR and the United States), economic (France), or restrictive (e.g., Sweden, which will not sell to states in conflict). Recipients are divided into those states seeking arms for security, for national integration, or for support of their military establishments.[1]

An early and widely cited study from the Massachusetts Institute of Technology focuses on military factors, such as mission requirements, environmental conditions, degrees of permissiveness or hostility to be encountered, inventory control, and modernization.[2] These factors are selected as keys to determining the size, form, rate, and quality of arms transfers. Others, influenced by the abundant, if conflicting, literature on the "military-industrial complex," emphasize the internal or domestic governmental, bureaucratic, and private industrial forces working to induce arms transfers.[3] Other researchers attribute arms transfers to more general economic factors within and between capitalist societies.[4]

Attempts have been made, moreover, to test the critical importance of systemic factors as determinants of arms transfers. Among the factors that have been examined are the degree of bloc cohesion (bipolarity, multipolarity, etc.), the ideological locus of conflict, the relation of modes of economic intercourse (free or monopolistic markets, etc.) to governmental and private controls over trade, the internationalization of business, and the impact of technological change. These clusters of factors are offered as a partial explanation for four dependent sets of relations: the structure of the supplier market and supplier behavior, donor-recipient patterns of arms transfers, the method or form of transfers dependent on a given type of arms, and the dependence or interdependence exhibited by states at different levels of economic development.[5]

These works, which are as varied and conflicting in conceptualizing arms transfers as in assessing their results, suggest that part of the confusion lies in the twin failure to distinguish sufficiently between the different levels at which arms-transfer relations occur and to integrate these levels into a general framework of analysis that would facilitate a systematic and comprehensive examination of the continuities and discontinuities that exist within and between these levels. A complete explanation of arms transfers, as a subsystem of the international system, requires that neither the special factors that bear immediately on arms-transfer transactions nor the inner dynamics of the arms-transfer subsystem can be sacrificed. Thus, the present chapter attempts to differentiate four levels of analysis, examine the factors that encourage or discourage arms transfers between and within levels, and integrate these elements into a general scheme which is useful for further study, research, and policy analysis.

The notion of arms transfers as a subsystem of international relations needs explanation. Such a subsystem can be conceived as the product of four sets of actor relations: national, subnational, transnational, and international. These relations may be systematically described and evaluated with respect to their contribution to subsystem creation and maintenance. If individual transactions cannot be easily foreseen or predicted—for example, the sale of U.S. arms to the People's Republic of China—there is a high probability, based on the recurring experience of the interwar and post-World War II periods, that actor initiative stemming from one or more of the four specified levels of action will continue to replenish the arms-transfer subsystem, despite the provisional and permutable character of any specific arms-transfer relation composing it.

Actors are distinguished by their composition, principal objectives, and targets of their activity; these are schematized in Figure 1.1. Composition refers to the internal organizational structure of each actor. The nation-state, as actor, primarily includes the ruling political elites of the state, however chosen or appointed, who are formally, if not always effectively, charged with defining the state's exterior relations.

Subnational actors are composed of the large, national private and public bureaucracies that make or use arms ostensibly in the pursuit of national objectives. This military-industrial-administrative-technoscientific complex is identified with the behavior, interests, and objectives of the managerial elites presiding over it. They include not only arms managers (military officer corps) but also managers of arms who design, develop, produce, and sell weapon systems and their support components.

Transnational actors may be divided into two different groups. The first is structured by the relations between multinational corporations, including state-run enterprises, that fabricate and market arms as parts of their economic activities. The second group of transnational actors comprises revolutionary movements, linked, at least in part, through arms transfers to outside third parties, primarily nation-states and their governing elites or other revolutionary groups. Two characteristics distinguish transnational actors, whatever their differences, from other actors: their relations cross national boundaries although their targets may be specific nation-states and their governmental institutions and decision makers and they do not officially possess international legal standing and legitimacy, however much they may influence recognized governmental units. The first element distinguishes them from subnational actors, the second from nation-states and their ruling elites.

International actors are conceived as collective bodies which, while composed of nation-states, have a unique international personality recognized as a single unity within the arms-transfer subsystem. The principal actors under this rubric are alliance organizations, such as NATO and the Warsaw Pact. The United Nations may also be included although its role is circumscribed and negligible.

In many instances the modalities of an actor's behavior, more than its composition, will determine how the actor should be conceived—for example, as a transnational or subnational actor. For example, ostensibly transnational actors, like Northrop, Thomson-Brandt, and Fiat, are also important subnational actors, respectively, in the United States, France, and Italy. Whether these multinationals are viewed as transnational or subnational actors depends critically on the formal quality of the relations they strike with other actors (whether within or between levels), on the substantive nature of these relations (whether political, economic, etc.), and on the targets of their action (whether national, subnational, or foreign elites).

Actor objectives concern the goals sought by a particular actor in

FIGURE 1.1: Arms-Transfer Subsystems

TARGETS: RECIPROCAL ACTOR INFLUENCE

ACTOR	AGENCY	OBJECTIVES
National	Nation-states and national governmental authorities	Security, political influence, economic growth, solvency, full employment 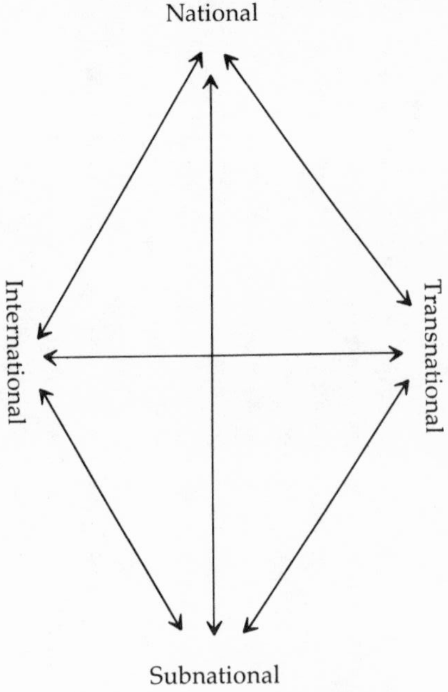
Subnational	Military organizations	Military security
	Industrial and corporate units	Maximum economic gain (profits in market economies or budgetary allocations in controlled economies)
	Technoscientific centers (research groups, universities, institutes)	Service functions for military and private sector in pursuit of new knowledge, techniques, and products
	Governmental bureaucracies	Surveillance and control of other subnationals
Transnational	Multinationals	Maximum economic gain
	Revolutionary movements, nation-states	Political change and new regimes
International	Alliance organizations: NATO, Warsaw Pact	Offense, defense, deterrence; collective political influence; internal management and policing of dependent states

Source: Compiled by the author.

6

entering into a particular arms-transfer agreement. The attribution of objectives to actors outlined in Figure 1.1 should be weighed with caution. These are suggestive and illustrative, and are designed neither to exclude nor to exhaust relevant factors. Under differing circumstances, other objectives than those cited as primary may animate an actor. For example, at one time maximum economic gain may largely explain the behavior of national and multinational corporations; at another, political influence, rather than economic profit, may be more pertinent as an explanatory variable; or, a mix of these and other objectives may explain why an actor behaved in a certain way. The objectives of an actor are operationalized in terms of the desired behavior sought from the targeted actor, and goals are achieved or advanced largely by controlling or manipulating the behavior of other actors. Since targets and objectives are linked by the behavior of the actor being influenced, targets—no less than objectives—change over time in relative importance and duration.

The effort of governmental officials to reestablish France's military production capacity after World War II illustrates the variability of objectives and targets over time. From the end of World War II to the beginning years of the Fifth Republic, the primary objectives of French arms-transfer policy were largely dominated by exterior factors, that is, French security and colonial interests. From roughly the end of the Algerian War to the present, French arms-transfer objectives have shifted to economic gain as a principal motivation. Meanwhile, elected governmental elites have experienced increasing difficulty controlling the military-industrial complex spawned partly by their initiative. As before, nation-states remain important targets of French policy, but the problem of controlling the behavior of subnational actors has also progressively become a target of concern for presidential and parliamentary action and decision. As the arms-transfer objectives of elected elites have become more complex and difficult to harmonize, the targets of their activity have correspondingly expanded in number and variety, horizontally and vertically.

The horizontal and vertical relations generated within and between levels of actors may be grouped into from one to four subcategories of substantive relations: strategic, economic, diplomatic or political, and scientific or technological. Unifying explanations that reduce so complex a phenomenon as arms transfers to one or a small group of factors, like capitalistic expansionism or national military-industrial complexes, ignore the web of real and perceived interdependencies between and within actor levels that are relevant to an understanding of them. In this context, interdependence may be defined as the effect of one actor's actions (or inaction) on the behavior of another, whether at the same level of action or at another; these effects may or may not be perceived by the initiating or receiving actor, or by either of them. The different levels of relations can be shown to be interdependent, but they need not be viewed by analysts or perceived by actors as consciously or purposely organized or directed. The fortuitous conjuncture of these relations often will be as relevant in explaining interdependencies as those intentionally motivated by actor purpose in support of arms transfers.

There is no necessary congruence or coherence between actor perceptions of the causes and conditions of arms transfers and the actual factors that may have been determinant. Real and perceived interdependencies must be accounted for in explaining actor behavior; thus, perceptions of interdependencies and the reactions they prompt, even where none may actually be present, create yet another layer of causality that poses an additional obstacle to our understanding of arms transfers. For example, U.S. shipments of F-5s to North Yemen, to match the Soviet arms buildup in South Yemen, can also be perceived as an effort either to strengthen the American negotiating position in the Strategic Arms Limitation Talks (SALT) by demonstrating the American president's resolve in responding to Soviet intervention in the Middle East and Africa or, at a subnational level of analysis, as a means to reinforce the president's position in Congress, or both. That there may be no effective impact of transferring arms on these intended (or attributed) outcomes is less relevant than that such linkages are perceived and acted upon as if they were real.

Given the limits of space imposed on this analysis, accent will be placed on horizontal relations, that is, on relations between actors at each level of action stipulated in Figure 1.1. This focus does not imply the lesser importance of vertical relations—those between actors at different levels— in explaining arms transfers. Rarely are crucial decisions and actions at one level uninfluenced by those at another. Global conflict between the United States and the Soviet Union at a national level cannot be easily separated from the demands of the military-industrial complexes of these states to develop more and better arms (subnational), from the transfer of weapons to revolutionary groups (transnational), or from interalliance cooperation and competition on arms production and sales (international). To a greater or lesser degree, actors usually aim simultaneously at targets at the same and at different levels of activity. The resulting horizontal and vertical relations, reciprocally reinforcing and intertwined, form the warp and woof of the arms-transfer subsystem, a resistant grid of relations that is stronger than the sum of the individual strands composing it. Concentration on the woof of these relations—their horizontal composition—should not obscure the critical functional importance of the warp—their vertical dimensions; much less is this narrower focus meant to deflect attention from the central object of this discussion, viz., the arms-transfer subsystem that is the evolving product of these myriad interactions.

The categories of actors and actor relations used in this *tour d'horizon* are admittedly porous and permeable; more work (and space) would be needed to perfect them. Notwithstanding these limitations, they still serve the immediate purpose of this analysis: to advance the paradoxical proposition that not only cooperation between actors composing the arms-transfer subsystem but also their competition and conflict encourage its further extension, consolidation, and significance for the operation of the international system.

NATIONAL ACTORS

Strategic Incentives for Arms Transfers

Viewed at the level of state suppliers and recipients in response to their security interests, arms transfers are essentially reciprocal, bargaining relations and cannot be understood, as they are often depicted, as separate unilateral acts of supplying and receiving.[6] Lost from sight in such a view is the fundamentally political character of each sale or transfer, the conjuncture of short- and long-run interests of the parties concerned, and the ongoing process of negotiation, consensus, and conflict within which a particular transfer occurs. Transfers, based on strategic grounds, have two general characteristics. First, suppliers and recipients use each other for their own strategic purposes which may or may not be compatible, that is, each manipulates the other for its own designs. Second, the exchange almost inevitably affects third states with differential impact on the supplier's and recipient's internal and external security relations. Listing strategic objectives on the part of supplier and recipient to explain their behavior obscures the reactive circularity of supplier-recipient behavior and the repercussions of these exchanges whose cumulative effect, ironically, may not be to maximize the security requirements of both parties.

Ideally, arms transfers between states, like alliances in general, mutually enlarge the military power, enhance the diplomatic position, and strengthen the respective regimes of the supplier and recipient. Supplying allies and clients is in principle economically less burdensome and politically less sensitive than stationing troops abroad. The weapons transferred by the United States and the Soviet Union to their allies in Europe since World War II have been based, albeit with different degrees of importance, on these assumptions. If the stationing of U.S. and Soviet armed forces on allied soil serves different aims (the police function of Soviet troops is greater), both have an interest in having strong military allies. On the other hand, European recipients of superpower arms, like West and East Germany in the case of the United States and the Soviet Union, respectively, have been willing to accept arms as a means of gaining access to the military power of their sponsors for their own local needs.

Numerous instances of arms transfers suggest the hypothesis that the divergence of security interests play as much a role in supporting arms transfers as their convergence. These divergences manifest themselves either in bargaining over whether, and in what form, a particular transfer of arms should be made, or in supplier attempts to control the use of weapons once they have been transferred. If the United States encouraged Pakistan, its SEATO ally, to accept arms in the 1950s as part of a global alliance structure to contain Soviet and Chinese expansion, Pakistan's motives in accepting them were focused more on countering Indian military power in South Asia. Similarly, it is very difficult to separate U.S. objectives in sending arms to Greece and Turkey to bolster NATO's southern flank from the conflicting interests of these traditional regional rivals and the utility of U.S. arms to support competing political claims. Soviet arms in Somalia in the 1960s may have served Moscow's varied security aims, but they simultaneously bolstered Somalia's revisionist designs on Ethiopia. The reversal of alignments in the 1970s, with the toppling of the Haile Selassie regime, produced the contradictory outcome of Soviet arms being pitted against each other in the Ogaden war. The Greek-Turkish and the Ethiopian-Somalian examples are repeated in the Pakistani-Indian and Arab-Israeli conflicts. The arming of both sides in a regional conflict risks becoming more the rule than the exception in superpower behavior.

Since alliance ties are essentially conditional, even when strong ideological affinities exist, suppliers often have little or no control over the use of their weapons for the strategic purposes and interests intended by the supplier. Breaking with an ally over unintended or even specifically proscribed use is limited by the interests that prompted the initial transfer. However these interests may be damaged by the untoward use of weapons, they are presumably still relevant despite strains on other issues. Turkey's invasion of Cyprus did not reduce the need for U.S. bases in Turkey, its contribution to NATO defense, or the access it provides to key communications facilities and logistics support. The cutoff of American sales and assistance to Ankara by Congress had more the effect of damaging U.S. security interests than of disciplining or cajoling Turkey to do Washington's bidding. This unintended result is reflected in President Carter's successful efforts to raise the embargo over strong congressional opposition.

If the materials transferred are highly sophisticated, like modern aircraft, or the recipient lacks adequate maintenance, repair capacity, and spare parts, or alternative supplies are not available, the supplier may be able to exercise some control over the recipient's use of its arms. The operability of $ billions of arms sold to Iran and Saudi Arabia depends substantially on the extensive training, maintenance, and support programs administered by American civil and military personnel. The difficulties experienced by Egypt in maintaining the advanced equipment sent by the Soviet Union between 1967 and 1972, before the expulsion of Soviet forces, also suggests some of the constraints of dependency. Egypt has had to seek, with mixed results, spare parts in Yugoslavia, India, North Korea, and even in some Eastern European countries.

Supplier controls can be exaggerated. The recipient may be willing to risk loss of arms support; delays or embargoes in reshipments may have only a long-run effect after the crisis conditions prompting illicit use have passed; the recipient may develop compensatory means to deal with short supplies, such as alternate suppliers, improvement of its own production facilities, or the cannibalization of military equipment for spare parts; or the recipient may be able to influence the decisions on resupply by bringing domestic pressures directly on the supplier.

Israel has been notably successful in using all these strategems. It has presented its suppliers with *faits accomplis* that, while unpalatable, left little room for effective opposition or reprisal. Even after the initial partial embargo against Israel in 1967 and the impounding of 50 Mirage Vs by France, Israel launched an attack against Beirut airport in 1968, using French Super-Frelon helicopters. Its use of cluster bombs in the strike against Palestinian settlements in 1978, in contravention of restrictive accords with the United States, suggests the inability to control a determined ally and client when it feels that its security interests are at stake. Similarly, Libyan Mirage fighters, which were prohibited from being reexported, were flown by Egyptian pilots in the 1973 "Yom Kippur" war.

The search for bases abroad (see, for example, Chapter 8) offers new possibilities for trade-offs between supplier and recipient. The spectrum of interests runs the gamut from a recipient's needs to ensure the supplier's protection and arms, on the one hand, to a simple exchange relation, on the other, in which the supplier's strategic basing needs are bartered for arms and other concessions. Whether arms or bases came first is not always easy to determine. Where strategic interests are shared, where a common adversary has been identified, where there is an agreed-upon military strategy on how to deal with an external threat, arms and bases will be of a fabric. The recipient, more than the supplier, may insist on the presence of foreign troops to guarantee its security. Arms may be accepted (or sought) to assure that the supplier will base its forces on the recipient's soil. U.S. arms in Europe after World War II preceded U.S. troops, and its armed forces and bases on the Continent were hostage to its intentions. U.S. bases in South Korea rest on similar assumptions; it is not surprising, therefore, that the client in Seoul should launch a covert operation to manipulate congressional opinion so that the arms and bases would remain.

Arms transfers are also used to promote regional security. Iran and

Saudi Arabia present contrasting cases for U.S. use of arms transfers to identify its interests with regional powers. Iran actively sought a regional role and in the 1970s has ordered more military equipment than any other NATO ally of the United States. Saudi Arabia, on the other hand, has been drawn into a regional role against its initial predispositions. Having assumed a leadership role, it has subsequently placed greater demands on its suppliers, particularly the United States, for sophisticated equipment than were anticipated. In responding to Saudi requests for F-15s, the United States raised the Middle East arms race to new levels of sophistication and potential lethality, whatever the compensating political advantages of these transfers may be.

Other states have had equally mixed success in developing regional pivot points through arms transfers. If Soviet ties with Cuba have risked nuclear war, they have survived sufficiently to undermine the Western position in Angola and Ethiopia without having necessitated the engagement of Soviet forces beyond an expanded advisory role. Military aid to India, however, has proved less fruitful, and Arab support for Soviet objectives has vacillated, depending on inter-Arab conflicts and fortunes and the status of Arab-Israeli hostilities. France's African position partly depends on its postcolonial basing network and security ties with segments of Francophone Africa, such as Senegal and Chad. The sale of French arms to Libya, however, poses a counterthreat to French troops fighting rebel forces in Chad which are being supplied by Tripoli.

The goal of arresting nuclear proliferation has also been incorporated progressively into the supplier-buyer calculus. Former Secretary of State Henry Kissinger reportedly pressured Pakistan, Iran, and South Korea to discourage the development of a nuclear military capability by alternately threatening to sell or not to sell conventional arms.[7] Opinion is divided on the relation between the proliferation of conventional arms and the enlargement of the nuclear club. Conventional arms are alternately viewed as a bar or a boost to nuclear proliferation. Both views were advanced, for example, in support and in opposition to the sale to Israel in 1975 of Pershing missiles, which are capable of firing nuclear warheads.[8] If there is little evidence to suggest that conventional weapons have encouraged the proliferation of nuclear weapons, there is also little basis for concluding that increasing conventional arms shipments or technology will blunt the threat of more recipients going nuclear. As long as decision makers believe that they will have such an effect and act on that conviction, the net result is likely to encourage more, rather than fewer, transfers.

Political or Diplomatic Incentives for Transfers

Strategic factors are so intimately related to political or diplomatic objectives that it is difficult to separate them without doing violence to the tissue of motives and interests abetting or resisting arms transfers. As an announced objective, regime support would appear to be one of the most pervasive motives underlying arms-transfer behavior of large and small state suppliers. U.S. and Soviet aid to their Western and Eastern allies has rested on the maintenance of friendly regimes in key states, and the cold-war struggle between the United States and the Soviet Union has assumed, through the linkage of arms transfers to regime goals, the equivalent of war by other means. The purchase by Nasser's Egypt of arms from Czechoslovakia in 1954, after the Western powers refused to supply Egyptian forces, appeared to be a Soviet victory since it permitted Moscow to penetrate more deeply into the Middle East than any previous Russian regime. Arms supplies also figured importantly in the Belgian Congo between supporters of Patrice Lumumba (the Soviet Union) and Colonel Mobutu (the United States). The superpowers supplying of rivals for power in Angola similarly fit the past pattern of regime support through arms and other aid. Ethiopia and Somalia in early 1978 may be seen as logical extensions of the ongoing and lethal global political campaign conducted by the United States and the Soviet Union to organize supporters into two loose coalitions divided along general ideological lines.

Small states play the same regime-support game with arms. Saudi Arabian support for the Yemenite monarchy, and for the Barre government in Somalia, or Iranian transfers to Oman suggest that regional powers are as concerned about regime change as the superpowers. Britain supplied indispensable assistance to Malaysia in its struggle with Communist insurgents. France supplies many of its former colonies in sub-Saharan Africa, like Senegal, the Ivory Coast, Togo, and Gabon, with arms to keep friendly regimes in power and has intervened in Gabon, Chad, Zaire, and in the western Sahara to bolster regimes of interest to Paris.

Recipient states, on the other hand, have increasingly attempted to diversify their supply sources to maximize their strategic and diplomatic independence, and in this the Arab states have led the way. Libya, acceding to Algerian counsel, purchased 110 Mirage aircraft from France rather than rely fully on Soviet supplies. Iraq made the same decision when in 1976 it ordered French F-1s and advanced naval aircraft to lessen its dependency on the Soviet Union. Latin American states, once the preserve of the United States, have also sought assistance elsewhere, partly because of the restrictive policies pursued by Washington. Peru has purchased military aircraft from five Western countries (Japan, United States, France, Canada, and Great Britain), but in 1976 the Soviet Union contracted to sell Peru SU-22 aircraft and a large number of tanks. Venezuela, Colombia, Argentina, and Brazil have equally sought to broaden their base of supply and, in the case of the latter two, to develop their own armaments industries.

France's reemergence as an arms producer after World War II was motivated initially by a long-run concern to become increasingly free of United States supplies. Between 1950 and 1964, France received $4.2 billion in military assistance, more than any other state. The creation of a strong defense industry and the *force de frappe* provided military capabilities relied upon by the de Gaulle regime to justify France's withdrawal from NATO, the opening to the the Soviet Union, and a steady attack on the expansionist policies of the United States, France's principal ally. Washington, not Moscow, was portrayed as the immediate threat to French and European interests, given its military and economic power and its global political influence.

Arms are also justified as a means of gaining access to political and military leaders, but the viability of this justification and its weight in the decisions of suppliers are difficult to measure. At a political level this factor would seem to have more significance in regimes ruled by a "strong man" or junta, than in a democracy where political participation is greater and influence more diffuse. The large stocks of Soviet arms—including fighter aircraft, surface vessels, and submarines—which were supplied to Indonesia in the 1960s appear to have been as much a tribute to President Sukarno as a response to Indonesian strategic needs. The fact that much of the equipment could not be operated or serviced effectively was less important than its symbolic and prestige value to the recipient and the subjective benefits derived by the supplier in furnishing Indonesian leaders with modern weapons, symbols of national unity and, paradoxically, self-determination. The subsequent counterrevolution launched against the Indonesian Communist Party by the supporters of General Suharto and the loss of Soviet influence in Indonesia suggest the thinness of the thread that holds arms and political influence together.

The employment of arms to influence the professional officer corps of a foreign state presents a wider range of targets to hit. In regimes run by the military, the subordinate officer of today may well be the strong man of tomorrow. Even if this vague political objective goes unrealized, however, there is always the possibility that the structure of the foreign army, its force levels, and its weapon systems will be shaped by the training programs and arms of the supplier country. Until the middle 1970s, Latin American aid was primarily linked to these overlapping political and military considerations.

Economic and Technological Incentives for Arms Transfers

If strategic and diplomatic factors appear to be the initial determinants of a state's decision to develop an independent armaments capacity, economic and technological considerations rapidly redefine the limits of these imperatives. The efficiencies of series production, balanced runs, and the spread of industrial, research, and development costs over a large number of units furnish powerful incentives to export. Without market outlets, choices must be made between purchasing fewer, and perhaps less advanced, weapons or absorbing these expenses at the cost of other desirable social objectives. In some states, like France, Israel, and Great Britain, the pressures for greater social and economic welfare reinforce the need to find customers for military products. From the perspective of these states, arms exports appear, paradoxically, to be an attractive means to resolve the conflict between internal socioeconomic and external strategic and diplomatic imperatives.

Since the pressures to sell arms are a function of the efficient use of scarce resources, they impact on all economies, liberal (United States), state interventionist (France), and socialist (Soviet Union). The response of a government to arms-sales incentives will vary according to a host of considerations and circumstances, including most immediately the development and the availability of productive resources, the willingness of the government and the population to absorb military expenses as a social cost, and the scale of the military production base that must be kept operating. This cycle of rising arms costs and pressures to export is repeated in greater or lesser degree in each country embarking on an independent armaments industry. The largely unanticipated result of these replications at a national level is the creation at a global level of an overcapacity of military production, the overstocking of weapons in national inventories, and the dumping of excess arms on world markets.

The economic incentives to sell are further reinforced by what might be termed a process of "banalizing" the sale of arms. Military weapons become increasingly perceived, particularly by those producing them, as any other product; arms have a market value and are a potential source of profit. Even when the arms industry operates at an economic loss, arms sales can minimize the losses suffered. From this perspective, promoting sales—in other words, stimulating demand abroad—is a requirement of their development if the means of armaments production are to be efficiently utilized. The arms fairs sponsored by France and Britain are outgrowths of the cost-export push in maintaining a national armaments industry. Depending on opposing domestic political pressures, the United States has, at different periods, actively pursued foreign markets. The Kennedy and Johnson administrations encouraged sales abroad. Despite the Vietnam war and rising demands to sell fewer arms, sales increased under the Nixon and Carter administrations. Strategic and political factors may well have played the larger roles in encouraging these transfers, but economic considerations and the pressures exerted by subnational actors appear to be relevant.

Selling arms is also viewed as a means of improving a nation's competitive position, especially in advanced technological industries.

Sophisticated weapons yield a higher value and more favorable foreign exchange than less processed goods or raw materials. They have increasingly been seen as a method of not only paying for imports but as providing access to critical materials such as oil. Trade imbalances between developed and developing countries, aggravated by the fourfold increase in oil prices since 1973, have accentuated the need to accelerate commercial exchanges to balance trade accounts and to earn currency. The tie between arms and oil, for example, has been explicitly stated in French arms policy and implicitly in American sales to Arab states.[9] Even the East European states and the Soviet Union drive hard bargains; sales to Egypt, Syria, and Iraq have been on a cash or barter basis.

Incentives arise, moreover, to make barter deals or swaps to assure employment and economic growth. Sweden, which has followed a restrictive arms-transfer policy, was reportedly prepared to make important economic concessions to Denmark, Norway, the Netherlands, and Belgium if those countries purchased the Viggen to modernize their air defenses. General Dynamics and Dassault, other competitors for the contract, proposed different schemes to share production and future sales. Arms are particularly important in maintaining employment in aeronautics and electronics, sectors that use a high proportion of the nation's advanced technological resources. Arms production in these industries assumes, as does road and bridge building, the character of public works and are, therefore, perceived as beneficial and worthy social functions.

Often overlooked is the modernization function attributed by decision makers to an armaments industry. A West German white paper of 1971–72 succinctly stated this point: "The German economy cannot afford to forego the benefits deriving from such defense projects [i.e., profits involving a high degree of technological innovation]...especially since national development of weapons and equipment, as well as collaboration in international armament projects, are dependent on a high technological standard...."[10] In 1976, West Germany replaced Great Britain as the fourth largest arms trader. For developed economies, arms production and sales are seen as the advanced thrust of the civilian expansion of the nation's economy and as a means of keeping pace in the technological race and in the search for markets. For developing states, an armaments industry, like the aeronautics industry in Brazil, is considered a key component of a nation's economic and political modernization. In addition to the nine developed states listed by the U.S. Arms Control and Disarmament Agency (ACDA) as major arms suppliers,[11] SIPRI lists 18 Third World states in 1977 as weapon producers in contrast to two in 1960.[12] An increasing number of arms-production centers, joined to expanding scientific and technological capabilities, accelerates the upward spiral of competitive lethality.[13]

The drive for new weapons arising from scientific discovery and technological advancement, on the one hand, and the economics of weapons production, on the other, have produced a synergistic effect, which has stimulated the quantitative and qualitative expansion of global arms production and sales. An important part of the problem of arms sales resolves itself then into the more difficult task of controlling the complex processes of economic, scientific, and technological change. These, moreover, overlay traditional security and diplomatic conflicts. The combination of these varied and powerful forces produces, on a global scale, an arms competition unparalleled in history. Viewed apart from these drives and incentives and the resulting intricate web of reciprocally reinforcing supplier-recipient relations that give them expression, arms sales as a political problem make little sense. They are more the result than the cause or the condition of growing supplier-recipient interdependencies which are driven, paradoxically, by a penchant of each state to maximize its independence in all significant areas of national activity. They are the product of the instruments of modernization that are attributes of advanced, national political structures and have roots that go deep into the psyche and dynamics of the nation-state.

SUBNATIONAL ACTORS

The donor-recipient relationship appears to be patterned in terms of the conflicting incentives that arise from the dynamics of military and political conflict and from the economic and technological competition of nations. This system of nation-state relations is not immune, however, from internal influences generated by the creation of a military-industrial-administrative-technoscientific infrastructure that is the mark of a developed armaments industry. These several interlocking bureaucratic groupings form the domestic organizational framework within which defense production and export occur. Depending on the political regime and economic system of a state, these structures are predominantly private, governmental, or mixed. In the United States, most research, development, and production of arms are left to private enterprises. France, on the other hand, has a mixed system: naval construction and heavy armor are largely produced in government arsenals; airframes, engines, and missiles are constructed in private and in nationalized associations (Société Nationale d'Etudes de Construction de Moteurs d'Aviation [SNECMA], Aérospatiale, Dassault-Bréguet, Matra); and electronics are largely left to the private sector (Thomson-Brandt, Dassault Electronique). The Soviet Union and East European states work through state instrumentalities.

These bureaucratic frameworks have their own sets of demands and claims on governmental defense and economic investment decisions. Space does not permit a review of the military-industrial-complex literature, but the influence of these complexes on governmental decision making remains in dispute. There is evidence that their different segments are often at odds with each other, and other demands and influences on governmental decision makers also often require cutbacks in spending, layoffs, restrictions on what may be produced or sold, and even net declines in certain defense sectors. Overall spending for defense relative to growth in GNP has declined for NATO countries over the past decade.[14] Base closings and unemployment in defense industries are perennials of the American economy; for example, between 1967 and 1972 Boeing, General Dynamics, Rockwell International, and Ling-Temco-Vought cut their total work forces from 383,000 to 170,000.[15]

Whatever the limits of subnational actor influence on arms and arms sales, their impact remains significant and, in many cases, decisive. The response of governmental elites to these bureaucratic structures derives from the critical role that they play in advancing their strategic, security, economic, and technological objectives and, inversely, from the pressures that these structures can exert on these elites, their actions and their policies. It is not surprising, therefore, that an inversion in announced national policies will result from the influence brought to bear by subnational elites on governmental decision makers. The image of a nation-state's political elites as insulated from internal pressures determining and controlling arms policy does not resemble the actual pattern of influence, for example, either in Western or in Eastern European states. Bureaucratic politics play a large, and in many instances the larger, role in defining a state's arms policy. The particular interests of subnational players, rather than their commitment to often distant and inarticulate goals (e.g. national security), shape and orient weapons decisions and subsequent arms transfers.

The objectives of national actors, characterized generally as the maximization of security, diplomatic influence, and economic benefit, are not always internally consistent or always compatible with those pursued by subnational actors. The latter are narrower and more particular, composed of specific organizational needs for survival and growth and the personal ambitions of individuals who occupy the varied perches and rungs of each bureaucracy. Moreover, the immediate demands of military security are not necessarily the same as those of national defense, which rest on broader considerations of diplomacy and economic stability and are usually cast in a longer time frame. Harmonizing these objectives with those of business enterprises interested in maximizing profits, controlling markets, assuring access to credit facilities and governmental subsidies and contracts, also poses serious problems of integration. Nor are any of these varied and conflicting goals congruent with those of actors focused on extending scientific or technological findings which may have implications for weapons design, military costs, and international security; the search for new knowledge or techniques may be pressed over concern for these latter considerations.

Operational, as distinguished from announced, national policy is thus often a derivative of the bargaining and negotiations between domestic elites within and between the national and subnational levels. These relations are patterned and can be described as forming separate, over-lapping, and interdependent sets of political games whose outcomes give content to national policy. What may pass as the response of national elites to external imperatives may be on closer examination little more than the projection of the domestic struggle for power, wealth, and privilege. From this perspective foreign actors are the occasion for domestic elite com-petition; they assume the role either as spectators, prizes, or both, of the multiple political games played primarily within the domestic arena.

The United States Army's decision to purchase Roland, a French-German ground-to-air missile, illustrates the play of subnational actors whose influence can be determinant in shaping a weapons program. The Roland was bought under license from Euromissile. Army habits and prevailing military requirements, based on the assumption of domestic control of arms production, ruled out the European manufacture of the missile. The Hughes and Boeing corporations, assigned the contract to produce the missiles in the United States, added their own modifications, partly motivated by market factors. An American all-weather version of Roland was developed in parallel with a follow-on European model, but at a cost that exceeded the original research and development costs of the system sold under license to the United States. Despite deliberate assur-ances by U.S. companies and the army that Euromissile's Roland would monopolize the European market, changes in Roland's European design proved sufficiently extensive to circumvent this understanding. Norway has already ordered the U.S. Roland, and other European states, including Switzerland, have shown interest in the U.S. version; Euromissile now finds itself in competition with its own missile. Meanwhile, the U.S. system is not as fully compatible with the French-German Roland as the ideal of standardization, pressed by successive U.S. administrations, would require.

What began as a joint United States-European weapon venture in pursuit of commonality and cooperation has strained political relations, raised European suspicions about the motives underlying pressures for standardization, and heightened military industrial competition on both sides of the Atlantic without appreciably advancing NATO military co-operation. The objectives pursued by national actors—standardization and a better and cheaper ground-to-air missile for the U.S. Army—were systematically modified, emptied of content, and even reversed, as the particular interests and needs of corporate and military subnational actors came into play. The Roland example may be multiplied by others, like the United States' refusal to buy the German Leopard tank, Air Force and Navy resistance to the F-16 as the standard lightweight NATO fighter, and the success of Dassault, linked to high political authority in the French government, in forcing the French air force to take options on its F-l M53 fighter to aid national efforts to sell follow-on fighter aircraft to other NATO states.

TRANSNATIONAL ACTORS

Another development that has radically changed the international environment in favor of increased arms transfers in quantity and quality is the increased role accorded to transnational actors in the international system. The arms-transfer relations struck between transnational actors assume either a technoeconomic or politicostrategic form.

Technoeconomic Relations

These refer to increased cooperation between developed and developing states in the design, development, production, licensing, and marketing of weapons.[16] The transnational actor is either a private or a semipublic enterprise (e.g. Aérospatiale in France). Their formal contractual arrangements and more numerous and multiform informal contacts with each other form a discernibly different set of relations from those associated with national and subnational actors; moreover, the variety and duration of these ties and alignments exhibit no single, simple pattern. They are functions of the technological, economic, and strategic capabilities and needs of the enterprises involved and of their dependence on, or influence over, the decisions and requirements of the national governments with which they deal in development, production, or export of weapons and support materials.

The multinationalization of the armaments industry stems from at least two imperatives: the need to minimize the national costs of new weapons and the demands to maximize the technological superiority of national armed forces. Although the costs of joint ventures are normally greater than nationally based programs, the expenditures required of each state are still less; also, an immediate market is assured by the participating states. Export possibilities are enhanced through the separate promotional efforts of the participating enterprises and states. Such programs, moreover, permit access and pooling of technical talent that would not otherwise be possible under strictly national auspices.

Governmental control of these joint ventures is difficult since they tend to fall between the oversight and control mechanisms of the states involved, a problem already well understood, if not resolved, with respect to multinational companies. The abrogation of such programs, once they have been set in motion, raises fundamental issues of national defense and political alignments between states whatever the significance of the techno-economic stakes. The crisis in U.S.-British relations, occasioned by the unilateral cancellation of the Skybolt program in 1962, illustrates the complexity, political volatility, and strategic importance of such common enterprises. It also suggests that governments are susceptible to increased internal and external pressures to make them work and bear higher costs if they fail. Alignments across national lines, between cooperating private and semipublic enterprises, are not necessarily compatible with the governmental policies and interests that may have initially led to their creation, especially if these involve threatened program terminations, like Skybolt or Concorde. Alternately, what one government may be constrained from doing (e.g., selling to countries at war) may be possible through sales initiated by the cooperating country. Euromissile was able to sell missiles to Syria through its French connection when its German partner was foreclosed from making the sale.[17]

Table 1.1 summarizes the findings of several surveys of joint West European or Atlantic cooperative programs, primarily in weapons development, since the 1950s. These include programs of shared research,

TABLE 1.1: European and Atlantic Cooperative Accords for the Development of Weapons

	European	Atlantic
Aircraft/helicopters	19[a]	20
Missiles	8	7[b]
Engines	11	12
Armor	4	3
Total	42	42

Sources: Mary Kaldor, European Defence Industries—National and International Implications (Sussex, England: Institute for the Study of International Organisation, 1972), pp. 71–79; R. Facer, The Alliance and Europe, Pt. 2: Weapons Procurement in Europe—Capabilities and Choices, Adelphi Paper No. 108 (London: Institute for Strategic Studies, 1974–75); Michael Klare, "La Multinationalisation des Industries de Guerre," Monde Diplomatique, February 1977; SIPRI, World Armaments and Disarmament: 1977 (Cambridge, Mass.: MIT Press, 1977); Assemblée Nationale Francais, Commission de la Défense Nationale et des Forces Armées, Avis sur le projet de loi de finances pour 1975, No. 1233, October 11, 1974, Défense: Dépenses en Capital, Vol. 1 (Rapporteur: M. d'Aillières), pp. 93–96.

Note: Of the 42 European programs, only five may be classified as civilian: Airbus (two versions), Concorde, Mercure, VFW-614.

a. Includes Gazelle in both U.S.-French and Yugoslav versions.

b. Includes U.S. version of Roland missile made in cooperation with Euromissile.

licensing, co-production, and co-development. Only one of the 42 projects listed in the Atlantic category involved a Canadian-European venture; all others included U.S. firms and one or more of their European counterparts. In only a few cases are the agreements between the U.S. government and a foreign firm. Inter-European cooperation is as active as the Atlantic network and in certain fields (e.g., aeronautics) more advanced and complex. Airframes, helicopters, and electronic design and development lead other forms of cooperation, followed by aircraft engines, missiles, and armor. Some programs are as large as the multibillion-dollar F-16 contract or as small as joint design efforts that amount to only a few millions of dollars.

Cooperative weapons agreements between the developing world (including Israel and South Africa) and the developed states of Eastern and Western Europe and the United States are also growing. In 1976, these amounted to approximately 90 different programs for major weapon systems, including 18 Third World states and 28 developed nations, among which were three communist states—Czechoslovakia, the Soviet Union, and China.[18] Most of these programs were for licensed production, but some included joint production and the transfer of technological capabilities. To these might be added the contract between Hughes aircraft and Iran for the construction of a missile plant and the agreement between Lockheed and the Greek government and privileged indigenous enterprises to construct a complete aeronautics industry in Greece. Also of note is European-Indian collaboration and the emerging arms consortium centered around Saudi Arabia, Egypt, the United Arab Emirates, and France.

Politicostrategic Relations

The arms-transfer relations struck between a legitimate government, as supplier, and a revolutionary movement may also be categorized as transnational. A characteristic of contemporary international politics, already discernible during the Spanish civil war, is the penchant of states to intervene in the internal strife of other nations. The ideological struggle between the United States and the Soviet Union globalized the intervention process and established precedents for smaller states to follow. The cold war may be dated from the Soviet Union's indirect intervention in the Greek civil war before the end of World War II. Soviet arms also found their way to the communist Chinese, North Vietnamese, and eventually to the Vietcong. These transfers were part of the larger Soviet strategy to increase the number of communist or progressive states more or less under Soviet tutelage. In the 1950s, the global balance of terror between the United States and the Soviet Union, the military stalemate in Europe, and the containment of the Soviet Union by a U.S.-led system of security alliances prompted a revision of Soviet strategic doctrine. Nuclear war was no longer declared inevitable, but wars of national liberation were sanctioned as a primary instrument for revolutionary change. Arms sent to the Palestinian Liberation Organization (PLO), the Neto regime in Angola, and Rhodesian rebels is consistent with this ideological thrust. The Western position in the Third World is presumably weakened, while the risk of nuclear war—arising from a direct confrontation of American power, such as those that occurred in a series of Berlin crises during the late 1950s and early 1960s—is minimized.

Since World War II the United States has a record of support for insurgent causes and has intervened on several occasions in civil strife by supplying arms to one of the contending parties. The overthrow of the Arbenz government in Guatemala in 1954 was aided by U.S. arms; intervention in the Belgian Congo and Laos in the early 1960s, in Cambodia, and, surreptitiously, in Angola illustrate further the perceived need to counter Soviet expansion in the Third World. U.S. support of the South Vietnamese government in its struggle with North Vietnam was similarly justified as a response to world communist expansion directed either by Moscow or Peking.

Lesser powers have also lent arms and supplies to groups which have an international impact although they may not have a juridical standing. Libya has sent arms and aid to rebels in Morocco, Chad, and the Sudan; Saudi Arabia provides financial support for the Palestinians; Iran has sent arms to the Kurds; the Greek and Turkish governments have supplied U.S. arms to their rival partisans in Cyprus. The Irish Republican Army (IRA) and Philippine rebels are also recipients of foreign military assistance, some of which, as in the case of the IRA, derives from private sources.

INTERNATIONAL ACTORS

The security alliances of NATO and the Warsaw Pact are the principal actors at the international level. Within NATO the division of labor in the security functions performed by member states has had the contradictory tendency of encouraging independent military production systems and of accenting the pressures to standardize military weapons, equipment, fuels, and logistics support. Within the Western group, the policies of several key states have been firmly grounded on the development and maintenance of separate weapons development and production capabilities for many of the reasons and with many of the effects already discussed.

The standardization initially achieved within NATO, based on U.S. equipment, was largely a function of the weakness of European economies to relaunch their defense industries after World War II and their dependence on the U.S. military guarantee. The increasing industrial, scientific, and technological strength of these economies, joined to political-strategic demands for a margin of maneuverability vis-à-vis other states, particularly the United States, has spawned a maze of new weapons that threaten the alliance's operational readiness and effectiveness. In 1974 the NATO commander, General Andrew Goodpaster, noted the existence of the following different families of weapon systems: 23 fighter aircraft, 7 battle tanks, 9 armored personnel carriers, 22 anti-tank weapons, 36 naval fire control mechanisms, 8 SAM systems for naval ships, and more than 20 different calibers for small-arms ammunition.[19]

The security risks of such diversity and the increased costs incurred in research and development in producing small runs of weapon systems, and in multiplying maintenance and service facilities have raised the issue of standardization. Discussion has evolved at Atlantic and European levels, and the European states have formalized the problem by organizing themselves, including France, into the Independent European Program Group; progress at either level has been slow. To the degree that standardization succeeds, it will spell more, not fewer, arms transfers, but presumably at a smaller overall unit cost. The sale of the F-16, the largest weapons production accord within the alliance, will replace four aircraft (the F-104, F-104G, F-5, and F-4). The terms of the contract will reinforce, rather than alleviate, pressures for exports. The weapons industries of the purchasing countries in Europe, as subcontractors, are expected to share in the future sale of the aircraft to other states. Meanwhile, the special fuel needed for the F-16, presently incompatible with NATO fuels, undermines the objective of standardization and increases costs and complicates military readiness.

The Soviet Union, less obliged to respond to allied demands, has made more progress in standardizing the Warsaw Pact on the basis of Soviet arms. East European arsenals—aircraft, armor, and missiles—are largely stocked with Soviet weapons. Thus, in both the Atlantic and Warsaw groupings, but for divergent reasons, arms transfers are encouraged and structured into the alliance bargaining and negotiation processes.

CONCLUSIONS

Arms transfers arise from the interaction of national, subnational, transnational, and international actors. These patterned and regular exchanges form a subsystem of the international system, and political and security conflicts between states and political groups, crystallized in discernible alignments, appear to be the initial determinants of arms transfers. The military-industrial-administrative-technoscientific structures created within each nation to respond to these security and foreign-policy imperatives of conflict further strengthen the international supports for arms transfers. These bureaucratic organizations have an interest in continued sales and transfers and, implicitly, in the security issues and conflicts that foster them. While the elimination of such weapons centers would not remove the sources of friction that animate nation-state differences, they often become as much a cause of, as a solution to, the problem of the control and elimination of armed conflict. Global and regional conflicts become anchored to them, and the institutionalization of these centers of production—an outgrowth of the incentives of sharing costs and advanced technological skills and knowledge—binds these separate national centers into an increasingly complex transnational superstructure that favors arms transfers. Regional alliances, pushed by the pressures of standardization, generate need for more, not less, traffic in arms. They also legitimize such exchanges by appeals to national and collective security.

The drive for national independence conspires with a growing interdependence between states with regard to their security, political status and influence, and economic and technological development to encourage more, not fewer, transfers. If the bipolar struggle between the United States and the Soviet Union has been the principal impulse for the diffusion of arms since World War II, the demands of superpower allies and neutrals to maximize their independence vis-à-vis the superpowers have nourished the formation of national weapons-production centers and catalyzed the search for a broader base of supply. The growing availability of resources with which to make or buy arms, thanks to rising global industrial capacity and a redistribution of wealth between the North and South, provides a salubrious climate for the proliferation of suppliers and recipients.

In the immediate future, there is little evidence that arms transfers will diminish in their significance as a characteristic of international politics. Highly fungible, they are viewed by relevant actors as an indispensable medium of exchange in their mutual trading and bargaining over key security, economic, political, and technological interests and objectives. Transfers occur, moreover, in a permissive international setting marked by the diffusion of political authority, the divergencies of regimes—separated by language, culture, and history—and the growing decentralization of economic and military power. These elements generate few effective countervailing forces to contain the boundaries of the arms-transfer subsystem. Like the common cold, arms transfers appear to be here to stay. The more irritating and debilitating symptoms can perhaps be alleviated and moderated, but the cure—and few of the key actors admit that there is even a sickness—is still a long way off.

NOTES

1. Stockholm International Peace Research Institute (SIPRI), *The Arms Trade with the Third World* (London: Paul Elek, 1971).

2. Amelia C. Leiss and Geoffrey Kemp, "Arms Transfers to Less Developed Countries," Report C/70–1, MIT Center for International Studies, Cambridge, February 1970.

3. See, for example, Françoise Sirjacques, *Determinanten der Franzoesichen Ruestungs-Politik* (Frankfurt: Peter Land, 1977).

4. Georges Menahem, *La Science et le Militaire* (Paris: Seuil, 1976) and Ulrich Albrecht, *Politik und Waffengeschaefte* (Munich: Carl Hanser, 1972).

5. Robert Harkavy, · *The Arms Trade and International Systems* (Cambridge, Mass.: Ballinger, 1975).

6. See, for example, Anne Hessing Cahn, et al., *Controlling Future Arms Trade* (New York: McGraw-Hill, 1977), pp. 27–101.

7. Leslie Gelb, "Arms Sales," *Foreign Policy*, no. 25 (1976–77), pp. 11–12.

8. Richard Burt, *Nuclear Proliferation and Conventional Arms Transfers: The Missing Link* (Santa Monica, Ca.: California Seminar on Arms Control and Foreign Policy, September, 1977), p. 2.

9. France, *Livre Blanc sur la Défense Nationale*, I, 1972.

10. Quoted in Roger Facer, *The Alliance and Europe, Part II: Weapons Procurement in Europe— Capabilities and Choices*, Adelphi Paper No. 108 (London: Institute for Strategic Studies, 1974–75), p. 13.

11. U.S. Arms Control and Disarmament Agency, *World Military Expenditures and Arms Transfers: 1966-1975* (Washington, D.C.: U.S. Government Printing Office, 1976), p. 77.

12. SIPRI, *World Armaments and Disarmament: 1977* (Cambridge: MIT Press, 1977), pp. 288–95.

13. See Harkavy, *The Arms Trade*, pp. 183–210. He suggests that there were more independent weapons-producing centers in the interwar than in the postwar period, while SIPRI findings, largely restricted to the postwar period, suggests greater independence following World War II. Both agree, however, that the development of independent centers poses increased international control and security problems for all states.

14. ACDA, *World Military Expenditures*, p. 15.

15. Facer, *The Alliance and Europe*, p. 26.

16. Michael Klare, "La Multinationalisation des Industries de Guerre," *Le Monde Diplomatique*, February 1977.

17. *Le Monde*, February 7, 1978.

18. SIPRI, *World Armaments*, pp. 295–304.

19. Quoted in Jean-Laurens Delpech, "La Standardisation des Armements," *L'Artilleur*, No. 126 (October 1976), pp. 20–29.

2 TWIXT CUP AND LIP: SOME PROBLEMS IN APPLYING ARMS CONTROLS

Richard H. Wilcox

It is clearly desirable to inhibit the peddling of implements of destruction to irresponsible despots in backward countries, for use in suppressing the citizens' rights and waging unnecessary wars with local rivals. It is also desirable to sanction the provision of defense equipment to responsible leaders of developing nations, for use in insuring the citizens' security and protecting national resources against predatory neighbors. Real situations, however, are seldom so clearly drawn. Proposed arms transfers frequently present some aspects of both of these images, and the image perceived tends to vary with the perspective of the viewer.

Few tangible criteria are available for assessing the probable impacts of prospective transfers, and no coherent body of knowledge exists to facilitate the dispassionate management of transfer programs. Other chapters of this book address a variety of theoretical relationships affecting the international transfer of arms, and they provide insight into possible conceptual frameworks for the subject. However, these theories and concepts must be applied in practice for any benefits to be realized in improved controls.

This chapter raises some of the questions that must be resolved in the development of effective arms-transfer controls. It is not intended here to

The views and opinions expressed herein are those of the author and do not necessarily represent those of the U.S. government or the Arms Control and Disarmament Agency.

advocate any particular concepts or theories or policies. The purpose is to explore and elucidate the dilemmas and complexities involved in putting into practice *any* bases or approaches that may be considered for the control of arms transfers. It is hoped that this chapter will provide some rough measures for evaluating the feasibility of the theories and concepts advanced in the remainder of the volume.

In practice, the control of arms transfers is a *legal* process: it is carried out under the authority of laws and in conformance with established rules. Transfers are not approved or disapproved arbitrarily, but rather must be judged objectively and decided consistently in accord with standing criteria. Because international laws or agreements for control of the arms trade have not yet emerged, the laws and criteria governing transfer decisions are those of individual countries. Ideally, the criteria are established to fulfill the overall objectives and interests of the national government, reflecting in turn the will of the populace. The criteria may be derived in part through theoretical analysis; at the very least they should be developed in accord with rational concepts. To be usable, the resulting rules need to be stated in commonly understood terms. But every rule that is established to carry out some ideal will most assuredly be carefully dissected by others whose goals or ideals differ from those of the rule makers, with the object of finding a loophole, an alternate reasonable interpretation, or an unforeseen detrimental aspect that can lead to abrogation. Thus, the implementation of sound and effective arms-transfer controls requires careful consideration of *all* the effects of the rules when applied to *all* types and classes of transfers to which they may be pertinent.

WHAT ARE ARMS?

To what transfers should arms controls be applied? The word "arms" conjures up a vision of lethal weapons. Unfortunately, many otherwise innocent items can become lethal weapons when misused. More important, many otherwise innocent items are essential for keeping modern lethal weapons operating. Thus, the simple concept of lethality provides inadequate discrimination. For example, it may be generally agreed that an army tank is a weapon falling within the purview of arms-transfer controls. A tank as sold to another country consists of many components and subassemblies, such as a transmission between the engine and the drive shaft. The tank cannot be operated without the transmission, so that in the event of failure of the original transmission sold in the tank, a replacement must be procured to keep the tank running. Does the replacement transmission fall within the definition of arms? Suppose the transmission is not unique to the tank, but is used also in heavy tractors? If the transmission itself is controlled as arms, what about standard roller bearings used in the transmission? Clearly, a practical line must be drawn at some point—but where?

Training and services present problems directly analogous to those of components and spare parts. For example, the provision of such maintenance services such as the replacement of tank transmissions would seem to lie in the same category as providing the transmissions themselves. But what about training citizens of a purchasing country to do their own maintenance? What about teaching them English so that they can take such technical training? What about training military officers of another country in general strategy and tactics? What about training foreign students in our engineering schools, which may provide them with the basis for indigenous design and production of tanks? Again, a practical line must eventually be drawn somewhere.

In general, the transfer of spare parts or the provision of training or services to a country is not as potentially disturbing to its neighbors as is the provision of major combat equipment such as tanks or attack aircraft. Yet, those who would exempt spares and services from controls would do well to consider the homely analogy of securing support for our private automobiles. A lack of parts can render our vehicles completely useless; at times we reluctantly agree to premium prices in order to obtain essential services, and when making new purchases our selections frequently take into account the manufacturers' or dealers' relative reputations for maintenance. And so it is with arms purchasers. They cannot maintain their military capability without logistics, and monopolistic control of their supply lines can provide powerful leverage over their activities, but a reputation for exercising such leverage is likely to lead to loss of clients.

In defining what to cover with arms controls, it is relatively easy to identify articles specifically designed, modified, or adapted for military use, together with associated technical data and related training.[1] Furthermore, in most cases purchases intended for the military services of the recipient country are identified as such. The difficult problems come from so-called "dual-use" equipment, services, and technology, for instance, inertial navigation systems usable in either commercial or military aircraft, construction of commercial airfields in strategic locations, or training for nuclear-power generation that may be applicable to weapons development.[2]

On a different scale, transfers of rifles for hunters and collectors, riot-control agents for police forces, and sidearms for palace guards are not likely to lead to any serious international complications. Unfortunately, it is difficult to phrase rules that will safely screen out such "minor" transfers for control purposes. Purchase of an excessive number of rifles may signal preparations for an uprising or smuggling for an ongoing insurgency. But how can "excessive" be defined? Preservation of internal peace and order is a legitimate function of any government, yet it also provides the rationale for most suppression of human rights. How can the coverage of controls be delineated to support the one and discourage the other?

Shades of Gray

In considering what to classify as arms for control purposes, it becomes evident that there is no simple definition that clearly separates all equipment and services into one category or the other. From the preceding discussion, it is obvious that the "lethal/nonlethal" criterion is inadequate. Furthermore, the design of effective controls inevitably requires that the context of the transfer be taken into account—the specific recipient nation, its neighbors, and the specific political situation existing at the time. Transfer evaluation criteria frequently include such terms as "instability," "arms race," and "ally," all of which are highly dependent upon time and place. A transfer of Soviet fighter-bombers to modernize the air force of a Warsaw Pact ally may attract little or no attention, but the same transfer to a Latin American or African nation will generate headlines worldwide. The ensuing reactions of other nations will also depend upon their interests in, and relationships with, the nations directly involved and on the current political environment locally and among the major powers.

There are several dimensions for sorting equipment and services within the overall category of arms. One that is particularly appealing is that of "offensive" versus "defensive" capabilities. Obviously, the acquisition of defensive weapons should be less disturbing to neighbors than offensive ones. Unfortunately, few items lie exclusively in one category or the other. It may be true that strategic bombers have little defensive use (except, of course, for deterrence); and that fixed surveillance radars have little offensive use. But the large majority of weapons represent possibilities for both applications. Tanks are a central element of the classic blitzkrieg attack; they are also a primary antitank defense. Strike aircraft are obviously useful for aggression, but they may also be invaluable for stopping invading forces. Destroyers soften up beaches for amphibious landings but also protect shipping. Military cargo aircraft supply offensive and defensive forces with equal facility. In the end, the *perception* of the equipment's purpose and the recipient's intent may be more critical than the actual military capability provided.

Nevertheless, it is possible to obtain general consensus on items constituting significant or major combat equipment. In essence, they are the weapons and munitions that are inherently more likely to aggravate a crisis by their arrival or, conversely, to increase stability by clearly signaling a determination to make any encroachment expensive. But, again, there are gradations of political impact likely to be generated by the transfer of different types of significant equipment; the U.S. "Major Defense Equipment List" includes not only tanks, destroyers, and strike aircraft, but also jet engines, rifles, and communications equipment.[3]

Perhaps the most difficult dimension for classifying arms transfers is that of the sophistication involved. There is no question that the modern fighter aircraft is highly sophisticated, and that the standard rifle cartridge is not. But what of the solid-state, portable radio-communications unit carried by the modern soldier? By incorporating the very latest electronic technology, this piece of gear has been made so automatic and rugged that it is almost foolproof for the unsophisticated conscript to operate. Again, the key to evaluation appears to lie in the circumstances of the transfer; that is, the degree of sophistication of weapon systems is important for transfer control purposes *if* the level of weapons effectiveness that is introduced significantly improves the combat capability of the recipient's armed forces. It is possible, of course, that attempting to evaluate significant improvements to armed forces may prove to be just as frustrating as trying to evaluate the sophistication of equipment directly.

A related problem arises in any attempt to control the transfer of militarily related advanced technology itself. Most science and much technology is equally applicable to civilian and military purposes. In modern society knowledge has a tendency to spread widely. Indeed, it is generally considered desirable to assist developing nations in improving their industrial bases and advancing their human skills. Yet to do so can also contribute to their development of indigenous arms-production capabilities. Several developing nations have already become nontrivial suppliers in the world arms market.

There are some arms that are not exceptionally destructive in comparison with most major weapons, but which nevertheless attract inordinate attention when transferred because they are susceptible to misuse in some ways that are particularly disreputable from a political, humanitarian, or diplomatic point of view. Typical examples are napalm and cluster bombs that could be indiscriminately applied against civilian populations, highly portable antiaircraft guided missiles that terrorists could use against commercial airliners, and riot-control agents that repressive regimes could use to suppress civil rights. Such weapons would appear to be prime candidates for transfer controls. But a workable definition of undesirable transfer circumstances for such weapons must be adequate to discriminate in individual cases between potential misapplications and legitimate defensive purposes. Unfortunately, such a definition is considerably more difficult to develop than the conceptual description attempted here.

QUESTIONS OF VALUE

The world arms trade is often described in terms of monetary value rather than military capability.[4] Certainly, dollar equivalents provide a common denominator for comparing the roles of various suppliers and the practices of various recipients. In addition, monetary value provides a measure of the resources expended on arms which, by and large, are lost to more beneficial social purposes.

On the other hand, the monetary value of arms transfers is seldom closely related to their potential for destabilization; the exceptions are the rare extremes—the billion-dollar sales of the most advanced modern weaponry. But even these differ drastically in the kinds of problems they present: F-16 co-production with NATO allies, Spruance destroyers for Iran, and F-15 interceptors for Israel are all politically different. Such cases are so unusual and so important economically and politically, however, that they will always be addressed at the highest levels of government, in contrast to the myriad of lesser cases that are processed routinely by the bureaucracy.

The U.S. government annually receives nearly 10,000 requests from foreign governments wanting to buy some equipment or service classified legally as arms. Many more requests are received for planning information about the cost and availability of weapons being considered for purchase. In addition, more than 20,000 applications are received annually from private firms for licenses to export equipment or services classified as arms or related technical data, or for advice as to whether a license would be granted if a potential sales effort were successfully carried out. Policy-level attention cannot be devoted to all of these requests, and thus some mechanism is required for selecting the cases that are particularly critical.

In the Arms Export Control Act, Congress adopted a monetary basis for selection: a proposed transfer of significant combat equipment worth $7 million or more, or any transfer worth $25 million or more, must be reported to the Congress. Somewhat more than 100 cases are so reported each year. The problem with establishing such monetary criteria lies in determining the essentially arbitrary level at which they should be set. The values chosen in this instance have proven to be successful in selecting the highly controversial cases, such as the Airborne Warning and Control Systems (AWACS) for Iran. But they also select many straightforward transfers, such as standard weapons for NATO, and some benign cases, such as a large sale of uniforms to Saudi Arabia. More important, these criteria could exclude a service contract with a developing country to modify previously sold aircraft so as to carry more lethal weapons. (This does not mean that such a transfer is likely to be approved—only that if it were it would not have to be reported to Congress under existing law.)

A monetary basis was also chosen by President Carter as one major tool for constraining U.S. arms exports. Specifically, he directed that the dollar volume of new commitments for government sales and grants of weapons and weapons-related items to other than major treaty allies in 1978 be reduced in comparison with 1977, after correction for inflation.[5] Such an approach offers several advantages: it is easily understood by the public, the arms manufacturers, and the other nations of the world, and it forces explicit consideration of the relative merits of major requests from prospective arms purchasers. However, these benefits of simplicity and definitiveness can be acquired only at the cost of insensitivity to other pertinent factors, particularly the likelihood of a specific transfer being destabilizing under the circumstances pertaining at the time.

Recognizing the lack of discrimination inherent in using monetary value as a control, the President invoked several criteria based upon the nature of weapons and the circumstances surrounding their proposed transfer. For example, no first introduction into a region is permitted of advanced weapons creating a significantly higher combat capability, nor may any commitment be made for sale of weapons so new that they have not yet even been deployed with U.S. forces (again exempting major treaty allies).[6] These two bases for controls—monetary value and substantive nature—serve different purposes and have different effects, and any development of arms-transfer limitations should consider them separately, though not independently.

In counting the monetary value of arms transfers, it is essential to differentiate between commitments and deliveries. Each serves an important purpose. The congressional reporting and presidential reduction criteria described above both pertain to new commitments. Because the objective of both is to identify for special review particularly significant obligations that the nation is considering undertaking, the estimated value of the proposed new commitments is the most appropriate monetary measure of significance. But in analyzing the actual impact of arms transfers, it may be less misleading to use the value of arms delivered. Particularly for major transfers, the delivery of goods is likely to delay the signing of contracts by several years. Thus, the value of deliveries provides a better representation of the actual product flow in the world arms trade. For purposes of economic analysis, however, serious inaccuracies may still remain because deferred payments are frequently involved and transfers are sometimes outright gifts from the supplier or from a wealthy benefactor. Nevertheless, for such computations as balance of payments determinations and GNP analyses, the value of deliveries made in a given year provides a much better approximation than the value of new commitments undertaken.

WHEN IS A TRANSFER?

A complex arms transfer may extend over quite a few years from onset to completion. For example, a developing country considering acquisition of jet fighters will review the various aircraft produced by different possible suppliers (or on their drawing boards), weighing requirements and resources and the political factors involved against the alternative capabilities, prices, and delivery schedules available. Technical and economic data are requested in increasing detail, and help may be requested in assessing military requirements. If a U.S. product is selected, a formal request for an offer to sell must be submitted; in fact, offers may be requested on several configuration options. For example, a potential buyer might be considering two different weapon complements: a lightweight one enabling extended flight duration to maintain deterrent patrols, and a heavier one providing greater lethality to defeat aggressors should deterrence fail. Considerable time and effort may be needed to work up detailed cost figures on such alternatives. The United States, if it decides to approve the request, then tenders a signed formal letter of offer and, if the prospective customer accepts the terms, a contract is established. Deliveries are then scheduled from the production line consistent with domestic requirements, training and support are arranged, and other aspects of implementation are initiated.

At the time the contract is established, a commitment to transfer arms clearly exists. For control purposes, however, it is important to determine whether some implied commitment may have been assumed earlier and, conversely, under what circumstances a commitment may be abrogated subsequently if conditions change. Whenever a manufacturer's advertisement for a given weapon or service appears in a technical journal, arms importers are likely to assume that the product displayed will be available under at least some circumstances. Any time a request for more specific information is honored, it is likely to reinforce the recipient's presumption of being an eligible purchaser. Thus, it is important that prospective transfers be reviewed and controls applied early, in order to avoid the development of momentum in an undesirable case that may become politically difficult to resist. Yet in the early stages of a prospective sale, the specific nature and magnitude of the transfer may be nebulous and the impact correspondingly difficult to assess. To explore with a friendly developing country its perceived defense requirements, without necessarily implying a willingness to transfer weapons associated with such missions, calls for diplomatic skill and tact of the highest order.

Once actual deliveries have commenced the recipient expects not only completion of deliveries as scheduled, but also provision of full support for as long as desired. Reliability of the supply line is a major barometer of the relations between the two nations. Because the recipient's security may be directly dependent upon the availability of spare parts, specialized consumables, and technical assistance, interruption of support must not be considered lightly; inconstancy will be viewed with alarm not only by the victim but, very likely, by all other clients. Thus, for major transfers it is essential that the implications of a long-term relationship be analyzed early in the process and controls exercised accordingly.

When, then, does the transfer "take place"? The purchaser is fully involved when the formal request is made. Within the executive branch of the U.S. government, the decision must be made before forwarding notification to Congress. In the eyes of other interested nations (including the purchaser), the United States is committed once Congress has had an opportunity to object and has not done so. Legally, the United States incurs an obligation when it makes a formal offer, and as noted previously a contractual commitment exists once both parties have signed. The purchaser normally acquires ownership upon payment, but nothing physical has been transferred until the first delivery takes place, and certainly the transfer is not completed before final delivery occurs. But if the overall transaction involves continuing support and subsequent modifications of a weapon system to avoid obsolescence, when is "final delivery"? If the terms of purchase involve credit, the economist may well argue that the transfer is not complete until the loan is repaid. In short, depending on the purpose it may be most appropriate to count transfers as requests received, as new commitments undertaken (at one stage or another), as transfer of title, as primary vehicle deliveries on major weapon transactions, as total deliveries completed during a year, or as payments received. Each of these involves a different time frame, and each portrays a different picture of the "arms trade."

SUMMARY AND CONCLUSIONS

This chapter differs from the others in the book in that it focuses on the *how* of controls for arms transfers, rather than on the *why*. It complements the theoretical and conceptual presentations by providing a basis for reflecting upon their relationship to "reality." In exploring the problems of defining arms, of providing for their great variety, of counting their value, and of timing their control, the purpose has been to illuminate some of the difficulty and complexity of decision making where real transfers must be approved or denied to real countries. The results are not intended to be discouraging, but rather to encourage the pursuit of promising new concepts and ideas beyond the theoretical stage to the development of practical controls—practical in the sense of effectively realizing the intended constraints without introducing unacceptable side effects. Only when this has been achieved will real progress have been made in controlling arms transfers in the modern world.

NOTES

1. See U.S. Department of State, *International Traffic in Arms Regulations (ITAR)*. 22 CFR 121-128 (Washington, D.C.: U.S. Government Printing Office).

2. J. W. Benson, J. G. Dunleavy, R. D. Minckler, and R. I. Widder, "Potential Criteria for the Determination of Items on the U.S. Munitions List," research report, Battelle Columbus Laboratories, Washington, D.C., June 1974, pp. 9–12.

3. U.S. Congress, House, Committee on International Relations, Subcommittee on International Security and Scientific Affairs, *Conventional Arms Transfer Policy: Background Information*, 95th Cong., 2nd sess., February 1978, pp. 154.

4. U.S. Arms Control and Disarmament Agency, *World Military Expenditures and Arms Transfers, 1967–1976* (Washington, D.C.: U.S. Government Printing Office, 1978).

5. U.S. Congress, *Conventional Arms Transfer Policy*, pp. 43–44.

6. Ibid.

3 UNDERSTANDING ARMS TRANSFERS AND MILITARY EXPENDITURES: DATA PROBLEMS

Edward T. Fei

Data on arms transfers and military expenditures are not easy to understand. For many, an understanding of the data on arms transfers often seems to have a half-life of about two weeks: one forgets half of what one knows in two weeks, half of what is left in two more weeks, and so on. This chapter attempts to explain what the data on arms transfers and military expenditures represent and examine some of the methodological choices which must be made in order to construct a data set.

DATA SOURCES

This chapter focuses on the data released by the U.S. Arms Control and Disarmament Agency (ACDA) in its annual publication, *World Military Expenditures and Arms Transfers (WMEAT)*. For comparison alternative approaches to measurement will be illustrated by references to the procedures used in the other two major, unclassified annual sources of information on arms transfers and military expenditures, *The Military Balance*, published by the International Institute for Strategic Studies (IISS),

The views and opinions expressed here are those of the author and do not necessarily represent those of the U.S. government or the Arms Control and Disarmament Agency and *World Armaments and Disarmament: 1978 (SIPRI Yearbook)*, published by the Stockholm International Peace Research Institute (SIPRI).

There are many different ways of describing an arms transfer. For example, Edward J. Laurence has provided the following list of measurable characteristics of an arms transfer:[1]

Variable	Values/Attributes
Type/number of equipment	5 T-62 tanks, 10 F-5 aircraft
Military utility	Payload, speed, combat radius
Logistics	Attributes depicting extent of logistic support accompanying transfer
Technical/training	Number of donor personnel to accompany equipment/number of recipient personnel to be trained in donor nation
Dollar value	Static valuation formula incorporating production costs, inflation, depreciation
Production arrangement	Package deal, assembly, license, co-production, co-development
Mode of payment	Cash, credit, gift, barter
Delivery stage	Rumor, agreement, delivery, ready for use in combat

Unfortunately, relatively reliable and comprehensive data are generally available for only one of these categories—the dollar value of arms transfers (see Chapter 2).

This poses serious problems for the analysis of the international traffic in arms. Many of the questions which an analyst asks cannot be answered with dollar data alone. For example, questions which relate to the transfer of military capability, technology transfer, or the economic burden of military transfers require more than just information on the dollar value of arms transfers.

In addition, even the dollar-value data on arms transfers is difficult to utilize. Inflation (or deflation) and changing currency exchange rates are two problems which affect dollar-value time series. Both problems—considered in greater detail below—must be solved to obtain a constant unit of measure against which arms transfers and military expenditures can be compared. Both ACDA and SIPRI data on arms transfers refer to the value of actual shipments and deliveries of arms, rather than agreements signed or financial transfers to pay for weapons. The logic of measuring the actual flow of weapons is that, in principle, the physical transfer of weapons should be easier to verify. In contrast, the signing of an agreement is not only harder to verify, but signed agreements may never be consummated. Payments for weapons are also difficult to verify and may be misleading as an indicator of the volume of arms transferred.

In *WMEAT* arms transfers are defined to include weapons of war, parts, ammunition, support equipment, and other commodities which are primarily military. This includes such items as uniforms, military vehicles, military communications and electronic equipment, and equipment for defense industries. Excluded by definition are nuclear, chemical and biological weapons, strategic-missile systems, foodstuffs, training, and technical services.

A consequence of this definition is that for the United States a large proportion of sales conducted under the provisions of the foreign military sales (FMS) program are not defined as weapons. For example FMS funds that are used for military training or construction would not be counted as part of the traffic in arms, since they do not involve weapons. Another consequence is that it may not always be appropriate to compare the value of arms transferred to military expenditure or GNP. The ACDA value of arms imported may not be representative of the cost to either the recipient or supplier of the weapons. For example, if U.S. troops withdrew from overseas bases, leaving their weapons behind as a no-cost transfer, this would be an arms transfer which would impose no direct burden on the recipient and would not show up in the recipient's data on military expenditures.

Another example is Honduras, which *WMEAT* shows with arms imports of $36 million and a military expenditure of only $21 million in 1976. It is a matter of public record that in this period Honduras received a shipment of Mystère-4A aircraft from Israel which would cause a large increase in the dollar value of arms imports. If Honduras either prepaid for these aircraft, purchased them on credit, or received them free, the aircraft delivery would not show up in 1976 military expenditures. This highlights the need for caution in using the value of arms imported as a possible indicator of military burden. It also follows that arms imports as reported by ACDA obviously should not be carelessly used as an indicator of relative military capability transferred since both the quantity and mix of weapons transferred are unknown.

ACDA does not produce the raw data on arms transfers; it receives the data from several official U.S. government sources.[2] A characteristic of this data which may raise problems for analysts is that the data for a given state's arms transfers in a given year is subject to revision. Where information is difficult to obtain, as is often the case with communist countries, the value of arms imported may be subject to upwards revision for several years as more information becomes available. For example, *WMEAT 1966–1975* shows North Korean arms imports for 1973 as $154 million, while the next year's edition showed $297 million for the same year.

The arms-transfer analyst must be aware that each edition of *WMEAT* is a slice in time which only describes the data as they are known at that moment. The data on arms transfers have an annoying habit of increasing; this reflects real-world problems, and revisions are likely to continue until no more additional information is received and all information received is processed. Alternatively, revisions may stop after the producers of the data lack the interest or resources to continue revisions.

SIPRI's coverage is considerably more limited since its annual yearbook covers only the arms trade to the Third World. In addition, SIPRI arms-transfer values are only an index and are therefore not directly comparable to the values used by ACDA. SIPRI does not attempt to measure the current value of weapons transferred, but instead uses price estimates as a trend-measuring device. Using 1968 prices SIPRI built a price list for every major weapons system transferred to the Third World in that year. This price list, now inflated to reflect 1978 prices, is used to value every recorded delivery involving major weapons systems. It is assumed by SIPRI that such an index is useful because major weapons systems are a fairly consistent proportion of the total arms trade and can therefore be used to measure the trend in the total flow of military goods to Third World states.[3]

A comparison of the SIPRI index of arms transfers to Third World states by region to the ACDA data for the same regions (using the SIPRI definition of which states constitute a region) reveals general similarity, but some points of considerable divergence. For example, Figures 3.1 and 3.2 compare ACDA and SIPRI data on arms flows into the Middle East and Africa. While the lines do tend to move together, there are periods of significant divergence, especially in the Middle East during 1972–74.

MILITARY EXPENDITURES

There are two categories of problems involved in assessing military expenditures: first, military expenditures must be defined; second, they must be measured in a fashion which facilitates interstate comparison.[*]

The first is solved relatively easily for NATO states as all three major sources, ACDA, IISS, and SIPRI, are in agreement; a NATO definition is used which includes military-like expenditures of all ministries and excludes those expenditures by the defense ministry which are of a civilian nature. The NATO definition, however, requires substantial fine print to define the civilian and military types. Examples of defense ministry expenditures which are not military expenditures include funding for

---

[*]This general subject is discussed further in Chapter 2, this volume. The comments here address the specific problems encountered when aggregating and comparing international data.

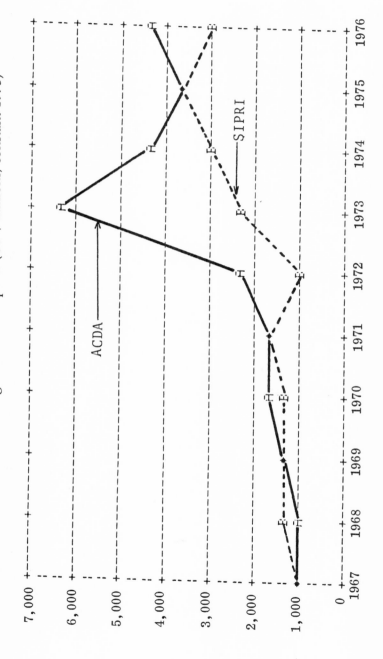

FIGURE 3.1: Middle East Regional Arms Imports (US $ millions, constant 1975)

Sources: A—U.S. Arms Control and Disarmament Agency, *World Military Expenditures and Arms Transfers, 1967–1976* (Washington, D.C.: U.S. Government Printing Office, 1978); B—Stockholm International Peace Research Institute, *World Armaments and Disarmament: SIPRI Yearbook 1978* (London: Taylor Francis Ltd., 1978).

41

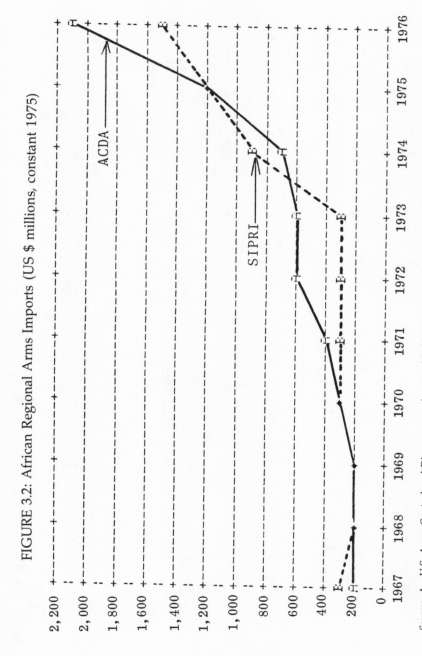

FIGURE 3.2: African Regional Arms Imports (US $ millions, constant 1975)

Sources: A—U.S. Arms Control and Disarmament Agency, *World Military Expenditures and Arms Transfers, 1967–1976* (Washington, D.C.: U.S. Government Printing Office, 1978); B—Stockholm International Peace Research Institute, *World Armaments and Disarmament: SIPRI Yearbook 1978* (London: Taylor Francis Ltd., 1978).

activities such as flood control, civilian-type space research, civil defense, stockpiling of industrial materials, and some pensions and medical services. On the other hand, expenditures by civilian ministries for some types of research, pensions, navigational aids, and medical services might all be counted as military expenditures.

For purposes of relating military expenditure to the arms trade, it is important to note that grant military assistance is included in the expenditures of the donor country. Also, purchases of military equipment for credit are included at the time the debt is incurred, not at the time of payment. It follows that in many cases the cost of an arms transfer shows up in expenditure data in a different year from that in which its value appears in arms-transfer data as hardware delivered.

For non-NATO states all three sources generally use some form of each state's officially announced military expenditures. This raises problems in the treatment of communist countries where ACDA, SIPRI, and IISS diverge in their use of officially declared budget figures.

In the case of the Soviet Union, the most recent version of *WMEAT* uses a dollar-costing methodology in which dollar prices are applied to detailed intelligence estimates of Soviet forces, weapons programs, and other activities.[4] This price series is intended to show what it would cost the United States to operate a military establishment similar to that of the Soviet Union. This calculation is obviously independent of the announced Soviet military budget. In contrast, SIPRI bases its estimating procedure on the officially declared Soviet military budget. To this base amount SIPRI adds 30 percent which is its estimate of Soviet defense expenditures that are not included in the announced budget. SIPRI then uses several different exchange rates to convert the ruble cost of Soviet milex into dollars.[5]

A problem with the SIPRI estimate is that since it is based on the announced Soviet budget, it only changes when the officially announced budget changes. Thus, in the period between 1970 and 1977 SIPRI shows constant or declining Soviet military expenditures. In contrast, while the ACDA data do not measure the ruble cost of Soviet expenditures, they can be a useful index of change in resources devoted to defense. In the same eight-year period in which SIPRI shows declining Soviet defense expenditure, ACDA shows a 30 percent increase in military expenditure.

The divergence between the ACDA numbers and the SIPRI and IISS numbers increases in the case of the non-Soviet members of the Warsaw Treaty Organization (WTO), which are Bulgaria, Czechoslovakia, German Democratic Republic, Hungary, Poland, and Romania. For these states both SIPRI and IISS simply take the officially declared budgets and then convert those figures into dollars using specially calculated conversion rates which differ from the official rate.

In contrast, the ACDA figures on the military expenditures of non-

Soviet Warsaw Pact states are produced by a modified version of the dollar-costing procedure used with the Soviet Union. The result is that the ACDA figures for non-Soviet WTO expenditures are significantly larger than those published by IISS or SIPRI. Again, as with the Soviet military expenditure estimates, the ACDA series show more variation—both increases and, on occasion, decreases—while the officially published budgets almost invariably show a series of incremental increases.

In addition to these definitional problems, there are measurement problems growing out of inflation and changing currency exchange rates which must be solved in order to obtain a constant unit of measure for interstate comparison of military expenditures and arms transfers. Determining the change in Austria's military expenditures between 1975 and 1976 illustrates this problem. A comparison of the three major public data sources shows the following:[6]

Austria's Military Expenditure ($ millions)

	1975	1976	Change (%)
IISS	410	433	5.6
SIPRI	327	313	−4.3
ACDA (current $)	434	440	1.4
ACDA (1975 $)	434	419	−3.4

While there is considerable variation in these numbers, all of them may be correctly derived from the value of Austrian military expenditures in Austrian schillings. Part of the difference in these numbers is accounted for by inflation. The IISS numbers are current year dollars, and include inflation. Both ACDA and SIPRI publish constant-dollar series on Austrian expenditures, showing that in real terms, Austria reduced her military expenditure between 1975 and 1976.

ACDA and SIPRI control for inflation by selecting a base year and then measuring the value of the military purchases of a state over time in terms of that base. Since the use of constant prices compensates for inflation, changes in the series should reflect real changes in resource commitments.

A problem is choosing which year to use for the base year. SIPRI uses 1973, while ACDA advances its base year in each edition of its publication. An accurate comparison of ACDA and SIPRI data on military expenditures or arms transfers would require that they be converted to a common base year. Even if this were done, however, there still could be differences between the two series which would reflect differences in computational procedures. Specifically, ACDA and SIPRI use different estimates of the rate of inflation. SIPRI generally uses the rate of inflation in consumer goods, while ACDA uses a measure of the inflation rate in the whole economy. This is calculated from data on the gross national product (GNP) which ACDA receives from the World Bank in both current and constant local currency. The difference between the current and the constant series allows the calculation of the rate of inflation from the GNP. In most instances the choice of using a consumer price index or a GNP price index is unlikely to produce great variance in the resulting constant-value series, but the accuracy with which either one represents the actual inflation rate in the arms industry remains uncertain.

There are also various procedures for converting different currencies into a common currency, such as dollars. Both ACDA and SIPRI use a similar procedure, although they differ in choice of base year and exchange rate. The ACDA procedure is first to transform a given state's military expenditure in local currency into a constant series with a base year, say 1975. The average annual exchange rate for 1975 is then used to convert the local currency values into 1975 constant-dollar prices. Using an analogous procedure, SIPRI uses 1973 as its base year and applies either official or weighted average exchange rates for that year.

In addition to a constant-dollar series which shows the real trend in defense expenditure, it may be desirable to know the value of a state's military expenditure in that year's prices. ACDA produces this series by applying the U.S. rate of inflation to the constant dollar series to "reinflate" the constant dollars. However, because the current-dollar series is derived from the constant-dollar series, the current-dollar values do not always remain the same from one edition of WMEAT to the next. This creates difficulties for the analyst who wishes to construct a time series longer than ten years by stringing together data from several editions. This problem occurs because, when the base year for constant dollars is advanced for a new edition of WMEAT, the process of deflating local currency values with the new base year price index, converting to constant dollars at the new exchange rate, and then reinflating to current dollars using the new base year U.S. price index, does not necessarily produce the same result given by the price indexes and exchange rate for the preceding year. The alternative is to convert directly from current values in local currency to current dollars, using the separate exchange rate for each year. This is the procedure used by IISS. A constant-dollar series, if desired, would then be derived from the current series. Changes in exchange rates, however, are then manifested as distortions in the dollar-time series, reducing the utility of the data for longitudinal analysis.

It would be desirable if more current data on military expenditures or arms transfers were available, since the most recent data published in WMEAT refer to events two calendar years before the date of publication. Actually, the question of more current information has different implications for arms transfers than it does for military expenditures.

ACDA military expenditure data refer to actual expenditures, not budgets or appropriations. Thus, by definition the total military expenditures for any given year cannot be compiled until after that year is completed. Especially for states with uncertain budgetary and accounting practices, establishing a firm figure for expenditures for the previous year may take a considerable period. Once the figure is established, however, it is unlikely to change significantly. In contrast, the ACDA numbers on arms transfers are generated by official U.S. government sources. More recent information in this case may produce sizable revisions in the figures reported in earlier editions of WMEAT.

CONCLUSION

It should be apparent that there are considerable problems in attemping to obtain valid and reliable data on military expenditures and arms transfers. Yet despite these problems, good data are essential to intelligent discussion of issues and policy concerning arms transfers and military expenditures. For the student of these questions a possible strategy for dealing with these data problems has three components. First, the nature and limitations of the data should be clearly understood. Second, the data should be used with caution; the analyst should not attempt to be too subtle in wringing out nuances of meaning from the data, since the numbers are subject to both error and revision. Finally, other sources of information should, if possible, be used in conjunction with the data on arms transfers or military expenditures. Multiple streams of evidence can be used by the analyst to increase or decrease one's confidence in one's findings.

NOTES

1. Edward J. Laurence, "The International Transfer of Arms: Problems of Measurement and Conceptualization," paper presented for delivery at the annual meeting of the Midwest Political Science Association, Chicago, Ill., April 1977, p. 3.

2. U.S. Arms Control and Disarmament Agency, World Military Expenditures and Arms Transfers, 1967–1976 (Washington, D.C.: U.S. Government Printing Office), p. 23.

3. Stockholm International Peace Research Institute, World Armaments and Disarmament, SIPRI Yearbook 1978 (London: Taylor & Francis Ltd., 1978), pp. 291–93.

4. U.S. Central Intelligence Agency, National Foreign Assessment Center, A Dollar Cost Comparison of Soviet and U.S. Defense Activities, 1967–77, January 1978, p. 2.

5. Stockholm International Peace Research Institute, 1974. World Armament and Disarmament, SIPRI Yearbook 1974 (Stockholm: Almqvist & Wiksell), pp. 172–204.

6. Sources: International Institute for Strategic Studies, The Military Balance 1977–1978 (Dovking: Adlard and Son, 1977), p. 82; SIPRI, Yearbook 1978, p. 147; ACDA, World Military Expenditures, 1967–76, p. 34.

PART TWO

THE INTERNATIONAL SYSTEMS LEVEL

4 SUPPLIER-CLIENT PATTERNS IN ARMS TRANSFERS: THE DEVELOPING COUNTRIES, 1967–76

Michael Mihalka

The global pattern of arms transfers reflects, focuses, and influences the changing character of international politics. Unfortunately, few studies have examined worldwide supplier-client arms-transfer patterns; that is, most efforts concentrate on a single region or discuss a single client or supplier and often make ill-informed comparisons with other regions. This chapter purposely adopts a global and statistical perspective and, in addition to describing broad trends in the importation of arms between 1967 and 1976, we examine trends in supplying arms. Beyond describing current attempts by developing countries to establish indigenous arms industries, supplier-client relations are outlined for specific classes in weapons systems between 1969 and 1976; the patterns emerging from this analysis are then compared with those of the period from 1955 to 1968. It is hoped that we will avoid using statistics as a drunken man uses lampposts—for support rather than illumination.

GENERAL TRENDS

Three trends appear in the pattern of arms imported by developing countries from 1967 to 1976: the decline in weapons flowing into Southeast

This paper has benefited from the comments and criticisms of Gloria Duffy, Tom McNaugher, David Ronfeldt, and Cesar Sereseres.

Asia, the more than compensating increase in imports by the members of OPEC; and the aggravation of conflict in the Middle East. Although the global dollar value of arms transferred has increased since 1967 in relative terms, the market in 1976 resembles the market of 1967. Military expenditures and the value of arms transferred as a percentage of GNP and arms imports as a percentage of military expenditures have roughly the same value in 1976 as they did in 1967; moreover, a real increase in the cost of weapons and the transfer of sophisticated weaponry to new countries (especially members of OPEC) has also contributed to the continuing increase in the aggregate value of arms transferred. In addition, the attempt by some countries to create an across-the-board indigenous arms industry has only partially succeeded; even the countries that have progressed the farthest—Brazil, Israel, and India—must still rely on foreign technology, especially for aircraft engines.

The United States continues to dominate the arms market, but estimates of the extent of domination vary. Many sales figures show the United States maintaining a two-to-one lead over its nearest competitor— usually thought to be the Soviet Union. The Soviet Union, however, supplies more combat aircraft and tanks to developing countries than does the United States. In part, this anomaly reflects different supply philosophies; the Soviet Union tends to replace a whole weapon system, while the United States emphasizes the replacement of system parts, accompanied by adequate training.

Although the two superpowers act as major suppliers for most countries, states have increasingly diversified their sources of supply. The characteristic pattern of multiple supply seems to involve securing hardware within a major weapons class primarily from one supplier but choosing different suppliers across weapon classes. Transport aircraft make up the only system countries seem to purchase from multiple sources with any frequency.

The character of each region differs as an arena for supply competition. Western suppliers dominate the Latin American market; until recent agreements with Peru, the Soviet Union supplied arms only to Cuba. Soviet-European competition characterizes sub-Saharan Africa. Soviet movement into the Horn of Africa leaves the United States without a major client in this area. Soviet-U.S. competition has virtually frozen out European efforts to penetrate the Asian market. The Middle East and North African region has become an "arms bazaar." Countries in the area with access to oil money (either directly, such as Libya or Iraq, or indirectly, such as Egypt) pick and choose among the many offerings of the arms exporters.

The fact that clients change suppliers rather frequently throws suspicion upon the argument that arms transfers give suppliers political leverage over clients. Arms imports seem to reflect more than to determine political orientation, and competition among suppliers has provided developing countries with considerable freedom of action. Latin America has moved a long way out of the U.S. orbit and now receives arms from a variety of Western suppliers and from countries within the region. Countries in sub-Saharan Africa apparently switch suppliers as the political exigencies dictate. The buying power of the OPEC countries allows them considerable freedom of choice. As a result of the Indochina war, the United States has lost a number of clients in Asia. Because the United States now requires payment for arms once provided free under the Military Assistance Program, developing countries have become more selective in their choice of suppliers. Overall, supplier-client relations will remain volatile as developing countries pursue their own policies independent of the interests of the countries that supply them with arms.

DATA SOURCES

Published by the U.S. Arms Control and Disarmament Agency (ACDA), *World Military Expenditures and Arms Transfers 1967–76 (WMEAT)* provides the major source of information on broad trends in arms transfers.[1] It contains statistics on the dollar value of goods actually delivered during the reference year, in contrast to the value of programs, agreements, contracts, and orders which may result in a future transfer of goods, or the actual payments made for such deliveries. *WMEAT* defines arms transfers as "the international transfer under grant, credit, or cash sales terms of military equipment usually referred to as 'conventional,' including weapons of war, parts thereof, ammunition, support equipment, and other commodities primarily military in nature." *WMEAT* includes the value of equipment transferred for defense industries but excludes training and technical services. Although *WMEAT* details the value of arms transfers that each state imports and exports by year, it provides that information only in aggregate form without detailing specific suppliers and clients for the given year.

The Stockholm International Peace Research Institute (SIPRI) provides much of the data on specific transfers of weapon systems.[2] These data have been aggregated here to describe specific supplier-client relationships in 11 different classes of weapon systems: combat aircraft, trainer aircraft, transport aircraft, utility aircraft, helicopters, tanks, armored personnel carriers (APCs), armored cars and reconnaissance vehicles, major surface combatants (e.g., destroyers and frigates), minor surface combatants (e.g., patrol boats and mine sweepers), and submarines. The present analysis is restricted to those states that Amelia Leiss included in her 1970 landmark study[3] so that changes in patterns can be readily identified (Table 4.1). Although the *WMEAT* information complements the SIPRI data,

TABLE 4.1: Countries in the Leiss Sample

Latin America and Caribbean

Argentina	Colombia	Nicaragua
Bolivia	Cuba	Peru
Brazil	Dominican Republic	Venezuela
Chile	Mexico	

Middle East and North Africa

Algeria	Jordan	Syria
Egypt	Lebanon	Tunisia
Iran	Libya	Northern Yemen
Iraq	Morocco	
Israel	Saudi Arabia	

Asia

Afghanistan	Korea, Republic of	Philippines
Cambodia	Laos	Thailand
India	Malaysia	Vietnam, Peoples
Indonesia	Pakistan	Republic of
Korea, Democratic		Vietnam, Republic of
Peoples Republic of		

Sub-Saharan Africa

Congo, Peoples Republic	Mali	Tanzania
Ethiopia	Nigeria	Uganda
Ghana	Rhodesia	Zaire
Guinea	Somalia	Zambia
Kenya	Sudan	

Source: Amelia Leiss, "Changing Patterns of Arms Transfers," Report C/70-2, Center for International Studies, Massachusetts Institute of Technology, Cambridge, February 1970.

these sources occasionally conflict, as will be seen in the discussion of supplier trends.

CLIENT TRENDS: 1967–76

Transfers

From 1967 to 1976, the top six arms recipients in the developing countries accounted for between 48 and 64 percent of the total value of arms transferred,* and the recipient of the largest amount of arms accounted for between 13 and 24 percent of that total. The countries among the top six in this period have remained roughly the same: the Republic of South Vietnam appeared in nine years; Iran and the Democratic Republic of North Vietnam each appeared in seven years; Egypt, six years; Turkey and Israel, five years; and the Republic of South Korea and Iraq, four years. No African or Latin American countries ever made the top six.

Three trends underlie the progressive increase in the value of arms transfers between 1967 and 1976. Figure 4.1 shows a decline in the value of arms flowing to the Southeast Asian countries but for which the OPEC countries more than compensate. The infusion of arms into the Republic of Vietnam largely accounts for the 1972 increase and the October War explains the jump in the 1973 figures. Two rather obvious conclusions are highlighted: that wars do indeed consume weapons and that the flood of oil money to the OPEC states assisted them in their quest for more arms.

The supply of arms to sub-Saharan Africa and Latin America remained of only minor consequence throughout this period. Two individual states outside the region in 1976, three in 1975 and five in 1974 received more in arms transfers than all of Latin America combined, while sub-Saharan Africa received an even smaller share of arms imports than Latin America. Perhaps the key way in which sub-Saharan Africa and Latin America differ from the Middle East and Southeast Asia is that they do not currently provide arenas for competition between the United States and the Soviet Union. Sub-Saharan Africa and Latin America also do not suffer from the intermittent interstate hostilities that afflict both East Asia and the Middle East, and these countries have neither possessed the flexibility provided by a favorable balance of payments nor occupied what the superpowers view as important geopolitical positions. This latter situation may now be changing; only the passage of time will reveal whether the appearance of Soviet Su-22s in Peru and the recent conflict in the Horn of Africa will increase superpower competition in Latin America and sub-Saharan Africa, respectively.

The progressive increase in arms transfers from 1967 to 1976 has given rise to the charge that we are witnessing an arms race that is out of control, but two important features of this period may modify this impression. First, the data in Figure 4.2 show the extent to which the complexion of arms trade in 1976 resembles that of 1967. Military expenditures as a proportion

---

*WMEAT classes as "developed" all states within NATO except Greece and Turkey; all states in the Warsaw Pact except Bulgaria; and Australia, Austria, Finland, Ireland, Japan, New Zealand, South Africa, Sweden, and Switzerland. The developing countries include all other states. Portugal and Romania, although listed as developed, possess characteristics more typical of developing states; Israel more closely resembles a "developed" state.

FIGURE 4.1: Value of Arms Received by OPEC Countries; Israel, Egypt, and Syria; and North and South Vietnam: 1967–76 ($ U.S. millions, constant 1975)

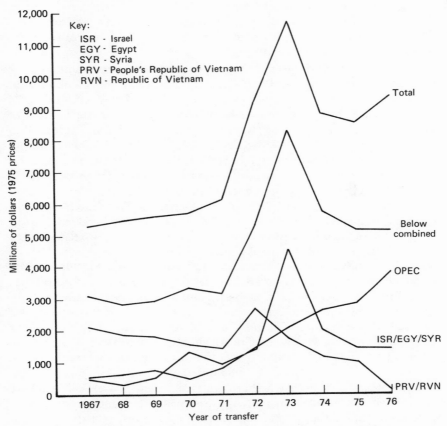

Source: U.S. Arms Control and Disarmament Agency, *World Military Expenditures and Arms Transfers, 1967–1976.* (Washington, D.C.: U.S. Government Printing Office, 1978).

of gross national product (GNP) have remained constant throughout the ten-year period. Arms imports and military expenditures as a percentage of GNP decline from 1967 to 1970, increase in 1972 and 1973, and fall back to 1967 levels in 1975–76.[4] Of course, countries do not necessarily pay for arms in the same year that they receive them. Nevertheless, the flow of arms has not induced countries to increase the proportion of their GNP that they spend on the military. Arms imports have increased in roughly the same proportion as GNP for developing countries as a whole.

FIGURE 4.2: Developing Countries—Arms Imports (AI) as Percentage of GNP and Military Expenditures (MILEX); and Military Expenditures as Percentage of GNP: 1967–76

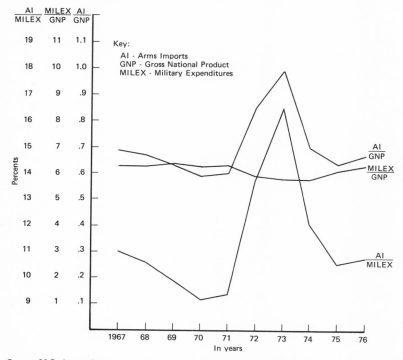

Source: U.S. Arms Control and Disarmament Agency, *World Military Expenditures and Arms Transfers, 1967–76.* (Washington, D.C.: U.S. Government Printing Office, 1978).

Second, the cost of arms has increased with time. Figures 4.3 and 4.4 detail cost increases in tactical aircraft and tanks, respectively. Commenting on cost trends in U.S. forces, one observer suggested that "we will reach a point in the year 2036 where the Defense Department will literally be able to afford only one aircraft."[5] If all countries replaced their obsolete inventory with modern equipment on a one-for-one basis, the trend line for the value of arms transfers would proceed ever upward without increasing the number of weapon systems in inventory. Cost escalation may create the impression of an "arms race" when, in fact, states are simply continuing to modernize their forces.

The recent increase in the value of arms transferred to OPEC states reflects not just an increase in quantity but the acquisition of relatively new and expensive weapons systems such as the F-14s that Iran received. The

FIGURE 4.3: Unit Cost Increase with Time: Tactical Aircraft

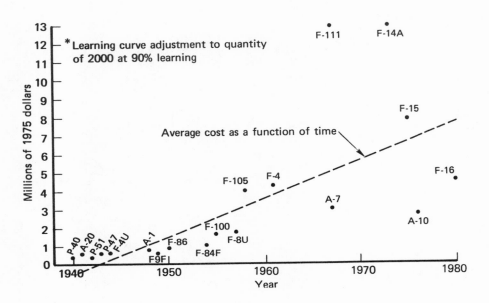

Source: Arthur J. Alexander provided the results from an unpublished analysis, W. D. White provided original cost data in *U.S. Tactical Air Power* (Washington, D.C.: Brookings, 1974).

increase in dollar value also reflects the U.S. and Soviet policies of providing relatively sophisticated equipment to areas that occasionally become embroiled in hostilities. For example, Israel has received 15 F-15s by 1976; the Republic of China (Taiwan) acquired 22 F-104B Starfighters from the U.S. in 1960, and Egypt received Tu-16s from the Soviet Union in 1961. The new purchasing power of the OPEC states has also led to the transfer of sophisticated weaponry; Libya has received Mirage F-1s from France and MiG-23Es from the Soviet Union.

Transfers of modern weapons do not necessarily signify any increase in military capability without the transfer of the requisite military infrastructure. Countries that have built a military infrastructure over the years can readily accommodate and effectively use sophisticated weapons. Israel, the Republic of China, and the Republic of Korea can incorporate new weapons within their force structure more readily than Iran or Saudi Arabia. In the near term, petrodollars in the latter two have bought the hardware

FIGURE 4.4: Unit Cost Increase with Time: Tanks

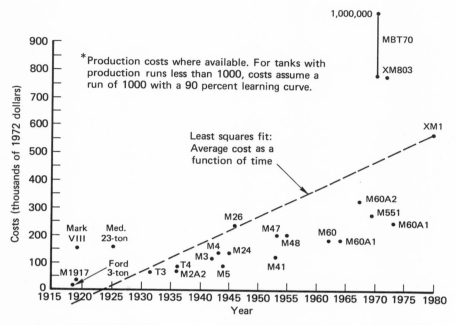

Source: Arthur J. Alexander, *Armor Development in the Soviet Union and the United States,* R-1860-NA (Santa Monica, CA: Rand Corporation, 1976).

and a large U.S. presence to assist in training.[6] Military effectiveness may come in time.[7] The transfer of sophisticated weapons to countries like Saudi Arabia and Iran, while not necessarily increasing their ability to operate their military forces independently, probably does serve an important political function in signaling a privileged supplier-client relation.[8]

Indigenous and Licensed Production

To avoid relying on the major arms exporters, some countries have attempted to establish indigenous arms industries or to produce weapon systems under license;[9] this trend will decrease dependence on the major exporters. These new arms-producing countries often meet their own military requirements and export to other developing countries. Although many countries have indigenous and licensed production programs, only three—Brazil, India, and Israel—have attempted to construct an across-the-board arms industry.

Brazil produces the Italian-designed M-326, an armed trainer and light strike aircraft, under license and has even exported its version, the MB-326G, to Togo under the Brazilian designation of AT-26 Xavante. Empresa Brasilera da Aeronautica SA (EMBRAER) produces a complete line of small to medium transports—the Bandeirante family—and has exported the maritime patrol version to Chile. Abu Dhabi, Libya, and Qatar have ordered the Brazilian Cascavel EE-9 armored car, although Brazil has not yet found a foreign buyer for the Urutu E-ll armored personnel carrier. Niteroi-class destroyers have been built in Rio de Janeiro shipyards. The Brazilians are clearly pursuing a policy to reach self-sufficiency in arms production.

Indian attempts to assure self-sufficiency in arms production predate Brazilian efforts. The first Indian-built Vickers Main Battle Tank rolled off the line in January 1969. Hindustan Aeronautics Limited (HAL) began development of the HF-24 Marut jet fighter in 1956. HAL currently produces a number of jet aircraft succeeding the Marut, has developed a light helicopter, and manufactures most of the components for the HAL 748, a transport aircraft. In addition, India has built Leander-class frigates at the Bombay shipyards.

The Israeli arms industry produces modern fighters such as the Kfir, and armored reconnaissance vehicles. Israel builds Reshef-class guided-missile patrol boats at the Haifa shipyards.

These countries have attempted to achieve self-sufficiency in arms production, but many of the weapon systems still require important components supplied by the major exporters. The United States was able to block an attempted Israeli sale of Kfirs to Ecuador because the plane used American engines and aircraft of the EMBRAER Bandeirante family use Pratt and Whitney turboprops. Although the Indians themselves produce the jet engines for the HAL Ajeet light attack aircraft under license from the United Kingdom, most countries rely on the major exporters to supply engines for their aircraft. The Cascavel and Urutu use Daimler-Benz engines and the French will fit H-90 turrets on the Cascavels that the Brazilians will supply to Qatar. Thus, with few exceptions, the developing countries have not progressed very far towards self-sufficiency in arms production. Even the programs that have achieved the greatest success still rely heavily on foreign technology.

SUPPLIER TRENDS: 1967–76

WMEAT does not unambiguously describe trends in the export of arms to developing countries. By not identifying the supplier for each recipient on a yearly basis, it cannot reveal whether the supply side of the market has changed significantly.

Most discussion on arms exports centers on sales rather than deliveries. Figures showing the dollar value of arms transfers agreements identify the United States as clearly dominating the arms market.[10] The Soviet Union barely succeeds in concluding more sales than either the United Kingdom or France. In terms of sales, the United States has even widened the gap, since 1972, between itself as a world leader and its trailing competitors in the supply of armaments. Critics have charged that the United States has leaped even farther ahead as a result of the Carter administration's current policy on arms transfers.[11] But the dollar value in sales and deliveries present an extremely misleading impression of the nature of the arms market.

The measurement of exports in terms of the numbers of major weapons actually delivered presents a different picture than sales. Table 4.2 illustrates the distribution of arms that major exporters have delivered to developing countries. The dominance of the United States appears less marked with the Soviet Union supplying the majority of combat aircraft and more tanks and self-propelled guns. According to WMEAT figures, the United States does dominate in exporting non-combat aircraft, helicopters, major surface combatants, submarines, armored personnel carriers, and armored cars. The delivery figures certainly temper the impression the United States provides twice as many arms as its nearest competitor.

A recent study contends that using WMEAT dollar values as a basis for comparing United States and Soviet arms transfers is "worse than meaningless."[12] According to the New York Times, the Central Intelligence Agency has prepared a report showing that the dollar value of Soviet transfers closely approximates the value of U.S. transfers.[13] Although very little of the U.S. program escapes notice, the Defense Intelligence Agency (DIA) estimates of Soviet transfers upon which the WMEAT assessments are based, depend heavily on the validity of intelligence sources. Although the United States transfers both services and equipment, the Soviets generally transfer only equipment. SIPRI, valuing arms transfers only by the cost of major weapons exported, assesses that the United States and the Soviet Union delivered respectively 14.8 and 14.6 billion dollars (in constant 1975 prices) worth of arms to developing countries between 1967 and 1976. WMEAT estimates that the United States and the Soviet Union delivered 30.0 and 15.5 billion dollars (in current prices) worth of goods and services respectively, during the same period. WMEAT juxtaposes a picture of two-to-one U.S. dominance to the image of rough equality between the United States and the Soviet Union conveyed by SIPRI.

OVERALL SUPPLIER-CLIENT PATTERNS: 1967–76

Table 4.3 portrays only a marginal and not overwhelming U.S. dominance of the arms market. A change in the accounting procedures used to estimate the value of arms transferred would not significantly change this

TABLE 4.2: Distribution of Major Weapons Delivered by Major Suppliers to Developing Countries, 1967–76

	Major Weapons Delivered (%)				Total Number of Major Weapons Delivered by Major Suppliers
	United States	Soviet Union	France	United Kingdom	
Aircraft					
Combat aircraft	35.9	54.7	5.7	3.8	6212
Noncombat aircraft[a]	59.0	13.3	13.3	14.5	3026
Helicopters	56.3	23.7	17.8	2.3	2972
Naval Vessels					
Major surface combatants[b]	70.0	12.4		17.7	113
Minor surface combatants[c]	23.0	32.7	17.2	27.0	640
Submarines	40.7	25.9	13.0	20.4	54
Land Armaments					
Tanks and self-propelled guns	41.6	47.5	3.9	7.0	18,607
Armored personnel carriers and armored cars	53.3	36.4	7.2	3.2	19,376

Source: WMEAT.

Note: Recipients include developing countries and the following developed countries: Australia, Japan, New Zealand, and South Africa. Excludes Soviet transfers to Vietnam and U.S. transfers to Indochina under the Military Assistance and Service Fund.

a. Reconnaissance aircraft, trainers, transports, and utility aircraft.

b. Aircraft carriers, cruisers, destroyers, destroyer escorts, and frigates.

c. Guided missile patrol boats, motor torpedo boats, subchasers, and minesweepers.

TABLE 4.3: Supplier-Client Patterns, 1967–76 of Transfers [*WMEAT: 67–76*] (by dollar value)

Sole Supplier		Predominant Supplier		Multiple Supplier	
Client	Supplier	Client	Supplier	Client	Largest Supplier
Western Bloc		*Western Bloc*		*Western Bloc*	
Dominican Republic	U.S.	Bolivia	U.S.	Argentina	U.S. (36%)
Republic of Korea	U.S.	Nicaragua	U.S.	Brazil	U.S. (43%)
Republic of Vietnam	U.S.	Iran	U.S.	Chile	U.K. (41%)
Republic of China	U.S.	Burma	U.S.	Colombia	U.S. (31%)
		Israel	U.S.	Ecuador	U.S. (16%)
Eastern Bloc		Jordan	U.S.	Honduras	U.S. (29%)
Mongolia	USSR	Tunisia	U.S.	Mexico	U.K. (57%)
Cuba	USSR	Cambodia	U.S.	Venezuela	France (33%)
Mali	USSR	Laos	U.S.	Lebanon	France (57%)
		Malaysia	U.S.	Morocco	France (35%)
		Philippines	U.S.	Saudi Arabia	U.S. (47%)
		Thailand	U.S.	Indonesia	U.S. (51%)
		Ethiopia	U.S.	Ghana	U.K. (43%)
		Guatemala	U.S.	Togo	Canada (40%)
		Paraguay	U.S.	Zaire	France (46%)
		Kenya	U.K.	Singapore	U.S. (44%)
		Uruguay	U.S.	Kuwait	U.K. (39%)

TABLE 4.3: *(continued)*

Sole Supplier		Predominant Supplier		Multiple Supplier	
Client	Supplier	Client	Supplier	Client	Largest Supplier
		Eastern Bloc			
		Algeria	USSR	Oman	U.K. (29%)
		Egypt	USSR	Ivory Coast	France (50%)
		Iraq	USSR		
		Syria	USSR		*Eastern Bloc*
		Democratic Republic of Korea	USSR	Congo	USSR (50%)
					Cross-Bloc
		Peoples Republic of Vietnam	USSR	Peru	USSR (25%)
				Libya	USSR (54%)
		Guinea	USSR	Northern Yemen	USSR (40%)
		Somalia	USSR	Afghanistan	USSR (32%)
		Uganda	USSR	Pakistan	People's Republic of China (40%)
		Southern Yemen	USSR	Nigeria	USSR (31%)
		Angola	USSR	Zambia	Canada (19%)
		Tanzania	People's Republic of China		
		Eastern Bloc with Cross-Bloc Ties			
		India	USSR		
		Sudan	USSR		

Note: Countries included in this table received over $25 million worth of arms between 1967 and 1976 according to *WMEAT* or were part of the Leiss 51 country sample (see Table 4.1). A country was considered as a cross-bloc recipient if it received at least 10 percent of its arms (estimated in dollar value from *WMEAT*) from each bloc. A predominant supplier provides more than 60% by dollar value of a client's arms.

Source: *WMEAT.*

pattern. Of the 65 states listed, the United States is the sole or predominant supplier for 20. The Soviet Union represents the sole or predominant supplier for 16. The United Kingdom and the People's Republic of China serve as the predominant supplier for Kenya and Tanzania respectively.

Latin America still receives most of its arms from the Western bloc; the United States is the sole or predominant supplier for six of 16 Latin American countries, and half of these 16 Latin American countries secure their weapons from a variety of Western sources, the United States being the major supplier for five of these eight. The Soviet Union has not yet penetrated the Latin American arms market to any significant degree, but it has supplied Cuba since the early 1960s and may expect to cultivate other clients if the Peruvians find their new arrangements satisfactory.

During the days of the Southeast Asian conflict, the United States served as the predominant or sole supplier for nine of the 17 Asian countries in Table 4.3. Only Indonesia and Singapore received arms from a variety of other Western sources. In South Asia, Pakistan, India, and Afghanistan secured weapons from both major blocs.

In sub-Saharan Africa, the United States served as the sole or predominant supplier only to Ethiopia. The USSR was the major sole or predominant supplier for the region. Even countries that opted for multiple Western sources of supply (four out of 16) did not secure the majority of their arms from the United States. Nigeria and Zambia acquired their arms from both Eastern and Western blocs, while the Soviet Union served as the predominant source of supply for four other African states. Sub-Saharan Africa provided an arena for arms-export competition between the Soviet Union and the former colonial powers—the United Kingdom and France.

The United States served as the sole or predominant supplier to four of the 16 Middle East and North African states listed, while the Soviet Union supplied five. Libya and Northern Yemen secured their arms from both blocs. The remaining five countries relied on multiple Western sources of supply.

Latin America and Africa have remained largely outside the arena of Soviet-U.S. competition. The United States competes primarily with other Western countries in Latin America, while the Soviet Union competes with the former colonial powers in Africa. In Southeast Asia and the Middle East, the clients of each bloc tended to be arrayed against each other between 1967 and 1976.

SUPPLIER-CLIENT PATTERNS BY MAJOR WEAPONS SYSTEMS: 1969–76

Because *WMEAT* does not describe specific transfers, the various SIPRI volumes must be relied on for identifying trends in supplier-client relations by the major weapon systems traded. Another analysis by the present author details the specific distribution of suppliers for each client in each of the weapons-systems categories listed earlier.[14] Countries were classed according to the proportion of weapons they have received from suppliers. If a country received weapons from only one supplier, that country was listed under the sole supplier. If a country received more than 60 percent of its arms from one supplier, it was listed under the principal or predominant supplier. The rest of the countries were identified as receiving arms from multiple suppliers.

The classification scheme obviously reflects a certain degree of arbitrariness. No attempt has been made to compare the cost of specific weapon systems within categories. Each weapon is implicitly assigned a weight equal to all others in a category. In Table 4.3 each weapon system is weighted according to its dollar value to develop an overall picture of supplier-client patterns. But this procedure has no more validity than the simple "bean counting" done in estimating the number of major weapons supplied within each class. The worth of a piece of military hardware depends on a number of factors outside the scope of this discussion. Bean counting must suffice to describe the distribution of suppliers.

The SIPRI data flesh out and sometimes conflict with the summary information found in *WMEAT*. For example, *WMEAT* indicates that Mexico has acquired its arms from a variety of Western sources, but primarily from the United Kingdom, yet SIPRI indicates that Mexico appears to have received combat and trainer aircraft and major and minor surface combatants from the United States and transport aircraft from the United Kingdom. Similarly, according to *WMEAT*, Algeria receives a negligible amount of arms from France, but the data derived from SIPRI suggest that France supplied Algeria with most of its combat aircraft and all of its helicopters, with the Soviet Union supplying all of its minor surface combatants. While on the whole SIPRI and *WMEAT* agree, enough inconsistencies appear to suggest that only broad generalizations about the nature of the arms market are justified.

When SIPRI data and *WMEAT* data (See Table 4.3) are combined, supply patterns are revealed for those countries that buy arms from a variety of suppliers. In general, the characteristic pattern of multiple supply seems to involve securing weapons from only one supplier for each major weapon class, but from various suppliers across weapon classes. Argentina received most of its helicopters and combat and trainer aircraft from the United States, but relied on multiple sources of supply for transport aircraft and armored personnel carriers. Morocco received combat and transport aircraft from the United States, but acquired its helicopters primarily from France. Zambia received combat aircraft from Yugoslavia; helicopters, trainers, and utility aircraft from Italy; transport aircraft from a variety of

Western sources, and tanks from the USSR. Even though a country may rely on multiple sources of supply for overall needs, it tends to maintain a single supplier for a given class of weapons.

Tables 4.4 through 4.6 highlight the observation that multiple supply has not generally occurred with regard to major weapon systems. Transport aircraft seem to be an exception to this general rule. But even in this class, only 11 out of 45 recipients relied on multiple sources.

The picture of trading patterns in particular systems that emerges from Tables 4.4 through 4.6 does not deviate significantly from the overall picture displayed in Table 4.3. Latin America remained a preserve for Western suppliers throughout this period; the USSR had only Cuba as a major client in the region. Sub-Saharan Africa remained an arena of competition between the Soviets, the Chinese, and the Europeans, with the United States supplying only the Ethiopians. East Asia and the Middle East-North Africa region display the interbloc competition that has reflected, if not exacerbated, the continuing conflicts in these regions.

The Middle East/North Africa region, however, differs from Asia as an arena for interbloc competition. The United States and the Soviet Union clearly dominated supply to Asia; only the supply of major surface combatants to Pakistan and Malaysia suggests any European penetration. In the Middle East and North Africa, on the other hand, the Europeans are major competitors with the Soviet Union and the United States in the "prestige" systems of combat aircraft, tanks, helicopters, and naval craft. Between 1969 and 1976, as noted before, trading patterns displayed a different character in each region: Western competition marked Latin America; Soviet-European competition marked sub-Saharan Africa; the United States and the Soviet Union competed virtually alone in East Asia; and the Middle East and North Africa provided a market for all, in part owing to the influx of hard currency from the sale of oil.

CHANGES IN SUPPLIER-CLIENT PATTERNS

The Leiss study provides the major source of information on the supplier-client patterns prior to 1969; it encompasses a broader span— 1945–68 for naval craft, 1959–68 for helicopters, 1955–68 for all other weapon systems—than the 1969–76 span examined here. But these last eight years have witnessed some important changes in the arms market; the recipient countries have become much more willing to shift suppliers both within and across blocs.

Tables 4.7 through 4.9 display the changes in supplier-client patterns from 1969 to 1976. A country's supply pattern remained the same if it continued to acquire arms from the same predominant or sole supplier. A

TABLE 4.4: Regional Distribution of Supplier Patterns: Aircraft, 1969–76 (number of countries)

	Sole and Principal Suppliers					Multiple Suppliers		
	U.S.	USSR	U.K.	France	Other	West	Cross-Bloc	East
Latin America								
Combat	4	1	—	3	—	1	—	—
Trainer	5	—	—	—	—	1	—	—
Transport	2	1	—	—	3	4	—	—
Utility	5	—	—	—	—	—	—	—
Helicopters	1	—	—	1	—	—	—	—
M.E. and N. Africa								
Combat	5	3	2	2	—	1	—	—
Trainer	1	1	3	1	1	—	—	—
Transport	6	1	—	—	2	1	—	—
Utility	2	—	—	—	2	—	—	—
Helicopters	4	2	—	4	—	—	1	—
Asia								
Combat	3	4	—	—	1	—	1	—
Trainer	5	—	1	—	3	—	—	—
Transport	5	2	2	—	—	3	—	—
Utility	5	—	—	—	3	—	—	—
Helicopters	8	2	—	1	—	—	1	—
Sub-Saharan Africa								
Combat	—	4	1	—	4	2	—	1
Trainer	1	1	4	—	4	3	—	—
Transport	1	4	1	—	4	1	—	—
Utility	2	—	—	—	3	1	—	—
Helicopter	1	2	—	5	4	—	1	—

Source: Prepared by the author from SIPRI data.

66

TABLE 4.5: Regional Distribution of Supplier Patterns: Armor, 1969–76 (number of countries)

	Sole and Principal Suppliers					Multiple Suppliers		
	U.S.	USSR	U.K.	France	Other	West	Cross Bloc	East
Latin America								
Tanks	—	1	—	3	—	—	—	—
APCs	1	—	—	—	—	1	—	—
Armored cars	—	—	—	—	1	—	—	—
M.E. and N. Africa								
Tanks	3	4	—	2	—	1	—	—
APCs	2	3	—	—	1	—	1	—
Armored cars	2	—	2	3	—	—	—	—
Asia								
Tanks	2	2	—	—	1	—	1	1
APCs	5	2	—	1	2	—	—	—
Armored cars	2	—	1	—	—	—	—	—
Sub-Saharan Africa								
Tanks	1	4	—	—	2	—	—	—
APCs	—	3	—	—	—	—	—	1
Armored cars	—	1	—	3	1	—	—	—

Source: Prepared by the author from SIPRI data.

TABLE 4.6: Regional Distribution of Supplier Patterns: Naval Vessels, 1969–76 (number of countries)

	Sole and Principal Suppliers					Multiple Suppliers		
	U.S.	USSR	U.K.	France	Other	West	Cross Bloc	East
Latin America								
Major surface combatants	4	—	1	—	—	2	—	—
Minor surface combatants	3	1	—	—	—	1	—	—
Submarines	2	—	1	—	1	2	—	—
M.E. and N. Africa								
Major surface combatants	1	—	1	1	—	1	—	—
Minor surface combatants	1	7	1	2	—	—	—	—
Submarines	—	2	—	—	—	—	—	—
Asia								
Major surface combatants	5	1	2	—	—	—	—	—
Minor surface combatants	5	3	—	1	2	—	—	—
Submarines	—	2	—	1	—	—	—	—
Sub-Saharan Africa								
Major surface combatants	—	—	1	—	—	—	—	—
Minor surface combatants	—	2	3	—	2	—	—	—
Submarines	—	—	—	—	—	—	—	—

Source: Prepared by the author from SIPRI data.

TABLE 4.7: Changes in Supplier Patterns: Aircraft, 1955–68 to 1969–76 (number of countries)

	Same	Other West	Other East	Changed Bloc	To Cross Bloc	First Received System in 1969–76
Latin America						
Combat	4	5	—	—	—	—
Trainer	3	3	—	—	—	1
Transport	5	5	—	—	—	—
Utility	3	1	—	—	—	1
Helicopter	1	1	—	—	—	—
M.E. and N. Africa						
Combat	6	4	—	3	—	—
Trainer	2	4	—	—	—	—
Transport	6	1	—	3	—	—
Utility	2	1	—	—	—	1
Helicopter	5	3	—	2	1	—
Asia						
Combat	5	—	1	2	—	1
Trainer	2	2	—	2	—	3
Transport	7	3	—	2	—	—
Utility	4	3	—	—	—	1
Helicopter	6	1	—	2	1	2
Sub-Saharan Africa						
Combat	3	3	—	2	—	4
Trainer	2	3	—	3	—	2
Transport	6	3	—	14	—	—
Utility	—	4	—	—	—	2
Helicopter	2	2	—	3	1	5

Source: Prepared by author from SIPRI data.

Note: 1959–68 for helicopters.

TABLE 4.8: Changes in Supplier Patterns: Armor, 1955–68 to 1969–76 (number of countries)

	Same	Other West	Other East	Changed Bloc	To Cross Bloc	First Received System in 1969–76
Latin America						
Tanks	1	4	—	—	—	—
APCs	1	1	—	—	—	—
Armored cars	—	1	—	—	—	2
M.E. and N. Africa						
Tanks	4	4	—	1	—	—
APCs	2	2	—	2	—	—
Armored cars	2	3	—	—	—	2
Asia						
Tanks	4	1	1	1	—	2
APCs	5	—	1	2	—	—
Armored cars	1	1	—	—	—	—
Sub-Saharan Africa						
Tanks	2	—	—	1	—	4
APCs	2	—	—	1	—	1
Armored cars	1	3	—	1	—	—

Source: Prepared by the author from SIPRI data.

TABLE 4.9: Changes in Supplier Patterns: Naval Vessels, 1945–68 to 1969–76 (number of countries)

	Same	Other West	Other East	Changed Bloc	To Cross Bloc	First Received System in 1969–78
Latin America						
Major surface combatants	3	4	—	—	—	—
Minor surface combatants	2	3	—	—	—	1
Submarines	2	3	—	—	—	1
M.E. and N. Africa						
Major surface combatants	3	1	—	—	—	—
Minor surface combatants	7	1	—	2	—	1
Submarines	1	—	—	—	—	1
Asia						
Major surface combatants	5	1	—	2	—	—
Minor surface combatants	4	1	2	4	—	—
Submarines	1	1	—	—	—	1
Sub-Saharan Africa						
Major surface combatants	—	1	—	—	—	—
Minor surface combatants	3	1	—	—	—	3
Submarines	—	—	—	—	—	—

Source: Prepared by the author from SIPRI data.

transition of the supplier's status from sole to predominant or vice versa was not considered to constitute a change. A country that acquired its military hardware from multiple sources did not change its pattern if two of its sources remained the same after 1969. The movement from multiple sources to a sole or predominant supplier and vice versa represented a change. Bloc changes occurred if a country shifted its supplier from a Western to an Eastern country—members of the Warsaw Pact, the People's Republic of China, and Yugoslavia. A shift from a cross-bloc supply situation to either Western or Eastern supplies also signaled a bloc change.

In Latin America, many countries are moving away from the United States and towards alternative Western suppliers. France, for example, has begun to supply a number of clients that formerly bought U.S. arms. French combat aircraft began to appear in the region with the transfer of Mirage-5s to Peru in 1968; Colombia began acquiring Mirage-5s from France in 1972, and Venezuela initiated acquisition of Mirage-3Es and Mirage-5s in 1973. France has supplied the AMX-13 tank to Argentina, Peru and Ecuador and the AMX-30 to Venezuela. The arrival of T-55s and An-26s to Peru mark the first Soviet penetration of this region since Cuba.

The countries of the Middle East and North Africa display changes between Western suppliers and between blocs. Algeria, after relying heavily on Soviet equipment until 1970, acquired 28 Fouga Magisters from France. Northern Yemen switched from Soviet to British supply in combat aircraft.

Asia does not show as many shifts in suppliers as the other areas. The Soviet Union and the United States continued to dominate the area from 1969 to 1976. India moved to a heavier reliance on the Soviet Union for imports of combat aircraft, but offset this dependence by continuing to develop its own arms industry. Indonesia had switched from Soviet to U.S. supply as early as 1965.

In sub-Saharan Africa, more countries have changed their major source of supply, especially in aircraft, than have remained with the same supplier. Only the pre-1968 Soviet clients—Mali, Guinea, and Nigeria—have continued to receive combat aircraft from the USSR. Somalia switched from a cross-bloc supply situation (Italy and the USSR) to relying more heavily on the USSR. Zaire moved from using the U.S. as sole supplier to multiple Western sources. Uganda received its combat aircraft primarily from Libya, whereas previously the Soviet Union had met all Ugandan fighter needs.*

The changes in the patterns of supplying armor reflect in part aggressive French marketing of their AMX series of tanks, but in general, bloc changes in armor mirror the changes for combat aircraft. In naval craft, the Soviet Union has actively entered only the competition for the supply of

---

*Retransfers are also a trend to watch. In 1977 Argentina transferred A-4Ps to Chile and F-86s to Uruguay; Cuba transferred MiG-21s to Peru; and Saudi Arabia transferred F-5Bs to the Yemen Arab Republic.

minor surface combatants. Thus, many of the changes in the supply of naval craft reflect competition between the Western states. The supply relationships for naval vessels display more stability than for either armor or aircraft.

Supplier patterns have become increasingly volatile, and recent years have seen many changes in the choice of suppliers. Table 4.10 shows some of the bloc changes that have occurred since 1968 and provides a tentative explanation for those shifts. The overthrow of Western-oriented regimes in Southeast Asia needs no further elaboration here. The Soviet Union embargoed arms to Egypt in 1974 and to Iraq in 1975. The Sudan followed Egypt's lead in changing suppliers. The Soviets abandoned Somalia to support Ethiopia. Bloc changes reflected either a change in the policy of the recipient or the desire of the supplier to woo other clients. Attempts by suppliers to manipulate a client largely failed and resulted in the client's securing alternative sources of supply; thus, bloc shifts cast suspicion on the argument that a continuing supplier-client relationship can confer leverage on the supplier. Bloc changes occur because a developing country desires less dependence on its supplier, wishes to pursue its own policy, or simply has experienced a change in regime. Soviet clients who wish to change suppliers virtually have to switch blocs, but Western clients can turn to other Western suppliers without being forced to secure arms from the Soviet Union.

Countries increasingly pay for the arms that in previous years they received for nothing;[15] this trend contributes to greater fluidity in the arms

TABLE 4.10: Some Bloc Changes in Arms Supply since 1968

Country	Supplier New	Supplier Old	Approximate Date of Change	Reason
Cambodia	China	U.S.	1973	Regime change
Laos	USSR	U.S.	1973	Regime change
Ethiopia	USSR	U.S.	1977	Regime change
Somalia	West	USSR	1977	Change in Soviet policy
Egypt	West	USSR	1974	Decreased dependence
Sudan	West	USSR	1974	Decreased dependence
Iraq	Cross	USSR	1975	Decreased dependence
Peru	Cross	West	1973	Decreased dependence
Libya	Cross	West	1970	Oil money
North Yemen	West	USSR	1974	Change in policy
Zambia	Cross	West	1971	Nonaligned policy
Congo	East	France	1968	Shift in regime's policy

Source: Prepared by author from analysis of this paper.

trade. The elimination of the U.S. Military Assistance Program has led to a decrease in the stability of the arms trade and the United States has maintained its dominance in the arms trade because of the purchases of a few countries. The saturation of these markets will only increase global competitiveness between major arms exporters.[16]

THE IDEOLOGY OF STATISTICS

Statistics can only go so far in advancing the debate over arms-transfer policy; unfortunately, that debate has given added credence to that old saw about "lies, damned lies, and statistics." Some individuals, viewing the same trends that we have examined, intone the familiar litany of "an arms race out of control," "the growing potential for cataclysmic destruction," and "the militarization of the world economy."[17] Such statements betray little except the author's ideological sympathies and perhaps expose a degree of liberal paternalism. Arms purchases may divert resources from other, more worthwhile pursuits, but they also communicate much about the political interaction among states.* To paraphrase Clausewitz, arms transfers can be viewed as the continuation of politics by other means. Numbers can point to arms purchases either as wasteful or as important instruments of political competition.

When used selectively, the numbers can support the contention of a global arms race, but the arms market has become more competitive also because oil revenues increase the ability of a few countries to pay high prices for sophisticated weapons. Nevertheless, the global arms market has only a few significant buyers and sellers. The major buyers do not acquire arms so much to offset purchases by others (the true meaning of an "arms race") as to achieve political objectives within their regions.

The military value of arms transfers has largely escaped quantification.[18] No one has yet provided a definitive measure of the political value of arms. Statistics can illuminate general trends in arms transfers, but the use of statistics to prove that an arms race has begun in the developing world burdens statistics with unjustifiable and needless ideological baggage.

NOTES

1. U.S. Arms Control and Disarmament Agency, *World Military Expenditures and Arms Transfers 1967–76* (Washington, D.C.: ACDA, 1978).

---

*The suggestion that arms expenditures represent an unproductive use of resources derives in part from a fundamental liberal belief that money or, by extension, reforms can ameliorate societal ills. Marxists, among others, would argue that such societal ills result from the structure of a society and that changes at the margins (e.g., "reallocation of resources") would have little effect.

2. Stockholm International Peace Research Institute, *Arms Trade Registers: The Arms Trade with the Third World* (Cambridge, Mass.: MIT Press 1975); SIPRI, *World Armaments and Disarmament, SIPRI Yearbook 1975, 1976 and 1977* (Cambridge, Mass.: MIT Press 1975, 1976 and 1977).

3. Amelia Leiss, "Changing Patterns of Arms Transfers," Report C/70–2, Center for International Studies, Massachusetts Institute of Technology, Cambridge. February 1970.

4. WMEAT makes no explicit comparisons between the value of arms transfers and estimates for GNP and military expenditures:

The disparity among national economic systems generates differences in the extent to which weapons prices represent true production costs in different nations. In particular, the relative economic value of arms to supplier and recipient may be considerably different. Furthermore, much of the international arms trade involves barter arrangements, multiyear loans, and partial debt forgiveness. Thus, acquisition by a nation of some given quantity of armaments does not necessarily impose the burden on its economy that is implied by the estimated equivalent U.S. dollar value of the shipment. Therefore, the economic value of arms imports should not be related in detail to the local economies (p. 23).

5. Norman R. Augustine, "One Phase, One Tank, One Ship: Trend for the Future?" *Defense Management Journal*, 2 (1975): 34–40.

6. U.S. Congress, House, Committee on International Relations, *United States Arms Policies in the Persian Gulf and Red Sea Areas: Past, Present and Future*, 95th Congress, 1st Session, 1977. "The advanced technology embodied in major U.S. programs in Iran has created the ancillary problem of considerable numbers of U.S. military and civilian personnel required to service the weapons systems and train the Iranian armed forces in their use. Short-term trends indicate a continued deep American involvement and presence in all aspects of the military expansion and modernization process in Iran..." (p. 159). "The U.S. presence in the Persian Gulf may number 150,000 by 1980" (p. 9).

7. In a personal communication to the author, an Israeli Air Force general has commented that the Saudis could only exploit 60 percent of the capabilities of the F-15 while the Israelis could exploit 95 percent. He suggested that prolonged training could increase the Saudis' ability to use effectively the F-l5.

8. David Ronfeldt, "Superclients and Superpowers," Report P-5945, Rand Corporation, Santa Monica, Calif., April 1978. On the diplomatic importance of arms transfers, see David Ronfeldt and Cesar Sereseres, *Arms Transfers, Diplomacy, and Security in Latin America and Beyond*, Report P-6005, Rand Corporation, Santa Monica, Calif., October 1977, esp. pages 37–39.

9. For an up-to-date account of indigenous and licensed production of weapons, see SIPRI, *World Armaments and Disarmament: SIPRI Yearbook 1978* (New York: Crane, Russak & Co., (1978), p. 203–22. See also *Defense and Foreign Affairs Handbook 1978* (Washington, D.C.: Copley & Associates, S.A., 1978); *Jane's Fighting Ships: 1977–78* (London: Jane's Yearbooks 1978); Christopher F. Foss, *Jane's World Armored Fighting Vehicles*, (New York: St. Martin's Press, 1976); F.M. von Senger and Etterlin, *Taschenbuch der Panzer 1976* (Mondien: J.F. Lehmanns Verlag, 1976); Peter Lock and Herbert Wulf, "Consequences of the Transfer of Military-Oriented Technology on the Development Process," *Bulletin of Peace Proposals* 8 (1977); and Signe Landgren-Backstrom, "The Transfer of Military Technology to Third World Countries," *Bulletin of Peace Proposals* 8 (1977).

10. *Report to Congress on Arms Transfer Policy Pursuant to Sections 202(b) and 218 of the International Security Assistance and Arms Control Act of 1976*, (Washington D.C. U.S. Government Printing Office, 1977).

11. Herbert Y. Schandler, et al., "Implications of President Carter's Conventional Arms Transfer Policy," Congressional Research Service, Library of Congress, Washington, D.C., September 1977.

12. Bridget Gail, "'The Fine Old Game of Killing': Comparing U.S. and Soviet Arms Sales," *Armed Forces Journal* (1978): 16–20.

13. Richard Burt, "C.I.A. Study Undermines Effort to Cut Arms Exports," *New York Times,* January 17, 1978, p.3.

14. Michael Milhalka, "Arms to the Third World: 1967–76," Report P-6207, Rand Corporation, Santa Monica, Calif., 1978.

15. Report to Congress, esp. p. 3–7.

16. For one examination of the consequences of this increased competition, see Anthony Sampson, *The Arms Bazaar* (New York: Viking Press, 1977).

17. Ruth Leger Sivard,*World Military Expenditures and Social Expenditures 1976*(Leesburg, Va.: WMSE Publications, 1976) p. 5.

18. For an attempt to assign "capability" scores to arms transfers, see Michael Mihalka, "The Measurement and Modelling of Arms Accumulations: The Middle East as a Case Study," Report C/75-8, Center for International Studies, Massachusetts Institute of Technology, Cambridge, April 1975.

5 THE IMPACT OF PRECISION GUIDED MUNITIONS ON ARMS TRANSFERS AND INTERNATIONAL STABILITY

C. I. Hudson, Jr.

Precision-guided munitions (PGMs) have been hailed by their most enthusiastic proponents as a quantum leap forward in military capability; yet, because of a number of current limitations, they have not delivered on this promise. The potential is still there for future systems, and some of today's PGMs are quite impressive. Both current and future PGMs have characteristics which deserve prudent attention when setting arms-transfer policies. Small groups of individuals can command increased firepower, with a high likelihood of destroying large, expensive targets. The desirability of placing such a capability in the hands of various groups depends on many variables which will be described in this chapter, which also offers some speculation on the effects of PGMs for the future of arms transfers and international stability.

DEFINITION AND DESCRIPTION

A PGM has been defined as a guided munition whose probability of making a direct hit on its target is greater than one-half when the weapon is employed at full range and is unopposed.[1] This is a useful definition for most purposes. A more complete analysis of a given weapon system would also consider the definition of the target, the damage capability of the weapon, and other characteristics, and might define as a PGM a system that does not rigorously meet the first criterion. Important characteristics of the PGM include weapon type; portability of the launcher, carrier, or firing platform; range, speed, probability of hitting the target, and likelihood of damaging the target, should it be hit. Cost, size, shape and weight, maintainability, and survivability may also be important. Other characteristics can be attributed to the weapon or can be external; these include finding and identifying the target, choosing and launching the weapon, guiding it to the target, and assessing the damage done by the weapon.

EARLY HISTORY OF PGM DEVELOPMENT

Many early PGMs were surface-to-air missiles (SAMs). A searching radar was used to find the target aircraft; a radar was also used to track the missile after launch and to keep track of the missile trajectory relative to the flight path of the target. Radio signals told the missile how to alter its course to intercept the plane (command guidance); other versions had on-board sensors and the necessary logic to steer the missile. Once launched in the general vicinity of the target, the on-board sensor would detect the heat of the engine or a reflected radar signal which might have been seen from the ground or the missile itself. The fuse was an important part of such missiles; its job was to pick the right instant to detonate the warhead to achieve the maximum amount of damage. Air-to-air missiles used similar techniques.

MODERN PGMs

The latest improvements in PGM technology are in air-to-surface and surface-to-surface weapons. Laser-guided bombs were demonstrated to have very impressive capabilities in Vietnam. Optically-guided air-to-surface weapons, such as Walleye and Maverick, are also highly effective in daylight during clear weather. Surface-to-surface antitank weapons have several methods for steering the weapon onto the target, including guidance signals transmitted by wire and by light. The Copperhead, a cannon-launched guided projectile, homes on the reflected light from a laser beam; the target can be illuminated by a forward observer or by a remotely-piloted vehicle. Another PGM under development is the Tomahawk cruise missile, which homes on a fixed target which is located relative to certain landmarks, terrain features, or map coordinates.

Homing torpedoes, anti-satellite weapons, and "smart" mines can also be considered PGMs, but this chapter is not intended to be a PGM catalogue or an exhaustive compendium of all existing PGMs. The examples chosen illustrate the breadth of PGM types and their widely varying characteristics; from hand-held, anti-tank weapons to expensive weapons weighing several thousand pounds with ranges of thousands of kilometers. Table 5.1 gives examples of some current PGMs, and lists some of their characteristics.

TWO EXAMPLES

It is almost impossible to make categorical policy statements on arms transfers involving PGMs because of the many complex factors involved. While specific examples do not necessarily lead to valid generalizations, they do provide a method for illustrating the various considerations involved in making arms-transfer policy choices. Two examples are presented from opposite ends of the PGM spectrum: a precision cruise missile and an antitank guided missile. One is expensive, the other cheap; one has a large payload, the other a small one; one is versatile with many potential uses, and the other is highly specialized. One has a long range and can be used quite effectively for offensive operations; the other has a short range and is primarily defensive in nature. When transferred to various recipients, these two types of systems can have very different implications for regional stability.

Precision Cruise Missiles

While the cruise missile may be an extreme case, it offers an example of one basic truth about weapon systems: You can't have everything you want. In a cruise missile, either a large payload or a long range is possible, but not both. Only a few hundred pounds can be sent a few thousand kilometers with today's cruise missiles; with the available delivery accuracy, this requires a nuclear warhead for a significant degree of target destruction. Conventional warheads of a thousand pounds or more could be effective, but this would reduce the range to several hundred kilometers.

Conventionally armed cruise missiles can have three effective delivery modes. First, weapons can be scattered over the target area, and if the weapon damage area, target area, and area-of-delivery error are comparable in dimension and shape, a cruise missile can be very effective. (This is basically a delivery mode analogous to that of a bomber with many bombs.) A second delivery mode involves submissiles launched from a cruise missile, with each submissile capable of acquiring and homing on the target; such submissiles can be launched sequentially or all at once. In this mode, the cruise missile is like an aircraft armed with terminally homing missiles. Finally, the cruise missile can be designed to acquire and home on its own target. This would probably not be worth the cost unless the target were

TABLE 5.1: PGM Characteristics

Name	Country	Designation	Type	Guidance	Max. Range (km)	Length (m)	Diam. (cm)	Wt. (kg)
Dragon	U.S.	M47	Antitank	Wire		1.1	24	14
TOW	U.S.	BGM-71A	Antitank	Wire guided, optically tracked	3.5	1.2	15	25
Shillelagh	U.S.	MGM-15C	Antitank	Infra-red guided, optically tracked	4.6	1.2	15	27
HOT	France/FRG	—	Antitank	Wire/IR	4.	1.2	12	20
Milan	France/FRG	—	Antitank	Wire/IR	2.	0.7	10	6.4
Swingfire	U.K.	—	Antitank	Wire	4.	1.1	15	—
Bantam	Sweden	RB53	Antitank	Wire	2.	0.9	12	7.6
Cobra 2000	FRG	—	Antitank	Wire	2.	0.9	10	10.
Mamba	FRG	—	Antitank	Wire	2.	0.9	12	11.0
Sagger	USSR	AT-3	Antitank	Wire	2.3	0.6	15	—
Maverick	U.S.	AGM-65A/B	Air-to-surface missile	Television	—	2.5	31	220.
Walleye 2	U.S.	GW-MK	Air-to-surface glide bomb	Television	—	4.0	46	1100
Tomahawk	U.S.	AGM-109	Cruise missile	Tercom	2800.	5.6	55	1200

Source: From *Aviation Week and Space Technology,* Aerospace Forecast and Inventory, March 13, 1978.

either extremely valuable or valuable but hard to destroy by any other means.

Why pay all this attention to precision-guided cruise missiles? For one thing, they are a member of the PGM family and they represent the cutting edge of new technology. They provide an ample illustration of the complexities of PGMs and point out the difficulty of simple categorizations. Finally, they provide interesting and important specific examples for developing arms-transfer policies.

The United States does not have a monopoly on PGM technology. Many other countries have effective surface-to-air and air-to-air missiles. The one area where the United States currently has a technology edge is in weapons delivered against land targets. Laser and electro-optically-guided weapons are in the U.S. weapon inventory and advanced systems are under development. Two versions of a nuclear strategic cruise missile are under active development. A ground-launched version is under serious consideration for use with conventional weapons, as is an antiship version.

A key question: To which countries would the United States be willing to sell or give cruise missiles, or with which countries would the United States be willing to share its cruise missile technology, and under what circumstances? The excluded cases are fairly easy. Countries which are viewed as current or likely future enemies of the United States would be definitely excluded from receiving either cruise missiles or the key technologies required to develop a precision cruise missile. (But this may only buy time in the case of developed countries which could develop their own technology, which could then be transferred according to their criteria.) Potential nuclear powers may well be excluded, even if friendly to the United States today. Terrorist or criminal groups, either national or transnational, would be excluded. This leaves allies, friendly countries, nonaligned and neutral countries, plus any others which do not clearly fall into the categories noted above.

Allies are a special problem, especially those in NATO. Current strategic-arms negotiations may lead to various types of bans or limits on cruise-missile performance. At the present time, U.S. allies in NATO are not pleased with these prospects.

If the United States decides to give or sell conventionally-armed cruise missiles to our NATO allies, to which NATO allies would these missiles be given or sold and where would the missiles be based? From the standpoint of insuring stability and minimizing unacceptability to the Soviet Union, the range with full payload should be limited to a value which will not threaten large amounts of Soviet territory from NATO bases. A quick glance at a map of central Europe reveals that a range of about 550 miles (880 kilometers) will reach very little Soviet territory from this area. If the same missile is based in northern Norway, however, it can reach a substantial number of valuable military targets on the Kola Peninsula. A missile based in eastern Turkey could reach a number of valuable targets in southern Russia. Clearly, then, the acceptability of such a weapon system to the Soviet Union would depend not only on what it can do, but the location from which it can be launched.

There is sometimes a thin line between being provocative and aiding deterrence and stability. The ability to deter attack depends heavily on having a credible capability to stop or repel an invader on the territory of a country under attack, and this credibility must exist in the minds of both the defender and the attacker. The ability to launch an effective conventional counterattack against limited but valuable assets on an attacker's own territory can also aid deterrence; a potential attacker would probably not welcome such a situation, but it would not be overly threatening if a response to an attack capability were limited by geography, types of targets, and numbers of missiles. Thus, the United States might make a decision to transfer limited numbers of conventional cruise missiles with limited range to Norway; the rationale would be quite different than in the NATO central front, where larger numbers of missiles could be deployed, but without the capability of threatening much Soviet territory.

With reference to other parts of the world with different geopolitical situations from that in Central Europe, South Korea provides an interesting case. As U.S. ground forces are withdrawn, the South Koreans may request many technologically advanced weapon systems to enhance their self-defense capability. The long range of even a conventionally-armed cruise missile would allow it to reach many countries other than North Korea; its precision would allow it to damage many valuable assets in these countries and could lead to an additional decline in regional stability. This is especially true if these weapons are perceived as a threat by other countries in this region.

In the Middle East or Africa, the introduction of precision cruise missiles could aggravate regional instability, intensify arms acquisitions, and subsequently amplify the likelihood of armed conflict. If the range of the missiles is sufficient to reach into countries that are recent or historical enemies, if the damage potential is great enough, and if no defense against the weapon is available, then the situation would be relatively undesirable. There can be exceptions to this, of course; if a country friendly to the United States is faced with an attack by a neighbor of greatly superior force, it may be desirable to provide that state with long-range, effective PGMs. The longer-term consequences of this should be carefully weighed.

This brief example illustrates a number of important points. Technical details of performance, geography, and the general military and political situation all make a difference. The perceptions of others affected in any way by an arms transfer can be important. Although not mentioned in the above example, economics make a difference. Precision cruise missiles are expensive—in the range of one-half million to one million dollars each; they will be expensive for the United States to give away and for others to buy. Their unit cost will, to a large extent, limit the numbers available and, there are a few cases where small numbers of cruise missiles would make a militarily significant difference. In addition, terrorists could create havoc with a handful of missiles and hundreds could make a difference for insurrectionists and some small military powers. Hundreds of such weapons would cost hundreds of millions of dollars and would constitute a major arms transfer that could not be taken lightly by supplier or recipient.

The example of the precision cruise missile raises another important issue. The infrastructure needed to support such a weapon system includes spare parts, resupply and repair, and the necessary intelligence data to use the weapon effectively as a precision weapon. The current Tomahawk missile requires detailed maps which include terrain features and the precise location of fixed targets. The potential exists for its use against movable targets, but only if current intelligence data are available. By providing a weapon which has maximum effectiveness only when current intelligence data are supplied, the United States could maintain some degree of influence over the use of such weapons by controlling the amount and type of intelligence provided. (It should be noted that the United States does not have a monopoly on intelligence-gathering methods, equipment, or techniques, so that improvements and growth in information-gathering technologies could give certain countries autonomous capabilities.)

Antitank Guided Missiles

The second weapon-system example has a number of characteristics quite different from the cruise missile. An antitank guided missile (ATGM) can be small, inexpensive, extremely portable, and lethal when used at close range against tanks. The simplest of such systems relies on the human eye for target detection, identification, and aiming of the weapon, and they are rugged, reliable, and easy to use. They have some serious shortcomings, however. Many require that the weapon be guided all the way to the target; thus, a single soldier is liable to feel disconcerted when the target (a tank) swivels its gun towards him before the ATGM arrives at the target. That is, the velocity of a projectile fired from a tank is much higher than that of the ATGM, and if the tank sees the missile coming, it can kill the ATGM launcher before the ATGM strikes its target. This is true for hand-launched ATGMs which rely on guidance signals from a wire attached to the missile or a "beam rider" missile which gets its information by electromagnetic radiation. This shortcoming can be overcome to some extent by putting the launcher under armored protection, or by using a "launch-and-leave" or "fire-and-forget" system, such as the TV-guided Maverick.

More complex systems illuminate the tank with a laser held by a forward observer, but detectors on the tank can tell when it is being illuminated, enabling the tank crew to take evasive or defensive action, or to attack the illuminator. Small, hand-held ATGMs also have limited lethality even if they hit the tank, especially with new techniques in armor protection. Larger systems, such as the air-launched Maverick, are highly lethal if they hit a tank and can be fired in a launch-and-leave mode. They rely on the contrast between the target and its background for homing, however, and if the contrast is lost by active countermeasures such as smoke or flares, or even by having a tank drive into a dark shadow, the missile can lose track and go astray.

In short, many of today's ATGMs either have some serious shortcomings or can have their effectiveness decreased by a variety of countermeasures. A number of technological options are available for improving ATGM effectiveness by removing some of today's limitations and decreasing their sensitivity to countermeasures. The cautionary remarks are to temper the enthusiasm of those who have been oversold on the capabilities of the current generation of ATGMs. They can be quite effective if the target can be seen, particularly if the tank is caught by surprise and takes no action to defend itself.

ATGMs are a good example of a weapon system which is primarily defensive in nature, and such weapons could be relatively beneficial in improving regional stability. Few weapons can be considered as purely defensive in nature, however, since offensive military operations rely on antitank weapons and defensive antiair weapons for their success. Moreover, an attacker often has periods of retrenchment or retreat and may need effective defensive weapons to hold territory, and in many tactical situations, the best response to an attacker may be an offensive counterattack, recalling the old adage of the best defense being a good offense.

A transfer of ATGMs would tend to increase regional stability if it would benefit a defender significantly more than an attacker. This would generally be the case, but there are a few exceptions. A country with a significant tank force, surrounded by other countries with comparable or smaller tank forces, could significantly increase its offensive capability with effective ATGMs. The general geopolitical situation and history of conflict must also be considered when evaluating potential shifts in regional stability. For example, a transfer of large numbers of ATGMs to Switzerland would be viewed quite differently than a transfer to potential conflict areas in the Middle East or Africa, both by neighboring countries and by the major developed countries.

Another facet of ATGMs is their relatively limited utility for destruction in the hands of small groups of criminals or terrorists. While all weapons can be dangerous when detonated nearby, the short range, low velocity, and specialized warheads of ATGMs limits their lethality in some applications. For example, terrorist attacks against commercial aircraft could be conducted effectively with a number of existing surface-to-air missiles (SAMs). These missiles, in addition to their launching and radar systems, may need special safeguarding to prevent such abuse. Most small ATGMs, on the other hand, would be unable to reach or catch a moving airplane–unless it was flying low and slowly and directly overhead—and even if the plane was hit, the result would not necessarily be catastrophic because of the specialized directed energy warheads used in ATGMs.

THE USE OF PGMs BY TERRORISTS

Terrorist use of PGMs is a problem which deserves special attention. Some countries would readily provide PGMs to terrorist groups and should probably be banned as recipients of any arms transfers as long as such behavior appears likely. Also, a country could lose PGMs by carelessness or lack of sufficient protection for the weapons; certain types of PGMs are inherently more dangerous than others and deserve to be more carefully protected in order to reduce the likelihood of their ending up in the hands of terrorists or criminals.

Highly portable PGMs that are easily used by one or two people and which can be highly lethal to high value targets or to large numbers of people are the types which should be carefully controlled and protected. A hand-held, surface-to-air missile which can threaten a large commercial aircraft with a full passenger load, is a good example. A weapon which is highly portable, however, generally has a limited lethal range, and would not lend itself to the type of indiscriminate killing which is typical of many terrorist attacks. Such a weapon could be dangerous when used against a source of stored energy which could cause more widespread damage. Fortunately, most sources of potential explosions are isolated or separated by buffer zones to prevent damage in the case of accidents.

The larger and more expensive PGMs can be more lethal and tend to be guarded and controlled more carefully; the control of their use could, perhaps, benefit from the same technology used to control nuclear weapons. Permissive action links which use, for example, combination locks and coded switches with penalty modes can deny use to unauthorized possessors of a PGM, but if they are too complicated, this may also inhibit authorized and desired use. There are a number of technologies for improving weapon-system security and a number of them are applicable to PGMs.

RELATIVELY SAFE AND RELATIVELY DANGEROUS PGMs

A number of combinations of PGM types and arms recipients can be classed as relatively safe and beneficial or relatively dangerous (or as relatively desirable or undesirable). These categories can change with time and circumstances as alliances shift and as PGM technology and PGM countermeasures continue to develop.

In this study, situations are judged to be relatively safe or desirable if they tend to lend stability in a crisis situation; they are considered relatively dangerous or undesirable if they tend to make a crisis situation unstable. A stable situation is one in which the participants would see disadvantages in resorting to military force and they would tend not to get involved in armed conflict; the tendency would be to pause and wait, rather than to strike first. An unstable situation occurs when there are apparent advantages to be gained by resorting to armed conflict. Of course, if armed conflict did occur, we would prefer that friendly countries have effective weapons for self defense. An ideal weapon for transfer would minimize the likelihood of conflict, but would also be very effective if conflict occurred. It is obvious that many ingredients are involved in determining whether a situation is stable or unstable. Levels of military force, past history of conflict, current political and economic conditions, and the particular nature of any current crisis can all be important. The nature of military equipment can also play a role; whether a given weapon system, such as a PGM, tends to improve stability depends to some extent on the characteristics of the weapon system, but it also depends on the other factors which include stability.

As was implied earlier, weapons that are largely defensive in nature can be considered "safe." Such systems are often anchored in place, such as coastal artillery and fixed antiaircraft systems. Movable systems that are highly specialized for defensive purposes, but whose mobility is restricted by their weight, also fall into this category—for example, a SAM system that can be moved in a few days—unless they are merely an accompaniment to a large-scale offensive buildup.

A moving attacker is at a relative disadvantage against a still defender, especially if the defender exploits terrain features and the local environment; antitank guided missiles and surface-to-air missiles used in this defensive manner can strengthen stability. If highly mobile, however, such weapons could also play a key role in offensive operations, so the degree of relative safety or danger must be judged on a case-by-case basis, which includes the consideration of geopolitical and other factors.

Weapons which require external information for their effective use, or which need a complex infrastructure or other supporting equipment, can be controlled to some degree if the supplier is the only one capable of providing the external information or if the recipient is dependent on the supplier for maintenance, spare parts, and replacements. Weapons with a technology which can be reproduced by the recipient and which can operate autonomously obviously cannot be controlled to the same degree; such autonomous weapons have the potential of taking on a life of their own, especially if transferred by the recipient to a third party.

The estimation of the effectiveness of PGMs must take into account the impact of countermeasures. Some can be technologically advanced and complex (such as certain electronic countermeasures), while others can be quite simple (such as smoke and flares). When evaluating the net advantage to attacker or defender, this can make a difference, depending on the type of PGM and the level of technology available to the likely potential parties in a conflict.

All other things being equal, however, long-range weapons are relatively more dangerous than short-range weapons. The definition of long range depends on the geography where the weapon will be most likely used. Weapons which are versatile and general-purpose can be relatively more dangerous than highly-specialized weapons.

The regional force balance should be considered in all cases of contemplated arms transfers. The history of confrontation and conflict should be examined and recent and current actions should be weighed for trends. The absolute magnitude of force is important; the degree to which PGMs make a difference is strongly dependent on how much military power is already in place. In some parts of the world, a relatively small amount of PGMs could make a big difference, while the same amount would be negligible elsewhere.

THE USE OF PGMs IN REGIONAL CRISES AND CONFLICTS

This chapter has concentrated so far on what should or should not be done with PGMs, assuming that maintaining regional stability is a desirable goal. There will be times, however, when such stability erodes and crises develop which may escalate into armed conflict. In a positive vein, PGMs offer a great deal of leverage in such situations for many areas of the world. For countries which are not heavily armed, a few PGMs could make a big difference; the most effective PGMs would be those which require little training for effective use and do not need an elaborate infrastructure. An impressive PGM capability (relative to the other military forces involved) could be rapidly provided by airlift. Additional weapons could be sent, if needed, and shipments could be terminated at the end of the crisis or conflict. Some control over the proliferation of PGMs can be exercised by sending additional weapons only to replenish those expended in training or combat.

In this context, PGMs could be transferred to friendly countries with relative ease. On the other hand, in a regional conflict between two countries which were not aligned with or unfriendly to one or more of the major developed countries, any of the developed countries might have vital interests at stake in the conflict, and might well want to influence the outcome. Their goal might be to have one side win or to terminate the conflict and restore stability as rapidly as possible, and PGMs provide a lot of military capability in a small package. They could be transferred to the countries involved (e.g., U.S. Mavericks to Israel), sent with advisors and technicians (e.g., Soviet SAMs in Egypt), used in the area by the armed forces of the supplier (e.g., the U.S. use of laser-guided bombs in Vietnam), or given to proxies (e.g., the Cubans in Angola). No simple rules of thumb will suffice for conflict situations; they have to be examined on an individual basis. There will be cases where the best choice is to provide effective PGM countermeasures rather than PGMs. Intelligence and tactical warning information can be easily provided or easily withdrawn to stabilize a crisis.

Certain types of PGMs have a great potential for mischief, while others have a great potential for improving stability and reducing the likelihood of war. This potential can be realized by a thoughtful arms-transfer policy which provides the right type of PGM in the right place at the right time, and in numbers appropriate to the situation.

NOTE

1. See James Digby, "Precision Weapons," in J. Holst and U. Nerlich, eds., *Beyond Nuclear Deterrence* (New York: Crane, Russak & Company, Inc., 1977), p. 158.

6 NUCLEAR PROLIFERATION AND THE SPREAD OF NEW CONVENTIONAL WEAPONS TECHNOLOGY

Richard Burt

Growing concern over the prospects of widespread nuclear proliferation in the next decade has sparked an energetic search for new mechanisms for containing, or at least managing, the process of nuclear proliferation. In the many approaches now being discussed, two different strategies
of nonproliferation can be broadly distinguished. The first, which aims at
influencing nuclear weapon *capabilities*, attempts to manage the transfer of
the technology, the expertise, and the resources which potentially could be
used by a nonnuclear state (one that does not currently possess a nuclear
weapon and delivery capability) to produce weapons.[1] The application of
international safeguards to nuclear fuel-cycle processes, the efforts of the so-
called "nuclear suppliers' club" to work out common understandings on the
transfer of technology, and the possible establishment of regional reprocessing facilities under international control can all be understood as
applications of this approach. The second strategy does not specifically
emphasize the control of technology or resources, but is directed towards
lowering the incentives for nonnuclear states to exploit them for purposes of
producing weapons. This strategy aims at influencing nuclear *intentions* by
focusing on the security concerns that might lead nations to acquire
weapons. In the past, the negotiation of arms-control agreements between

This chapter was originally published in *International Security* 1 (1977): 119–39.

existing nuclear states, policies designed to enhance the credibility of nuclear commitments to allies, and the establishment of "nuclear-free" zones have all been understood as methods of reducing incentives for proliferation.

Curiously, the impact and possible utility of conventional-arms transfers for strategies of nonproliferation is a policy area that has traditionally received little attention. In those cases where the issue has been addressed, arguments have been only vaguely articulated; for instance, it has been argued that the transfer of some military equipment, such as advanced aircraft, could influence nuclear capabilities by providing an attractive means of nuclear weapons delivery. This concern influenced U.S. opposition to the delivery of the nuclear-capable Pershing missile to Israel in 1975. It has also been maintained, however, that the supply of conventional military equipment could influence nuclear intentions by providing an alternative to nuclear weapons acquisition. Again, U.S. arms policies towards Israel have provided a basis for the fear that a sudden curtailment of U.S. support might lead to an Israeli emphasis on nuclear defense.

Little effort has been expended on exploring the relationship between nuclear proliferation and conventional-arms transfers. In part, this may be because the spread of conventional weapons is viewed as a serious problem in its own right, possessing its own dynamics and its own bureaucratic and academic constituencies. It also certainly reflects the fact that conventional-arms transfers are seen to fulfill foreign-policy objectives other than merely stemming nuclear proliferation.[2] With the exception of certain specific cases, the tendency has been either to ignore the implications of the diffusion of conventional military power for nuclear proliferation, or to note simplistically that nuclear proliferation "has increased the risk that a local conflict involving conventional arms might escalate into a nuclear conflagration."[3]

Two recent developments—one technological, the other political— suggest that this will not remain the case for long. First, the growing availability of a new generation of conventional weapons has raised the possibility that an expanded menu of nonnuclear options might not only be used to bolster the defensive capabilities of insecure, would-be nuclear powers, but that new conventional weapons might be substituted in roles that were previously thought to require nuclear weapons. This has resulted in schemes in which the introduction of new conventional weapons is linked to such nonproliferation measures as the establishment of nuclear-free zones. Second, there is growing interest in using conventional-arms transfers (or more precisely, the threat of restricting arms transfers) as a means of gaining leverage over the decisions of recipients of nuclear technology. It has been suggested, for example, that the threat of an American arms embargo might be used to induce non-signatories of the

1968 Non-Proliferation Treaty (NPT) to adhere to the regulations of that agreement.[4] Under a provision of the 1976 Arms Export Control Act, U.S. military and economic aid has been formally linked to constraining the use of nuclear technology by recipient states. The provision does not require NPT membership, but threatens an embargo on economic and military aid and sales to states that deliver or receive nuclear reprocessing technology without international safeguards.[5] Thus, more by accident than design, the relationship between conventional-arms transfers and the spread of nuclear weapons has become more important and more controversial.* The question of whether conventional-arms transfers can be usefully incorporated into a strategy of nonproliferation is based on the assumption that the proliferation of nuclear weapons poses a graver threat to international order than the spread of conventional arms, and that little progress is likely to be made in severely limiting the spread of conventional weapons. Thus, priority is given to manipulating the arms trade in order to meet other objectives—in this case, nuclear nonproliferation. Using different assumptions, it would be just as appropriate to investigate the possibility of using nuclear arms to stem the proliferation of conventional capabilities. Four questions are addressed:

1. What new nonnuclear weapons technologies are becoming available to would-be nuclear states and what will be their likely impact on security considerations that might lead to the acquisition of nuclear arms?

2. Will certain of these technologies provide effective substitutes for nuclear capabilities and thus serve to dampen incentives to acquire nuclear arms?

3. While possibly replacing nuclear weapons in some roles, will a new class of conventional deterrent weapons create special problems of its own?

4. What are the political costs and benefits of using conventional-arms transfers as a lever to influence the nuclear decisions of recipient states?

DEVELOPMENTS IN NONNUCLEAR TECHNOLOGY

As the above questions indicate, there are two distinct arguments of how developments in conventional weapons technology might reduce

---

* This was vividly demonstrated in the apparently contradictory discussions held by the United States Secretary of State with the Shah of Iran and Prime Minister Bhutto of Pakistan during August 1976, where, in the case of Iran, interests of nonproliferation were said to be served by the continuance of American conventional sales; but in the case of Pakistan those same interests were said to necessitate the threat of an American arms embargo. The threat of withholding military equipment from Pakistan was used to dissuade the government from going ahead with the purchase of reactor and reprocessing technology from France. Secretary of State Henry Kissinger reportedly justified this action by referring to his obligations under the language of the Symington provision. See note 5.

pressures for states to acquire nuclear weapons. The first is that a wide range of high-performance but relatively cheap and serviceable weapons is now coming on the market and that these systems will work to significantly bolster the military viability of insecure would-be nuclear nations. The second is that a class of more advanced systems could become surrogates for nuclear weapons, providing states with credible conventional deterrent capabilities. Each of these possibilities will be considered separately.

It is widely accepted that new military technology is now changing significantly and that a cluster of new weapons and support systems could have a dramatic impact on military tactics, organization, and the actual outcome of conflict over the next ten to twenty years.[6] The implications of the new weapons for the character of modern war are unclear, but some observers have argued that in the future weaker states should generally be better able to provide for their own defense, particularly against such older military technologies as aircraft, armored forces, and amphibious craft.[7] It is useful to note four areas where technological change appears to be working to the advantage of the defender:

1. *Battlefield-guided weapons:* The deployment of precision-guided, mobile, and in some instances, portable antitank missiles and air defense systems has significantly increased the vulnerability of tanks and aircraft on and over the battlefield. Because these systems are not expensive and require little training and maintenance, they appear well suited to the defensive needs of developing nations. When wedded with improved target-engagement technology, longer-range precision-guided weapons can be used to strike lucrative targets beyond the battlefield, such as troop concentrations and artillery emplacements.

2. *Area weapons on land:* The ability to rapidly and efficiently deliver mines and cluster munitions from aircraft, missiles, and artillery tubes will enable states to erect formidable barriers to large-scale armored and infantry penetration. At the least, by slowing down and channeling the movements of attacking units, a new family of area weapons will complement the deployment of precision-guided weapons by easing the task of target acquisition.

3. *Sea denial and coastal defense weapons:* A new generation of highly accurate antiship missiles will provide small naval vessels and coastal defense installations with the capability to threaten large naval combatants. Advances in naval mines and torpedo technology, meanwhile, could allow coastal states to close off maritime approaches and strategic straits to incursion.

4. *Surveillance and warning:* The use of small, remotely piloted vehicles, remote sensors stationed on land, and reconnaissance aids (night-vision devices, moving-target indicators) will improve tactical intelligence gather-

ing and thus will improve strategic warning against surprise attack. This should increase the confidence of states having tense borders.

It is frequently suggested that the combined effect of these developments will be to shift the balance of the offense-defense duel in the favor of the defender. This notion is not only based on the argument that offensively oriented weapons, like tanks and strike aircraft, are likely to become more vulnerable, but that inherent benefits accruing to the defender, such as concealment and knowledge of terrain, are likely to become more salient as small units come to possess greatly increased firepower. Precision-guided munitions (PGMs, see Chapter 5) are seen to have an especially important role, for in a "one-shot, one-kill" era, the collateral damage associated with intense conventional warfare could decline dramatically. This would not only mean that states could more effectively employ defense-in-depth strategies, but that they might also find it easier to adjust psychologically to the idea of intense conventional conflict, rather than opting for deterrence-only defenses based on the uncertain nuclear threat. Thus, some observers have speculated that the introduction of new conventional weapons technologies could enable existing nuclear powers to adopt nuclear "no-first-use" policies, while nonnuclear states might be more willing to agree to establishing nuclear-free zones. In essence, by providing nations the means to guarantee their security without nuclear force, new weapons technologies are said to reduce substantially the military advantages attached to nuclear weapons procurement.

This is an intriguing argument, but it must be approached with considerable caution. Several crucial questions need to be resolved before any general claims concerning the military impact of new weapons technologies can be stated confidently. One important group of questions concerns the actual ability of the new systems to perform as advertised: How well will PGMs function under fluid battlefield conditions, where target acquisition and designation will offer special problems? Will developing states be able to cope with the elaborate command, control, and communications infrastructure that in some cases is essential to the efficient use of the new weapons? Will an even newer generation of reliable and inexpensive countermeasures nullify the apparent advantages flowing from contemporary technological developments? Answers to these questions will not be attempted here, but it is important to note that no general consensus yet exists on the operational implications of the new technology. Moreover, if and when these questions are resolved, a host of equally difficult problems will still have to be addressed. While it is possible to distinguish between defensive and offensive strategies of war, neither conform to any precisely defined set of operations on the local, tactical level; in combined-arms warfare, defensive strategies are a composite of offensive and defensive tactics, and it is necessary to examine specific military relationships before making judgments as to who is likely to benefit most from the introduction of new technologies. In the case of the NATO-Warsaw Pact balance in central Europe, for instance, there are indications that the Soviet Union is seeking to exploit the defensive advantages of new antitank weaponry for offensive ends.[8] The reverse case seems to apply to Israel, which has used tanks and aircraft in offensive roles in the service of a defense-dominated strategy. It might be argued that the movement of technology in favor of the defender will result in a net decline in Israeli security, which could act to foster a decision to emphasize nuclear weapons for defense.

Another important dimension of this problem concerns the argument that during wartime the use of PGMs will increase the consumption of ordnance and the intensity of combat. This contention is not only based on the actual experience of the 1973 war in the Middle East, but also on the observation that the decentralization of established forces implicit in widespread deployment of PGMs will require larger stocks of weapons. When the possibility of higher consumption rates is coupled with the higher attrition rates expected from the use of PGMs, three consequences could follow. First, rather than favoring the defense, the new technologies could merely work to favor the side possessing larger forces-in-being. Thus, the emergence of a "one-shot, one-kill" era would appear to especially benefit military forces, like those of the Warsaw Pact and the Arab states, which are equipped and organized to sustain heavy losses. Second, by accelerating the pace of conflict, the new technologies could reduce the time available for techniques of crisis management through tacit bargaining by controlled escalation. Rapid, intense conflicts could create an atmosphere in which unconsidered or premature escalatory responses became more likely.[9] Third, the high consumption of stocks, and the rapid attrition of forces could result in making states more, rather than less, dependent on outside suppliers to secure their defenses. This may be seen by some states to be politically unacceptable while large-scale aid might be unavailable to others.

The impact, then, of the spread of new nonnuclear weapons could be very different from the commonly held view that they would promote military stability between potential adversaries. In some circumstances, the result could be to exacerbate numerical asymmetries between weaker and stronger forces, to introduce new incentives for escalation in time of conflict, and finally, to increase the dependency of weaker states on stronger allies. Any one of these outcomes could serve to reinforce tendencies toward nuclear proliferation.

Until the implications of PGMs and other new technologies are better understood, it will be difficult to argue convincingly that a new generation of conventional weapons will act together to secure the defenses of threatened states. But there may be some cases in which the introduction of new weapons would solve specific defense problems confronted by would-be nuclear nations. The widespread acquisition by Yugoslavia of modern antitank weapons, for instance, would probably go a long way to counter the existing threat posed by Soviet armor. If systems like the United States Army's TOW missile were made available to the Tito regime, this might have some impact on what appears to be a growing interest in the acquisition of a tactical nuclear weapons capability.[10] Moreover, the debate over the implications of new technologies has generally centered around their impact on the military balance in Europe and the Middle East, regions in which states possess a full panoply of modern equipment and where the lessons of combined-arms warfare are most apt. In other regions (e.g., Latin America or sub-Saharan Africa) where stocks are smaller and balanced forces almost nonexistent, and where gaps in capabilities might be more easily exploited, the introduction of PGMs, barrier weapons, and improved surveillance and warning systems might have a far greater impact than in more densely armed areas: the options that were open to Israeli commanders in countering the Egyptian use of antitank weapons in the Sinai are unlikely to be available to a Peruvian tank commander who confronts Chilean forces armed with TOW.

THE SURROGATE TECHNOLOGIES
AND INCENTIVES FOR PROLIFERATION

While new conventional weapons do not seem to promise to make nuclear weapons unattractive or unnecessary to would-be nuclear states, this does not rule out the possibility that a narrower range of nonnuclear systems could be used for roles that were previously assigned to nuclear weapons. There are already several instances in which new conventional weapons are being used to lessen reliance on older, nuclear systems. Advanced medium and high-altitude air defense missiles, such as the United States Army's Patriot, are scheduled to replace the nuclear-armed Nike Hercules during the 1980s. Conventionally armed, scatterable land mines and cluster munitions could serve as effective substitutes for atomic demolition mines in appropriate areas in Western Europe. Laser-guided artillery systems, meanwhile, might provide a convincing capability against forward-deployed artillery and rocket forces in Eastern Europe or North Korea, and thus could provide an effective substitute for nuclear rounds.*

Perhaps the most interesting and important of these surrogate technologies from the standpoint of nuclear substitution is the new family of

---

*Rocket-assisted, guided artillery rounds have been tested by the United States at ranges exceeding 30 miles.

long-range, precision-guided cruise and ballistic missiles now under development in the United States, such as the Navy's Tomahawk cruise missile, the Air Force's air-launched cruise missile (ALCM), and the Army's Pershing II and improved Lance ballistic missiles. Deployed with new point and area munitions, these systems will be capable of performing a variety of missions in the European theater, including deep interdiction strikes and attacks against high-value, hardened targets in Eastern Europe. In South Korea, precision-guided missiles, equipped with earth-penetrator warheads, could be targeted against underground aircraft shelters in the North. In the Middle East, missiles armed with fuel air explosives could be used to destroy hardened, dispersed airbases.[11] Missiles armed with submunition packages, meanwhile, might provide an effective means to suppress air defense installations, a role that has been projected for Israel's conventionally armed Lance. During the next decade, then, highly accurate delivery vehicles armed with specialized warheads are likely to be used to supplant nuclear weapons in many tactical roles and, more importantly, might be deployed to perform strategic missions against military command centers, vulnerable economic assets, and high-value civilian targets.

But if conventional weapons can increasingly be used to replace nuclear arms in specific roles, can we be at all confident that this development will arrest tendencies towards nuclear proliferation? This cannot be answered in isolation from an analysis of the reasons that motivate states to seek nuclear weapons. While the existence of direct security threats is a crucial variable in determining the timing and the nature of specific decisions to acquire nuclear weapons, the costs and benefits of going nuclear cannot be calculated in purely military terms, but ultimately must be related to domestic political factors and the wider characteristics of the international system. These include the nature of the East-West military balance, the state of alliance systems and commitments, the role of regional powers, and norms concerning the use of force. As Edward Luttwak has persuasively argued, both the security and the prestige value of nuclear weapons acquisition have usually been relatively low.[12] This was primarily the result of the strength of U.S. power and the credibility of U.S. commitments. In the bipolar international system, some would-be nuclear states were provided with credible nuclear guarantees, while others, lacking such protection, were constrained from providing for their own nuclear defense by a rigid international pecking order.

With the passing of the cold war's bipolarity, both incentives for acquiring nuclear weapons have increased. Superpower strategic parity has gradually diminished the credibility of the U.S. nuclear commitment, particularly in the case of such peripheral allies as South Korea, Taiwan, and Pakistan. Coupled with the emergence of strategic parity, the elaboration of the so-called "Nixon Doctrine," which acted to qualify American commitments to Third World nations, created new pressures for nuclear proliferation. These pressures have been reinforced by the decay and dissolution of security arrangements such as SEATO and a tendency within the United States to reexamine nuclear-deployment policies and foreign commitments.

As nations huddling under the U.S. nuclear umbrella have been forced to consider new security alternatives, neutral states have come to view their nonnuclear status as just another manifestation of an international system that is politically, economically, and militarily rigged against them. Arrangements like the NPT system are increasingly seen as efforts by the major powers to perpetuate what is said to be an unjust international order.[13] At the same time, the technology for obtaining weapons-grade material—enriched uranium and plutonium—is becoming increasingly accessible to a new group of potential regional powers (e.g., India, Brazil, Iran) who aspire to and, unlike in earlier periods, are actually able to achieve positions of greater status in an increasingly pluralistic and fragmented international system. The result is a vicious cycle which increases incentives to go nuclear: U.S.-Soviet nuclear parity makes it difficult for the superpowers to make good on guarantees to nonnuclear allies, raising the incentives for these states to obtain their own nuclear shields. When this occurs, residual superpower nuclear commitments become riskier and thus more uncertain, setting off new pressures to proliferate.

The availability of a growing class of nuclear-surrogate technologies is just one additional factor to consider in calculating the impact of the erosion of postwar alliance systems in the West. In the case of South Korea, for example, a continued U.S. willingness to supply new conventional weapons is likely to be accompanied by a growing interest in withdrawing troops and/or nuclear weapons from the peninsula. This points to an important distinction that must be made in considering the impact of the surrogate technologies: while the new weapons may be able to perform in roles now assigned to nuclear weapons, their ability to replace the elements of psychological deterrence and political commitment stemming from the stationing of nuclear weapons and troops on Korean soil is questionable. If linked to the removal of U.S. bases, the transfer of surrogate technologies to South Korea would bear an uncomfortable resemblance to "Vietnamization."

In Western Europe, the situation is somewhat different, for the transfer (or the indigenous development) of surrogate technologies is unlikely to foreshadow a large-scale U.S. withdrawal from NATO. Their deployment, however, could be coupled with a drive to deemphasize the role of theater nuclear weapons in alliance strategy. This development could disturb the fragile consensus within NATO over military doctrine, especially if the consequences of downgrading the role of nuclear weapons for deterrence were perceived as increasing the likelihood of protracted conventional war should deterrence fail. At the same time, the availability of a new generation of long-range conventional strike systems, capable of attacking high-value targets deep in Eastern Europe or in the Soviet homeland itself, could provide Western European governments with a new means of escalation autonomy—the ability independently to raise the stakes attached to Warsaw Pact aggression. But these new conventional options are better understood as deterrent links rather than military ends in themselves, for even the most fully developed, conventional strategic capability would be incapable, by itself, of deterring a nuclear-armed Soviet Union. Instead, surrogate technologies could provide some European states with a mechanism for threatening escalation, which could come to encompass a strategic exchange between the superpowers. Long-range conventional strike systems could thus come to possess a quality similar to the one commonly ascribed to the *force de frappe*—a trigger mechanism for insuring that in the event of war in Europe the superpowers would not remain as sanctuaries, safe from the ravages of war. Viewed in these terms, the surrogate technologies would not offer Europeans escalation autonomy, for deterrence would ultimately reside with the strategic arsenal of the United States. Instead, their deployment would enable the alliance to parcel out control of the escalation process.[14] Thus, paradoxically, the effect of surrogate technologies would not be to diminish the role of nuclear weapons in alliance strategy, but to sustain the credibility of extended deterrence in a period of superpower strategic parity.*

For the United States, increased escalation autonomy for Western Europe would come at the expense of decreased escalation control. This price might be seen as worth paying if the alternative is understood to be the further proliferation of independent European nuclear capabilities.

STRATEGIC CONVENTIONAL WEAPONS AND THE NONNUCLEAR WORLD

The possible spread of nuclear-surrogate technologies to nonnuclear, nonaligned states raises a different set of problems. At present, over 60

---

*This argument tends to highlight the more general tension between the efforts to maintain the credibility of extended deterrence and the possible impact of these policies on the nuclear decisions taken by nonnuclear, nonaligned states. A common criticism of Western reluctance to renounce the first use of nuclear weapons and the American "flexible options" nuclear targeting doctrine is that these policies tend to emphasize the salience of nuclear threats for securing defense which are liable to be emulated by would-be nuclear states. While this argument might contain an element of truth, the alternative would be to restrict the role of nuclear weapons in Alliance strategy. This would not have unpredictable consequences vis-a-vis the Soviet Union, but it would set off new pressures for proliferation within the Alliance. The tension between managing intraAlliance and extraAlliance proliferation was perhaps most acute in the late 1960s when Secretary of Defense Robert McNamara, while elaborating a narrower role for strategic weapons via the assured destruction concept, pressured allies to sign and ratify the NPT.

states, many of them nonaligned, possess supersonic strike aircraft that might be used to deliver nuclear weapons against strategic targets in the homeland of an adversary. Many of these aircraft, of course, can also deliver punishing strikes against urban, industrial, and military targets with conventional munitions, but during the next decade the proliferation of a new generation of precision strike systems—air and surface-launched cruise missiles and remotely piloted vehicles—could usher in a new era of strategic conventional warfare. Armed with fuel-air explosives or advanced point munitions, these weapons will enable states to threaten intolerable damage against soft and even hard targets of an adversary without resort to nuclear blackmail. As shown in Table 7.1, the technology for creating such delivery capabilities is becoming widely available in the form of several categories of advanced missiles now under development in the West and the Soviet

TABLE 6.1: Development of Advanced, Conventionally-Armed Missiles (1976)

Country	Surface-to-surface Ballistic	Long-Range Cruise	Air-to Surface	Antiship	Surface to-Air	Anti-submarine
U.S.	D	D	S	S	S	S
USSR	D	S	S[a]	S	S	S
France			S	S	S	S
Britain			S	D	S	
W. Germany				D	D	S
Israel			D[b]	S		
Italy				S	S	
Sweden				S	D	
Australia						S
Japan				D	D	
Norway				S		
Canada					S	

Note: D = under development; S = in service. These are missiles under development or in service which potentially could be used in roles now assigned to nuclear-armed systems. "Advanced" refers to systems using seeker guidance, precision positioning, correlation guidance, and stellar-inertial guidance (but not other forms of inertial guidance). Not shown are advanced systems which the countries listed have in service, but which were obtained from abroad and not developed indigenously.

a. Includes only long-range, command-guidance missiles, though the AS-5 Kelt may have an active radar-seeker.

b. A TV-guided missile, the Rafael, is reported to be under development.

Source: Richard Burt, "New Weapons Technologies: Debate and Directions," *Adelphi Paper* no. 123 (London: IISS, 1976).

Union. While most of these missiles are not being procured for strategic missions, the guidance systems, the engines and the airframes of many of them could be exploited for such roles. And as the list of suppliers of advanced missiles has grown, so has the number of recipients. In just one category—antishipping missiles—over thirty-five nonnuclear states either possess or have on order advanced systems under production by the nations shown in Table 7.1[15].

Will nonnuclear states rush to deploy conventional strategic weapons and, if so, how will the rules of conventional deterrence operate? As Roberta Wohlstetter has pointed out, the essential quality of nuclear weapons is that they are understood to be weapons of mass destruction; they possess the quality of indiscriminateness.[16] In the past, other avenues of mass destruction such as biological weapons have been open to nonnuclear states, but these alternatives have generally not been exploited. This taboo against the acquisition and use of weapons of mass destruction remains relatively strong (perhaps even increasing) despite the growing systemic incentives to acquire nuclear weapons, and it could have a paradoxical effect on the introduction of conventional weapons capable of attacking strategic assets. While it is unlikely that states will obtain conventional weapons for "city-busting" operations, the discrimination offered by precision-guided, specialized warheads may not be viewed as violating existing norms of warfare. Surrogate technologies will not come to possess the psychological or the status value of nuclear arms, but the lack of stigma attached to their acquisition is likely to lead to their widespread proliferation.

At first glance, the spread of strategic conventional weapons might be received with relative calm, for the ability of weaker states to increase the risks of aggression would appear to raise the threshold for conflict in nonnuclear regions. A stronger power, for instance, would be forced to think twice before precipitating an incident along a border with a weaker neighbor who, while inferior in overall military terms, possessed the capability to destroy an air base or a hydroelectric plant within the stronger state's interior. But many of the familiar dilemmas one confronts in thinking about deterrence with nuclear weapons also apply in this case, if only on a lesser scale. If the stronger state chose to initiate a limited border conflict, the weaker state would be faced with a difficult choice: lacking an effective local-defense capability, it could either submit to the stronger power or escalate by striking valuable targets in the enemy's homeland. If this latter alternative were chosen, a local conflict would thus develop into a full-scale war; and the weaker state would then feel the full brunt of its adversary's power.

Between more evenly matched adversaries, greater stability might be injected into military relationships by the mutual adoption of conventional deterrent capabilities that promised to raise the costs of minor conflicts. But the introduction of the deterrence-defense dichotomy into the design of conventional forces could foster "defense on the cheap" tendencies on the part of governments, resulting in an emphasis on longer-range strike capabilities at the expense of battlefield defense forces. The effect of such trip-wire conventional strategies, of course, might be to breed greater caution on the part of would-be aggressors, but it would also result in greater violence in the event of deterrence breaking down. In the case of potential adversaries possessing asymmetrical capabilities, the introduction of conventional deterrent forces could produce far more unsettling effects. If a weaker state's decision to acquire long-range, precision strike options were met by a similar move by a stronger adversary, the weaker state would be likely to find itself doubly deterred: the threat of strategic retaliation would seem to rule out the actual use of long-range systems in wartime, while inferior battlefield forces would still be unable to cope with local attacks. In this situation, the mutual acquisition of conventional forces could act to heighten a state's sense of military inferiority, which could ultimately lead to what the procurement of conventional deterrent forces sought to avoid— the acquisition of nuclear weapons.

But the introduction of conventional deterrent capabilities need not reinforce tendencies towards proliferation, rather, this would very much depend on regional circumstances. Some writers have speculated, for instance, that the desire of some states to achieve regional superpower status could play a major role in the decision to acquire nuclear weapons. It can also be argued, however, that states aspiring to regional hegemony possess strong interests in keeping nuclear weapons out of regional politics. Because of their destructive power, nuclear weapons tend to function as "equalizers" in relations between weaker and stronger powers. For this reason, a would-be regionally dominant power, such as Iran or Brazil, might be expected to oppose the acquisition of nuclear weapons by neighbor states. Under these circumstances, potential regional superpowers might be prepared to countenance the procurement of conventional deterrent forces by their neighbors, recognizing that this is the lesser of two evils.

If nuclear weapons do spread to new regions, strategic conventional forces might still fulfill important functions. As in the East-West context, long-range conventional options could raise the threshold for nuclear use in regional conflicts by providing nuclear powers with an additional step on the ladder of escalatory responses. It is even possible to imagine that these weapons could enable nonnuclear states to obtain some form of conventional counterforce capability. In this role, strategic conventional forces might be used by a regional or outside power to destroy, in a preemptive strike, the nuclear weapons fabrication and launch centers of an incipient nuclear state. It is difficult, however, to conceive of this actually happening. The logical candidates for the conventional preemptor role are the two superpowers, working together or alone. If working alone, it is unrealistic to expect either the United States or the Soviet Union to sit by and watch the other carry out a counterforce blow against an incipient nuclear power; witness, for example, the opposition the United States reportedly expressed to possible Soviet plans to destroy Chinese nuclear facilities in the late 1960s.[17] While, in certain circumstances, the superpowers might be able to agree on the necessity of preemptive action, this would undoubtedly be viewed as an intolerable step by the rest of the world. On the regional level, the introduction of conventional preemptive capabilities could raise a host of uncertainties, particularly during a period when the task of distinguishing civilian nuclear programs from weapons-production activities is likely to become more difficult. The existence of conventional preemptive capabilities, moreover, would create strong incentives for an incipient nuclear state to accelerate the production of weapons in time of peace and, during severe crisis, to entertain using them in a preemptive strategy of its own against the conventional disarming capabilities of an adversary.

If it seems that (1) incentives to acquire nuclear weapons, while growing, remain relatively low; (2) the impact of new conventional weapons technologies may not necessarily add to the security of weaker states, and (3) strategic conventional weapons raise as many problems as they solve, then it is tempting to conclude that conventional arms transfers should be discouraged in their own right. This would be a mistake. While the linkage of new conventional technologies and nuclear ambitions is unclear, the impact of decisions by supplier states to reduce substantially or to cut off arms exports to would-be nuclear nations can be forecast with much greater precision. The changing nature of U.S. military commitments has created new security concerns for such peripheral allies as Taiwan, Pakistan, and South Korea that, in turn, have led to an increased demand for U.S. military equipment. In some cases, national leaders such as Pakistan's former Prime Minister Bhutto and South Korea's President Park have publicly warned that the decision to go nuclear will be taken in the light of their success in obtaining adequate supplies of conventional equipment. Thus, arms suppliers appear to be caught on the horns of a dilemma in attempting to use conventional arms as a means of influencing the nuclear intentions of recipient states. It may be that making available new conventional weapons will provide no guarantee against states developing nuclear options, but a decision to deny conventional capabilities to would-be nuclear nations will probably hasten the process of proliferation.

Concern over the conventional arms trade as a problem in its own right has spawned several suggestions of how supplier nations might reduce the volume of equipment moving into the nonindustrial world. One recent report has argued that it is important that major arms suppliers cut back on the sale of high-technology weapons because these weapons are more destructive than earlier models and because their transfer often entails an unwanted identification in interest between the supplier state and the recipient.[18] But as we have seen, the ultimate military impact of a new generation of antitank missiles, air-defense systems, and area weapons is unclear. While they are unlikely to offer a panacea to the defensive problems of threatened states, the interest in obtaining them shown by states such as Yugoslavia, Sweden, and Pakistan points to the real possibility that their deployment would not only raise the cost of aggression but, by minimizing collateral damage, might also reduce destruction in the event that conflict breaks out. The availability of longer-range, precision strike systems, in addition, would constitute a more effective deterrent to attack and, if employed, a less destructive alternative than crude, widescale conventional bombing and shelling operations. New weapons are not, by definition, more destructive weapons; by reducing unwanted damage, they are often more efficient.

A more troubling problem is created by the impression of political commitment often fostered by the transfer of advanced military technology. The most visible sign of U.S. support for Iranian objectives, of course, was the massive sales program conducted in recent years. But arms sales can also herald the decline of commitment; the United States' transfer of billions of dollars of equipment to South Vietnam in the early 1970s symbolized the reduction of U.S. support. If arms transfers do indeed convey a sense of commitment, it is all the more important to examine the possible impact of introducing constraints on such transfers. This is particularly true for the cluster of states—Taiwan, South Korea, Israel, South Africa, and perhaps Chile—who currently face major threats to their continued existence. These "pariah states" are nuclear candidates not only because they might be forced to fight for survival, but also because other avenues to security—alliances, security guarantees, and arms transfers—are increasingly unavailable. It would be an exaggeration to argue that the United States and other arms suppliers must decide whether they choose to live in a world armed to the teeth with conventional weapons or crowded with nuclear powers, but the objective of nonproliferation must be balanced against desires to limit arms sales and decrease commitments.

DIRECTIONS FOR POLICY

Not unexpectedly, the relationship between conventional-arms transfers and nuclear proliferation appears enormously complex. The fact that there do not seem to be any hard and fast principles for using conventional arms in a strategy of nonproliferation does not mean that the two processes are not linked, but only that the relationship is part of a more complicated equation involving the structure of the international system, the future of alliance guarantees, and the character of military technology. Consequently, the problem varies enormously from country to country and is best approached on a case-by-case basis. Nevertheless, some general guidelines for policy do emerge.

First, it is essential to distinguish between the ability of conventional weapons to be substituted for nuclear *roles* and their ability to replace nuclear *commitments*. New conventional weapons may offer alternatives to the use of nuclear weapons, but they are unlikely to offer an effective substitute for the maintenance of nuclear guarantees. Indeed, an important contribution of improvements in nonnuclear weaponry may be to make existing guarantees more credible by providing nuclear guarantors with greater flexibility and discretion in extending nuclear protection. Conventional weapons, including the surrogate technologies, lack the deterrence value of nuclear weapons, and attempts to justify the withdrawal of nuclear arms from Western Europe or East Asia by pointing to the capabilities now available from nonnuclear weapons could have unpredictable consequences. This seems especially true in the case of South Korea, where a growing desire to withdraw nuclear weapons is coupled with a wish to reduce the military presence of the United States generally—actions that could trigger a decision by the Seoul regime to go nuclear. A possible means of balancing the desire to reduce the U.S. military presence on the Korean peninsula while curbing tendencies toward proliferation might be to decouple the issues of nuclear weapons and U.S. forces. Under one approach, most of the forty-two thousand U.S. troops might leave the mainland, leaving behind the nuclear weapons under the custody of a small American force. In this case, the withdrawal of the bulk of the U.S. contingent could be justified by making new conventional weapons available to the South Koreans. Another approach would be to take the opposite tack: the nuclear weapons could go, but U.S. forces would stay. In this way, the removal of nuclear weapons could be justified by the added punch provided by new conventional systems while evidence of the continuing U.S. commitment would be provided by the maintenance of existing force levels. Neither of these strategies could guarantee that the Park regime would not be tempted to exercise a nuclear option at some time in the future, but both alternatives seem preferable to simply offering technology in lieu of weapons and personnel. As this case illustrates, there is no painless solution to the problem of proliferation, and a successful nonproliferation policy must seek to reconcile conflicting foreign-policy objectives.

Second, the argument that new conventional weapons may be better suited to enhancing, rather than replacing, the credibility of existing guarantees points to another paradoxical conclusion: that arms transfers may have a more important role to play *after* proliferation has occurred than *before*. While the availability of specific items of conventional equipment is unlikely to satisfy many of the desires that might tempt a state to go nuclear, their existence could have an important impact in determining whether nuclear weapons would actually be used in the event of conflict. Thus, the transfer of conventional arms may have more utility in managing the process of proliferation than in halting it. Since the mid-1960s, the emphasis that France has placed on nuclear weapons, in both force design and doctrine, has generally been seen by other Western governments as a destabilizing factor in Alliance defense planning. It is feared that France—lacking balanced conventional forces able to respond to aggression in a graduated manner—would be forced to use nuclear weapons prematurely, thus setting off a more widespread nuclear exchange. As a result, Western observers have applauded the recent decision to expand spending on conventional forces revealed in the 1976–81 defense plan and statements by leading officials that French forces must be able to respond to a wider spectrum of threats.[19] Similarly, a suggestion that is increasingly heard is that the United States and other Western nations should supply China with advanced military equipment. The argument is made that improved Chinese conventional capabilities would lessen the likelihood that a Sino-Soviet conflict would quickly pass the nuclear threshold. If and when new states acquire nuclear weapons, there will be a natural tendency for arms suppliers to punish them by, among other things, reassessing arms-sale arrangements. If such a decision were to deprive new nuclear powers of their primary sources of conventional weapons, they could be driven to adopt a trip-wire nuclear posture.

Third, while there is a case to be made for manipulating conventional-arms transfers to lower the incentives to acquire and to use nuclear weapons, this should not lead to a neglect of other avenues of nonproliferation. The emphasis now given to influencing the intentions of would-be nuclear powers largely results from a popular view that it is no longer possible to constrain nuclear capabilities; the technology, materials, and expertise for fashioning crude weapons, it seems, are already in the hands of many. But while this is true for some states, it is not true for all. In endeavoring to alter nuclear intentions, it would be a mistake to abandon efforts to agree on more rigorous safeguards for the transfer of nuclear technology, to establish multinational fuel-reprocessing facilities, and to explore mechanisms for greater cooperation among nuclear supplier nations. At the same time, a clear distinction should be maintained between attempts to limit capabilities and strategies to change intentions. This is clearly illustrated in the case of the Symington provision of the 1976 Arms Export Control Act, which, as outlined previously, calls on the government of the United States to withhold economic and military assistance from a state that receives nuclear technology without appropriate international safeguards. Clearly, by linking U.S. assistance with the acceptance of restrictions placed on the use of nuclear technology, the provision is meant to control the transfer of capabilities. Yet, if used indiscriminately, it could also influence nuclear intentions. Deprived of U.S. military equipment, an insecure, would-be nuclear state might be driven to exercise that option. In this way, the legislation could bring about the very outcome it sought to avoid. In the same way, the acquisition of the expertise and equipment to produce weapons-grade material should not necessarily be seen as a state's desire to obtain weapons. Premature efforts to manipulate nuclear intentions and capabilities by decreasing or increasing supplies of conventional equipment could backfire badly. A sudden embargo on arms transfers could foster nuclear ambitions that did not otherwise exist, while a rapid infusion of new arms to a near-nuclear power could spark off similar ambitions on the part of rival powers. It is useful also to distinguish among the types of weapons that nonnuclear states are likely to acquire over the next decade. Despite the attention lavished on PGMs, cruise missiles, and remotely piloted vehicles (RPVs), the bulk of the arms trade will continue to be in traditional weapons such as tanks, aircraft, and unguided munitions that are not only more destructive, but appear more aggressive than antitank and air-defense missiles. Proponents of conventional arms control, therefore, might be better rewarded by focusing their energies on regulating "old" rather than new technologies. Among the newer weapons, some systems are more provocative than others, and it would not be prudent to offer long-range cruise missiles to meet defense requirements that could be satisfied by the deployment of precision-guided artillery.

Finally, more attention should also be given to the impact on proliferation of treating the transfer of conventionl arms as a problem in its own right. It is often noted that the sale of advanced aircraft has resulted in the spread to numerous nations of nuclear-capable delivery vehicles. Yet it is also recognized that acting unilaterally, states are unlikely to be successful in restricting the transfer of sensitive equipment in what is increasingly a buyers' market in arms. The Johnson administration's embargo on supersonic aircraft to Latin America for example, failed to keep these systems out of the region because other suppliers moved in to fill the gap. But the limited progress of the suppliers' group of nuclear-technology-exporting nations has led to the suggestion that a similar mechanism should be established to agree on guidelines for conventional arms like those being discussed in the context of nuclear exports. Reflecting the discussion in the nuclear area, some observers have also called for the creation of a conventional-arms control cartel in order to blunt competition in the sale of equipment. For delivery vehicles and support systems, which are limited to use with nuclear (rather than conventional) explosives, these ideas might have some merit, although this is a small and steadily shrinking class of weapons. For dual-capable and conventional weapons generally, a suppliers' group arrangement not only appears politically infeasible, but also undesirable. It has already been seen that appearing to withhold conventional arms could serve to stimulate nuclear appetites. If undertaken on a multilateral basis, constraints on arms transfers would also heighten the general sense of discrimination felt so acutely in the nonindustrial world. The nuclear suppliers' group discriminates, but, unlike the NPT system, it does so in private. The ability of this body to operate at the fringes of the international spotlight would be sacrificed by giving it, or a related group, such new responsibilities as dividing up the market for conventional arms. A relatively innocuous, informal group would soon be perceived as a condominium of "have nations" working against the "have nots." Moreover, the task of achieving consensus on conventional arms transfer issues would be far more difficult than in the nuclear area. If the group became seriously divided over conventional-arms policies and, at the same time, became a target for dissatisfied members of the international system, attempts to regulate effectively the transfer of nuclear technology could easily go by the board.

NOTES

1. See American Enterprise Institute for Public Policy Research, *Nuclear Threat in the Middle East*(Washington D.C.: AEI, 1975), p. 31.

2. As late as October 1975, the impact of conventional-arms transfers on nuclear proliferation does not appear to have been an official criterion for U.S. arms-sale decisions, despite the fact that this consideration has seemed to play a role in certain isolated cases. In testimony to Congress, Sidney Sobers, Assistant Secretary of State with special responsibilities for the Middle East and Southern Asia, listed ten major criteria that were applied to requests for the sale of U.S. arms during the early 1970s. These ranged from determining whether a weapon was "offensive" or "defensive" to whether alternative sources were available to supply the system. Absent was any reference to whether the state was thought to harbor nuclear ambitions. [*Atlantic News*, No. 772 (Brussels), October 31, 1975].

3. United Nations Association of the United States,New York,*Controlling the Conventional Arms Race*, National Policy Panel Report, November 1976, p. 4

4. See Anne Hessing Cahn and Joseph J. Kruzel, "Arms Trade in the 1980s," paper prepared for The 1980s Project of the Council on Foreign Relations, pp. 19-20.

5. The International Security Assistance and Arms Export Control Act was signed into law by President Ford in July 1976. The provision referred to here was introduced by Senator Stuart Symington (D-Mo.) and prohibits the furnishing of economic or military assistance (with the exception of food grants) and military sales to countries that "deliver or receive nuclear reprocessing technology materials, equipment or technology unless they adhere to International Atomic Energy Agency or other international safeguards." This is qualified, however, by the provision that the president can waive the prohibition in specific cases, if he determines that vital security interests are involved and obtains assurances that nuclear weapons will not be fabricated from American supplied nuclear material.

6. For a comprehensive introduction to the prospects for new weapons technologies, see G. Kemp, R. Pfaltzgraff, and U. Ra'anan, eds., *The Other Arms Race* (Lexington, Mass.: Lexington

Books, 1975); and J. Holst and Uwe Nerlich, eds., *Beyond Nuclear Deterrence: New Aims, New Arms* (New York: Crane and Russak, 1976).

7. See especially James Digby, "Precision Guided Weapons," Adelphi Paper no. 118, International Institute for Strategic Studies (IISS) London 1975; Col. Edward B. Atkeson, "Precision Guided Munitions: Implications for Dètente," *Parameters* 5 (1976): 75-87; and Peter Wilson, "Battlefield Guided Weapons; The Big Equalizer," *Proceedings of the Naval Institute,* February 1975.

8. See Philip Karber's arguments concerning the use of antitank weapons in "The Soviet Anti-Tank Debate," *Survival,* May-June 1976.

9. See James L. Foster's arguments in "New Conventional Weapons Technologies: Implications for the Third World," paper presented at the Fletcher School of Law and Diplomacy Conference on Implications of the Military Buildup in Non-Industrialized States, 1976.

10. For a statement of Yugoslav interest in both new nuclear and nonnuclear technologies, see the article by Dimitrije Seserinac Bedza in the party newspaper *Borba,* December 7, 1975 and reprinted in *Survival,* May-June 1976.

11. See Steven J. Rosen and Martin Indyk, "The Temptation to Pre-empt in a Fifth Arab-Israeli War," *Orbis* 20 (1976): 279-80.

12. Edward Luttwak, "U.S. Foreign Policy in a Proliferating World," paper presented at California Arms Control and Foreign Policy Seminar's Conference on Prospects for Proliferation: The Impact on U.S. Foreign Policy. 1976, p. 2

13. The most eloquent presentation of the Third World's case against the NPT system and other nonproliferation mechanisms has been presented by Hedley Bull. See "Rethinking Non-Proliferation," *International Affairs* 51, no. 2 (April 1975): 175-89, and "Arms Control and World Order," *International Security,* Summer 1976.

14. Not all NATO members possess a perceived interest in obtaining a modicum of escalation autonomy. The smaller states, especially those in exposed positions like Norway, are wary of acquiring long-range systems that could potentially strike targets in the Soviet Union. For a discussion of the idea of "parceling out" deterrence, see J. Holst in Holst and Nerlich, *Beyond Nuclear Deterrence.*

15. See "New Naval Weapons Technologies," *Strategic Survey 1975* (London: IISS), p. 23.

16. Roberta Wohlstetter, "Terror on a Grand Scale," *Survival,* May-June 1976, p. 101.

17. John Newhouse, *Cold Dawn* (New York: Holt, Rinehart and Winston, 1973), pp. 164-65.

18. United Nations Association of the United States, National Policy Panel on Conventional Arms Control, New York, "Controlling the International Arms Trade," Interim Report, April 1976.

19. For an outline of the new French defense spending plan, see *The Observer* (London), May 23, 1976, p. 9. For evidence of greater emphasis in French doctrine on conventional contingencies, see statements by President Giscard d'Estaing and Chief of Staff Gen. Guy Mery reprinted in *Survival,* September-October 1976, pp. 226-29.

7 THE PROLIFERATION OF NEW LAND-BASED TECHNOLOGIES: IMPLICATIONS FOR LOCAL MILITARY BALANCES

Steven J. Rosen

Will the proliferation of new land-based weapons systems—including tactical ground weaponry, land-based air power, sophisticated early warning and target acquisition systems, and surface-to-air and surface-to-surface artillery and missiles—significantly affect the political stability of recipient countries and their regions? The global arms traffic now consists of the movement of larger quantities of equipment to smaller powers at an accelerated rate, as well as the introduction of technologically more advanced weapons to Third World countries and other states outside the compass of the great powers earlier in their production and deployment life cycles. The purpose of this chapter is to review briefly some implications of the proliferation of land-based systems for regional politicostrategic relations.

THE CENTER AND THE PERIPHERY

The global arms production and distribution network can be characterized as a flow system having a center and a periphery, with the United

The present article is based on research by the author before joining the staff of the Rand Corporation, and does not represent the views of the Rand Corporation or the sponsors of its research.

States, the Soviet Union, France, and Great Britain (the center) accounting for over 85 percent of production and distribution and the 110 states of the periphery depending primarily on imports from the metropolitan powers for the greater part of their essential military requirements.* Moreover, the driving forces of military research and development are the perceived strategic, economic, political, and bureaucratic imperatives of the countries of the center, rather than of the periphery. New technologies are developed primarily to affect the European military balance and the global strategic balance between the superpowers. The subsequent introduction of these technologies into the peripheral regions is often an incidental by-product or a mere "spillover" effect of the Eurocentric system. In short, the global system is characterized by patterns of structural *strategic* dependency not unlike the relationships of structural *economic* dependency that have been described by students of world trade and capital flows.

The fact that research, development, production, and distribution are dominated by the Europeans and the superpowers and that the spillover effects to the Third World countries are secondary and often uncoordinated and unanticipated is, in one sense, quite irrational for the contemporary world. There have been fifty or more substantial wars in the peripheral countries since 1945, depending on how one counts, but not a single instance of large-scale fighting in Europe or between the superpowers since the end of World War II. Today, the stability of the European balance is reinforced by redundant levels of deterrence and military equilibrium, including (1) substantial inventories of conventional arms, making it unlikely that an aggressor could achieve a theater-wide superiority or even sustain a local breakthrough; (2) thousands of tactical nuclear weapons, acting both to strengthen the "correlation of forces" in the central theaters and to provide a signaling device linking the conventional deterrent to the strategic nuclear deterrent; and finally (3) the panoply of strategic atomic weapons themselves, including submarine-launched ballistic missiles, land-based ICBMs, long-range strategic bombers, and the new strategic cruise missiles. Central war in the European theater or between the superpowers is highly unlikely in the foreseeable future. On the other hand, further rounds of active fighting in the peripheral areas are only too easy to predict: the ongoing insurgency in Eritrea; potential Somali irredentist actions in the Ogaden district of Ethiopia, the Northern Frontier district of Kenya, and possibly Djibouti; the eruption of large-scale fighting in Rhodesia-Zimbabwe; the increasing possibility of renewed conflict in Korea; the

---

*The indigenous arms production and co-production industries of such peripheral states as India, South Korea, Taiwan, Singapore, Iran, Israel, and Egypt are growing in scale and importance; a more detailed analysis would need to distinguish between states which are essentially self-reliant, wholly dependent, and dependent upon a combination of home production and imports. It should be noted, however, that the advanced technologies discussed here are still primarily under the control of the countries of the center.

struggle between Morocco, Mauritania, Algeria, and the Polisario in the former Spanish Sahara; the recrudescence of the Arab-Israeli conflict; possible Guatemalan actions against Belize; instability on the South Asian subcontinent; conflict between Thailand and the new communist powers of Indochina; and many other cases. A survey of world conflicts conducted in 1969 identified no fewer than 160 significant disputes having some potential to erupt into large-scale violence within fifteen years, and the vast majority of these were in the peripheral areas.

We have, then, technologies developed primarily in response to perceived European needs with only incidental attention to the implications for the Third World, but technologies whose most direct and important effects are likely to be seen in these peripheral countries rather than in the center. What are the consequences of this anomalous system?

ASYMMETRICAL PROLIFERATION AND REGIONAL STABILITY

First, as already noted, the periphery should not be viewed as a world of settled political relations and recognized borders, but rather as a collection of simmering conflicts and potential wars involving separatist and irredentist territorial claims, competition over geopolitical assets and natural resources, internal challenges to incumbent regimes, and other disputes. In many areas, such peace as exists has not been achieved because the regional actors have become reconciled to the existing political relations or regard them as equitable or optimal, but rather depends on delicate balances of power that dissuade challenges to the status quo. In situations where stability is fragile, large-scale changes in relative military capabilities or perceived capabilities may tempt those dissatisfied with the existing situation to resort to a trial of strength.

The redundancies of the European balance make it unlikely that marginal additions of new technologies or augmented quantities of combat equipment can upset the basic balance of power there within a short period. But in many peripheral areas, existing inventories of tanks, artillery, advanced combat aircraft, missiles, and other hardware are small, and relatively minor shipments of equipment can produce rapid and decisive changes in the local correlation of forces. Two recent examples are the Soviet shipments to the Popular Movement for the Liberation of Angola (MPLA), which are credited with the decisive victory of that faction in the civil war, and the bolstering of the Dergue regime in Ethiopia. Similarly, the reliance of many peripheral states on technologically obsolete equipment means that the local balance of power can be affected rapidly by the sudden introduction of an "off-the-shelf" system closer to the frontier of technological possibility, such as a superior antitank system to neutralize a neighbor's preponderance in armor or the provision of night-vision equipment to one side only. Thus, local balances in the periphery are more sensitive to fluctuations in the arms trade than are the central balances in Europe and between the superpowers, and the uncontrolled traffic in arms has the potential to unhinge the delicate deterrence relationships upon which the stability of political arrangements in many regions depends.

Moreover, there are gross asymmetries in the capacities of various neighboring states in peripheral areas to acquire, deploy, and effectively use various systems. The ability to acquire weapons may be affected by a state's balance-of-payments position, the degree of support it enjoys from great-power allies or petrodollar-endowed sponsors, its geopolitical position in relation to the perceived interests of potential suppliers, the indigenous technological base limiting a state's ability to absorb arms, the level of inventories available in the supplier states with whom the consumer is politically associated, by the degrees of restriction placed on arms exports by the principal supplier state, by the lead times required to obtain a given system from a certain source, and other factors. Neighboring states may be favored quite unequally by these factors, and a thorough analysis of the contemporary flow of arms from the center to the periphery would show many cases of asymmetry in the quantities of equipment going to each side in various regional conflicts, altering the respective balances of forces.

One of the types of asymmetry that deserves special note is the subclass of regional balances in which one side is supplied by the United States or the West Europeans and the other side is supplied by the Soviet Union. In most of these cases, it is becoming apparent that the Soviet Union has demonstrated a capability to deliver larger quantities of tanks, armored personnel carriers (APCs), and artillery pieces out of existing inventories on schedules that could not be achieved by the Western countries even if they had the will to do so. For example, Libya, Syria, Egypt, and Iraq, four secondary allies of the Soviet Union, have received almost 5000 Soviet tanks since 1970, a number half as large as the total NATO armored force in the central European theater. U.S. armor production during this period for all purposes, domestic and foreign, for major and minor allies, was less than 3000. The Soviet export advantage is rooted in the higher levels of output of general-purpose land forces produced by Soviet military industries in recent years. According to former United States Secretary of Defense Rumsfeld's final report to Congress, the following were the average annual production rates of selected general purpose forces from 1972 to 1976:[1]

	Tanks	APCs	Artillery	Tactical Aircraft
USSR	2770	4990	1310	1090
USA	469	1556	162	573

It might be objected that this comparison excludes the production of the United States' European allies, several of whom are major suppliers. But a comparison of NATO aggregates with those of the Warsaw Pact yields substantially similar results. The following figures are from a statement by Representative Les Aspin (Democrat, Wisconsin), a leading critic of military spending in the U.S. Congress:[2]

	Tanks	APCs	Artillery	Tactical Aircraft
Warsaw Pact	2800	4350	1400	938
NATO	983	1678	330	821

It may even be argued that the primary relationship between the Soviet Union and the Third World is one of arms supply. The USSR is not a major nonmilitary trading partner of the developing countries; the entire Eastern bloc typically absorbs less than 5 percent of the exports of developing countries and provides just over 5 percent of their civilian imports.[3] Nor is the communist superpower a major source of economic aid—accounting in 1975 for only 10 percent of agreements and 3 percent of aid actually delivered[4]—or cultural influence—most Third World elites and media being oriented to Western languages, educational influences, films, and publications. This means that the Soviet Union's one major concrete form of influence in the Third World is its ability to deliver arms in quantity and when they are needed, particularly to states and insurgencies whose purpose in acquiring arms is to challenge the existing political status quo. In material terms, the Soviet Union's status as the world's largest conventional arms producer gives it a unique role as a supplier and an identifiable interest in the maintenance of tense conditions in regional conflicts. It also means that, in quantitative terms, friends of the Soviet Union will tend to enjoy some significant advantages over neighbors who tie their interests to the West. For example, Somalia received from the Soviet Union, prior to its withdrawal of support, some 250 tanks and 310 APCs by the end of 1976; neighboring Kenya, with four times the population and eight times the GNP, had no tanks and 13 APCs, and Ethiopia, with nine times the population and eight times the GNP had 62 tanks and 50 APCs before Soviet supplies began arriving in 1978. It should also be noted that, should war erupt in the Horn of Africa, the most likely battlefields (Ogaden, Djibouti, and the Northern Frontier district) are soft-surfaced, open areas where tracked vehicles will be important. Peru, during its long years of association with the United States, accumulated 60 M-4 medium tanks; in the few years it has been associated with the Soviet Union, it has received an estimated 200 T-55s, while neighboring Ecuador has 40 American and 41 French light tanks. Cuba has over 600 tanks, and Angola has more tanks (over 200) than South Africa(160). Even Israel has received from the Soviet Union, in the form of captured equipment, half as many usable tanks as they have received from the United States—615 compared with 1250.[5]

On the other hand, Western equipment continues to outperform many Soviet items on a unit-comparison basis, and in most categories of hardware the technologically superior Western supplies are preferred by many Third World consumers. It is true that Soviet research and development expenditures now exceed those of the United States by a margin of from 25 to 50 percent, and if these trends continue the USSR could eventually compound its quantitative preponderance with superior quality as well.[6] But the present Western advantage in computers and microelectronics, radars and sensors, and precision guidance technologies would take some years to overcome even if Western research and development efforts stopped altogether or failed to respond to the stepped-up pace of Soviet investments. Assuming that the West retains its qualitative lead, the theoretical possibility exists that in areas where the Soviet Union provides larger quantities of weapons to one side the West could react to restore the military balance by providing offsetting, technologically superior equipment to the other side. Whether such a system of counterbalances can be sustained and whether quality can always offset quantity are of course arguable, but it is clear that without such compensatory actions the system of regional deterrents is in peril. There will even be some states (Libya, Iraq, and Kuwait providing current examples) who will have the best of both worlds by shopping for "brawn" in the East and "brains" in the West.

Of course, it is possible to take the view that the sensitivity of regional balances to the introduction of greater quantities of arms will be reduced over time as local inventories accumulate and further increments have a smaller percentage effect on the correlation of forces. Such a condition of relative immunity to numbers has probably already been achieved in the Arab-Israeli case, where the stocks on hand are so large as to reduce the significance of additional acquisitions. For example, the 4,600 tanks fielded by the Arab armies against Israel in 1973 represented a number two-thirds as large as the entire peacetime inventory of NATO in the vast northern and central European theater (7000), and the 1,225 combat aircraft of the Arab confrontation states was, again, nearly two-thirds of the 2,050 combat aircraft in north and central NATO. It seems unlikely that additional numbers of tanks or aircraft would fundamentally alter the balance in this region unless the new equipment also had performance capabilities significantly greater than the old ones. Similarly, there may be a self-correcting element in the qualitative or technological side of the arms trade; as the inventories of the peripheral states are improved to incorporate new technologies and advance closer to the existing state of the art in military equipment and aircraft, the possibility that a regional balance will be disturbed by the sudden introduction of an advanced system will be to that degree reduced, though never eliminated. After a certain point is passed in arms proliferation, the global system of local deterrents may achieve a dynamic equilibrium, with a resilience that will insulate it, to some degree, from the destabilizing effects of further arms transfers, though it is unlikely that any regional balance will be able to keep pace with all developments in technology.

The problem with this view is the long unstable period during which the low-technology, low-inventory states will be transitioning to high technologies and high inventories. Moreover, the new balances of forces achieved at the end of the transition may be qualitatively different from the balances that existed before the proliferation process began, since the comparative capabilities of the parties may be altered in the evolution from one relatively stable force ratio to another. In many cases, this can mean that states enjoying new military advantages will insist on significant border alterations or they may even absorb neighboring states in their entirety; separatist and autonomist peoples who happen to be favored by the changed balance of power may insist on secession. In short, even if proliferation finally results in a new military equilibrium, it may well mean increased political turbulence and a heightened possibility of war in many peripheral areas, particularly during the transitional decades, if states and movements that were dissatisfied with the political status quo that existed before the large-scale arms transfers happen to emerge in a more favorable position than before. The chances for war can also increase during the transitional period if some actors believe that their own military positions are rapidly deteriorating because of their adversaries' mounting accumulation of weapons, and they choose to resort to preventive war before their military positions are eroded completely.

None of this is to argue that the proliferation of tanks, APCs, artillery, missiles, and land-based aircraft necessarily and invariably will lead to political instability; it is rather to develop the theme that periods of rapid change in capabilities have this potential unless the relative balance of forces between contentious neighbors is managed with care. There are some circumstances, of course, under which the supply of arms to recipients in areas of tension can make the outbreak of war *less* likely. Furnishing a status quo power with a sizable and unambiguous superiority in military strength may help regional rivals with anti-status quo aspirations to recognize the futility of starting a war. Examples here might include the effects of the Shah's massive arms imports in dampening the expansionist ambitions of Iraq against Kuwait and other neighbors. Perhaps another example is Korea, where the strengthening of the South seems to be effective in deterring Kim Il Sung from exercising military options for reunification. Sometimes, arms transfers can reinforce stability by altering the position of a threatened state from one of military inferiority to one of parity with its potential adversaries, thus making it a less tempting and vulnerable target for attack. These are, however, exceptional cases. In most regions, there already exists some correspondence between the present balance of military forces and the distribution of territory and other valued assets. More often than not, alterations in these existing military balances will not serve to correct unstable force ratios but rather will tend to undermine such stability as has been achieved.

THE EFFECTS OF NEW TECHNOLOGIES

Are there some technologies that are inherently defensive and, hence, will tend to reinforce existing military balances, as opposed to others that are favorable to the offense and therefore destabilizing? This section singles out a number of particular new technologies most likely to proliferate widely and assesses their effects on regional stability in areas of the periphery. Four systems are considered, three of which (antitank weapons, surface-to-air missiles, and airborne and over-the-horizon radar early warning systems) have the prima facie image of favoring the defense and one (surface-to-surface medium-range weaponry) which seems offensive in character; the analysis shows that the actual pattern of offensive-defensive interaction that might result from the proliferation of these systems will be more complex than first impressions indicate. This new hardware is then related to the aspect of "human technology"—the effects of the equipment in relation to existing levels of technological competence in the affected countries, and the effects of training programs and technological cooperation in altering the relative competence of personnel in various regional adversary relationships.

Antitank Guided Munitions

Probably the most benign of the new land-force technologies from the offense-defense point of view are the antitank guided munitions (ATGM), including missiles and artillery shells with terminal guidance capabilities and vastly improved, single-shot kill probabilities. Large and costly offensive systems like tanks and armored fighting vehicles are becoming more vulnerable to detection and targeting by relatively inexpensive systems that can be acquired by defensive forces in large numbers and operated by personnel with relatively low levels of technical skill. These are labor-intensive, intermediate military technologies that are well suited to developing countries and have been evaluated as inherently defensive in nature by many commentators. Offensive forces entering areas where the defense has been well planned in advance will tend to suffer very substantially in the lethal hail of fire. For example, a tank that betrays its location to a small defending force of missile-armed infantry whose own positions are concealed by ground cover or terrain undulations has a high probability of being hit and destroyed. The difficulty of assaulting prepared positions on the ground was already evident in the 1973 Middle East conflict, where every offensive or counteroffensive by either side against fully mobilized and alert enemy strongholds found unexpectedly fierce resistance and sustained higher loss rates than had been expected even when the local force ratios strongly favored the attacker. Small defending units will not only be able to threaten and destroy larger armored units in more situations, but they themselves will be more survivable because of their lower "all-media signatures," that is, their lower visual, radar, electronic, thermal, and acoustical contrasts with the surrounding environment. A great premium will be attached to hiding, blending with background, and remaining motionless, and this will tend to serve the defender, who can play a more passive role while the attacker is obliged to move aggressively forward often over open terrain in unfamiliar territory.* Against such antitank defenses, the aggressor will require much larger amounts of suppressive supporting fire, artillery barrages, organic mechanized infantry attached to the armored corps, and other elements of the combined arms offensive. The scale of mobilization and concentration required to achieve a breakthrough against even relatively small defending units armed with precision guided munitions (PGMs, see Chapter 5) will raise the costs of offensive operations considerably, both in terms of the numbers of men and equipment necessary to execute a given operation and in terms of the levels of battle attrition that will have to be tolerated. Another new antitank technology worth mentioning in this connection is a cluster munition fired by rockets or artillery or dropped from aircraft and consisting of a canister of small minelets which are scattered instantly over a relatively wide area upon impact. Dispersible minelets do not destroy tanks, but they do immobilize armored vehicles passing over them by destroying their tracks. Effectively, they are instant area-denial weapons that can be used to close certain approaches to an aggressor, to force the concentration of attacking forces and their exposure to attrition by precision guided fire, or to canalize offensive movements into certain routes rather than others. Here again, countermeasures are available to the offensive forces, but the net effect of this technology is to slow the enemy advance and to raise the scale of the operation required to achieve a breakthrough.

---

*Future developments may include robotized, self-initiating antitank missiles which can be prepositioned in areas the enemy is expected to enter and fire automatically when targets whose signatures match precoded profiles approach. The possibilities for concealment and camouflage of such systems are endless.

There are a few special cases in which the tactically defensive orientation of antitank guided weapons could be used to support the strategic offense rather than the defense. One is an adversary relationship in which the attacker depends primarily on guerrilla foot soldiers and the defender depends on highly mobile fighting vehicles (tanks, armored personnel carriers, mechanized infantry fighting vehicles, or even soft-wheeled vehicles). Here, the high hit probabilities of the new PGMs might serve to enhance the effectiveness of the guerrilla units and at a minimum force a change in tactics by the defenders. Depending on the nature of the terrain and the political orientation of the surrounding civilian population, antitank guided weapons could change the balance of forces in some regions in favor of the insurgents.

The other exception that should be noted with regard to antiarmor weapons is the class of cases in which an aggressor successfully seizes a piece of territory and then turns the PGMs to "defensive" purposes to hold it against counterattack. More generally, it may sometimes be necessary for an army which is defensively oriented in the political and strategic senses to adopt offensive means in a particular tactical engagement: to carry the way to the territory of the enemy, to strike along the line of least expectation, to execute a pincer operation to isolate and encircle an enemy unit that has managed a breakthrough, to force the diversion of enemy battalions from areas of weak defense to more favorable positions, or for other reasons. The defensive army may be forced to use offensive tactics, and ATGMs, by making such operations more difficult, may in particular cases actually work against the strategic defender and in favor of the aggressor.[7] These are exceptional cases and circumstances, however, and the net effect of the proliferation of ATGMs in the majority of cases should be to enhance the ability of small states to defend themselves at relatively low cost, in some cases against adversaries whose preponderance in armor might have been much more threatening in the past.

Surface-Based Air Defenses

Another relatively benign class of weapons whose proliferation is often regarded as favorable to the defense is the new generation of antiaircraft artillery with sophisticated fire control and high rates of fire—such as the Soviet ZSU-23 quad guns—and a wide array of surface-to-air missiles (SAMs) with radar and infrared terminal guidance. In theory, the effect of these systems is similar to that of the ATGM: they make it difficult for offensive strike aircraft to enter a certain lethal envelope without risking high rates of attrition. Protective measures against the surface-to-air systems, such as evasive maneuvers and electronic countermeasure jamming pods, can reduce sortie loss rates for the aircraft, but only at the cost of system degradation—which results from displacing part of the ordnance-carrying capability of the aircraft—or reducing its mission performance capability—by forcing it to fly at unusual altitudes or in nonoptimal flight profiles—and to lose some accuracy in weapons delivery. As long as the surface-to-air systems are operative, their effect is to raise significantly the active attrition of enemy aircraft or to degrade the system effectiveness of the attacker's equipment (sometimes called "passive attrition"). Ron Huiskin has shown the speed with which these systems are being introduced in a large number of Third World countries; those possessing SAMs, for example, grew from 8 in 1965 to 26 in 1976 (though during the same period the number of Third World countries possessing supersonic combat aircraft increased even more rapidly—from 14 to 44).

It is somewhat less clear, however, that there is an organic link between surface-to-air weapons and the defense than in the case of antitank guided weapons. In addition to the caveats noted already for the antitank weapons (strategic defense versus tactical offense, seize-and-hold operations, guerrilla forces) effective surface-to-air weapons may be used to construct a defensive umbrella protecting offensive ground forces which are moving forward from aerial interdiction (for example, the Egyptian and Syrian offensives of October 6, 1973). In cases where the offensive side is preponderant on the ground and the defense leans on its air force to restore the balance, this has the net effect of enhancing the offense. This argument might apply especially to the cases mentioned earlier in which one side is supplied by the Soviet Union, and therefore is likely to possess larger numbers of tanks and field artillery as well as surface-to-air missiles and guns, while the other side depends on the West and tends to be air intensive.

Relatively Long-Range Air-to-Surface and Surface-to-Surface Weapons

Surface-to-air missiles and artillery may affect the offensive-defensive balance in another way, by forcing the attacking air force to acquire long-range, stand-off defense-suppression weapons such as air-to-surface missiles and glide bombs with terminal guidance, surface-to-surface ballistic missiles with ranges in excess of 40 miles, and perhaps eventually tactical cruise missiles. Combined with precision radar-emitter location systems, remotely piloted vehicle (RPV) reconnaissance, and other means of acquiring SAMs as targets, these weapons can be highly effective in suppressing the larger and longer-range, radar-dependent surface-to-air defenses, though they cannot eliminate infantry-portable missiles if proliferated on the battlefield in huge numbers.[8] After the defense-suppression missions are completed, the air force will have relatively wide freedom of the skies at altitudes above two miles (the approximate limit of infantry SAMs and smaller antiaircraft artillery). At this altitude, the aircraft will require terminally guided missiles and bombs to support friendly ground forces, interdict enemy units, and conduct strikes against enemy targets in the interior. For these reasons, the net effect of the proliferation of SAMs may be to accelerate the proliferation of longer-range air and surface-based missiles and bombs of an unambiguously offensive character.

Delivery vehicles that enable an attacker accurately to strike fixed and mobile targets relatively deep within an adversary's interior, while firing from platforms within the attacker's own territory and air space, are among the most offensive of the new weapons because the defender's army can no longer act as a shield against attacks on the homeland even if it is superior to the attacking forces. Fixed targets whose locations are known, such as factories, refineries, generating and pumping stations, communications facilities, and bridges, will be particularly vulnerable, as will the civilian population unless extensive civil-defense measures are undertaken.

It is important to distinguish here between the older, "beyond-the-battlefield" weapons—such as the Soviet Scud surface-to-surface missiles—with long ranges but low accuracy (circular error probability of the Scud is estimated to be several hundred meters) and the coming generation of surface-to-surface and air-to-surface weapons that combine range with precision terminal guidance. While the former systems could have a psychological effect, they were not efficacious in the performance of primary military tasks unless armed with nuclear warheads. Moreover, their psychological effect has often been the reverse of that intended. The Germans fired over 10,000 V-1 buzz bombs and V-2 rockets—carrying warheads as large as 1000 kilograms—against Great Britain late in World War II, only to find British resistance stiffened by the "hail of blows" rather than weakened, as it had been by smaller air raids in 1940–41.

However, the new generation of medium-range weapons—including tactical cruise missiles, terminally guided submunitions carried by tactical ballistic missiles, kamikaze drones and RPVs, rocket-assisted artillery shells with extended ranges, and air-launched glide bombs and missiles with ranges in excess of fifty miles—will enable the attacker to be far more selective and effective in choosing targets. Moreover, the unit costs of the new systems are coming down as research and development outlays are spread over longer production runs, modular guidance and propulsion systems are adapted to a multiplicity of weapons, microminiaturized electronic components reduce both weight and cost, and economies of scale are achieved in production. The United States is now developing a 500-pound buzz bomb with its own booster engine and a simplified laser guidance system with a range in excess of 50 miles and a unit cost of only $6,500.* The unit cost of the GBU-15 glide bomb is expected eventually to

---

*However, surface-based laser designation of Smartroc will be limited by the horizon—22 miles at sea—but RPV designators could extend the range.

drop from $150,000 to under $50,000, as is the tactical range cruise missile.[9] Expendable attack RPVs and kamikaze drones are expected to reach a unit cost in full production of $10–20,000, and have ranges of 200 miles and more.* Unguided, rocket-assisted artillery projectiles with ranges in excess of 30 miles are already in production at unit costs of $500 to $1,000.[10] Cannon-launched guided projectiles will soon be available for a few thousand dollars per round. Taken altogether, these systems, should they become off-the-shelf items, will be affordable by many peripheral countries in substantial quantities.

If both sides in a regional adversary relationship possess the means to strike each other's interior, the possibility exists that a system of deterrents may operate during conflict if reason can restrain the temptations to action. Referring to the Scuds in his possession, President Sadat addressed a warning to Israel at the height of the October war:

> We realize the responsibility of using certain kinds of weapons and we control ourselves. But the Israelis have to remember what I have said: An eye for an eye, a tooth for a tooth, and interior aggression for interior aggression.[11]

Following the 1973 war, Israel proposed an agreement through the International Red Cross under which it would join Syria and Egypt in a pledge to refrain from striking at each other's population centers if another war erupts.[12] It is conceivable that, if stand-off and beyond-the-battlefield weapons do proliferate to peripheral regions, tacit and explicit restraints on deployment may follow.

Historical analogies suggest, however, that rational interest alone can fail to arrest the escalation from limited to total war, even when there is a highly developed process of signaling and tacit bargaining. There are bound to be some factions who will call for the use of a prohibited weapon to turn the tide of battle, to bring a more decisive victory, to end the war earlier, or to break the morale of the enemy. The advocates of escalation will play upon the belief that eventually the other side intends to use beyond-the-battlefield weapons anyway or, conversely, that it has only a limited means to do so. Accidental violations of limiting principles by an enemy may be misread as intentional acts signaling the end of restraint. As the distance between "allowed" and "disallowed" weapons and targets narrows, as both sides try to bring within their disallowed sanctuaries an increasing number of targets regarded as legitimate military objectives by the enemy, and as the "fog of war" thickens, the boundaries between permissible and impermissible actions will be eroded. There may be a sequence of small, escalatory steps whose end result the leaders are unable to foresee, but which will lead

---

*The Northrop Low Cost Expendable Harassment Vehicle, for example, weighs 90 pounds, flies at 120 mph, and has a total endurance of five hours, including ferry and loiter.

incrementally, to unlimited warfare. And, in the heat of battle, restraint may fail under the pressure of anger that demands expression. Once the hounds of war are unleashed, the decision makers may be overwhelmed by the social forces that they have activated.[13] Once long-range weapons are in the hands of belligerent states, it may be more difficult to restrain their use through mutual deterrence than a purely rational theory of behavior would suggest. On the other hand, the number of states manufacturing and aggressively marketing aircraft with weapons fits capable of delivering stand-off ordnance, as well as the wide variety of stand-off systems being introduced, will make an effort to arrest the proliferation of these weapons exceedingly difficult to realize in practice.

Early-Warning Systems

Early warning surveillance systems are not in themselves weapons systems at all, but large-scale reconnaissance aids designed to provide near real-time information on enemy deployments. Two principal types are of interest here: airborne early warning (AEW) aircraft, and over-the-horizon (OTH) radars. The principal mission of AEW aircraft is to loiter in a holding pattern over a particular region and, by the use of long-range radars and other sensors to conduct surveillance well beyond the limits of ordinary ground-based radars lacking OTH capabilities. In the case of the Hawkeye E-2C, the effective surveillance cylinder has a radius of about 250 miles and extends from the surface to 100,000 feet. AEW aircraft also enhance interception capabilities; the Hawkeye is capable of following the move-ments of as many as 300 enemy aircraft at a time and can simultaneously vector-in intercepting aircraft or missiles against as many as 30. Its greatest appeal is the possibility to act as a force multiplier for the defender, providing oversight of the entire area of the enemy's potential attack and, based on the "big picture" of the enemy's deployments, allowing allocation of scarce defensive resources earlier and far more effectively than was formerly possible with piecemeal intelligence and without downward-looking radars and real-time communication. Grumman claims that the Hawkeye can enable a fighter force to reduce friendly losses by 400 percent and increase enemy attrition by 200 percent when full-scale hostilities are initiated. It makes surprise attack harder to achieve and increases the losses that the attacker must be willing to sustain while reducing those of the defender.[14]

The problem with this seemingly benign system is that it also has the potential to assist one's fighters and ground-attack aircraft operating on the enemy's side of the front line, by identifying and locating lucrative targets in the air and on the ground. Hawkeye's Passive Detection System, for example, can identify SAM radars from as far as 400 miles, facilitating air-defense suppression while its radars can acquire and locate enemy tank and artillery concentrations over a large area. In summary, while the primary mission of AEW is defense, it can substantially enhance the offensive capabilities of air and ground forces as well. This kind of system is going to be very attractive to reasonably well-heeled armed forces, and both Grumman and Hawker Siddeley will be happy to have export orders to take up idle capacity in their Hawkeye and Nimrod production lines, respectively. The British firm is said to be looking to the Middle East, the Persian Gulf, Australia, and Japan, while it is expanding the capabilities of the Nimrod by outfitting it with the avionics (*aviation electronics*) suite of the E-2C and especially by adapting the APS-125 overland radar.[15] The Soviet Moss is an airborne warning and control system (AWACS) with capabilities an order of magnitude below the Hawkeye or U.S. AWACS, but its effectiveness in defense and offense was evident during the December 1971 Indo-Pakistani war when it was on loan to India. Flying at night, Indian strike aircraft repeatedly succeeded in making low-level penetrations of up to 160 kilometers into Pakistani air space, locating and attacking targets with great precision, while at the same time providing gap-free detection of aircraft entering India.[16] As in the case of antitank guided weapons and surface-to-air missiles, the implications of proliferations of AWACS aircraft for offensive-defensive interaction in particular regions are more complex than initial impressions may indicate.

Ground-based, over-the-horizon radars are an alternative means of performing many of the early-warning functions of airborne systems, but at the present time they do not appear to have the same degree of bonus offensive potential. Recent "backscatter" radar developments make it possible to bounce high-powered signals off the ionosphere to detect targets at ranges of between 800 and 3200 kilometers, or even farther around the curvature of the earth, and to "mirror" the signals back to separate receiver stations located in the home country. Aircraft, large cruise missiles, and some types of surface shipping can be detected and, with some refinements now under development, intercepted by defensive systems vectored into a general envelope by the ground radar. The early-warning range of OTH backscatter radar is much greater than that of present airborne systems. This enhances the defensive function, but at the same time OTH has several limitations that make its offensive potential less threatening: first, the known capability of OTH to acquire targets on the ground is considerably less than the comparable capabilities of Hawkeye and AWACS; second, aircraft detected by the system are not, as yet, located with the precision that is possible with existing AEW systems; third, while some writers have suggested further developments of OTH radar that would enhance its offensive applications, these are probably beyond the ability of developing countries to realize and exploit on their own. The possibility exists, however, of providing some peripheral states—particularly those with deep interiors and long frontiers—with an alternative to AEW systems that is less expensive and has wider coverage with fewer offensive temptations.[17] OTH is also likely to gain in importance with the adoption of the 200-mile economic zone.

The Human Factor

The highly selective and cursory examination of a few technologies confirms what is already common knowledge: there are no hard and fast distinctions between offensive and defensive weapons and systems, and much depends on the particular strategic and tactical applications for which the hardware is used. Another factor at least as important is the unequal capacity of military personnel in different recipient states of the periphery to effectively maintain and operate given sets of equipment and obtain the greatest combat utility from them. Differences in social and cultural environment, prevailing levels of human technological competence, past combat experience, the quality of officer corps and of the political leadership and other human factors will impact greatly upon the effectiveness with which different technologies are adapted to the particular needs of recipient states. While differences in personnel are less quantifiable than differences in equipment, a considerable body of historical evidence points to the conclusion that sound training, well-considered tactics, and the individual competence of personnel have a much greater effect on combat outcomes than any normal differences in weapons hardware.[18]

This is illustrated by the experience of U.S. Navy pilots in Indochina who during the first phase of the air war (1965–68) achieved kill ratios in air combat of F-4s against MiG-21s of 2.3:1. This was considered unacceptably low by Navy officials, who sought to correct it during the bombing phase of 1968–1970 by instituting the so-called Dissimilar Air Combat Pilot-Re-training Program (nicknamed Topgun). When intensive air combat was resumed in the 1970–73 period, Topgun pilots flying essentially the same planes against the same adversaries improved their kill ratios to 12.5:1—a 500 percent improvement based primarily on improved human performance.[19] Similarly, the air-combat superiority of the Israelis, evidenced by dogfight kill ratios of 20:1 in 1967 and 40:1 in 1973,[20] is explained far more convincingly by differences in pilot skill and tactics than by objective disparities between the Israeli Phantoms and Mirages and the Arab MiGs and their respective weapons and avionics fits. (Indeed, on some measures the Russian platforms were regarded as superior by the Israeli pilots.) These and other evidences, as well as many first-person accounts, suggest that differences in equipment and hardware technology are minimized by differences in human skill and training in the circumstances of all but the most unfavorable force ratios and technological imbalances.

It follows that even if identical quantities and qualities of equipment were introduced to both adversaries in a local conflict, the effective balances of force might be altered simply because one side could absorb and utilize the materiel better than the other. It also follows that personnel training programs and other forms of "human technology" transfers from the center to the periphery may be as important as or even more important than, the arms transfers themselves. Technical skills, systems of military management, methods of logistical planning and operations analysis, strategic and tactical conceptions, and other "intangible arms transfers" have the same potential to alter local military balances and thereby destabilize regional deterrent relationships as transfers of weapons, though the weapons themselves may be more highly regarded by both the supplier and the recipient, not to mention those who monitor arms flows at the Stockholm International Peace Research Institute (SIPRI). Yet military advisory missions and training programs are one of the largest components of the global military flow. In 1976, the United States alone had military missions and groups in forty-four countries,[21] including 132 technical assistance and training teams either contracted for or actually in 34 countries.[22] The Vinnell Corporation, for example, has contracted through the U.S. Army to provide 1000 U.S. civilians, mostly former military personnel, to train the Saudi Arabian internal security forces.[23]

THE RELATIONSHIP BETWEEN NEW TECHNOLOGIES AND OPERATOR COMPETENCE

In some respects, the introduction of weapons systems that are highly sophisticated but simple to operate, will reduce the impact of human skill in military operations. The closer we come to the mythical automated battlefield, with pushbutton "fire-and-forget" weapons, the less individual competence and initiative will count. The new systems vary greatly in the expertise they demand of the operators, but they do tend, with some exceptions, to simplify the skills required of the actual users on the front line. For example, the second-generation ATGMs (TOW, Dragon, Milan) come closer to truly automatic guidance than the first generation missiles that they replace,* and the coming introduction of laser-homing, cannon-launched

---

*The first-generation systems require the operator to align the horizontal and vertical coordinates of both the target and the missile until impact, while operating under fire. Second-generation systems either autonomously home in on infrared or electro-optical signals or call upon the operator to fix a single set of cross hairs on the target alone.

guided projectiles will require even less of the target designators and artillery crews. As the tactical subtlety and technical sophistication required to operate the new systems is on the average lower than for the systems they replace, it may be argued that the revolution in military equipment will reduce the advantage of "brainpower" in the operation of weapons on the battlefield and act to some degree as an equalizer between armies of unequal skill. And this is yet another way in which proliferation will alter existing military balances.

On the other hand, although many of the systems themselves are easier to operate, the overall effect of the technological revolution will probably be to increase the demands on a core of highly trained personnel and to increase the advantage of an officer corps that can adapt and improvise. Because effective firepower is becoming increasingly light and compact, mobile and relatively independent small units will be used in the future to threaten and destroy larger units in many situations. This is expected to lead to a proliferation of small units and to a "molecular" pattern of deployment on the battlefield.[24] A larger degree of authority will have to be delegated to lower command levels, and the quality of junior officers and the intermediate ranks from captain to colonel will have a greater impact than before on the effectiveness of the fighting forces. Improvisational tactics and operational flexibility will find their widest scope, and the net effect of the new technologies will be to enhance rather than reduce the importance of the human qualitative factor. On the higher levels of strategy and war planning, the very speed of technological change and innovation may reward the side that is able to modify its organization and force posturing more rapidly and to absorb and integrate new equipment on shorter lead times. The former head of U.S. military research and development, Malcolm Currie, offered the hypothesis that in the coming years, a technological breakthrough or surprise is less likely to take the form of an unforeseen new weapon per se than of the innovative use of a known technology on the basis of a superior understanding of its ultimate significance on the battlefield.[25] So the relationship between the new equipment technologies and human technology may enhance the advantage of states favored by the balance of skills at the higher levels.

CONCLUSION

The world system of local military balances, like the global ecosystem, is the product of many years of mutation and adaptation leading to a delicately tuned equilibrium. The system has some homeostatic resilience, and can tolerate moderate amounts of change introduced at a reasonable pace, but sudden and large-scale changes in the environment run the risk of upsetting the basic equilibrium. Just as rapid and uncontrolled industrialization can upset the planetary bio-system, the present anarchic and uncontrolled pattern of proliferation of advanced weapons technologies has the potential to upset the ecology of military relationships on which regional political systems rest. In some cases, it may be desirable to alter political relationships and, therefore, it may be necessary to change the existing military balances. But the present phenomenon of largely indiscriminate proliferation, both quantitative and qualitative, lacks a guiding hand and may well have consequences unforeseen by the principal actors.

This chapter briefly reviewed some of the ways in which the present pattern of proliferation threatens to alter delicate regional balances. Neighboring states are unequally favored by the possession of resources with which to pay for arms, by the geopolitical assets they can offer to potential suppliers, and by the degrees of support they enjoy from great-power allies or petrodollar-endowed sponsors. States are also unequally affected by the levels of inventory maintained by the suppliers with whom they are associated, by the different restrictions placed on arms exports by the various suppliers, and by the lead times required to obtain particular systems when they are needed. States supplied by the Soviet bloc tend to receive larger volumes of equipment, while those supplied by the West tend to receive technologically more advanced systems. There is no assurance that all these assymmetries will cancel each other out; indeed, in many cases, there are reasons to believe that the asymmetries will worsen over time.

On the qualitative side of the arms trade, some important differences have been noted in the destabilizing potential of various new technologies that are likely to proliferate, but it has not been possible to identify any technologies that are purely defensive in practice. The most benign of the systems examined were the antitank guided munitions (ATGMs), but even these could aid an attacker by facilitating seize-and-hold operations, impeding the use of offensive tactics by the strategically defensive side, and enhancing the opportunities for guerrilla incursions. Surface-to-air missiles (SAMs) can aid the attack by degrading the interdiction capabilities of the defending air force, operating offensively to cover the defender's own air space, and by encouraging the proliferation of stand-off SAM-suppression weapons which themselves have considerable offensive potential. Medium-range surface-to-surface missiles, rocket-assisted projectiles and stand-off air-to-surface missiles and glide bombs have many offensive applications and are likely to become off-the-shelf items from many suppliers and, in some cases, will be relatively simple technologies for indigenous production. Airborne and surface-based early warning systems have an offensive bonus in their ability to vector attacking aircraft, missiles, and other weapons systems against enemy forces, once the latter are located.

Finally, the ability of states to absorb and integrate the quantities and qualities of weapons that become available to them is highly unequal. Military skills are distributed across the globe asymmetrically, and some states will obtain greater net utility from given inputs of equipment than will others. Moreover, the distribution of military skills is itself being disturbed, as human technology transfer proliferates in patterns as asymmetrical as the equipment flows.

It would be impossible and in many ways undesirable to freeze the global arms system at a certain moment in time solely to stabilize the existing complex of political relations in all parts of the world. But even those who seek large-scale political change cannot be sanguine with the present pattern of arms proliferation, because the actors who come out on top may not be the "good guys" from their point of view in every case. The world is a picture with some aesthetically pleasing areas and some areas whose arrangement is not delightful to the eye. But the solution is not merely to scramble the pieces of the image in the hope that the new arrangement, randomly arrived at, will be more satisfactory. This, in effect, is what the present pattern of arms proliferation threatens to do. On the other hand, it is not clear that a conventional arms-control regime imposed by the exporting states will be any more satisfactory, nor that one can be established effectively.

NOTES

1. Donald H. Rumsfeld, *Annual Defense Department Report, Fiscal Year 1978* (Washington, D.C.: U.S. Government Printing Office, 1977), p. 11. For trends in U.S. and Soviet production of ground-force equipment for 1966 to 1976, see p. 27. These simplified tabulations aggregate in broad categories equipment with widely varying performance characteristics, comparing, for example, the U.S. M-113 armored personnel carrier with the more sophisticated Soviet BMP mechanized infantry fighting vehicle, or classing the MiG-21 with the F-15. It is virtually impossible to quantify in a simple and comprehensive way the wide array of systems under production without comparing incommensurables. For instance, tanks vary in mobility, protection, accuracy, range, rate of fire, target acquisition, location aids, etc. Fighters differ from ground-attack aircraft and themselves vary in acceleration, maneuverability, range, payload, avionics, and weapons fits. Obviously, aggregate comparisons can be highly misleading. However, available evidence based on more detailed and exhaustive studies tends to support the broad point made here. Soviet production of these land-based, general-purpose forces has, in the net assessment, exceeded that of the West in recent years.

2. Representative Les Aspin, "Comparing Soviet and American Defense Effort," reprinted in NATO's *Fifteen Nations*, June–July 1976, p. 41.

3. United States Department of State, "Communist States and Developing Countries: Aid and Trade in 1972," State Department, Bureau of Public Affairs, Washington, D.C., August 1973, p. 19.

4. U.S. Central Intelligence Agency, "Communist Aid to Less Developed Countries of the Free World, 1975," Washington, July 1976, p.5.

5. All figures from International Institute for Strategic Studies, *The Military Balance, 1975–76* and *1976–77* (London: 11SS).

6. Malcolm Currie, former Director of U.S. Defense Research, Development, Testing, and Evaluation, in *Aviation Week*, February 16, 1976 and May 17, 1976. See also Robert Perry, "Comparisons of U.S. and Soviet Technology," Report R-827-PR, Rand Corporation, Santa Monica, Calif., 1973.

7. Richard Burt makes the case still more generally, arguing that the defender is often required to adopt mobile tactics. Compare "New Weapons Technologies: Debate and Directions," Adelphi Paper No. 126, International Institute for Strategic Studies, London, 1976, pp. 8–14

8. The next generation of medium- and long-range SAMs may reduce vulnerability by separating the radar transmitter from the receiver (the bistatic principle) or by replacing radars altogether with passive (non-emitting) detection systems dependent on infrared sensors. See S. J. Rosen, "Surface-to-Air Missiles and the Future Value of Air Superiority in the Middle East," *Survival*, September–October 1977.

9. See Kosta Tsipis, "Cruise Missiles," *Scientific American*, February 1977, p. 25; and Richard L. Garwin, "Effective Military Technology for the 1980s," *International Security*, No. 2, Fall 1976:67. Both authors are aware that the present unit costs of tactical cruise missiles are vastly in excess of this figure (e.g., $500,000 and more).

10. See Rumsfeld, *Annual Defense Department Report*, p. 173.

11. Speech of October 16, 1973, in Egyptian Ministry of Information, *Speeches and Interviews by President Anwar El Sadat, July–December 1973* (Cairo: State Information Service, 1974), p. 207.

12. "Israel Seeks Pact on Sparing Cities in Any Future War," *New York Times*, April 5, 1975, p. 3.

13. On the failure of efforts to limit strategic bombing of cities during World War II, see Frederick M. Sallagar, *The Road to Total War* (New York: Van Nostrand Reinhold, 1969). For a more optimistic view, see George Quester, *Deterrence Before Hiroshima* (New York: John Wiley, 1966).

14. See J. Philip Geddes, "Airborne Early Warning for the U.S. Navy," *International Defense Review* No. 5 (1975), pp. 679–82, and Philip J. Klass, "E-2C Radar to Provide New Flexibility," *Aviation Week and Space Technology*, July 12, 1976, pp. 51–53.

15. See David A. Brown, "Nimrod Early Warning Version Pushed," *Aviation Week and Space Technology*, March 14, 1977, pp. 47–50 and "British Order Nimrod AEW Development," *Aviation Week and Space Technology*, April 4, 1977, p. 15.

16. See Nikolai Cherikew, "Moss: AWACS with a Red Star," *International Defense Review*, No. 5, 1975, pp. 677–78.

17. It should be noted that, since OTH-Backscatter is generally reported to be not effective at ranges of *less* than 800 kilometers, it is most applicable to island states widely separated from their national adversaries or to states with territory deep enough to move the emitters a considerable distance inland. For a general description of OTH-B, see Desmond Ball, "Jindalee: Over-the-Horizon Radar in the Defence of Australia," *Pacific Defence Reporter*, February, 1977 and his "Some Further Thoughts on Jindalee" in *Pacific Defence Journal*, May 1977.

18. See Jack N. Merritt and Pierre M. Sprey, "Negative Marginal Returns in Weapons Acquisitions," in Richard G. Head and E. J. Rokke, eds., *American Defense Policy*, 3d ed. (Baltimore: Johns Hopkins University Press, 1973), p. 491.

19. See Philippe Grasset, "Dissimilar Air Combat Training,'" *International Defence Review*, June 1975, pp. 823–27; and Andrew Hamilton, "Topgun: The Navy's 'MiG-Killing' School," *U.S. Naval Institute Proceedings* 102 (1971): 95–97.

20. Edward Luttwak and Dan Horowitz, *The Israeli Army* (London: Allen Lane, 1975), pp. 299, 302, 347.

21. U. S. Congress, Senate, Committee on Foreign Relations, International Security Assistance and Arms Export Control Act (Washington, D.C., U.S. Government Printing Office, 1976), p. 23.

22. U.S. Congress, House, Committee on International Relations, *U.S. Defense Contractors' Training of Foreign Military Forces* (Washington, D.C.: U.S. Government Printing Office, 1975), p. 5.

23. Ibid, pp. 51–53.

24. See James F. Digby, "Precision Guided Munitions: Capabilities and Consequences," Report P-5257, Rand Corporation, Santa Monica, Calif. Ross Babbage developed the implications of the dispersal and concealment of small units in "Technological Trends on the Conventional Battlefield Till the Turn of the Century," Strategic and Defence Studies Centre, Australian National University, 1976.

25. *Aviation Week and Space Technology*, February 16, 1976, p. 38.

8 THE NEW GEOPOLITICS: ARMS TRANSFERS AND THE MAJOR POWERS' COMPETITION FOR OVERSEAS BASES

Robert E. Harkavy

BACKGROUND

Whereas the past few years have witnessed an increasingly intense debate over the rationales for the conventional-arms supply policies of the United States and other countries, curiously short shrift has been given to traditional geopolitical rationales for arms sales, that is, to the use of arms transfers as a major instrument in the global competition for acquiring and maintaining strategic military access and, conversely, for diminishing or denying the access of others. These rationales are often cited almost as an afterthought at the end of long lists of reasons for arms transfers.[1] The omission is particularly surprising because such rationales are being relied upon with increasing frequency, if quietly, within the U.S. government, where there now often exists a stark conflict with competing conventional-arms-control goals.

This conflict has arisen at a time when the postwar basing network of the United States is contracting and in considerable jeopardy. Amid an overall withdrawal of commitments, the United States has been engaged in difficult negotiations over renewal, acquisition, or removal of facilities in a number of dispersed areas: Spain, Greece, Turkey, Thailand, Morocco, and Ethiopia, among others. Previously obscure place-names, like Ramasun, Incirlik, Kagnew, Rota, Sigonella, Souda Bay, and Cockburn Sound have recently become daily fare on the nation's front pages, very often in relation to arms supply or control policies.

The Soviet Union, meanwhile, has accelerated the use of arms transfers for acquiring strategic access, expanding a once limited basing network to near global dimensions during an era which is witnessing the withering of previous ideological bars to many arms-transfer client relationships. Its efforts have been supported by a massive conventional-arms production base, which presently turns out far more tanks, artillery pieces, and aircraft annually than does its U.S. counterpart.

The heightened interest in the linkage between arms transfers and strategic access comes at a time of increasing attention—both in the scholarly literature and the policy-making milieu—to what might be described as "traditional" geopolitical concerns.[2] Resource shortages, both existing and expected—most notably in oil but involving numerous other commodities—have served to focus renewed attention on real or hypothetical requirements for protecting sea lanes and for controlling maritime chokepoints and on the importance of staging areas for military intervention contingencies. The apparently declining salience of cold-war ideological conflict, following upon the final collapse of former colonial empires, has rendered base acquisition and retention a more competitive business. Various forms of strategic access have become important, tangible items of exchange, providing considerable leverage for smaller powers in bargaining over military and economic aid. Meanwhile, the Soviets' development of a blue-water navy and a long-range, air-transport logistics capability has expanded the superpowers' competition to global dimensions, involving all three oceans and their littorals. Finally, there is the greatly increased sensitivity on the part of smaller nations to the symbolic import of compromised sovereignty inherent in granting strategic access to others, which often provides a visible target for internal political opposition groups.

Bases and staging points for extended logistics have entered the news in numerous contexts. These have included the role of the Azores Islands in the U.S. arms resupply of Israel in 1973, the Soviet utilization of lengthy staging networks to supply its clients in Angola and Ethiopia, and the diplomacy and propaganda battles surrounding Somalia (Berbera), Diego Garcia, and the related ongoing U.S.-Soviet negotiations over Indian Ocean demilitarization. Other notable examples are the U.S.-Turkish and U.S.-Greek imbroglios over bases amid the unending Cyprus crisis; Arab attempts at nudging the West out of bases in the Azores, Malta, Bahrain, and Masirah; Soviet basing problems in Egypt, Syria, and Libya; and Israel's use of Kenyan staging facilities on the return from Entebbe.

Meanwhile, ongoing developments in military technology and associated changes in military requirements have created the need for new types of overseas facilities and have changed the importance of traditional ones.

Both superpowers, and some other states as well, continue to maintain "forward" garrisons involving the stationing of army units, aircraft, and naval vessels. Such deployments may be for either offensive or defensive purposes in relation to general war contingencies, and are often used to provide credibility for the deterrence of attacks on weaker client states or alliance partners. There are also the many traditional uses of facilities: training (often where uncongested space or certain kinds of terrain or weather are available); staging of arms, personnel, aircraft, and spare parts; refueling of aircraft; naval repair, replenishment, refueling, and shore leave; forward contingency positioning of war materiel and POL (petrol, oil, and lubricants); antisubmarine (ASW) monitoring and other reconnaissance operations; and port visits, which allow for "showing the flag," maintaining a presence, and demonstrating resolve.[3]

On a less visible and, hence, less sensitive level, there is the matter of aircraft overflight privileges, involving a range of practices and traditions. Some allied or friendly nations allow others more or less full, unhindered, and continuous overflight rights. In other cases, ad hoc formal applications for permission to overfly must be made well ahead of time; approval may or may not be granted depending upon the purpose and situation. Turkey and Yugoslavia, for instance, granted the USSR overflight rights during the 1973 airlift to the Arab states, while some U.S. NATO allies did not grant similar access to the United States on behalf of Israel.[4]

In addition to the traditional uses of basing and staging facilities, a variety of mostly new technical functions have come to require strategic access to the territory of others, varying in their applicability to strictly military purposes. These facilities for the most part can be broken down into functions relating to intelligence, surveillance, and communications. Among the numerous activities included here (utilizing terminology specific to the United States, but duplicated elsewhere) are communications (COMINT), signal (SIGINT), and electronic (ELINT) intelligence; naval and presidential or executive communications networks; LORAN and OMEGA navigational aid systems, satellite tracking networks, deep-space surveillance, oceanographic research, nuclear-test detection (seismographic and air-sample collections), and underwater submarine detection. There are also a variety of esoteric facilities involved in monitoring both strategic and tactical missile tests. Many of these activities, while periodically cited and briefly discussed in the press, are shrouded in considerable secrecy and mystery and are thus technically obscure to the general public.[5] Also, as with many staging bases, the functioning and importance of these facilities can often only be gauged in terms of global or regional networks, involving matters of complementarity and redundancy again usually beyond the view of casual observers.

Some overseas facilities may fall into a gray area between civilian and military use. The Soviet Union, for instance, has developed an extensive network of access for its large fleets of fishing vessels, some of which may have less benign than advertised roles. Stations capable of tracking satellites but with predominantly civilian utility may also involve functions blurring into the military domain.

It is only in recent years that access to all of these types of facilities has been clearly linked to arms supply. Also, it is only recently, with the growing aspiration for controls on conventional-arms transfers (at least in the United States), that an ironic dilemma has been produced with respect to overall arms-control requirements. Arms transfers have often been used to acquire facilities necessary to implement arms-control arrangements in other domains, for example, SALT and test ban verification and the monitoring of suspicious nuclear activities by as yet nonnuclear, as well as nuclear powers.

BASES, ARMS TRANSFERS, AND SYSTEMIC CHANGE: AN HISTORICAL NOTE

From the early nineteenth century until World War II, the strategic access afforded the major powers was primarily a function of their colonial possessions, protectorates, and mandates. During the interwar period, for instance, very few permanent bases were provided to anyone by integrated security alliances. There was nothing equivalent to NATO or the Warsaw Pact or to the kinds of overseas access now routinely provided the United States and the Soviet Union by formal defense-alliance agreements in the developing areas. Since most of these areas were colonial possessions, and since the shifting diplomatic alignments of the major powers in a multipolar, balance-of-power system were less dominated by ideological grounds, there existed a different context for basing diplomacy.[6]

Furthermore, prior to World War II there was hardly any discernible connection between arms supplies and base acquisitions. The arms trade of those days was virtually the private bailiwick of free-wheeling producers and traders, and arms-transfer patterns often appeared divorced from the prevailing and shifting lines of diplomatic alignment. Also, gratis military and economic aid was then very rare, and, hence, it could not be used as a *quid pro quo* for strategic access as is commonplace today. As a result, there was not, prior to 1945, a very close correlation between national power, arms production, and arms-supplier roles, on the one hand, and the extent of the big powers' overseas basing systems on the other.[7]

Great Britain, of course, had the world's most powerful navy, as well as the most elaborate basing network, extending into virtually every corner of the globe. It was intended to protect "lifelines" to its most important possessions—particularly India—and its structure suggested a Mahanesque rimland strategy, with an extensive ring of naval and air facilities around the southern arc of the Eurasian mainland directed against Germany and Russia. None of it, however, depended on arms transfers or military aid as a trade-off, nor upon alliances or leases.[8]

Earlier, France had the second most extensive system of access, even though it did not possess a significant global naval capability. It maintained numerous garrisons and bases throughout its empire, most notably in North and West Africa, and in Indochina; again, access was totally independent of arms supplies.

Late in the race for empire, the United States possessed a rather weakly defended network of overseas bases in Cuba, Puerto Rico, the Canal Zone, Hawaii, Midway and Wake Islands, Guam, Samoa, and the Philippines.[9] Again, arms-supply relationships were not involved in their acquisition, and the same was the case for Japan's far-flung Pacific-island basing network and for Holland's rather extensive air and naval installations in the Dutch East Indies.

During the first few years preceding the outbreak of World War II, there were some changes in the previously casual diplomacy of base acquisitions which—particularly in connection with arms transfers—presaged what was to become the hallmark of postwar diplomacy. It was during this period that most governments began to assume control over arms-transfer policies and to integrate them into the broader lines of strategy.

The late 1930s also saw some adumbrations of the granting of military aid, as well as the onset of government-to-government barter arrangements involving arms and raw materials. There was also some mutual granting of the use of facilities between friends as alliances hardened into wartime coalitions. Germany was granted use of Italian air bases in Tripoli and Rhodes, while Axis arms supplies to Franco's Spain achieved some strategic access, particularly for submarines, in North Africa and in the Canary Islands. Japan's heavy arms supplies to Siam (Thailand) allowed it to acquire naval bases menacing British supply lines in the Andaman Sea. The United States took over British bases in Bermuda, the Bahamas, Jamaica, Trinidad, Antigua, Newfoundland, and Labrador, in exchange for the military assistance provided by the lend-lease agreement. And, on the very eve of its entry into the war, the United States vied with Germany over access throughout Latin America, where many states were demanding arms as a payoff for providing bases or for denying them to others.

After 1945, as the cold war lines hardened, the East-West competition assumed the spatial nature of the heartland-rimland confrontation antici-pated in the geopolitical theories of Halford MacKinder. The West still had extensive bases all around the Eurasian periphery, as long as Great Britain and the other Western colonial powers maintained hold of their colonial possessions. In addition, the United States forged defense alliances with a ring of anticommunist friends in NATO, CENTO, and SEATO. These were underpinned with extensive military and economic aid, and U.S. bases and garrisons were welcomed as a deterrent to Soviet or Chinese aggression or subversion.[10] The Western-led alliances peaked in the 1950s and early 1960s, however, after which the accelerating process of decolonialization, anti-Western ideological shifts, and declining perceived need for American protection all contributed to the withering of the West's available basing assets. Meanwhile, massive arms aid came to an end in the early 1960s and, with it, one very useful lever for maintaining access. After this, basing assets would have to be bargained for with cash-purchase arms supplies, some limited outright aid, leases, and the remains of shared security concerns. For the USSR, however, long without overseas bases and also long without a global navy or long-range air-logistics capability, things began to move in the opposite direction, paced by an aggressive arms-selling effort.[11]

THE DEVELOPMENT OF SOVIET OVERSEAS BASING FACILITIES: ARMS TRANSFERS AND STRATEGIC ACCESS

During the first decade of the cold war, up to the mid-1950s, the USSR was almost totally lacking in overseas facilities (leaving aside the forward deployment of a massive land army in Eastern Europe). The only significant Soviet facilities apart from the Warsaw Pact were the navy bases at Porkalla, Finland and at Port Arthur in Chinese-controlled Manchuria, both of which were returned to indigenous control during the 1950s. Later, during 1958-61, some use was made of submarine bases in Albania, which ended with the Sino-Soviet and Albania-Soviet break around 1961. The Soviet Union was essentially constrained, in terms of strategic access and overall geopolitical strategy, within the interior lines of a heartland empire, although some submarines were early deployed in both major oceans. Also, up to 1955-56, Soviet arms transfers were limited primarily to the Warsaw Pact and China, that is, within the then aptly designated Sino-Soviet bloc. The still relatively weak Soviet arms-production base was almost entirely occupied with equipping Soviet-bloc forces, while the United States and Great Britain controlled most of the arms markets in the developing world.

Beginning in the mid- and late-1950s, however, the Soviet Union became a weightier factor in the arms markets of the developing world. Arms deals with Egypt and Syria in 1955 were followed by the initiation of arms relationships with North Yemen (1957), Indonesia (1958), Guinea (1959), India (1961), and, indirectly, the Algerian rebels in the late 1950s.[12] Soviet arms supplies tended during this period to be large and concentrated in a few key client states which served as initial wedges in cracking the iron ring of alliances set up around the USSR by Secretary of State Dulles; but, still, these initial arms client relationships did not immediately translate into overseas basing facilities for the USSR.

A watershed was reached around 1964 when, in the wake of the Cuban missile crisis, the humiliated Soviet military leadership attempted to both rectify its exposed naval shortcomings and close the overall strategic-nuclear gap.[13] The Soviet Union began its naval expansion in a modest way, with a limited deployment of submarines and surface ships to the Mediterranean, at a time when it had only limited access to port facilities. For the most part, its small Mediterranean fleet cruised for limited periods from the Black Sea, making use of auxiliary ships for fuel, water, and other stores and routine maintenance.

After the 1967 Middle East war, during which the United States held clear naval superiority in the Mediterranean, the USSR expanded its Mediterranean deployments and began to make greater use of foreign ports and offshore anchorages.[14] The ports were primarily in Egypt, but also in Syria, Yugoslavia, Algeria, and Morocco, all of which were then heavily reliant on Soviet arms supplies. In 1968, in a further step, there was a formal agreement with Egypt providing access for Soviet naval forces in Alexandria, Port Said, and Mersa Matruh, as well as the use of Egyptian airfields by Soviet reconnaissance aircraft monitoring the eastern Mediterranean. The agreement corresponded with the massive Soviet arms shipments to Egypt between 1967 and 1972.[15]

In 1972, however, President Sadat expelled most Soviet personnel and curtailed access to the facilities, in part because of disappointment over denials of requests for more and better arms and over Soviet demands for payments for previous shipments. Soviet access was completely terminated, and its arms supplies to Egypt dropped off sharply, leaving the Egyptians to scrounge about for spare parts through third-party transfers from Yugoslavia, India, North Korea, and some Eastern European countries. In early 1976, Egypt apparently closed all Soviet access rights to Alexandria.

As their access to Egyptian facilities was curtailed after 1972, the Soviets attempted to compensate with expanded access to Syrian facilities, involving regular use of the ports at Tartus and Latakia after the 1973 conflict. Ships used as floating repair and maintenance bases were transferred from Egypt to Syria. Between the 1973 war and the Lebanese crisis in 1976, the USSR poured massive quantities of weapons into Syria (including MiG-23 Flogger and SU-20 fighters, Scud surface-to-surface missiles, SAM-3, 6, and 7, T-62 tanks, modern artillery, and armored personnel carriers—APCs). Among its motives was to demonstrate to clients the benefits derived from providing them with desired strategic access.

Then during the Lebanese crisis in 1976, Soviet arms shipments to Syria were temporarily curtailed, as was Soviet naval access to Syrian ports.[16] The USSR then began to concentrate its Middle Eastern arms supplies in Iraq. In addition to all of the usually supplied modern systems, including Scud missiles, they provided TU-22B Blinder bombers—otherwise sold only to Libya in the Middle East— and MiG-25 Foxbats. They also concluded an agreement which apparently allowed full Soviet access to Iraqi air and naval bases.[17] Simultaneously, greatly increased Soviet arms shipments to Libya (and also the sale of some nuclear technology) well beyond that country's absorption capacity (supplemented by considerable French, Italian, and British arms) seemed aimed at achieving naval and/or air facilities further west in the Mediterranean. By early 1978, however, full access to Tobruk and Benghazi had not yet been granted.[18]

Still farther west in the Mediterranean, Soviet arms supplies to Algeria and Morocco had also achieved some strategic access. Algeria had long been primarily reliant on Soviet arms and received increased imports in 1976-77 as tensions with Morocco over the Spanish Sahara mounted. Some Soviet access to Algerian ports has been granted (though not full use of the large ex-French base at Mers El Kebir). The Soviet Union has also apparently used Algerian, as well as Libyan, airfields for staging military supplies to Angola and Mozambique. Morocco, an important Soviet arms client in the early 1960s which, until recently, still received some Soviet arms, now relies primarily on the United States and France, but it has allowed Soviet port visits. Meanwhile, the Soviets have made extensive use of offshore anchorages throughout the Mediterranean, near both its own arms clients and NATO countries, such as Greece.[19]

All around the vast Indian Ocean littoral, the USSR has also judiciously utilized arms transfers as an opening wedge leading to the granting of strategic access. As a result, the Soviet naval presence in the Indian Ocean, negligible up to 1968, has grown steadily in the interim.[20] For the most part, arms-client relationships have preceded the granting of strategic access; India, Indonesia, Pakistan, Iraq, both Yemens, Sudan, and Tanzania were significant recipients of Soviet arms during the early and mid-1960s, before the deployment of a Soviet Indian Ocean naval force. Arms-transfer relationships can thus, in some cases, be perceived as chips which were later, gradually, cashed in for strategic access.

The Soviet Union has availed itself of some degree of strategic access in a number of Indian Ocean locales; major naval base facilities are now in South Yemen and Iraq. Somalia, of course, long provided the USSR with its major air and naval facilities in the region, after having received massive (for the region) Soviet arms shipments. These began with transfers of MiGs in 1963 and tanks and APCs in 1965, and then extended to a wide range of weaponry which menaced more lightly armed regional rivals in Kenya and Ethiopia. Port facilities at Berbera and Chisimaio, and an airfield at Hargeisa, provided the USSR with POL, maintenance, shore leave, a floating drydock, landing fields for TU-95 Bear D reconnaissance aircraft, communications facilities, and a facility for handling ship-to-ship missiles.[21] The facilities and the preceding arms-client relationship have now been terminated, but it is assumed that massive, current Soviet arms aid to Ethiopia, believed to be in excess of $800 million, is intended to achieve naval and air bases there to replace those lost in Somalia astride the strategic Bab el Mandeb straits.

South Yemen has received Soviet arms since 1967, acquiring its first tanks in that year and then MiGs in 1969. It began to allow the Soviet navy use of strategically located Aden in 1968. Later, refueling facilities for Soviet naval aircraft as well as some use of the island of Socotra were provided.[22]

Iraq has been an important Soviet arms client since 1958. It has recently escalated its purchases but has also utilized its oil wealth to diversify suppliers, making considerable purchases of French arms. The new agreement with the Soviet Union apparently allows use of naval facilities on the Persian Gulf at Umm Quasr and Basra, as well as several inland air bases.[23] Iraqi air staging bases were reported crucial to the recent Soviet arms airlift to Vietnam during the latter's border conflict with China.

The USSR has used its arms largesse to acquire lesser degrees of strategic access at a number of other points around the Indian Ocean. Massive arms shipments and also licensing of MiG-21 technology to India has resulted in some use of the major Indian naval base at Vishakhapatnam, which the Soviets apparently helped to build. Limited use has also been made of facilities in Sri Lanka—site of the former major British naval base at Trincomalee—which receives arms both from the Soviet Union and Great Britain. Mauritius has allowed Soviet ship visits at a key location in the Indian Ocean, which as yet are not apparently tied to arms shipments. Large deliveries of Soviet arms to Mozambique, however, some for transshipment to Zimbabwean guerrillas, have now resulted in an initial Soviet naval visit to Maputo and the threat of subsequently expanded access in close proximity to South Africa.

Until very recently, the Soviet Union was virtually bereft of foreign strategic facilities in the West and South Pacific. Nuclear submarines have long been deployed in Pacific waters, however, and some offshore anchorages have been used for surface craft. More recently, however, there have been auguries of Soviet use of Vietnamese facilities—among other things, of considerable worry to the People's Republic of China (PRC)—particularly Cam Ranh Bay, in consonance with the Soviets' continuing role of primary arms supplier to Vietnam. That role was underscored during the recent China-Vietnam conflict. Further, there have been some hints of aspirations of achieving access in the South Pacific; the Soviet Union has reportedly been angling for fishing-boat facilities in Tonga and Western Samoa, with either arms or economic aid to serve as a *quid pro quo*.[24]

On the eastern side of the Pacific, the Soviet Union has now made the first steps toward strategic access in Peru, after being frustrated by Allende's overthrow in Chile, which might otherwise have provided naval port facilities. Some reports indicate impending Soviet use of Peruvian ports in the wake of massive arms deals involving modern SU-22 fighter bombers, SAMs, tanks, and artillery.[25]

Soviet arms supplies have judiciously been used to construct what is now a significant network of strategic facilities around the Atlantic Ocean, particularly along the West African coast. The USSR has, of course, long been installed in Cuba and Guinea, both major arms recipients. More recently, Soviet development of numerous arms-client relationships in West Africa, both with coastal and inland states, has resulted in a significant expansion of strategic access. This was well demonstrated by the routes of supply used to provision Cuban and MPLA forces in Angola.

The Cuban connection dates from the immediate aftermath of Castro's revolution, with initial Soviet arms shipments having arrived in 1960, and the USSR began deploying both surface ships and submarines there during the 1960s. They made particular use of the naval base at Cienfuegos, of communications and intelligence facilities, and also of Havana airfield facilities for Bear D reconnaissance aircraft which conduct surveillance over the Atlantic Ocean.

Along with Ghana, Guinea was the first really significant Soviet-bloc arms client in sub-Saharan Africa, receiving Czech tanks as early as 1959 and Soviet aircraft a year later. Ever since, it has been provisioned with modern arms (now including modern armor and MiG-21 aircraft) at a higher level than any of the other smaller West African states. In return, Soviet naval patrols have operated off the coast of Guinea and Bear Ds out of its airfields; in addition, Guinea was a major staging point for Soviet supplies to Angola.

During and since the peak of the Angolan war, Soviet transport aircraft have also apparently made use of facilities in Benin, Guinea-Bissau, Equatorial Guinea, the Republic of the Congo, Mali, and perhaps Nigeria, as well as Algeria further north. Each is primarily a Soviet arms client, and each is now far more heavily armed than any of its surrounding "moderate" neighbors which still lie within the Western arms orbit. The facilities now available to the Soviets are probably somewhat redundant, providing "fallbacks" if some traditionally volatile African states should undergo changes of regime or shifts in ideological orientation. Meanwhile, the USSR is thought to be pressuring Angola for still newer facilities, in return for shipments of arms measured in hundreds of millions of dollars. These facilities, if they eventuate, would provide an additional threat to the white regimes in southern Africa.

Thus, by 1979 it was clear that, mainly through the organized use of arms-transfer diplomacy, the Soviet Union had achieved a vast expansion of its global basing network since 1955, if only slowly and almost imperceptibly. It is clear that its vast expansion of basing assets has been achieved at a relatively low cost, for, although data on the mix of Soviet arms trade and aid in various places is not easy to come by, many bases certainly have been acquired merely by allowing extensive cash arms sales. At the same time, it is often the case that the USSR has provided clients access to weapons that are sufficiently sophisticated in the regional context so as to achieve qualitative advantages over rivals. This has been most evident throughout Africa, where in the face of some Western efforts to control qualitative levels of arming, the Soviet Union has provided significant numbers of supersonic jets and tanks to its clients first, for example, in Somalia, Uganda, Guinea, Angola, Mali, and Nigeria.

Of course, the strategic value of a given nation to a major power may not—and normally will not—bear any relationship to the size of its arms markets. That is determined by location (access to the sea, control over key chokepoints, etc.) and land area. The Soviet Union has thus been able to acquire some major strategic assets—for instance, in Somalia, South Yemen, and Mali—in exchange for arms sales at a very modest level relative to those in some of the world's more heavily armed hot spots, that is, in the Middle East and South Asia. Soviet arms sales to some key major basing hosts in the decade 1965-74 were as follows: South Yemen ($114 million), Guinea ($42 million), Mali ($12 million), Somalia ($134 million), and Cuba ($310 million). Egypt—where Soviet access has now been curtailed—and Syria accounted for $2.5 billion and $1.8 billion, respectively, during the same period. Again, these were *mostly arms sales*, not aid.[26]

In pursuing a purposive strategy of utilizing arms supplies to achieve strategic access, the Soviet Union has, of course, encountered some tricky dilemmas and has been ensnared in complex subregional conflicts and rivalries. For instance, after having established major bases in Somalia (acquired by arming the Somalis against rival Ethiopia), the Soviet Union became a major arms supplier to now radically oriented Ethiopia, resulting in the alienation of Somalia and the loss of its bases. A somewhat analogous situation almost arose with respect to Ecuadorian requests for Soviet arms; if granted, these might have soured Soviet-Peruvian relations at a time when the USSR seemed to have been anticipating the use of Peruvian facilities. Soviet dilemmas regarding arms supplies and alternative basing facilities in Egypt and Libya, and in Syria and Iraq, have already been noted.

U.S. ARMS TRANSFERS AND STRATEGIC ACCESS

The previous postwar and current development of the relationship between U.S. basing facilities and arms transfers has, of course, been very distinct from the Soviet experience. As noted, in the immediate wake of

World War II and at the onset of the cold war, the United States and its allies were provided an extensive global basing system by colonial remnants, through alliances and economic and military aid relationships, and generally, as a consequence of the force deployments emerging from World War II. While the Soviet Union has gradually—accelerating after 1960—built a global basing system mostly through new arms client relationships, the West has experienced a gradual degradation of its strategic assets. It has also been forced to assume considerable and increasing economic and political costs in order to cling to its still very extensive and dispersed positions.[27] Unlike the Soviet Union the West, including the United States, has had to bear the onus of its colonial-imperial past. Its infringements on national sovereignty have encountered great sensitivity and resistance even where arms-sales relationships have constituted the primary objective remnant of dependency.

The United States is, of course, availed of numerous facilities in Western Europe through its NATO alliance. Some of these, however, as indicated during the 1973 war, may not be available for purposes not directly connected with NATO, that is, anti-Soviet defense. The Turkish-Greek imbroglio over Cyprus has also indicated the precariousness of some U.S. base facilities, certainly to the extent that their continued use depends heavily on a continuing flow of arms supplies to the host countries. Bases in Iceland, which are critical for, among other things, antisubmarine activities, have also been under considerable pressure, although the arms-supply relationship is not terribly important. By and large, however, the continuing U.S. security relationship with Western Europe (of which arms transfers is one aspect) does assure some solid strategic assets which are usable for a wide range of purposes and contingencies.

The United States is also still able to make use of some facilities in areas outside Europe controlled by its closest NATO allies, hence routinely available for most purposes. Most notable here are Greenland (owned by Denmark), the Netherland Antilles, and British possessions including Ascension Island, the Phoenix Islands, and the islands of Turks, Caicos, and St. Lucia in the Caribbean. Ascension is potentially valuable as a staging point and as a base for surveillance activities with respect to contingencies in southern Africa or in the South Atlantic.

The United States still retains considerable strategic access within and around the North Atlantic, in places where arms supplies are not relevant, or at least not yet, and where, in several cases, leasing arrangements are now being negotiated. The newly independent Bahamas, as well as Bermuda, Antigua, Barbados, and Trinidad and Tobago—all former or remaining British possessions—have a variety of U.S. facilities involving tracking, surveillance, radar, missile-testing, ASW, and other functions, and the Lajes base in the Azores is also still used by the United States. It is not clear, however, whether it could be used for staging another resupply operation to Israel, even despite the resumption of heavy military aid from the United States and other NATO nations to now quiescent, but still shaky Portugal.[28]

Around the Mediterranean, U.S. strategic access has been dwindling as Soviet assets have been enhanced. For example, many of the bases used by U.S. forces now would not be available for Middle Eastern operations on behalf of Israel, and it is not clear whether they might be available for a post-Tito crisis in Yugoslavia. Still, important bases are maintained in Spain (strategic and tactical air bases, aerial refueling, submarine maintenance), and in Italy (the U.S. Sixth Fleet homeport plus numerous other facilities on the mainland and on Sicily and Sardinia). Greece provides airfields and communications and intelligence facilities, both on the mainland and on Crete, while Turkey tentatively provides similar facilities. The connection between access and arms transfers is most obvious in the latter two cases, where maintained or increased arms supplies—for forces now partially deployed against each other—have become a regional price for continued access to vital facilities.[29]

The U.S. navy also visits Moroccan and Tunisian ports and maintains a naval communications facility in Morocco. Both moderate North African states now rely primarily on U.S. arms to balance massive Soviet shipments to rivals in Libya and Algeria. (Morocco also receives weapons from France and the Soviet Union; Tunisia, from France and Italy.) Here, continued access is a primary U.S. rationale for continued supply. Both nations have been requesting more sophisticated weaponry (modern aircraft, missiles, helicopters, air-defense systems) to match those possessed by their rivals. North Africa is a good example of an area where U.S. interest in impeding escalated arms races conflict with that of continued strategic access.

Around the Indian Ocean, U.S. arms transfers have been used to maintain scattered enclaves of strategic access to match the expanding Soviet basing network, most notably in Oman, Kenya, and Singapore (and earlier in Iran and Ethiopia). Iran, in conjunction with massive U.S. arms shipments including an impressive array of modern, sophisticated systems such as the F-14 fighter, Spruance-class warships, TOW antitank missiles, and so forth, earlier had allowed the United States access to crucial communications and intelligence facilities, now apparently irrevocably lost. That loss has made the now recovered Turkish facilities all the more crucial, though apparently they are only partly redundant to those in Iran.

The long-term U.S. arms-supply relationship with Ethiopia previously assured the use of the Kagnew communications complex which is now considered virtually superfluous in the light of new, surrogate satellite technology. The growing U.S. supply relationship with Kenya, including the transfers of F-5E fighter aircraft, has allowed for continued U.S. naval visits to Mombasa and for possible use of Kenyan airfields for staging P-3 Orion surveillance flights over the Indian Ocean.[30] Oman, now a significant recipient of U.S. arms, may also allow continued P-3 staging out of Masirah Island after the British departure from a long-held base.[31]

In Southeast Asia and in the Pacific, the United States maintains a ring of bases around the Asian mainland, and most are backed up by continuing arms-supply relationships. The recipients include Singapore, Thailand, the Philippines, Australia, Taiwan, Japan, and South Korea. Singapore does not provide major facilities but allows regular transit of military air transport and P-3 flights, as well as naval maintenance facilities. Most U.S. bases in Taiwan, meanwhile, have been deactivated in line with the now lower profile required by the abrogation of the formal defense treaty, though some technical facilities will perhaps remain. The major bases are at Clark Air Base and Subic Bay in the Philippines, Okinawa, various air bases in Korea and Japan, and now in Western Australia, all supported by broader military relationships (including arms sales), as well as essential ideological affinity. To the extent that some of these facilities may be under increasing political pressure, fall-back positions are provided by the island network in the U.S. Trust Territories in the Marshall, Caroline, and Marianas Islands; these, however, may themselves later come under pressure if Micronesian independence drives should escalate, but are not now subject to arms-sales policies.[32]

There is not, of course, always a one-to-one correspondence between arms supply and strategic access. Both the United States and Soviet Union have numerous arms clients where weapons have not been translated into access. This is because of a sensitivity to sovereignty, low supplier leverage, resentment of supplier support of rivals (the Arab states and Israel), or even lack of a supplier's need for the bases. U.S. arms supply has not resulted in significant basing rights in Jordan, Israel, Kuwait, Indonesia, Saudi Arabia, Pakistan (after 1965), Zaire, and in a number of Latin American nations. Likewise, Soviet arms have not produced such trade-offs in, for instance, Finland, North Korea, China (prior to 1961), Algeria, Pakistan, Nigeria, the Sudan, and Uganda. In some of these cases, however, arms supply may have been useful in assuring overflight privileges, port-visiting rights, and minor technical facilities, but not in major staging bases, permanent facilities, or garrisons.

The most significant aspect of current U.S. basing problems involves the vastly increasing economic and political costs being demanded by formerly willing hosts, some of whom no longer perceive their security problems as altogether congruent with U.S. interests and who may also be under considerable domestic political pressure to reduce the visible U.S. profile. Needless to say, the U.S. defeat in Vietnam has contributed to this process by reducing its prestige and credibility and by emboldening indigenous, radical political forces to push for U.S. withdrawal.

During the recent past, the United States has been involved in strenuous negotiations and political struggles over key basing facilities, particularly in Spain, Greece, Turkey, and the Philippines. A Treaty of Friendship and Cooperation was signed in 1976 with Spain which extended the use of most critical U.S. facilities, with the exception of the Rota submarine base, which will be phased out in 1979. The price for the United States was something over $1 billion in military and economic aid over five years (plus additional Export-Import Bank loan guarantees), as well as commitments for modernizing Spanish forces with advanced weapons systems such as the F-16 fighter.[33]

Similar negotiations were in progress with Greece, enmeshed in some serious status-of-forces issues. Here, the United States seemed willing to provide a military aid package in the neighborhood of $700 million to extend the use of its numerous facilities.[34] A Defense Cooperation Agreement has also been consummated with Turkey, despite the impasse created by the ongoing Cyprus crisis. The restoration of access to Turkish bases is expected to cost the United States on the order of $1 billion in military and economic aid over a four-year period. Similar arrangements with the Philippines, which hosts important U.S. facilities at Subic Bay and Clark Field, also will involve a "rental" cost of something in the neighborhood of $1 billion over a period of years.

The leverage possessed by host governments over an increasingly embattled United States has also resulted, in some cases, in increased demands for qualitatively more sophisticated arms, parallel to the Soviet experience in Iraq, Libya, and elsewhere. Greece and Turkey have bargained for more modern fighter aircraft, armor, missiles, and other items; these are ostensibly for use within the NATO defense structure, but it is also inevitable that they are to be deployed against one another. The Philippines, meanwhile, has used the base negotiations to press for deliveries of, among other things, more effective attack aircraft.

The several nations now negotiating new basing agreements with the United States are not the only places where U.S. bases are under pressure. Internal political factors have also placed increased pressures on U.S. facilities in many other countries. These include, among others, Japan, Australia, Thailand (where U.S. facilities were withdrawn, then partly reinstated after a rightist coup), Oman, Bahrain, Iceland, Italy, Panama, and in Portugal, where U.S. facilities in the Azores were in jeopardy during Portugal's radical interregnum. With the leverage exhibited by Turkey, Greece, the Philippines, and Spain in prying massive aid packages (existing or in negotiation) out of the United States in return for the extension of basing privileges, others were expected to follow suit. This could perhaps bring the overall costs for the U.S. global basing system close to prohibitive.

In some areas where restraints on U.S. arms sales have jeopardized existing access, one result may have been to increase pressures for sales elsewhere to acquire substitute facilities. The earlier temporary loss of Turkish bases increased reliance on those in Iran; the subsequent loss of the latter has clearly increased Turkish leverage in bargaining with the United States over arms supplies. Loss of access in Ethiopia may produce a military requirement for substitutes in Sudan, which is now pressing for an enhanced U.S. arms-client relationship. There is a parallel here with the progression of the Soviet quest for bases in Egypt, Syria, Libya, and Iraq.

The global competition for basing rights, largely acquired as a *quid pro quo* for arms-transfer relationships, has pretty much been a two-nation game. This reflects the fact that only the United States and the Soviet Union now have global security interests and responsibilities and a global military reach. For the other major powers, the arms trade has primarily been an economic matter.

France, as the world's third largest arms supplier, but without a really global navy or long-range intervention capability, has not often, if at all, used its arms supplies as a wedge for gaining strategic access. Many or all of its major arms clients—Saudi Arabia, South Africa, Iraq, Libya, Brazil, Pakistan—provide it no bases at all, although very recently it has acquired bases for its Jaguar aircraft in Senegal, Chad, and the Ivory Coast in connection with military assistance.[35]

Britain too no longer sells or gives away arms to maintain strategic access; like France, its sales rationales are primarily economic. Its now constricted basing system (with Malta, Mauritius, and Masirah being phased out and Cyprus precarious) is essentially divorced from arms-transfer policy.

SOME GENERALIZATIONS ON BASES AND ARMS TRANSFERS

Amid the welter of detail describing the connection between big-power strategic access and arms transfers, a number of broad generalizations are suggested, all requiring much more extensive investigation. Among them are the following:

- the correlation between various types of arms-transfer acquisition patterns and degrees of access provided the major powers;
- big-power spatial strategies and related cognitive maps, connected to the gradual ongoing shift from a mutual heartland-rimland configuration to much more diffuse and less ideological competition; and
- the conflict, for the United States at least, between geopolitical strategies and conventional arms control goals.

The preceding analysis has demonstrated the obvious truism that there is a significant correlation between arms-transfer acquisition patterns and the granting of strategic access. Of course, given the current importance of arms transfers as an instrument of diplomacy, they may be described as an intervening variable measuring overall association, which is supported by ideological affinity and the facts of alliances and other kinds of security arrangements. The precise nature of the correlation involved does require further investigation.[36]

Most basing arrangements appear to co-exist with sole- or pre-dominant-supplier acquisition styles, that is, where a recipient acquires all or most of its arms from one supplier.[37] Conversely, the multiple-source acquisition of arms, particularly if across the major power blocs (i.e., the recipient receives both Western and Soviet-bloc arms simultaneously; see Chapter 4, this volume), more often than not occurs where no major power has significant strategic access, indicating a degree of neutrality or ideological "even-handedness."

Virtually all of the dependent nations which have granted the Soviet Union major basing facilities have received most of their arms from them: Syria, South Yemen, Somalia (earlier), Angola, Cuba, and Iraq. Iraq, however, has now begun to acquire some French materiel (including Mirage F-1 fighters) while vastly increasing its acquisitions from the Soviet Union. It is also noteworthy that those major Soviet clients which have maintained diversified arms sources across the blocs—Libya, Nigeria, India, Sri Lanka, and Algeria to a lesser extent—have demonstrated some reluctance to grant the USSR major facilities. This may in some cases have less to do with ideological affinity than with the availability of alternative sources of arms; size, wealth, or both may be other factors. The contrast between Libya and India, on the one hand, and Somalia and Angola, on the other, may be instructive, although the impact of a Soviet presence in deterring external threats may also have played a role in the latter cases; but in no case does the Soviet Union have major basing facilities where U.S. or other Western arms predominate.

The same generalizations hold for the hosts to major United States bases; Greece, Turkey, Spain, Portugal, the Philippines, Japan, and so on, have all relied primarily on U.S. arms. Many U.S. bases, however, are located in nations which are tied in one way or another to the U.S. security orbit, but where arms-market leverage is not critical. This is true of Australia and Iceland, for instance, and also for numerous facilities located in British possessions or lingering spheres of influence: the Caribbean, the Bahamas, Bermuda, Ascension, and Diego Garcia. There have been only a few cases where U.S. and other Western basing rights have co-existed with some Soviet arms supplies to the host, most notably Iran, Cyprus, and Morocco.

What could earlier have been described as a competition for strategic access fitting the heartland-rimland model has now become a much more complex and less definable game, with both sides seeking crucial, dispersed points of access all around the globe. Both superpowers, as indicated, now have at least some naval and air points of access in virtually every area of the world. The vast and dispersed proliferation of Marxist regimes, most of which are Soviet arms clients, has long since shattered the old U.S. policy of containment.

In conclusion, it is clear that the combined effects of decolonialization and the weakening of the alliances of the period of tight bipolarity have produced a closer relationship between arms-supply policies and strategic access, one perhaps characterized by more symmetrical bargaining positions between suppliers and recipients than had existed earlier. The expansion of the Soviet basing system and the contraction of its Western counterpart has produced still another dilemma for those searching for conventional-arms controls, one which might sharpen the contradictions between arms control and overall national-security policies.

NOTES

1. See, for instance, Leslie Gelb, "Arms Sales," *Foreign Policy*, no. 25 (1976–77). In placing this factor eighth in a list of nine general factors said to propel arms sales, Gelb states that "obtaining these rights used to be a major rationale for past grant military aid; but it may no longer be a compelling reason for special sales arrangements. The principal base-rights countries now place so many restrictions on American use that the whole policy of bases for aid requires review" (p. 8).

2. A good analysis of the postwar lack of attention to traditional geopolitical modes of analysis is in Geoffrey Kemp, "The New Strategic Map: Geography, Arms Diffusion, and the Southern Seas," paper delivered at the Fletcher School's conference on the Implications of the Military Build-up in Non-Industrial States, 1976. See also Robert E. Walters, *The Nuclear Trap* (Baltimore: Penguin, 1974), and Colin Gray, *The Geopolitics of the Nuclear Era* (New York: Crane, Russak, 1977), for lengthier expositions of some of the same themes.

3. For general material on the breakdown of various types of facilities and associated definitions, see Herbert G. Hagerty, "Forward Deployment in the 1970s and 1980s," National Security Affairs Monograph 77-2, National Defense University, Washington, D.C.: 1977; Richard B. Foster, "Implications of the Nixon Doctrine for the Defense Planning Process," Stanford Research Institute, Menlo Park, Calif., 1972; and B. M. Blechman and R. G. Weinland, "Why Coaling Stations are Necessary in the Nuclear Age," *International Security* 2 (1977): 88–99.

4. For analyses of the overflight access problem, see P. M. Dadant, "Shrinking International Airspace as a Problem for Future Air Movements–A Briefing," Report R-2178-AF, Rand Corp., Santa Monica, Calif., 1978; and Richard G. Toye, "The Projection of U.S. Power by the Air Force in the Western Pacific and Indian Ocean," paper delivered at the Fletcher School's conference on "Security and Development in the Indo-Pacific Arena," 1978.

5. A glimpse of what is involved here is given in Frank Barnaby, "On Target with an Omega Station," *New Scientist*, March 25, 1976. See also Albert Langer, Owen Wilkes, and N. P. Gleditsch, *The Military Functions of Omega and Loran-C* (Oslo: Peace Research Institute, 1976).

6. For data and general analyses of interwar basing systems, see George Weller, *Bases Overseas* (New York: Harcourt, Brace, 1944); and R. Ernest Dupuy, *World in Arms* (Harrisburg, Pa.: Military Service Publishing Co., 1939).

7. See Robert E. Harkavy, *The Arms Trade and International Systems* (Cambridge, Mass.: Ballinger, 1975), esp. Ch. 2.

8. See Brig. D. H. Cole, *Imperial Military Geography* (London: Sifton Praed and Co., 1950); Paul M. Kennedy, *The Rise and Fall of British Naval Mastery* (London: Allen Lane, 1976); and Gerald S. Graham, *The Politics of Naval Supremacy* (London: Cambridge University Press, 1965).

9. On U.S. bases prior to World War II, see Weller, *Bases Overseas*; and Buel W. Patch, "American Naval and Air Bases," *Editorial Research Report*, Washington, vol. I, No. 7, February 1939.

10. See Roland Paul, *American Military Commitments Abroad* (New Brunswick, N.J.: Rutgers University Press, 1973).

11. This trend is best depicted in Avigdor Haselkorn, "The Soviet Collective Security System," *Orbis* 17 (1975).

12. The dates of initiation of Soviet arms client relationships can be pinpointed in the Stockholm International Peace Research Institute (SIPRI), *Arms Trade Registers* (Cambridge, Mass.: MIT Press, 1974), broken down by recipients and by armed services (army, navy, and air equipment).

13. On Soviet naval expansion aims, see Sergei G. Gorshkov, *Red Star Rising at Sea* (U.S. Naval Institute, Annapolis, 1974), translated by T. A. Nelly, Jr., particularly the final chapter entitled "Some Problems in Mastering the World Ocean."

14. See C. Joynt and O. M. Smolansky, "Soviet Naval Policy in the Mediterranean," Research Monograph no. 3, Department of International Relations, Lehigh University, Bethlehem, Pa., 1972; and the chapters by A. Z. Rubinstein, U. Ra'anan, R. O. Freedman, and G. S. Dragnich in M. MccGwire, K. Booth, and J. McDonnell, eds., *Soviet Naval Policy* (New York: Praeger, 1975).

15. See Robert O. Freedman, "The Soviet Union and Sadat's Egypt," pp. 211–31, in MccGwire, et al, op. cit.; and R. G. Weinland, "Land Support for Naval Forces: Egypt and the Soviet Escadra 1962–1976," *Survival* 20 (1978).

16. See "Syria-U.S.S.R.: Soviets Asked to Leave Syrian Naval Port," *Defense and Foreign Affairs Daily*, January 14, 1977.

17. See "Iraq: Defense Protocol with U.S.S.R.," *Defense and Foreign Affairs Daily*, October 13, 1976.

18. See "Libya: Soviets Building up Tobruk," *Defense and Foreign Affairs Daily*, August 25, 1976.

19. For information on Soviet offshore anchorages in the Mediterranean, see "Instability in NATO Examined," *Washington Post*, April 18, 1976, pp. A-17, 18.

20. See, among others, M. MccGwire, Ken Booth, and John McDonnell, eds., *Soviet Naval Policy* (New York: Praeger, 1975); Geoffrey Jukes, *The Indian Ocean in Soviet Naval Policy*, Adelphi Paper no. 57 (London: IISS, 1969), W. Adie, *Oil, Politics and Seapower: The Indian Ocean Vortex* (New York: Crane, Russak, 1975); and George E. Hudson, "Soviet Naval Doctrine and Soviet Politics, 1953–1975," *World Politics* 29:1 (1976).

21. Among numerous articles on Soviet facilities in Somalia, see "Somalia-U.S.S.R.: Major Naval Complex Nearly Ready," *Defense and Foreign Affairs Daily*, January 7, 1977; and J. Bowyer Bell, "Strategic Implications of the Soviet Presence in Somalia," *Orbis* 19:2 (1975): 402–14.

22. Note of Soviet use of an intelligence facility on Socotra is made in "U.S.S.R.: Intelligence Ship Deployment: Naval Deployment in Mozambique," *Defense and Foreign Affairs Daily*, August 3, 1976.

23. See "Iraq: Defense Protocol with U.S.S.R."

24. See Stephen Ritterbush, "Resources and Changing Perceptions of National Security in

the Central and Western Pacific," paper delivered at the Fletcher School's conference on "Security and Development in the Indo-Pacific Arena," 1978.

25. See, *inter alia*, "Peru: More Reports of Soviet Deal," *Defense and Foreign Affairs Daily*, January 26, 1977, wherein it is claimed that Peru's naval and air bases are already under "effective" Soviet command.

26. These data are drawn from the U.S. Arms Control and Disarmament Agency's *World Military Expenditures and Arms Transfers* (Washington, D.C.: U.S. Government Printing Office, 1976), an annual publication. It should be noted, however, that Soviet transfers to some of these African countries have accelerated since 1974.

27. For a somewhat pessimistic analysis of the decline of U.S. basing assets, see Alvin J. Cottrell and Thomas H. Moorer, "U.S. Overseas Bases: Problems of Projecting American Military Power Abroad," Washington Paper no. 47, Georgetown Center for Strategic and International Studies, Washington, D.C., 1977.

28. See "High Stakes in the Azores," *The Nation*, November 8, 1975; and "In-Flight Refueling to Aid C-5 Wing Life," *Aviation Week and Space Technology*, July 12, 1976, pp. 32–34.

29. On U.S. Spanish bases see, *inter alia*, Stephen S. Kaplan, "The Utility of U.S. Military Bases in Spain and Portugal" (unpublished paper, Brookings); "Spain Pact Has Plusses for Both Sides," *Washington Star*, March 4, 1976, p. A4; "Secret U.S.-Spain Airlift Accord Told," *Washington Post*, October 11, 1976, p. A24; and "No Secret Pact on Bases, Spain Says," *Washington Post*, October 14, 1976, p. A25. On U.S. bases in Greece, see "Rising Hatred of U.S. in Greece is Imperiling a Vital Defense Flank," *Wall Street Journal*, January 6, 1976; and "U.S., Greece Initial Pact on Military Bases and Aid," *New York Times*, April 16, 1976, p. 3. On U.S. bases in Turkey, see "The Turkish Bases: A Turning Point in Ties with U.S.," *New York Times*, July 31, 1976, p. 9; "Turks Expect to Close U.S. Bases if Congress Rejects Military Aid," *New York Times*, September 28, 1976, p. 12; and "U.S., Turkey, Renew Talks on Bases," *Washington Post*, March 25, 1976, p. A14. See also Library of Congress, Congressional Research Division, Foreign Affairs and National Defense Division, "United States Military Installations and Objectives in the Mediterranean," report prepared for the Subcommittee on Europe and the Middle East of the Committee on International Relations, Washington, D.C., 1977.

30. "Kenya Offers New Flexibility to U.S. Indian Ocean P-3 Patrols," *Baltimore Sun*, July 30, 1976, reprinted in *U.S. Naval Institute Proceedings* 102 (1976).

31. On U.S. base activities on Masirah, see "Oman: U.K. to leave Masirah by March 1977," *Defense and Foreign Affairs Daily*, July 21, 1976; and "Masirah: Oman Denies Possibility of U.S. Presence." In the same issue, see also "Bahrain: NATO Warships Welcome in the Gulf." See also "U.K. Keeps Persian Gulf Fleet Small as Nations in Region Build Strength," *New York Times*, July 17, 1976.

32. See Ritterbush, "Resources and Changing Perceptions," for an analysis of this possibility.

33. See "U.S., Spain Agree to Sign Full Treaty," *Washington Post*, January 23, 1976, p. A18; "Spanish Treaty Contains Terms for F-16 Sales," *Aviation Week and Space Technology*,105 (1976): 69–70; and "The Spanish Connection: A Wider Commitment in the Making," *The Defense Monitor* 5 (1976).

34. See "U.S., Greece Initial Pact on Military Bases and Aid," *New York Times*, April 16, 1976, p. 3.

35. For an analysis of French aims at finding a new home for its Indian Ocean fleet to replace Djibouti, see "France: Moves Into Indian Ocean to be Backed by Bases," *Defense and Foreign Affairs Daily*, April 1, 1976.

36. For a start, with an analysis involving various kinds of Soviet presence or penetration in the Third World, see Michael L. Squires, "Soviet Foreign Policy and Third World Nations," Professional Paper no. 155, Center for Naval Analyses, Arlington, Va., June 1976.

37. For a pathbreaking typology of donor-recipient arms acquisition styles, see Amelia C. Leiss, Geoffrey Kemp, et al., "Arms Transfers to Less Developed Countries," C/70–1, Massachusetts Institute of Technology, Center for International Studies, Cambridge, Mass., 1970.

PART THREE

THE NATION STATE
LEVEL I—
SUPPLIER STATES

9 HOW THE UNITED STATES MAKES FOREIGN MILITARY SALES

Jo L. Husbands

INTRODUCTION

Policy tools, if they appear even moderately successful, tend to acquire a life of their own; their traditional uses remain accepted practice, while new advocates promote them for new purposes in new arenas. In one sense, foreign policy is simply the sum of the instruments—trade, cultural exchange, the use of force—used to achieve its broad goals. The potential problem arises when the policy tools become so intimately woven into a nation's foreign relations that altering their role threatens the entire fabric of policy. Decision makers may then be forced to make policy to control their own policy instruments.

Bringing such instruments back to the status of mere tools requires considerable effort and tenacity. The attempt of the Carter administration to reduce the role of conventional-arms "transfers" (sales plus aid) in American foreign policy illustrates these difficulties very well. It also provides the focus for an examination of the way decisions about arms sales are made and, more generally, of the importance of the decision-making process as an influence on eventual policy choices.

As a candidate, Jimmy Carter was a forceful critic of the size and direction of U.S. arms transfers. The United States, he declared, could not be "both the world's leading champion of peace and the world's leading supplier of the weapons of war."[1] As president, he continued his condemnation of the arms trade, telling the United Nations General Assembly in the fall of 1977, "The ever-increasing trade in conventional arms subverts international commerce from a force for peace into a caterer for war."[2]

Measured against this rhetoric, the Carter policy itself is a modest program in both its goals and its coverage. Announced in May 1977 after an extensive interagency review, the policy seeks to restrain the sale of advanced weapons to countries outside the primary U.S. alliance network[3] in six ways:

- The dollar volume (in constant Fiscal Year 1976 dollars) of new commitments under the Foreign Military Sales and Military Assistance Programs for weapons and weapons-related items in Fiscal Year 1978 will be reduced from the Fiscal Year 1977 total... and will be reduced in Fiscal Year 1979 from the total in Fiscal Year 1978.
- The United States will not be the first supplier to introduce into a region newly-developed, advanced weapons systems which could create a new or significantly higher combat capability. Also, any commitment for sale or coproduction of such weapons is prohibited until they are operationally deployed with U.S. forces...
- Development or significant modification of advanced weapons systems solely for export will not be permitted.
- Coproduction agreements for significant weapons, equipment, and major components...are prohibited...
- ...the United States, as a condition of sale for certain weapons, equipment, or major components, may stipulate that we will not entertain any requests for retransfers....
- An amendment to the International Traffic in Arms Regulations will be issued, requiring policy level authorization by the Department of State for actions by agents of the United States or private manufacturers, which might promote the sale of arms abroad. In addition, embassies and military representatives abroad will not promote the sale of arms...

The President also pledged:
- to "continue our efforts to promote and advance respect for human rights in recipient countries," and
- to "assess the economic impact of arms transfers to those less developed countries receiving U.S. economic assistance"[4]

The exceptions to the policy generated almost as much attention as the policy itself. The restrictions do not apply to sales to the NATO nations, to Japan, Australia, or New Zealand. Such sales have not been controversial, and there is little sentiment to reduce them, except perhaps in pursuit of NATO weapons standardization and the "two-way street." Nor does the policy cover services such as military construction, "non-weapons-related" advice, training, technical assistance, and some overhead administrative costs. The largest U.S. construction program, in Saudi Arabia; thus remains unaffected ($8 billion to date for airfields, port facilities, and other infrastructure investments needed to support a full-fledged modern military force).[5]

Beyond this, the Carter policy does not apply to all the channels through which American arms move overseas. The dwindling Military Assistance Program involves direct grants of money, weapons, and military equipment; only weapons and weapons-related items are subject to the policy. Arms sales go through two channels: Foreign Military Sales (FMS) and commercial sales. For FMS, the U.S. Government functions as a middleman, in effect buying military equipment from U.S. companies and reselling it to foreign buyers. FMS comprise the bulk of American arms transfers—$11.3 billion in fiscal 1977; $13.5 billion in fiscal 1978[6]—but only sales of "weapons and weapons-related" items are covered by the Carter policy. These sales amounted to $8.7 billion for fiscal 1977 and $8.4 billion in fiscal 1978.

Commercial sales, where U.S. defense industries sell directly to foreign governments, currently account for another 10 percent of total arms transfers. Most commercial sales are the literal nuts and bolts of military hardware—spare parts, helmets, camouflage nets, and so forth—but they are also the channel for small arms and police equipment purchases by foreign governments. Thus commercial sales restraint has been of particular concern to human rights activists.[7] Commercial sales are not covered by the Carter policy, although the State Department's Office of Munitions Control must issue export licenses for each sale. The Arms Export Control Act of 1976 tightened the definition of which cases go through FMS and which through commercial channels. Now the total value of a commercial sales case may not exceed $25 million, except to NATO, Japan, Australia, or New Zealand.

Congress is the other major source of arms-transfers regulation, with a long-standing role in shaping the outlines of policy. In recent years, some members and committees have sought a direct part in making specific arms-transfers decisions. Their primary vehicle is the Security Assistance Act and Arms Export Control Act, which prescribes certain institutional roles, decision-making rules, and reporting requirements.* Under its most important procedural prescription, Congress has given itself 30 days from the time of formal notification by the executive branch to disallow certain FMS by concurrent resolution. Taken together, these congressional and executive policies set the pattern for arms-transfers decision making.† The

---

*This act amends and updates the FMS provisions of the Foreign Military Sales Act of 1971 and the military assistance portions of the Foreign Assistance Act of 1961 which in turn had replaced the Mutual Assistance Act of 1954.

† Originally, this provision was added to the Foreign Assistance Act in 1974 by Senator Gaylord Nelson and then incorporated into the Arms Export Control Act.

next section mixes an institutional history of the arms sales program with a brief review of the major participants; to set the stage for a description of the decision-making process and provide a context for evaluating the experience of the Carter administration.

BACKGROUND

Until the explosive growth of arms sales in the early 1970s, the Department of Defense had firm control of the formulation and execution of policy.[8] Decision making was ostensibly an interagency process, but the Pentagon's monopoly on information, its expertise, and its command of administrative machinery gave it a natural advantage. Controversy surrounded the military *aid* program, but while the sales program remained small there was little pressure to change the Pentagon-dominated system.[9]

The Pentagon's control was broken well before the Carter administration took office. As arms sales increased, more and more agencies and individuals demanded a genuine role in choices about a suddenly important policy tool. The State Department and the National Security Council staff became steadily more involved in the process as Henry Kissinger made generous use of arms transfers in his diplomatic initiatives.[10] Arms transfers were widely accepted as a policy tool, so the end of the Pentagon's dominance changed the formal structure more than the outcome; few sales were rejected, but the number of consenting voices swelled.

On taking office, President Carter and his advisers thus faced a bureaucratic apparatus in which arms sales were regarded as a valuable and necessary instrument of policy. With the optimism natural to a new administration, the president and his advisers seem to have been confident of their ability to shape the decision-making process to their own ends. Instead, sporadic bursts of bureaucratic guerrilla warfare highlighted the resistance to even modest attempts to restrain arms transfers.

The difficulty of initiating restraint can be better appreciated after a brief review of the agencies, departments, and organizations now involved in arms transfers. The principal institutional actors are the Defense Department, the State Department, the Arms Control and Disarmament Agency (ACDA), the National Security Council staff, the Central Intelligence Agency (CIA), and the Defense Intelligence Agency (DIA), with the Agency for International Development (AID), the Office of Management and Budget, and the Treasury and Commerce Departments drawn in for specific purposes. Within each, of course, a long list of offices and individuals may become involved. All told, a single arms-sales case might require as many as twenty signatures before it is cleared and Congress, whose own participation is constantly expanding, is notified.[11]

Any policy process involving so many participants easily generates controversy. Even so, the particular intensity of the conflict over the Carter arms-transfers program cannot be underestimated. On one level, the moral tone of President Carter's statements has offended many who work on arms transfers in what they believe is the pursuit of U.S. national security and interests. Much more importantly, there remains a consensus that some arms transfers, if not always desirable, are absolutely necessary to U.S. foreign policy. Arms sales form the core of U.S. relationships with many important allies and friends, and no ready substitute seems available.[12]

There is also a widespread reluctance to undertake unilateral reductions in U.S. arms transfers without comparable actions by other arms exporters.[13] When the policy was announced, the President explicitly noted, "I am initiating this policy of restraint in the full understanding that actual reductions in the worldwide traffic in arms will require multilateral cooperation."[14] Talks with various Western European nations and with the Soviet Union have so far not produced substantial progress toward a suppliers' accord, although the Conventional Arms Transfers (CAT) talks continue and some optimistic reports emerge.[15] In announcing his arms-transfers ceiling figure for fiscal 1979, President Carter explicitly linked continuing American restraint to progress in the CAT talks:

My decision on U.S. arms transfers levels for FY 1980 will depend on the degree of cooperation we receive in the coming year from other nations, particularly in the area of specific achievements and evidence of concrete progress on arms transfers restraint.[16]

To complicate matters further, U.S. arms sales, at least in terms of sheer dollar volume, are concentrated among a few key client nations.[17] Reducing sales to these countries is thus an important measure of the policy's success, but some of our best customers are also some of our most important friends. The central role of arms in U.S. relations with these nations guarantees that their requests will be extremely difficult to refuse.

Taken together, these reservations regarding restraint point up just how unlikely it was for the Carter policy to be readily accepted by those charged with its design and implementation. A minority would want more stringent reductions, and more would wish for—if not a return to the laissez-faire approach of the Kissinger years—a much less restrictive policy. In the face of such widespread reluctance, implementing the policy requires careful attention to each case and a great deal of sheer persistence from those committed to its success. As one State Department official ruefully commented, "You'll fight and fight a particular sale or amendment to the policy and think you've won, but if you turn your back on it for even a few days, the thing is back on its feet and already approved at a higher level."[18]

MAKING POLICY

Deciding whether or not to make particular sales is only part of the arms-transfers decision-making process.[19] There is, in addition, a continuing need to create and refine policy and guidance. Arms-sales decisions have traditionally been made on a case-by-case basis, with the general predisposition over time to approve most cases. One purpose of the Carter policy was to provide, almost for the first time, a set of standards by which to evaluate individual cases.[20] Decision making would remain case by case, but the guidelines developed from the policy would insure greater consistency and restraint.

The vague wording of the Carter policy created an immediate need to define its terms. To be effective, phrases such as "advanced" or "sophisticated" weapons systems and "operational deployment" required working definitions. Much of the initial interagency time spent on arms sales policy was devoted to this task.[21] With Congress already using it as the standard for required reports from the executive branch, the U.S. Munitions List, started over twenty-five years ago to regulate military exports, provided the logical source for "weapons and weapons-related items." Months of interagency negotiation and wrangling, however, failed to produce exact definitions of "advanced weapons systems" or "a higher combat capability," and the list of "lethal" and "non-lethal" military equipment requested by Congress in the International Security Assistance Act of 1977 has never appeared. [22]

President Carter revamped the Security Assistance Program Review Committee (SAPRC) left over from the Ford Administration, giving it the interagency mandate for arms transfers policy definition and coordination. Chaired by Undersecretary of State Lucy W. Benson, the new Arms Export Control Board (AECB) permanent membership includes representatives from the Defense Department, Department of State, Joint Chiefs of Staff, ACDA, the NSC staff, the CIA, the treasury and commerce departments, OMB, and AID. With membership deliberately set at a high level—assistant or undersecretary—the AECB does not meet often as a full committee. When they occur, such meetings usually only put the AECB's stamp on decisions taken through other channels.

Most of the work of the AECB is actually done through its working groups,* whose staff-level membership carries out the inter- and sometimes intraagency negotiations. The working groups handle another continuing concern of the AECB: requests for exceptions to the policy. For all the attention to definition and the creation of guidelines, much *de facto* policy is

---

*These are the Arms Transfers Policy Planning Group, the Security Assistance Program Review Group, the Administration and Management Review Group, the Middle East Arms Transfers Group, and the Arms Control Impact Group.

made through decisions about particular cases. There have been several requests for exceptions each month since the policy's announcement, usually relating to restrictions on coproduction or the transfer of sophisticated military technology.[23] Most of the exceptions are approved; the advocates of arms-sales control see themselves in a constant struggle to prevent the exceptions from nibbling away the substance of the Carter policy.

MAKING SALES

Foreign Military Sales

The Executive Branch

The process of making a foreign military sale can last from six months to several years by the time all the decision-making steps are completed. All sales of major defense equipment items worth $7 million or more, or of major weapons systems totaling $25 million or more must be reported to Congress for their potential disapproval. All sales over $25 million must go through FMS channels.

Even without U.S. legal requirements, many foreign governments prefer FMS channels for major weapons sales because the Defense Department role includes assembling all the components of a weapons system into a single coordinated package. Involved Pentagon personnel gain considerable information about a nation's needs and intentions, and have considerable opportunity to influence its eventual choice. This access has been used on occasion to promote the purchase of particular weapons in order to keep a production line open, lower the unit cost of a weapon, or recoup research and development expenditures. The Carter administration has sought to discourage these promotional activities as well.

A major thrust of the Carter policy has been to move up the point of initial decision. The first serious review of a potential sale now occurs much earlier than ever before, in the hope that if cases are reviewed while only inquiries and not formal requests, it will be easier to turn down questionable sales.[24] Thus, an inquiry by a foreign government about a weapons system is now the first point in the decision-making process. These inquiries are generated in a number of ways: through an air show or other display of U.S. weapons here or abroad; from contact with U.S. military advisers or the representatives of American manufacturers in foreign countries; or as the result of a study by a Defense Department survey team. Such inquiries now come directly to the State Department through embassy channels rather than through the Pentagon.

U.S. companies may also initiate contact with prospective foreign buyers. One of the accomplishments of the Carter policy has been to restrict drastically the promotional activities of military advisers and personnel on behalf of U.S. manufacturers. Companies must now obtain clearance, as described below, before making any contact about a possible sale. The cable outlining these procedures is referred to in the defense industry as the "leprosy letter."[25]

Whatever the source of the request, the release of information about a weapons system now requires an export license from the State Department's Office of Munitions Control (OMC).* More attention is given to requests from a foreign government, as turning these down have more direct impact on bilateral relations; requests for these licenses are now treated as the first step toward a possible sale, and the evaluation rests upon whether, in the future, the United States genuinely would be willing to sell the equipment in question to the requesting nation.[26] Notification of requests is circulated among the relevant offices in the State Department, the Pentagon, and ACDA. These offices then have a limited time in which to file their reservations, if any, to the proposed release of information. The State Department's Bureau of Politico-Military Affairs, of which the OMC is a part, has the task of coordinating the review, and if reservations are filed, the director of the bureau makes a determination. Any challenges to his decision work their way up the policy hierarchy until a solution is found or imposed.

If the initial request for information is approved—and most still are—the next formal step is the request by a foreign government for the United States to issue a letter of offer and acceptance (LOA). Months of negotiations between the manufacturer and its potential client may go by from the time of the initial release of information.

Once a request to purchase is made by a foreign government, another interagency process begins. In response to the requirements of the Carter policy and of the Arms Export Control Act, sales cases divide roughly into two categories. The bulk of arms sales are routine, time consuming to process, but almost certain to be approved. Cases become routine because of the country involved, not because of the equipment to be sold.[27] Sales to countries exempt from the Carter policy—NATO, Japan, Australia, New Zealand—are generally noncontroversial. A case becomes controversial because of (in order of importance) the country involved, the equipment to

---

*Requests are generally for two types of data: "price and availability" and "price and budgetary." The various military departments prepare this information, and thus have an early impact on the process and a chance to assess the impact of a sale on their own supply and logistics requirements. According to the Director of DSAA, General Ernest Graves, the Air Force Logistics Command now services more foreign-owned than U.S. aircraft.

be purchased, and/or the size of the sale.* In practice, most attention focuses on sales to four major U.S. customers: Israel; Taiwan; South Korea; and Saudi Arabia;[38] Iran's new position is unknown.

The primary participants in the decision-making process are the offices within the State Department and the Department of Defense. The Defense Department, with its command of information and the administrative machinery, would appear to have a natural advantage in pressing its point of view. There is, however, no *single* Pentagon viewpoint. At a minimum, one must distinguish between the "military" and the "civilian" portions of the Defense Department. †

The primary responsibility for arms transfers within the office of the Secretary of Defense lies with the office of the assistant secretary of defense for International Security Affairs (OAS/ISA) and the Defense Security Assistance Agency (DSAA). Very simply, ISA is in charge of formulating arms-transfers policy, while DSAA is in charge of administering sales once they have been made. In practice these functions have tended to become fused; during the Ford administration, one man, Lt. General Howard Fish, headed both offices. ISA has both functional and regional offices, although its Policy Plans Section has the primary role in deciding general policy questions.

For the military, the major responsibility rests with the office of the Joint Chiefs of Staff which, in conjunction with the various service departments when necessary, produces the military analysis of the proposed sale. It is responsible for analyzing the military needs and capabilities of the would-be purchaser and the capabilities of the equipment proposed for sale. The DIA prepares the "threat" analysis of the military challenge facing the prospective buyer.

The office of the Joint Chiefs has shown a continuing concern for the transfer of certain sensitive, sophisticated military technology; there is no blanket endorsement of all arms sales from the military analysts. For example; asked why the Navy appears to be the hardest line service in objecting to foreign military sales, Adm. David H. Altwegg (director of the Security Assistance Division in the Office of the Chief of Naval Operations) replied that the Navy did not want to see sales of AIM-9 missiles to other than approved countries, nor in particular its antisubmarine warfare equipment, in which the United States maintains a strong lead over the

---

*The most important sources of anticipated controversy for executive branch officials are the would-be customer, Congress, various agencies within the executive branch, and nongovernmental organizations.

† In practice there are many civilian analysts within the military departments and the Office of the Joint Chiefs of Staff and many military personnel within the Office of the Secretary of Defense. The distinction therefore rests on the formal lines of authority and not on the composition of the staff.

Soviet Union. He said: "we will fight every micro-inch of the way to preserve this ASW superiority."[29]

The military's primary advantage in the bureaucratic bargaining is its expertise; its judgment may be challenged but, particularly for weapons systems in current use, it has a natural credibility which no alternative source can muster. In addition, military personnel on assignment in other offices or agencies provide a major source of support and information for civilian analysts. Very few civilians can match the expertise and familiarity with weapons systems of a career military officer. Fewer still will have access to a network of contacts for information about the actual performance of a system. Nor are all military officers unstinting advocates of arms sales; a good number may question the military utility of particular sales, worry about the transfer of sophisticated U.S. military technology, or about the creation of potential equipment shortages among U.S. forces when first-line equipment is sold right off the production line. A picture of the arms-transfers decision-making process in which military "hawks" oppose civilian "doves" would be completely misleading.[30]

Within the State Department, the Bureau of Politico-Military Affairs (PM) has policy control; it is roughly comparable to ISA, and the fortunes and power of the two offices have seesawed in recent years. PM is now clearly in ascendence.[31] The bureau is the center of arms-transfers decision making within the executive branch. It has sought to build up its own expertise and information sources independently of the Defense Department, for example, by using military officers on loan to supplement formal information channels.

Other offices in the State Department become involved in arms transfers as required. The regional bureaus are major participants when countries under their charge are affected. For bureaus such as Near East and South Asian Affairs this means an almost permanent participation in the process. The Legal Adviser's office is brought in on matters of law, while the Policy Planning Staff has a role in the resolution of issues with long-term implications for U.S. foreign relations. The Bureau of Human Rights and Humanitarian Affairs is to be involved when the would-be purchaser has a questionable record on human rights. The bureau's role and influence are not widely accepted, however, and its impact has been felt primarily in cases involving relatively unimportant countries.[32]

ACDA is a relatively new participant in the arms-transfers process, and is seeking a more active role. At one time there was only a single officer assigned to arms transfers, but its Weapons Evaluation and Control Bureau is now more fully staffed. One indication of ACDA's increased role in arms sales is its inclusion in the review of requests for technical information. Its capacity is still, by statute, an advisory one, but it is now a regular participant.

Other agencies and departments are involved in the decision-making process either less regularly or less formally. AID, for example, is invited in when the customer receives U.S. economic assistance and the impact of the sale on the country's economic development is a consideration. As already mentioned, the DIA and sometimes the CIA are asked to supply "threat" analyses as a supplement to the assessments of the Office of the Joint Chiefs of Staff. The Treasury Department becomes involved when the sale would be financed using the FMS Credit Program. Given the president's continuing concern with restraining arms transfers, the National Security Council has an important role in policy making and in day-to-day decisions on important cases. With only two staff members to monitor arms transfers regularly, however, the NSC has not been as active on this issue as on, for example, nuclear proliferation. An exception is the Conventional Arms Transfers (CAT) talks, with Jessica Tuchman, the NSC staff member for "global issues," actually serving on the American delegation.

Under the formal procedures worked out for processing FMS cases, the Office of Security Assistance and Sales in the Bureau of Politico-Military Affairs (PM/SAS) receives a weekly computer listing of requests for LOAs from the Department of Defense. A copy of the list is given to ACDA and to the other relevant offices or agencies, with PM again taking responsibility for coordination. The interested agencies then have five days to file any reservations to a proposed sale. They may also request more information, which PM/SAS is responsible for getting from the Pentagon, but at some point a memorandum detailing the reasons for the reservation must be filed. To guard against bureaucratic inertia clogging the process, time limits are imposed on all stages. Any case which becomes the subject of controversy is resolved through an interagency negotiating process, moving gradually up through the layers of the policy-making hierarchy.

There are several formal and numerous informal channels for the interagency decision-making process. Consider, for example, the typical progress of a nonroutine case which falls under the requirements for eventual reporting to Congress. If a particular sales case appears likely to generate controversy, it will probably be discussed by the director of PM and the assistant secretary for ISA at their weekly "brown-bag" lunch. Their respective staffs prepare the agenda for the meeting, and they strive to anticipate the politically important cases.

The primary decision at the lunch meeting is whether to hold an immediate AECB meeting. If the case is not urgent, an interagency paper is ordered instead, to summarize the pros and cons of the sale and set out the institutional positions of the participants. This paper defines options rather than recommending a policy choice; either the proponents or opponents of a sale may be assigned to take the lead in the paper's preparation.

Once the paper is assigned, the process becomes more formal. A month may pass in the search for a consensus; if one can be achieved, the paper will be circulated among the AECB members for approval. If not, the case may be considered by the AECB, with its chairperson, Undersecretary of State Lucy

W. Benson, empowered to take the sense of the board and make its recommendation to the secretary of state. The secretary may then make a recommendation to the president.

If any of the participants still have strong objections, a meeting of the NSC's Policy Review Committee (PRC) will be held. An urgent case might be taken directly to the PRC, but this is a rare occurrence. The membership of the PRC includes the secretary of state, the secretary of defense, the president's national security adviser, the chairman of the Joint Chiefs, the director of ACDA, and any other cabinet-level official whom the NSC staff decides should be present. The secretary of state chairs PRC meetings concerned with arms transfers. The secretaries of state and defense and the national security adviser also have lunch together once a week, so informal discussion and coordination of a case before or outside the PRC is possible. Only a very small number of arms-transfers cases ever generate enough controversy to reach this level. Losers at a lower level, of course, may try to appeal a decision farther up in the hierarchy in hopes of a more favorable outcome.*

The final step in the executive branch process is a decision by the president. The president may either be presented with the consensus recommendation of the AECB or the PRC or receive a summary of the positions in the unresolved controversy surrounding a case. The NSC staff is responsible for synthesizing the material on the case provided by the State Department and other actors into a short memo. The president personally makes the final decision on all cases that must be reported to Congress. The president may also become involved in significant cases of policy definition. This level of intimate presidential interest and involvement in the details of arms transfers is unprecedented.[33]

Congress

For major arms sales cases, the executive branch process is only the first step. Under the terms of the Arms Export Control Act, sales of major defense equipment over $7 million and all sales over $25 million must be reported to Congress. The Congress then has 30 days in which, by concurrent resolution, it may disallow a sale. Arrangements have been worked out to give Congress another 20 days of advance notice before the formal notification. The Senate Foreign Relations Committee and the House International Relations Committee have the primary responsibility.

Congress has never disapproved an arms sale since giving itself a veto in 1974, but this is not a true measure of its impact on the process. The

---

*The ability to appeal a decision higher and get it on the agenda of a policy maker is both an important informal bureaucratic tactic and, if successful, a measure of an actor's power.

reporting requirements and regulations have shaped the way in which arms-transfers decisions are made and define in large measure the cases which will receive significant attention. In view of this concern for the anticipated reaction of Congress, extensive informal consultation and discussion has grown up between various offices in the executive branch and congressional staff members.[34] Its formal role gives Congress a presence within executive branch decision making it would not otherwise have.

Congressional pressure has forced modifications in certain sales, such as the transfer of the Boeing E3-A airborne warning and control systems (AWACS) to Iran and the 1978 Middle East jet aircraft package deal. In another sense, however, the failure of Congress to disallow any sale reflects the difficulty of arousing resistance to a policy tool which enjoys wide acceptance.

Reflecting the integral role arms transfers still play, certain members of Congress and their staffs are seeking to become involved, or at least informed, earlier in the decision making process. The Security Assistance Act for 1979 gives Congress access to almost all the information compiled by the executive branch for its own decision making. The Foreign Relations and International Relations Committees have a direct computer-terminal link to the data sources in DSAA, giving them much improved monitoring capabilities. Even with all this, however, by the time an arms sale reaches Congress for formal review, it has invariably developed too much momentum to stop it. Congress can build checks and hedges around arms transfers, but it is unlikely to have a direct role in controlling weapons exports.

If an arms-transfers case survives this process, an LOA is issued to the potential client. The deal may still not go through, as the would-be buyers may change their minds while the United States is making its internal decision. Only when the LOA is signed by both U.S. officials and the foreign purchaser is the sale complete and the case added to the tally in the Defense Security Assistance Agency's accounting.

Commercial Sales

The commercial sales process is similar to that for FMS, but the State Department's Office of Munitions Control (OMC) takes charge. An even smaller percentage of commercial cases generate controversy. Since the U.S. government has no formal role in commercial arms sales, negotiations between a U.S. manufacturer or supplier and a foreign government or private firm are usually near completion when the request for an export license is filed with the OMC. Issuing the license, thus, represents the only U.S. government participation before the equipment is sent overseas. With control tightened on the kinds of equipment and the size of sales that can go through commercial channels, the role of these sales as a "back door" to evade export controls has more or less disappeared. The only sales likely to be contested now are those involving the sale of police equipment and small arms to "repressive" regimes. The Bureau of Human Rights and Humanitarian Affairs in the State Department reviews all export-license requests from countries with a record of human-rights violations.

NASA, the Federal Aviation Administration, the Department of Energy, and the National Security Agency may review license applications for equipment of interest to them. ACDA sees cases in which it has expressed an interest, and AID reviews those involving an economic aid recipient. The Commerce Department sometimes becomes involved in cases of equipment, such as computers and cargo aircraft, which have both civilian and military applications.* If any of these actors file a reservation, OMC is in charge of seeking a resolution through the same interagency process used for disputes over FMS, and cannot issue an export license until the dispute is resolved. There is no formal congressional role in commercial arms sales, although reports of all cases over the $7 million/25 million level must be sent to Capitol Hill within 30 days of issuing an export license, and routine general reports are presented by the OMC every quarter.

CONCLUSIONS

The process described above is not a simple interinstitutional conflict with, for example, the Defense Department zealously promoting arms sales and ACDA firmly in opposition. The reality is one of shifting coalitions and alliances across institutional lines, with a predisposition to approve most sales most of the time. For any given sales case, the supporters will be a mixture of staff members from the State Department, the Pentagon, and scattered other offices, while their opponents will be other staffers from different offices in the same departments.

If a generalization about alliance patterns can be made, it is that the conflicts tend to divide into regional versus functional interests. Bureaucrats who deal with arms transfers as a substantive issue tend to be somewhat more interested in developing guidelines and standards of practice. Their ideal guidelines might be very different from those found in the current Carter policy, but they are still more likely to regard arms transfers as a policy tool which requires management. For those with regional responsibilities, on the other hand, the day-to-day task is the maintenance of good relations with the countries in their charge. This creates a focus on short-

---

*The role of the Commerce Department in organizing and supporting trade fairs overseas gives it an important source of intelligence about market trends in weapons and potential sales.

term problem solving and often makes the staffs of regional offices the staunchest supporters of arms transfers as a proven means to that end.

Over the years, the major customers for U.S. weapons have developed powerful interagency groups of advocates. These groups spring to the defense of any proposed sale and have a formidable record of success in guarding their clients' interests. As already noted, one recognition of the strength of these coalitions is the decision of President Carter and his advisers to move the first point of choice earlier in the process in the hope support for a sale will not have solidified. The efforts of Congress to obtain information about potential sales early in the evaluative process reflects a similar feeling that arms sales quickly acquire a momentum which makes them very difficult to turn down. This in turn reflects their continuing acceptance, in spite of the Carter policy, as essential instruments of U.S. foreign policy.

Evaluation of the Carter policy now focuses on the dollar ceiling on arms transfers to the countries it covers. Very quickly, the ceiling became established as the standard by which the success of the Carter administration in restraining arms sales is measured. Decision making thus has become increasingly centered on the management of the ceiling. During the final quarter of fiscal 1978 the list of pending arms sales cases and the amount of room remaining under the ceiling was distributed three times rather than the routine once per week. The merits of a particular sale became clouded by its potential impact on the ceiling. There has been continuing pressure to establish regional or national subceilings, formally or informally, to insure all the important customers their fair share. One potential result of this may be to reduce sales to nations without the political clout to press their interests or needs to the front of the line.

So far, however, there have been no substantial reductions in arms sales. One Defense Department policy maker commented, "I couldn't name more than two handfuls of cases which have been rejected in the name of arms sales restraint."[35] Fiscal 1978 was another record year for foreign military sales (13.5 billion), and predictions of even further increases for 1979 were heard before the upheavals in Iran.[36]

President Carter and his advisers have apparently accepted that arms transfers are not an "exceptional" tool of American foreign policy, but an "important" and even relatively routine one. The president appears increasingly aware of the political utility of arms transfers and of their central role in U.S. relations with some of its most important friends and allies. In many ways, the 1978 package deal of jet aircraft to Egypt, Israel, and Saudi Arabia was an acknowledgement of this. The Carter Administration has imposed some order on the process, set some standards, and corrected some abuses, but it is not certain how long the policy outlined in May 1977 will survive.

The decision-making process itself helped to mold the current form of arms-transfers policy, but the assessment of its impact must be carefully qualified. The president's policy did not simply founder on the rocks of a recalcitrant bureaucracy. The policy was modest in conception, in spite of the rhetoric in which it was packaged, and the political realities of the importance of arms transfers have been responsible for its limited effects. The decision-making process reflects the importance of arms transfers and thus is a constant reminder and reinforcement for their central role. The recommendations emerging from the process are still most likely to offer the president support for arms sales, and the procedural changes enacted so far have not altered this predisposition.

The political "realities" are not immutable, however; the role of arms transfers could be reduced and the decision-making process revamped over time to minimize arms sales. New actors and greater attention to agencies or offices likely to oppose arms sales would have an eventual effect, but the overhaul would require a major effort by the executive branch and meet bitter resistance. It would also mean little without corresponding attention to the substance of the policy. Without such an effort, however, the process will continue to reflect the current "reality" and arms transfers will remain common coin in American diplomatic commerce.

NOTES

1. Speech to the Council on Foreign Relations, New York, July 1976.

2. Speech to the General Assembly of the United Nations, October 1977.

3. Public attention has focused on Carter's goal of restraining arms transfers to unstable, developing regions such as in the Middle East. Non-NATO European countries such as Sweden, Spain, and Switzerland are also subject to the ceiling, however, and this has reportedly been the source of some friction in U.S. relations with these nations (author's interview with staff member in the office of the assistant secretary of defense for International Security Affairs).

4. *Arms Transfers Policy*. Report to Congress for use of the Committee on Foreign Relations, United States Senate, July 1977.

5. U.S. Congress, House, Committee on International Relations, Subcommittee on International Security and Scientific Affairs, *Review of the President's Conventional Arms Transfers Policy*, 95th Cong., 2d sess., p.30.

6. U.S. Defense Security Assistance Agency, *Foreign Military Sales and Military Assistance Facts*, December 1978; *Wall Street Journal*, October 19, 1978.

7. See, for example, Michael Klare, *Supplying Repression* (New York: Field Foundation, 1977).

8. The material for this section was collected in part through interviews with staff members in the State Department, the Department of Defense, ACDA, the Office of Management and Budget, and the National Security Council.

9. Author's interview with a staff member in the Office of the Assistant Secretary of Defense for International Security Affairs.

10. In an interview with the author, a staff member of the State Department's Bureau of Politico-Military Affairs (PM) commented, "Henry used to hand weapons out like hostess gifts. We would think we had sales to Country X sealed off and then Kissinger would come back from some trip and tell us he had just agreed to supply another billion or so in arms to them."

11. House Committee on International Relations, *Review*, p. 48–80.

12. See, for example, U.S. Congress, Senate, Committee on Foreign Relations, *Middle East Arms Sales Proposals*, 95th Cong., 2d sess.

13. These sentiments emerged clearly in a conference on foreign military sales for defense-industry executives. See American Defense Preparedness Association (ADPA), *Meeting Report*, Third Annual Executive Seminar on Foreign Military Sales and International Logistics Support, November 28–29, 1977.

14. Senate Foreign Relations Committee, *Policy*, p.1.

15. Testimony of Leslie Gelb, Director, Bureau of Politico-Military Affairs, Department of State, before the Committee on International Relations, House of Representatives, October 3, 1978.

16. Jimmy Carter, "Statement by the President," White House press release, November 29, 1978.

17. U.S. Congress, House, Committee on International Relations, Subcommittee on International Security and Scientific Affairs, *Conventional Arms Transfers Policy: Background Information*, 95th Cong., 2d sess., February 1, 1978.

18. Author's interview with staff member, Bureau of Politico-Military Affairs, Department of State.

19. Very little has been written about arms-transfers decision making except "how-to" accounts for the defense industry. Unless otherwise indicated, therefore, all the information in the following section is taken from William H. Cullin, *How to Conduct Foreign Military Sales* (Washington, D.C.: American Defense Preparedness Association, 1977) and House Committee on International Relations, *Review*, p. 48–80.

20. Author's interview with staff member, Bureau of Politico-Military Affairs, Department of State.

21. Author's interview with staff member, National Security Council.

22. Harold J. Logan, "Bureaucracy Still Struggling to Restrain U.S. Arms Sales," *Washington Post*, November 12, 1977.

23. Author's interview with staff member, Office of the Assistant Secretary of Defense, International Security Affairs.

24. Author's interviews with staff members, ACDA and Office of the Assistant Secretary of Defense, International Security Affairs.

25. "Washington Roundup," *Aviation Week and Space Technology*, June 5, 1978, p. 13.

26. Author's interview with staff member, ACDA.

27. Author's interview with staff member, Bureau of Politico-Military Affairs, Department of State.

28. Ibid.

29. "Relaxed Air Show Restrictions Forecast," *Aviation Week and Space Technology*, December 11, 1978.

30. One former ACDA staffer described a period under former Director Fred Ikle when many arms-transfers cases would find conservative, pro-arms-sales civilian analysts opposing military officers critical of the sales.

31. Author's interviews with staff members, PM and OASD/ISA.

32. Author's interview with a staff member, OASD/ISA, who commented, "I've never yet seen a 'human rights' arms-transfers case."

33. Author's interview with staff member, National Security Council.

34. Author's interviews with staff members, PM, OASD/ISA, and House International Relations Committee.

35. Katherine Johnsen, "Congress to Expand Arms Sales Monitoring," *Aviation Week and Space Technology*, August 14, 1978.

36. A report in the *Wall Street Journal* predicted U.S. arms sales will increase further to $14.4 billion in fiscal 1979 (October 19, 1978).

10 THE ECONOMICS OF ARMS TRANSFERS

Anne Hessing Cahn

It seems abundantly clear that what is not known about the causes and consequences of global arms trade far outweighs what is known; beyond this, much of what *is* known is based on incomplete, inadequate, or inaccurate data. This is especially true for the economics of arms transfers. It is frequently alleged that arms sales ameliorate balance-of-payments deficits, spur increased commercial transactions between recipient and supplier, aid alliance standardization, reduce unemployment, lower per unit production costs, and contribute to the viability of defense industries. This chapter will examine these assertions.

INTERNATIONAL ASPECTS

We begin our analysis of the international economic aspects of global arms transfers by examining the role of arms transfers in the overall economies of the four major arms suppliers. As can be seen from Table 10.1, these four major suppliers—the United States, the Soviet Union, France, and Great Britain—perennially account for more than 80 percent of the global arms trade.

The views expressed are solely the author's and do not represent those of ACDA or any other executive branch department or agency.

TABLE 10.1: Comparison of Four Major Arms Exporters ($ U.S. billions, constant 1975)

	GNP	Exports	Arms Exports	Exports/ GNP (%)	Arms Exports/ Total Exports (%)	Arms Exports/ GNP (%)	Arms Exports/ World Arms Exports (%)
1967							
United States	1282.0	50.0	3.5	3.9	7.0	.30	43.8
Soviet Union	653.0	15.3	3.1	2.3	20.3	.50	38.8
Great Britain	195.0	23.0	0.2	11.8	0.7	.08	1.9
France	239.0	18.2	0.1	7.6	0.7	.06	1.7
1970							
United States	1369.5	59.3	4.3	4.3	7.3	.30	53.4
Soviet Union	764.0	17.6	2.1	2.3	12.0	.30	26.0
Great Britain	208.0	26.6	0.1	12.8	0.4	.05	1.4
France	278.0	25.0	0.3	9.0	1.1	.10	3.4
1973							
United States	1571.0	85.0	6.0	5.4	7.1	.40	38.5
Soviet Union	861.0	25.4	6.0	3.0	23.6	.70	38.5
Great Britain	232.5	36.6	0.7	15.7	1.9	.30	4.5
France	327.0	43.7	1.0	13.4	2.4	.30	6.6
1976							
United States	1611.4	109.5	5.0	6.8	4.6	.30	39.1
Soviet Union	960.0	35.3	3.6	3.7	10.2	.40	28.1
Great Britain	231.1	44.1	0.6	19.1	1.4	.30	4.8
France	353.5	54.5	0.8	15.4	1.5	.30	6.2

Source: U.S. Arms Control and Disarmament Agency, *World Military Expenditures and Arms Transfers 1967–1976* (Washington, D.C.: U.S. Government Printing Office, 1978).

Note: Arms exports figures refer to deliveries, not orders or commitments, and exclude training, construction, and technical services.

There are at least three measures of the role of arms transfers in a nation's economy: the relative importance of exports in relation to the gross national product (GNP), the ratio of arms exports to total exports, and the ratio of arms exports to GNP. Table 10.1 confirms that Great Britain and France are much more export dependent than the United States and the Soviet Union. At the beginning of the decade exports accounted for just over 10 percent of Britain's GNP; ten years later nearly 20 percent was attributable to exports. The percentage of France's GNP derived from exports doubled from 7.6 to 15.4 percent. Despite its role as the world's leading trading nation, the United States' exports accounted for only 6.8 percent of GNP in 1976.

Although it is common wisdom that "arms sales are important to the defense production and economies of the United Kingdom and France in particular,"[1] the contribution of military exports to total exports is much greater for the Soviet Union and the United States than it is for Britain or France. Even for the Soviet Union, however, in 1976 arms exports constituted only 10 percent of total exports and .4 percent of GNP. Comparable figures for the United States, Great Britain, and France are 4.6, 1.4, and 1.5 percent, respectively, for total exports and .3, .3, and .2 percent for GNP. Thus, for the major arms suppliers, arms exports have relatively little impact on aggregate economic output.

For balance-of-payments considerations, it is useful to distinguish short– and long–term effects. Short-term advantages accruing from increasing military sales to countries with foreign-exchange constraints may be partially offset by reductions in purchases of capital equipment and other nonmilitary imports by these countries. Suppose the United States were to reach a policy decision to limit arms sales to the Persian Gulf area to the yearly average delivered between 1968 and 1977 ($1.3 billion in current dollars, instead of the $4.4 billion delivered in fiscal 1977).[2] In such a case, one economist argues, countries like Iran "would probably spend less in total on arms imports, because other suppliers would not be able to sell either as much or as sophisticated equipment as Iran is obtaining from the United States."[3] He reasons that Iran would, therefore, probably spend more on nonmilitary imports of which a portion would be U.S. civilian products. These increased civilian sales "would partially offset U.S. economic losses from the reduction of its arms exports." These considerations, of course, would not apply to countries like Saudi Arabia which have few foreign-exchange constraints.

In the longer term, increases in U.S. arms sales (or any exports) bring about an appreciation of the exchange rate. The strengthened U.S. dollar would eventually cause exports of nonmilitary goods to decline, a condition which might cause lower employment in nondefense industries. With a fully recovered economy, total U.S. employment would be approximately the same with or without increased arms sales, but the relative positions of specific firms and of the military and civilian industries would be different.

Balance-of-payments justifications for arms sales are pernicious for several reasons. First, arms constitute only a minor component of the major arms suppliers' exports. Second, they provide open-ended rationales since they can be used to justify any arms sales. Lastly, sales of any domestic products help the balance of payments; civilian goods produce the same balance-of-trade benefits as military exports. For these and other reasons the present administration does not use balance-of-payments arguments as justifications for any arms sales.

A second economic justification often used for arms sales is that they spur commercial transactions. Analysts such as Geoffrey Kemp often argue that countries which buy large amounts of arms from the United States are also "some of our best customers for non-military exports."[4] However, the data in Table 10.2 raise doubts about the validity of the "foot in the door" economic rationale for arms sales. Since the fourfold oil price increase in 1973, Japan's total exports showed the largest increase—82 percent—compared to increases of 51 percent to 61 percent for the other leading Western nations. Yet for the same period Japan's negligible arms exports actually declined from $17 million in 1973 to $8 million in 1976. Looking at total exports to the largest purchasers of arms, the OPEC countries, we see that the German Federal Republic demonstrated the greatest percentage increase—264 percent—in the five-year period. Yet there is no indication that German arms sales to OPEC countries increased comparably before or during that time. In fact, given that the only major German arms sales to OPEC countries—submarines and, possibly, frigates to Iran, occurred subsequently to the general increase in German exports, it may be that in this case arms sales resulted from, rather led to, commercial sales.

A third economic rationale for arms sales, particularly in the United States, has been alliance standardization. The economic savings attributable to standardization have been estimated at $10–15 billion a year (or about 10 percent of the approximately $110 billion which the 14 nations of NATO spend annually on general-purpose forces).[5] While the total economic costs of nonstandardization are the subject of some debate, there is little dispute about the need to remedy the present situation.

Senator John Culver (D-Ia.) recently wrote that NATO's forces today are a museum of different weapons. There are seven different main battle tanks, 23 different types of combat aircraft, over 100 types of tactical missile systems, numerous guns of different caliber and some of the same caliber that cannot fire the same ammunition, and many different radars including 36 in naval forces alone. Communications problems were dramatically illustrated a few years ago when over half the theoretical kills of NATO naval patrol planes in one exercise were attributable to NATO's own weapons.[6]

TABLE 10.2: Total Exports of Major Western Countries
($ million current)

		Exports to (FOB)	
		World	OPEC
United States			
1973		71,339	3,602
1974		97,908	6,690
1975	44	107,191	10,768
1976		114,997	12,552
France			
1973		35,859	1,730
1974		46,388	3,164
1975		53,005	4,952
1976		55,680	5,080
Japan			
1973		36,885	2,711
1974		54,480	5,446
1975	31,00	54,882	8,406
1976		67,364	9,278
United Kingdom			
1973		30,542	1,754
1974		37,160	2,567
1975		41,731	4,553
1976		46,352	5,133
West Germany			
1973		67,531	2,259
1974		89,188	4,268
1975		90,063	6,777
1976		101,989	8,227

Source: Central Intelligence Agency, *Resource Aid—Handbook of Economic Statistics, 1977,*
p. 58.

There are many approaches to standardization. Common equipment
may be obtained through joint development (as with the multiple-role
combat aircraft); co-production of components (F-16 fighter); licensed
production (Hawk missile), or direct purchase (Lance missile). Standardization may result from prior planning, as with the Franco-German

development of the Roland missile, or from later decisions, such as the United States' subsequent participation in the Roland program.

Different approaches carry different costs and benefits. Direct purchase results in longer production runs and avoids duplicative research and development. For individual nations the corresponding disadvantages may be negative balance of payments, loss of domestic employment, or dependence on a foreign source (albeit an ally) for national-security materials. The approach favored by the Department of Defense is competitive research and development followed by licensed production;[7] this approach requires duplication of research and restricts economies of scale. Cooperative research and development reduces some costs, but may add others associated with the difficulties of coordination and the lack of competition.

In the past, the alliance-standardization justification of arms sales mostly was used to justify U.S. sales to European allies. Now, however, the need for a "two-way street" is widely recognized in the United States. The term refers to the value or number of arms which the United States sells to NATO countries compared with what the United States purchases from them, and up to the present the flow has been predominately (10 to 1) in one direction—from the United States to NATO. President Carter and Secretary of Defense Harold Brown have declared that the two-way street concept is U.S. policy. Carl Damm, a member of the Bundestag of the Federal Republic of Germany, warned participants at a NATO conference in July 1978 that if the United States wanted to retain 50–70 percent of the European military market in the 1980s, it would have to allow European industries to share in the U.S. market.[8] Although the two-way street concept is declared official U.S. policy, contemporary political realities are such that implementation of that policy will be slow and tortuous.

DOMESTIC ASPECTS

The relationship between arms sales and unemployment, like so many of the other economic variables examined so far, is subject to a great deal of uncertainty and dispute among economists. Basic concepts and methodologies vary from study to study, and valid comparisons are difficult to obtain. The problem is compounded since arms-transfer data, as data for most exports, are generally based on deliveries although the impact on employment occurs earlier; that is, employment will rise or fall when a given arms transaction is ordered or cancelled, while the arms transfer is often reported when the goods or services are delivered. The time between the order and delivery may be years. To compound the problem, some data use the date the export license is granted, others the date the contract is signed, and a few the date at which the weapons become operational; thus, different studies often lead to different conclusions.

For example the Congressional Budget Office in 1976 concluded that under a total ban of U.S. foreign military sales (FMS), and if no ameliorative offsetting remedies were enacted, by 1981 the unemployment rate would be approximately 0.3 percent higher than otherwise projected, total employment would be about 350,000 jobs lower than if the FMS program were continued.[9] The study is based on an annual FMS program of $8.2 billion; thus, in this calculation, $1 billion FMS accounts for about 42,000 jobs.

Later studies prepared by the Carter administration point to $1 billion in arms sales accounting for about 38,000 jobs. An often quoted Bureau of Labor Statistics study in 1975 found that $1 billion spent on defense creates 74,000 jobs, but this study differs from the others in that it is based on total defense expenditures and not just arms transfers. Since much of defense expenditures are for personnel-related functions (wages and pensions), the intuitive guess might be that employment effects of FMS would be greater than those for total defense expenditures, but the various studies are not consistent with this conventional wisdom.

Averaging the two figures cited for the U.S. arms transfers results in $1 billion in sales accounting for 40,000 jobs. This figure can be compared with the job-creating potentials of other federal programs which indicate that $1 billion spent on the space shuttle program (NASA) generated 57,000 jobs, the same $1 billion created 84,000 jobs if spent on the National Institutes of Health, 89,000 jobs if spent on Veteran's Administration health care, and 136,000 jobs if spent on occupational training.

Data for other supplier countries are scanty, but the conventional-arms industry employs between 1 and 1.5 percent of the working population in the major West European arms-supplier countries. In 1976 Jacqueline Grapin estimated that of the 270,000 workers in the French armaments industry, 75,000 were engaged in supplying foreign markets (excluding subcontractors and those in procurement services).[10]

Regardless of the absolute size of the European labor force resulting from arms sales, their political clout is enhanced by the fact that all but a few of the major armaments producers in France and Britain are wholly or partly government owned. Thus, as Lawrence Franko points out, "decisions to lay off workers in the European defense industries necessarily involve direct and visible government (and therefore political) responsibility."[11]

Another facet of the employment arms-sales relationship is that, while defense expenditure is not as labor intensive as other forms of public expenditure, those workers that are employed are disproportionately highly trained and skilled. According to a recent British study, 50 percent of the 200,000 employees in the aerospace industry are highly skilled technical workers.[12]

As for the other economic benefits, four sources of potential savings can be identified: research and development recoupment, learning curve effects and economies of scale, overhead reduction, production-line stability without termination and start-up costs. Based on a study of 35 major weapons systems, the Congressional Budget Office (CBO) found in 1976 that in a given fiscal year an $8 billion FMS program would generate savings of $560 million or about one-half of one percent of current defense outlays.[13]

The celebrated "contract of the century" competition to sell a new combat aircraft to Belgium, Holland, Denmark, and Norway has been used to illustrate the possible effects of arms exports on unit costs. Sweden is the only country which both maintains a state-of-the-art technological capability in many weapon systems and restricts its arms exports severely. (Total Swedish arms exports average about $25 million yearly for the last five years). According to Lawrence Franko, "the net effect of limited exports on the per-unit price of Sweden's most advanced tactical aircraft, the JA-37 Viggen, has, it seems, been substantial."[14] Table 10.3 shows that Viggen's per unit price is considerably higher than that of the major aircraft with which it is roughly comparable.

The 1976 CBO study found that most substantial savings from foreign

TABLE 10.3: Comparative Prices and Outstanding Orders: Attack Aircraft

	Approx. Unit[a] Price Range, 1977 ($ million)	Approximate Orders, January 1978 (units)	
		Total	For export
Viggen (Sweden)	8.0–10.0	180	0
Jaguar (France-U.K.)	6.8–8.5	402	24
Mirage F-1 (France)	4.5–4.7	533	186
F-16 (U.S.)	6.1–7.7	1896[b]	558

Source: Lawrence Franko, "Restraining Arms Exports to the Third World: Will Europe Agree?" *Survival* 21: 1 (1979): 14–25.

a. Prices estimated to be those paid by home-country authorities, and vary with specific equipment ordered with each aircraft, as well as with attack versus interceptor models.

b. Includes not only firm orders by U.S. Air Force, but also "planned procurement," giving a total estimated production run for U.S. domestic procurement of 1388.

sales, about 14 percent on procurement and about 4 percent on research and development recoupment, occurred with "recently developed, high-technology systems—particularly new fighter aircraft and missiles."[15] The U.S. arms-sales mix of weapons, construction, and services has shifted somewhat from those where savings are high (aircraft and missiles) to those where savings are negligible or nonexistent (ships, ammunition, construction, and services). In 1972 aircraft and missiles accounted for 59 percent of the value of U.S. foreign military sales; by 1975 this had dropped to 41 percent.[16]

In contrast, French and British military exports consist mainly of those high-technology items for which substantial domestic procurements savings can be expected. French arms exported in 1976 totaled about $800 million. According to Franko, nearly 80 percent of French arms exports consist of aerospace and electronics, and French export of these items is 50–60 percent of production.[17] Therefore, French defense-procurement savings from high-technology exports must have been on the order of $96 million in 1976 or about six-tenths of one percent of total French military expenditure.

While British and French views tend to emphasize the benefits of defense spending and arms exports, the Japanese often express a contrary opinion. Many Japanese feel that their modest defense expenditures have contributed importantly to their phenomenal economic growth by freeing resources for industrial investment that would otherwise have been spent on the armed forces. Total Japanese defense spending is less than one percent of GNP and as already stated, Japan's arms exports are miniscule.

As can be seen from the above, short-term impacts on balance of payments, increased commercial transactions, alliance standardization, employment, and per unit production costs are not likely to be the major considerations in economic calculations of arms transfers. What makes arms exports economically important is their importance to individual defense sectors or particular companies. For the United States as a whole, foreign military sales are only 15 percent of U.S. procurement. For individual firms, however, the data are very different: Northrop Corporation lists foreign sales, including FMS, at 59 percent of its total sales for 1976;[18] Bell Helicopter derives 42 percent and Grumman 26 percent of their revenues from foreign military sales.[19]

Defense-firm dependency on arms exports is much more pronounced in Europe. Dassault-Breguet, the French producer of the Mirage, regularly exports more than 60 percent of its production (70 percent in 1976) and more than 80 percent of those exports are military.[20] When British Aerospace was created in 1977 by merging British Aircraft and Hawker-Siddeley, 70 percent of all orders on hand were for export.[21]

For arms exports, as for so many other foreign-policy issues, numbers alone never provide enough information either to explain policies or to guide policy makers; for a variety of reasons, arms exports are more important than they appear to be in simple economic terms. The British and French view military exports as vital to the continued viability of their national defense-production lines. In addition to wanting to maintain their own aircraft and missile industries for reasons of national political independence or prestige, Europeans also perceive a link between technological developments in aerospace with medium- to long-range industrial growth, "both directly and through spin-offs and linkages to other sectors."[22] In the United States the major defense exporters often employ large numbers of people, making arms sales an important issue for particular labor unions, as well as for their representatives in Congress.

Although economic considerations undoubtedly play a role in arms-sales decisions, they are seldom, if ever, paramount. The international trade in arms has become such a prevalent implement of foreign policy for many countries, both recipients and suppliers, that economic criteria are subordinated to political considerations. If there is to be effective control of the international transfer of arms, the political context in which arms sales are negotiated and implemented has to be acknowledged, analyzed, and made amenable to joint recipient-supplier restraint.

NOTES

1. U.S. Congress, Senate, Committee on Foreign Relations, *Arms Transfer Policy*, 95th Cong., 1st sess., July 1977, p. 10.

2. Department of Defense, Defense Security Assistance Agency, "Foreign Military Sales and Military Assistance Facts," December 1977, pp. 4, 13.

3. Edward K. Fried, "The Economics of Arms Transfers," Washington, D.C., Brookings Institution, p. 13.

4. Geoffrey Kemp, "The Arms Transfer Phenomenon and Its Course," draft paper, p. 27.

5. U.S. Congress, Senate, Committee on Armed Services, *Department of Defense Appropriations Authorization for Fiscal Year 1977*, 94th Cong., 2d sess., May 14, 1976, p. 167.

6. John Culver, "Comment: The Argument for Standardization" *Foreign Policy* 31 (1978): 91–94.

7. Dewey F. Bartlett, "Standardizing Military Excellence: The Key to NATO's Survival," *AEI Defense Review* 6 (1977): 6.

8. "Reduction in US Arms Dominance Urged," *Aviation Week and Space Technology*, July 3, 1978, p. 15.

9. Congressional Budget Office, "The Effect of Foreign Military Sales on the U.S. Economy" Staff Working Paper, July 23, 1976, p. 1.

10. "French Arms Sales," *Le Monde*, November 9, 1976, cited in *Bulletin of Peace Proposals* 2 (1977): 179.

11. Lawrence Franko, "Restraining Arms Exports to the Third World: Will Europe Agree?" *Survival* 21:1 (1979): 16.

12. Lawrence Freedman, "Arms Production in the United Kingdom: Problems and Prospects," Royal Institute of International Affairs, London, 1978, p. 7.

13. U.S. Congressional Budget Office, "Budgetary Cost Savings to the Department of Defense Resulting from Foreign Military Sales," Staff Working Paper, May 24, 1976, p. ix.

14. Franko, "Restraining Arms Exports," p. 19.

15. Congressional Budget Office, "Budgetary Cost Savings," pp. 13–14.

16. Ibid, p. 16.

17. Franko, "Restraining Arms Exports," p. 20.

18. Steven Lydenberg, "Weapons for the World: Update: The U.S. Corporate Role in International Arms Transfers," Council on Economic Priorities, New York, 1977, p. 19.

19. Anne Cahn et al., *Controlling Future Arms Trade* (New York: McGraw-Hill, 1977), p. 68.

20. Franko, "Restraining Arms Exports," p. 13.

21. Ibid.

22. Ibid., p. 18.

11 POLITICAL INFLUENCE: THE DIMINISHED CAPACITY

William H. Lewis

The prevalent view of the United States by foreign-affairs specialists and practitioners is that of a deeply wounded nation. Vietnam, the scars of Watergate, and the shifting basis of international power are all identified as factors that contribute to the diminished capacity of the United States to play a significant leadership role. Whatever the causes—which are invariably held to be multiple—the U.S. sense of mission as the "free world's" defender and armorer is at a low ebb and, according to most impartial observers, so too is the capacity of the United States to provide the equipment and military weapons that its friends and allies require.

Paradoxically, available statistical data suggest the contrary. During fiscal 1978 (October 1, 1977–September 30, 1978), U.S. arms transfers to other nations topped $13 billion,* which is roughly comparable to previous year levels. Despite the *dictat* of President Carter in May 1977 that the United States should curtail its conventional-arms sales abroad and that it would place severe controls over the provision (or sale) of advanced or sophisticated weaponry to Third World nations, the United States actually heightened both the *scale* and degree of sophistication of weapons sold in

---

*The term "arms" here includes military equipment, usually referred to as "conventional," comprising weapons of war, parts, ammunition, support equipment, and other commodities considered primarily military in nature—tactical guided missiles, military aircraft, armored and unarmed military vehicles, tanks, infantry small arms, and the like.

1977–78. If the level of such sales is a measure of influence, it would appear that U.S. capacities were barely diminished. Closer examination would reveal, however, that the *geographic scope* of U.S. sales had contracted; the principal recipients of American weapons were Iran, Saudi Arabia, and Israel—nations which either had a moral claim on the United States for security support or on which the United States is heavily dependent—for petroleum and monetary stability.

U.S. dependence on Saudi Arabia is a reflection of the complex linkages that take place in arms-transfer relationships. Where the United States has become the principal or sole supplier, all too often the political or economic factors that have fostered such a relationship lead to mutual dependence and a diminished U.S. capacity to sustain its influence on the recipient government's policies for an appreciable period of time.

The degree of American dependence was reflected in the lengths to which the Carter administration was reportedly willing to proceed in evading its self-imposed arms-transfer ceiling of $8.6 billion for fiscal 1978. The president apparently has agreed to meet Iran's request for costly frigates, while at the same time appearing to honor his sales ceiling, by having European shipbuilders develop the hulls, superstructures, and power packages, the most expensive segments of the sale; for its part, the United States has agreed to sell the less expensive weapons systems.[1] Comparable subterfuges by the Carter administration have come to light elsewhere. For example, the sale of F-5E aircraft to Egypt is to be phased over a period of several years to meet existing arms-ceiling constraints; the same practice was being followed in the sale of airborne early warning (AEW) equipment to Iran.

From a symbolic point of view, however, nothing appears to underscore the diminution of the will and influence of the United States more than the decision of the Carter administration and the Congress to repeal the 1974/75 arms embargo against Turkey, imposed after the illicit use of U.S. arms by Turkish forces to seize control of 40 percent of Cyprus. The fact that both Turkish forces and U.S. arms remain on Cyprus, in clear violation of existing U.S. military assistance legislation and in contravention of international law, carried no weight with the president or Congress. The embargo had failed to move the Turkish government and, in the interim, Turkish commitment to the NATO alliance had eroded, as had Turkey's erstwhile indulgence in permitting U.S. access to intelligence facilities upon which the U.S. military had become heavily dependent for the monitoring of the Soviet strategic-weapons development program. Through the lifting of the embargo, it was argued that the United States would gain the following immediate advantages: renewed Turkish participation in NATO, readmission of the United States to essential intelligence facilities, and reinvigoration of the Cyprus negotiating process.

The curious strategy by the Carter administration on the Cyprus issue raises profound questions about the significance of arms as an instrument of foreign policy. Having declared in May 1977 that arms would no longer be treated as a key foreign-policy bargaining chip, the administration reversed itself one year later on Turkey by taking the position that the sale of weapons is indeed important to the NATO alliance, to the Cyprus negotiating process, and to the ability of the United States to influence the future course of events in the eastern Mediterranean. In 1978, confusion reigned concerning the importance and role of arms transfers as an instrument of U.S. foreign policy.

"INFLUENCE" IN THE MATRIX OF POLICY

Part of the difficulty confronting efforts to assess the importance of arms transfers to the foreign-policy goals of the U.S. Government may be attributed to uncertainty that surrounds the term "influence." Part of the international political process involves the efforts of a state, through a wide variety of acts and activities, to change or sustain the policies, goals, or behavior of other states. Inducements may involve diplomatic persuasion, economic assistance, alliance support, agreement to serve as an assured source of arms, or direct threats. It is the ability to influence the policy goals or orientations of other governments that is the quintessential test of power, as opposed to military capabilities.

"Influence" must be viewed in instrumental terms—that is, as a means to an end. Statesmen use influence to achieve a specific goal or to defend a goal already attained. These goals, in the context of arms transfers, may include alliance support, deterrence, access to bases, protection of lines of communication, or accommodation to such needs as resource availability, commodity pricing, or trading advantages.

Since arms enhance the recipient's capabilities, the degree of the recipient's dependence on an external supplier is a most serious national-security concern. An arms-supply relationship, by its very nature, is both sensitive and intrusive. Nations stake their power, capabilities, and weight in the international community on their arms-supply relationships. Hence, the transfer of arms is a process which binds nations together, but only imperfectly. For instance, the process often evolves into an "exchange of influence." Dependency ensues—as in the case of U.S. ties with Israel, NATO, Korea, and Taiwan—but the resulting web of interdependence diminishes the leverage of supplier on a recipient's policies. Second, influence can become attenuated because recipient nations have a clear threshold of national interests which they will not sacrifice in favor of the supplier nation. The experience of the Soviet Union in Egypt, Somalia, and

Indonesia, as well as that of the United States in Ethiopia, Turkey, and Latin America—where military advisory missions were thrown out as a result of policy disputes between suppliers and recipient nations—attests to the importance of nationalism as a natural check on superpower political manipulation. Finally, there is the process of "reverse influence," in which the recipient involves the supplier in sharing regional or extraregional objectives, tempers confrontations, and often leads to accommodations which appear to blur original supplier goals in the recipient country. Soviet willingness to turn a blind eye to repression of local communist parties in Syria, Iraq, and other Arab countries reflects this accommodationist approach.

Where there is a potential conflict with a recipient nation over its misuse of U.S. equipment, the United States has sometimes shown a disposition to recede from the direct confrontation or to acquiesce rather than "squander" what limited influence it has over the recipient government's actions. Thus, the United States has ignored, until recently, the stationing of F-5 aircraft in the western Sahara by the Moroccan government. The use of these aircraft in Mauritania to cope with Polisario guerrilla raids appears to be in substantial violation of military-aid agreements between Washington and Rabat covering the area and terms of usage of U.S. weapons; however, Morocco's moderate position on Middle Eastern questions has induced the Carter administration to adopt a relatively passive position on the violations. Similarly, the United States has blinked away past excesses by the Mobutu regime in Zaire because of the sizable Cuban military presence in neighboring Angola and the strategic importance of both countries in shaping and influencing nationalist forces in adjoining regions of Africa.

Thus, arms serve as an instrumental vehicle for achieving certain specific foreign-policy outcomes: they establish or sustain necessary relationships; they create a process of interaction; they add to the capabilities of supplier and recipient; and they often create mutual dependencies. These interactions help to shape the responses of supplier and recipient to local and regional problems or crises. Dependence is not, however, a certain gauge in determining the lengths to which recipient nations will go when vital national interests are involved. Compelled to choose between ongoing dependency, which involves a sacrifice of these interests, and seeking other sources of supply, most nations will opt for the latter course.[2]

This chapter identifies the reasons why U.S. leverage or influence in the arms-transfer field is diminishing from a zenith in the period immediately following World War II. It traces the historical evolution of U.S. transfers and explores the reasons why the U.S. effort became amorphous in terms of doctrine, bloated in scale, and increasingly lacking in effective management and control—all of which has tended to dilute the amount of U.S. influence associated with the U.S. military assistance program. In addition, it will be demonstrated how the growing oversight role demanded by the U.S. Congress could have restored a semblance of balance to the program but, paradoxically, by supporting the general thrust of Carter administration initiatives on sales abroad and insisting on increased orthodoxy (with respect to human rights and other precepts), the Congress has further contributed to the diminished capacity of the administration to effectively utilize arms transfers as an instrument of policy. Some general cautionary hints and normative prescriptions are then offered for the future foreign-affairs practitioner of the art of diplomacy and suasion.

The decline of the United States from its post-World War II position as the free world's principal armorer is part of a natural and essentially uncontrollable historical process which takes place on the world stage and interacts with domestic forces within U.S. society. The result for U.S. policy has been an increasingly ambivalent posture of arms sales; it is a natural by-product of the international forces which seem to encourage both increased arms transfers and the public debate and skepticism about the benefits to U.S. purposes and policies arising from such sales.

HISTORICAL BACKGROUND: THE RISE AND DECLINE OF U.S. PROGRAMS AND INFLUENCE

Military assistance has been an integral part of U.S. national-security policy for more than a quarter of a century. Begun with special programs of military aid to the Philippines and Western Europe in 1946, Greece and Turkey in 1947, and Nationalists in China in 1948, the manifold efforts of the U.S. government were finally united in a single body of legislation, the Mutual Defense Assistance Act, which was enacted in 1949. As outlined by the act, military assistance was viewed as "essential to enable the United States and other nations dedicated to the purposes and principles of the United Nations to participate effectively in arrangements for individual and collective security." The area of geographic concentration for military assistance was to be Western Europe and it was to serve as tangible proof of the importance assigned by the United States to the North Atlantic Treaty Organization (NATO) which was formed on April 4, 1949.

The impetus for the collective security efforts of NATO came from mounting evidence that the national interests and aspirations of the Soviet Union were antithetical to those of Western Europe and the United States. The Soviet refusal to withdraw Russian troops from northern Iran, the Greek Civil War and Soviet pressure on Turkey for joint control of the Dardanelles, events in Czechoslovakia, the Berlin "blockade" of 1948—all these events moved the West and the Soviet Union towards a prolonged period of cold-war confrontation. What emerged in the United States to counter the Soviet threat was a military strategy of deterrence; its foreign-policy counterpart was containment, and military assistance was to be the mortar of the NATO alliance.

In time, the concept of containment escaped its original geographic confines and was extended to other areas; following the Korean war, the focus of U.S. policy gradually shifted from Europe to Asia. Economic recovery in Western Europe had buttressed the capacity of most NATO countries to finance their own defense needs, and the seriousness of military threats to potential allies in the Asian area appeared to mount with the consolidation of Communist Chinese power on the mainland. In time, military assistance was directed towards supporting bilateral security arrangements with South Korea, Taiwan, Japan, Thailand, and Pakistan. In some instances, aid was also extended to "unaligned" countries such as Indonesia and India.

As the geographic and policy reach of U.S. military-aid programs expanded in the 1950s and 1960s, the official rationale for these programs also expanded. The prodigious military and economic relief efforts, originally intended to rehabilitate the war-ravaged economies of U.S. allies in Europe and to buttress their capacity to act in concert with the United States to meet perceived military threats from the Soviet Union, now enfolded nations and leaders in Asia, the Middle East, and Africa who shared few beliefs and interests with their counterparts in Europe. As a result, the rationale for U.S. assistance burst the original conceptual bounds of deterrence and containment and came to encompass such broad desiderata as the following:

1. To assist allies and other states in the maintenance of an effective defense posture in order to defend against external aggression (Israel, South Korea, Turkey); contribute to a common defense effort (NATO, SEATO); replace arms within levels established by international agreement (South Vietnam under the 1973 Paris Accords); and enable or facilitate the withdrawal of American troops from overseas positions (Vietnam, South Korea).
2. To provide a source of leverage in pursuit of important diplomatic objectives (the Cyprus and Arab-Israeli disputes).
3. To acquire base rights and access to local facilities on a regular or emergency basis.
4. To provide a symbol of U.S. commitment to, or expression of concern with the security of, recipients of U.S. equipment and services (Iran, Saudi Arabia, Ethiopia).
5. To support a pro-U.S., independent orientation by politically or strategically (geographically) important countries and, thereby, to exclude Soviet or other influence or dominance.
6. To maintain access or influence with key leaders and groups in countries that are recipients of military assistance.

7. To assist a government or particular regime that the U.S. favors, on its merits or as being inherently more pliable or attractive than alternative regimes.

The inflation of the program's rationale and goals, in due course, was reflected in the number of beneficiaries that came within the ambit of U.S. military assistance—at one point, 80 countries—and the level of funds requested by successive administrations.

However, although Congress became increasingly concerned with the vast expenditures associated with the arms-transfer effort, it had reason to believe that the financial burden would decline when the economic infirmities of allies and friends had been overcome. Western Europe had recovered and was expected to serve as a model. In the case of Iran, the Republic of China (Taiwan), Greece, Zaire, and other nations, their graduation from grant assistance was reassuring. By the early 1970s Congress made it clear, and most recipients of grant military aid realized, that the program had a finite time limit. Virtually all recipients planned on increased recourse to credit-sales arrangements for the acquisition of military equipment and associated services.

Simultaneous with the reduction in grant aid in the 1970s, military assistance became the object of a continuing debate in the United States. During the trauma of Vietnam, certain shibboleths about the American role of international policeman came under attack, as did the efficacy of military assistance as an instrument of policy. Nevertheless, under the stewardship of Secretary of State Henry Kissinger, military aid was accorded a nonpareil position as a means for achieving foreign-policy ends. Kissinger held such aid to be vital to U.S. influence abroad—to preserving ties with allies, forging more rational relationships with its adversaries, maintaining regional balances of power, and creating a new era of cooperation with all nations. Whatever the nature of the regimes it supported, security assistance was viewed as the first step toward a positive U.S influence and as a hindrance to other, undesirable sources of supply. On the other hand, the Kissinger approach had obvious defects:

...the Kissinger propositions offered little ground for discrimination, and critics of his policy suggested that security assistance ought to be one of the alternatives in an array of policy choices. It should be the policy followed only when it could be defended as wise for the United States, for the benefiting country, and for other countries affected by it. Assistance might buy only the illusion of influence. It could commit the United States to the further support, or even defense, of another country; certainly, if the United States views military help as a principal means of influencing countries, it opens itself to easy blackmailing by them....[3]

By 1977, there was reason to believe that Kissinger's critics had prevailed. It seemed that President Carter had drastically altered U.S. policy by severely curtailing arms sales. Shortly after his inauguration in January 1977, Carter's staff conducted an intensive policy review, the results of which were new guidelines for the bureaucracy, hallmarked by professions of self-restraint and limitation. The actual performance, however, of the Carter administration since then has closely paralleled that of its predecessor, fueling widespread confusion and cynicism regarding the president's goals and tactics.

Part of the difficulty may be attributed to the fact that the hegemony of U.S. economic and military power is at an end. The United States has not become a "have not" nation economically, but it is becoming a nation with a shrinking domestic natural-resource base readily at its disposal. United States arms-transfer policies should, in such circumstances, be brought into balance with economic and security realities. Instead, however, the Carter administration has injected a moral dimension which creates a measure of ambiguity, is perplexing to traditional friends and allies, and effectively neutralizes the comparative advantage the United States has enjoyed in weapons technology.

The interplay of morality and economic dependence are exemplified in the Middle East. In May 1978 the president contended that the sale of advanced weapons to Israel and Saudi Arabia would serve the cause of peace; he was also prepared to set aside moral issues on the Cyprus question in an effort to secure congressional support for the termination of the 1974/75 arms embargo against Turkey. Elsewhere, most particularly in the African Horn region, the president appeared ready to provide "defensive" arms to Somalia, a nation which several months previously had outraged its African peers by invading the Ogaden area of neighboring Ethiopia. For most observers, the questions of selective morality and policy inconsistency have become issues demanding early resolution by the president.

CHANGING FRAMEWORK FOR ASSISTANCE

The way the Carter administration made policy further reduced U.S. ability to use grant military assistance and sales to gain influence. As the administration completed the initial period of its tenure in 1978, it had yet to make rational the arms-transfers policy-making process, effectively managed and controlled by the White House. Decisions were made on a case-by-case basis; existing interagency coordinating mechanisms operated only intermittently; scrutiny and oversight by middle-level policy managers were haphazard at best. But, of particular significance, the policy approach of the Carter team did not appear to take into full account the changes that were occurring internationally in the arms-transfer community. These deficiencies were at least a decade in the making; indeed, by the time the

Carter administration had arrived in Washington, it was already evident that the organization, content, and thrust of U.S. arms-transfer programs were losing their capacity to cope with those changes.

What the Carter administration has contributed to the process is a refusal to recognize that the international arms trade has taken on a life of its own, one which the United States had virtually no prospect of controlling, constraining, or otherwise influencing. Among the factors contributing to this change were the following:

1. *Shift from Grants to Sales.* This is an ongoing process. Grants and credit sales are winding down in programs with most countries and phasing out in others. While the need for grant military assistance may persist for the indefinite future in the case of countries where the U.S. has base rights or in Israel and Jordan, ongoing grant military-assistance programs are likely to prove the exception rather than the rule. The shift to sales has reduced the leverage which the United States has on purchasing countries.

2. *Shift in Rationale.* With the shift to sales, national-security rationales began to carry less weight with Congress and the public than in the past. As a result, both felt less constrained in challenging the position of the executive branch on proposed sales cases. Indeed, the Congress, in time, came to claim a co-equal right with the executive branch in making arms-transfer policy.

3. *Reduced Capacities.* Economic and commercial exchanges between nations have come to figure more and more importantly in the economies of all. In the United States, exports and imports, which accounted for just over 5 percent of Gross National Product in 1960, now make up over 15 percent. However, the growth of trade, and of military exports as an important factor in GNP, has also added to demands on the U.S. production base and on the Department of Defense at a time when the latter wishes to undertake extensive force modernization for the U.S. armed services. Moreover, the Defense Department faces other problems: the number of MAAG (Military Assistance Advisory Group) personnel assigned abroad is under constant reduction as a result of Congressional fiat. The availability of specialists as advisers for service abroad is limited because of the priority needs of U.S. forces; the U.S. production base for high-priority items—tanks, aircraft, and missiles—has narrowed in recent years, thus putting U.S. forces in competition with foreign purchasers for procurement and early delivery, and such competition tends to degrade the preparedness of U.S. forces. Production problems are assuming worrisome dimensions. The narrow U.S. production base of some military items is extending delivery lead times, which adversely affects the competitive position of the United States abroad. Constraining foreign sales would have unfavorable economic and foreign policy consequences; on the other hand, to proceed as in the past—using on-the-shelf stock or deferring U.S. military priorities—would degrade U.S. force readiness.

4. *Availability of Other Suppliers.* As the U.S. program has shifted from nonreimbursable transfers to a sales base, the ability of the United States to influence the policies and postures of other governments has diminished commensurately. Foreign purchasers now weigh carefully the costs of equipment, as well as the costs of continuing dependence on the United States for military supply. The availability of other suppliers, many of which are willing to make their equipment and services available at political and financial discount, further diminishes Third World willingness to rely solely on the United States as a source of supply.

5. *Widening Range of Policy Questions.* Decisions on sales now include not only questions of military final products and services, but technology, production know-how, planning and programming, and provision of specialized military training. Given the nature and complexity of these decisions, and their relationship to other U.S. commercial objectives abroad, the question arises whether existing U.S. bureaucratic machinery and processes are adequate to meet future needs. Thus far, the performance of the bureaucracy has been uneven, almost hesitant, reflecting a wide measure of uncertainty concerning administration goals and strategy.

6. *Groping Improvisation.* The net impression of the Carter administration approach is that of groping improvisation. Until a coherent overall strategy is adopted, the machinery at hand is likely to sputter along as best it can. The infirmities of the bureaucracy were outlined in an administration report to Congress, in June 1977, in the following terms:

Major decisions on arms transfers under the existing institutional system have been made at a high policy level. The system has been generally effective and reasonably efficient but has met with the following problems:
Its essentially ad hoc and fragmented character;
The multiplicity of decision channels;
The lack of a single document or coherent series of documents on policies, planning, and procedures;
Difficulty in controlling all significant decision points;
Inadequate interagency planning.[4]

As recent reports indicate, the Carter administration has been unable to correct these deficiencies. The discovery by the Department of Defense of a one-billion-dollar shortfall in arms-sales accounting, late in 1977, is only the most glaring example; the Departments of State and Defense continue to develop their own separate and distinct military-sales program with little effective supervision by the White House. Perhaps most disturbing, the Carter administration continued to dispatch military survey teams abroad as of mid-1978 with little if any policy guidance from senior levels within the executive branch. Their reports, which ultimately are transmitted to foreign governments and serve as planning baselines by these governments for the purchase of military equipment, frequently commit the U.S. government to sales which it has not examined with any degree of depth. The survey-team process has become so diffuse and undirected that members of Congress have expressed growing concern and have begun to discuss the necessity for legislative oversight.

DECLINING INFLUENCE: CONGRESSIONAL ROLES

Issues regarding U.S. policies and actions on arms sales have become a serious bone of contention between the executive branch and the Congress; the identification and debate of public-policy issues occur most often when sales programs are presented to Congress. With rare exceptions, the press and other media deal only with individual cases with political overtones, and other public attention is minimal; major arms sales can be newsworthy and are sometimes reported and commented on editorially. But Congress itself has begun to assume a more vigorous and continuous policy role in arms-transfers decisions.

Until recently, security assistance* has been subjected to more attention and more controversy than arms sales, but this is only partly because security assistance has been the larger program. Security assistance has required annual appropriations and authorizing legislation whereas until 1974 cash sales, government and commercial, were made or licensed at executive branch discretion, subject only to after-the-event reporting to Congress often months later or in general or aggregate terms. Not only did the annual budget request afford Congress the opportunity to decide on the amounts of money to go into military aid, it offered the best opportunity for congressional discussion and action on U.S. foreign policy. The annual debate on the foreign-aid legislation has thus dealt not only with the rationale for security assistance and the relative priorities for such assistance, U.S. defense forces, and domestic needs as expressed in allocation of budgeted funds, but also with the rightness and effectiveness of U.S. policy in Turkey, and Chile, and Korea, and Indochina.

Current debate and soul searching over security assistance can be related to two principal issues: congressional control over the program and, more fundamentally, the extent to which the program continues to make sense in a world of evident political and economic change. The congressional assertion of a larger role in defining the program and supervising its implementation has been explicit in recent years, particularly on the part of both the Senate and House Foreign Affairs Committees. Their general

---

*The term "security assistance" is more comprehensive than "military assistance"; it has four main parts: grant military assistance (MAP), military training, foreign military sales, and security economic supporting assistance, the last program being administered by the Agency for International Development.

objectives have been, first, as in the case of the War Powers Act, to reassert the co-equal rights of Congress regarding formulation (as distinct from conduct) of foreign policy and foreign-aid programs and the contracting of new national commitments and, second, to specify more precisely the purposes and recipients of U.S. arms and then to ascertain that congressional directives and guidelines are adhered to in the obligation and expenditure of funds. In opposition to this, the Carter administration and its supporters in Congress have insisted on the critical need for presidential flexibility for quick and decisive reaction to unexpected challenges in a changing and dangerous world. Restrictive congressional provisions have at times been general, for example, on presidential authority to transfer funds within accounts; other specific restrictions have reflected a congressional view on policy regarding particular issues (such as human rights performance by arms recipients) and corresponding limits or requirements on spending (Turkey, Israel, Chile, South Korea, etc.). These latter specific restrictions serve, by accretion, to define foreign policy as it relates to arms sales. Over the past two years, they have been presumed to support the broad human rights and arms-control doctrines enunciated by the president. But, in the congressional zeal to establish absolute standards of performance by other countries, the ability of the administration to influence congressional policies has actually been strait-jacketed.

There have been distinct schools in Congress with respect to the future of security assistance. The Senate has questioned the general rationale and effectiveness of the program and has been explicit that it wants to end grant military assistance as a "habit" and bureaucratic "addiction." It has twice voted (in 1973 and 1974) to terminate grant military assistance and military advisory groups at the urging of the Senate Foreign Relations Committee: "The United States should provide grant military aid to foreign countries not as a habit, but rather only in specific instances where such assistance is clearly warranted." The House International Relations Committee, on the other hand, has viewed military assistance as "an important tool of foreign policy," and the House has not been willing to join in legislating its phase-out. The House has, however, been active in framing and imposing its position on particular issues at variance with the executive branch on human rights questions. In sum, the assertion of a broadened congressional role in the formulation of arms-transfer policy has diminished the Carter administration's flexibility, led to the growth of constituency policies in the policy area, and thus added to the doubts and confusion of nations dependent on the United States for their security.

RESIDUAL POLITICAL INFLUENCE

Arms sales have been used to political ends throughout the history of the program. The objectives listed earlier might be grouped under the following rubrics: U.S. diplomatic leverage in negotiations, influence with countries, regimes, or leaders; encouraging a pro-U.S. or at least neutral orientation and precluding hostile or uncooperative influences; symbolizing U.S. commitment, and heightening confidence in U.S. support. At present, the political case for arms sales is controversial. As the international arms trade takes on a life and momentum of its own, the political viewpoint that gains will have to be one that recognizes the current, greatly diminished capacity of the United States to influence the decisions or actions of other governments.

Judicious use of military equipment for political purposes can be good diplomacy, moreover. It works when the aid helps recipients do what they want or find to be in their own interests: enabling a moderate Arab ruler to survive (Jordan); proving U.S. even-handedness between Arab states and Israel so the former can more easily negotiate with the United States (Egypt); or providing an alternative to reliance on the Soviet Union (Sudan). Use of aid as pressure, blackmail, or penalty is likely to produce few successes; these uses often have no measurable effect either as warnings or as sobering penalties, and where U.S. administrations have tried to use delays in making military equipment transfers to soften tough negotiating positions (e.g. Israel), they have not been notably successful.

When the United States tries to buy anything carrying political costs to the other country, it again runs into difficulty; the "trading" value of military aid can be limited or illusory. For example, the United States wants allies to stay in alliances (Greece and Turkey), or wants them to stay out of the communist orbit or to reject regimes which are leftist or anti-U.S. (Chile); the United States also desires facilities or overflight rights (Spain, Portugal, Turkey, and Greece); and finally, the U.S. government wants to have "influence," a respectful hearing, or good relations (Indonesia). In practice, this means that the other party, even if it seeks the increment that U.S. security aid can add to its own defense resources, will soon see that it has considerable leverage in this kind of bargaining.

Once the United States has given aid (equipment, supplies, training) it becomes at best a precedent and an argument for continued aid, and at worst a resource at the disposition of the recipient for domestic or external use regardless of the stated purpose for which given. In either case, the United States is not in a strong position to exert political influence. Since, for example, the United States cares more than Greece and Turkey that they stay in NATO, the U.S. government has shown that it will pay a high price for bases, political influence, or harmonious relations with countries which it traditionally maintains friendly ties.

What is often overlooked by the present administration and its supporters is the complex relationship between arms transfers and political influence. The United States still uses military equipment sales to obtain important political or military ends. In particular, U.S. forces need bases, access, or other facilities for which rights are bought rather than provided by the host country as part of its alliance contribution. If payment is sought at rates which are politically rather than economically calculated, on the grounds that a U.S. presence carries domestic or foreign political costs and risks for the host country, that should be the warning signal for a hard reassessment by the executive branch of its need for the facility: first, to see whether its value is really proportionate to the cost and, second, to determine whether the United States can, in such a situation, really have confidence that the facility will be available when needed in a crisis.

The case is similar where arms transfers are being used to buy alliance or other political commitments, "influence," or good relations. When such commodities are put on the auction block—cases in which the support and goodwill of the United States should presumably be in themselves of great security and economic value—the U.S. government should ask why it must pay and whether by paying it is, in fact, obtaining anything beyond the likelihood of having to continue to pay.

These observations do not suggest that arms transfers are always and everywhere without value as a political instrument, but the policy maker must recognize that they are not an effective instrument of general application, nor are they always likely to produce desirable policy results. Moreover, purposes can at times conflict. The United States may have an interest in the security of a nation facing external aggression or internal instability; at the same time, it can have a general interest in personal freedom and representative government and a repugnance for persecution and violent repression.

Sanctions, including the use or threat of aid cutoffs or reduction, are often ineffective; furthermore, there may be cases in which a country has such special ties to the United States, or is the victim of so flagrant an aggression, that the character of the current regime has little weight. In addition, cutting off assistance may well harm the people who are the victims of repression, rather than the repressive regime; the likelihood of this may be increased under the current economic foreign-assistance program, with its emphasis on development activities directed to the poorest strata of society.

Military assistance, conversely, is directed in the first instance at the government rather than the people; as instruments of power, military equipment can actually or in appearance strengthen the capacity of a regime which rules by force to retain its authority. Any conspicuous sanction, such as the cutting off of aid, can serve to distance the United States from a regime engaged in violation of human rights, and to withdraw from such a regime the possibility of arguing that its policy and acts meet no meaningful objection, have no costly consequences, or are condoned in fact by major democratic states. If sanctions are judged in a particular case to be the right course for the United States, cutting off military aid (in the absence of immediate external menace) should be most appropriate, because it does not hurt the people and hits the instruments and status symbols of the regime itself.

The United States cannot dictate to other countries what kind of government or leaders they have, and it should not try to do so, either openly or covertly. Normal diplomatic and commercial relations are in order with any legitimate regime in the absence of active hostility or exceptional viciousness. Aid represents, however, not only substantial support but a political symbolism of some mutual interest as well. Unless it is very clear what the mutual security interest is, the United States has every right to refrain from providing military equipment to a regime which is not merely authoritarian but actively and even cruelly repressive of human rights. Determinations in such matters may be difficult and disputed, but they are worth the time and effort to make, in order that United States purposes in granting assistance not be subject to misrepresentation at home and abroad.

CONCLUSION

Justifications for arms transfers often embody the implicit assumption that constructive purposes related to general U.S. interests constitute sufficient reason for launching a program with a particular country. Even if the purposes and interests are spelled out carefully and fully, more is required: the United States has political and economic interests in varying degrees almost anywhere in the world; there is actual or potential instability in most areas; and the maintenance of peace and stability is an important concern. When arms transfers are proposed, harder tests must be met.

- Will military aid in itself really improve the net security of the recipient or will it lead to a matching buildup by rivals to no net gain?
- Will the benefits correspond to the costs to the United States, costs not only in dollars but in involvement in area problems and the fate of the client, in tensions with other states, in its association with nondemocratic regimes?
- Are there alternative approaches to stability and security—that is, settlement of disputes rather than reciprocal military buildups, recourse to regional or U.N. mechanisms, economic aid or political commitments by the United States when support is essential?
- If questions such as these get uncertain or discouraging answers, is it possible that instabilities will have to work themselves out (perhaps even in a local military test of strength), and is it better to let this happen than to make a local issue into a major one by U.S. involvement commencing with security assistance?

Security assistance is not a prescription for every security or stability problem of a country in which the United States has even major interests. While there are few alternative tools of United States foreign policy available, however, the results of arms transfers can be uncertain, mixed, or, at times, outweighed by the costs.

NOTES

1.*Washington Post*, August 20, 1978, p.1.

2. See K. J. Holsti, *International Politics* (Englewood Cliffs, N.J.: Prentice-Hall, 1977).

3. See P. Farley, S. Kaplan, and W. Lewis, *Arms Across the Sea* (Washington, D.C.: Brookings Institution, 1978), p. 34.

4. U.S. Department of State, *Arms Transfer Policy*. Report for use by the Committee on Foreign Relations, U.S. Senate. Washington, D.C., June 30, 1977, p. 32.

12 ARMS DEALS: WHEN, WHY, AND HOW?

Ingemar Dörfer

INTRODUCTION: ARMS TRANSFERS ARE COMPLEX

In the most perceptive analysis of the arms trade of recent years, Leslie Gelb states, "The arms trade market is virgin territory for diplomacy." In contrast to most do-gooders who think up various schemes to curb the conventional-arms trade, Gelb approaches arms sales as a foreign-policy problem, rather than as an arms-control problem: "Sales are so intertwined with other matters that they have to be treated on a country-by-country basis with decisions based on pragmatic trade offs."[1] Despite the rhetoric of the Carter administration, this has indeed been the policy of the United States recently, a policy largely directed by Gelb.[2] Yet various prescriptions and recipes analyzing the arms trade out of its political context continue to flourish,[3] and although most of these studies are read only by other social scientists about to embark upon similar endeavors, the injection of a modest amount of realism into a study might not be a totally wasted effort; it might even be read by policy makers.

A major arms transaction is an extraordinarily complex affair, often the outcome of years of negotiating between governments. The diplomacy involved is certainly not virgin territory, even if the *study* of such diplomacy is. But not only does the diplomacy of arms transfers remain unexplained, the domestic dimensions of most such transactions have not been explored either; and, more often than not, these dimensions determine the origin, the process, and the outcome of major arms deals. The domestic dimensions not only determine when and how nations wish to buy arms, they also decide what arms are offered and eventually bought. In the case of the advanced industrial nations, where most arms are to be found, the domestic politics of the major states are all-important to the outcome.

This chapter reviews the intricacies that go into any arms deal between advanced nations. When it comes to rich, developing nations, such as Iran or Saudi Arabia, we get to know only the United States' side of the story; but, for example, if the Shah made all the decisions in Iran, there was not that much more to know, and for all practical purposes the point of departure has to be the United States. In fiscal 1977, U.S. arms exports amounted to over $11 billion, more than 50 percent of the world total.[4] Next to the oil-producing nations, by far the largest market is Western Europe, Canada, Japan, and Australia;[5] yet arms deals between these nations are the least studied.

The United States is so important because what happens in Washington often determines what Bonn or Rome or Tokyo (to cite three World War II enemies) in the end buys, but, of course, what happens in Bonn and Rome and Tokyo is also important. It is also very difficult to find out,[6] and that is exactly why so few studies exist of how various capitals perceive the same problem in a specific, rather than a general, sense. In an in-depth study—of which the present analysis, for limitations of space, can only be a preview— the issue must be scrutinized from as many angles as there are capitals and major corporations involved. The capitals and their relations are obviously multifaceted, and we are dealing with what Richard Neustadt has called in an apt phrase, the "friendship of machines."[7]

Most of the examples used here are from the "arms deal of the century": the selling of 348 General Dynamics F-16 air-combat fighters to Norway, Denmark, the Netherlands, and Belgium in 1975 for a price of $2.1 billion. When Secretary of Defense James Schlesinger signed the Memorandum of Understanding with his four European colleagues on June 10, 1975, much had happened in Washington that a naive observer would not link to the memorandum at all. In order to proceed in a logical fashion, axioms relating to the weapons-acquisition process in the United States are established first; the implications for other advanced nations buying their weapons abroad then will also be shown. In doing this, the primary unit of analysis will be the political institutions involved.

THE UNITED STATES AS PROVIDER: MILITARY SERVICES

Services Want New Weapons Systems

Military services try to find missions in life and navies and the air forces are, in particular, strongly dependent on expensive new weapons systems to fulfill those missions. Especially in the United States, with its traditional emphasis on the cheap technological fix and firepower, this has been the tradition.[8] Both services have glamor weapons systems: the aircraft carrier* and ballistic-missile submarine for the navy and the manned bomber for the air force. Since those weapons systems are the symbols of a superpower, they do not usually figure in arms deals, although one of the most publicized arms deals was of this nature: the conversion in 1962 at Nassau in the Bahamas of the Skybolt missile to the Polaris ballistic-missile submarine, with all its implications for the U.S.-British alliance.[9] The foremost power symbol of medium and small powers, on the other hand, has been the jet fighter, and the transfer of combat aircraft is the most prominent and expensive part of the arms-trade business.

The U.S. Air Force and the U.S. Navy obviously plan, develop, and procure jet fighters without much concern for the international market; in this, their focus is different from that of the corporations that produce the fighters. Because of new missions, new demands of old missions, or simple obsolescence of old inventory, the services are constantly planning new combat aircraft. Within the services, the "brown-shoe" navy (the 13 carrier navy admirals) and the Tactical Air Command (TAC—the generals in charge of the 26-wing Tactical Air Force) are the ones interested in new jet fighters, but rarely are they interested in the same fighter.

Services Always Have Favorites

"True" services have a flagship: the Dreadnought of the British Navy of 1910, the Panther tank of the Wehrmacht Panzer Army of 1943, the B-52 bomber of the U.S. Strategic Air Command (SAC) in the 1950s. The brown-shoe navy and the Tactical Air Force of 1975 had the Tomcat and the Eagle. The F-14 Tomcat, with a planned procurement for the U.S. Navy of 509 (as of 1978), suggests the essence of the carrier navy since its purpose is the most essential of all, to protect the carriers against enemy attack. † At a current unit-program cost (in fiscal 1975 dollars) of $23.3 million, the F-14 remains a technologically marvelous weapons platform for the Phoenix missile, and in the carrier navy only budgetary restraints will lead to the procurement of lesser aircraft. The F-15 Eagle is the air force's answer to the Tomcat as the all-weather, main fighter plane of the TAC. With 733 planes to be procured, the unit-program cost of the F-15 is $13.7 million. Efforts to force the navy and the air force to choose one plane or to buy one together have always

---

*Traditionally, there are 13 capital ships in the U.S. Navy; formerly these were battleships and now they are carriers.

† To someone not grounded in navy thinking the glamour plane of the carrier fleet would be the strike aircraft, not the guardian planes. This goes to show the pitfalls of not having a Navy training.

failed, as Secretary McNamara failed in forcing the services to pick the F-111 in 1962.[10] The services, after all, thrive on such rivalry, and the F-14 and the F-15 will remain service favorites until something more advanced comes along.

Innovative Systems Pose Threats to Favorites

Once a favorite is established the services want as many as possible; weapons systems that pose a threat to the favorite are avoided and, if forced upon the service, are kept on the "back burner." Since the services are traditional and not innovative, such systems have difficulty finding supporters in the higher echelons of the services, and they become, so to speak, orphans. Often the orphans are pushed by a group not in the mainstream of the service, for example, the "fighter Mafia" in the air force and the Marine Corps in the navy; such was the case with the F-16 in the air force and the F-17/18 in the navy. The air force at first insisted in calling the YF-16* a technology demonstrator and refused to fund it beyond April 1975. When it finally was made clear to the generals by the Secretary of Defense that one of the lightweight fighter prototypes would go into the air force inventory, the air force as an institution immediately began to take measures to make the orphan respectable: the designation was changed from lightweight fighter to air-combat fighter, and a special Fighter Modernization Study Group was assembled to bless the orphan. After the F-16 was formally selected by the air force, the colonel managing the program was exchanged for a brigadier general who, when the program grew even further, was promoted to major general, a program-management rank reserved for the major programs (favorites) of the air force, such as the F-15 and the B-1.

Timing is very important here. Once a favorite has been established and production is well underway, it is easier to adopt the orphan since it no longer poses such a threat to the favorite. Once an orphan is adopted by the services every effort is made to accommodate it. A configuration steering group had already been appointed for the lightweight fighter *before* the choice had been made between the competing YF-16 and YF-17. The task of the steering group was to give the new fighter missions in the air force, since none had been thought of for the technology demonstrator. Another purpose was ostensibly to prevent the engineers from "growing" the plane, adding specifications and avionics (*aviation-electronics*) so that it would become heavier and more expensive. In fact, the air force told the traditional field commanders at TAC that they would grow the aircraft at the same time they told the Office of the Secretary of Defense that they would not do so; as a result, the air force has grown the aircraft, but not substantially.

---

*The Y designates a prototype.

The reason that the F-16 has not grown very much has to do with its relationship to the favorite F-15. Although it is quite feasible to do so, the air force has not put Sparrow radar missiles on the F-16. If one did, the F-16 could do almost everything the F-15 does (and some better), but since the F-16 costs $7.6 million and the F-15 costs $15.5 million (unit procurement cost in 1977 dollars)[11] that would make the favorite look bad, and its production line might be shortened. Moreover, the fact that the YF-17 had a higher growth potential in its air frame in 1975 was one of the reasons, although far from the major one, why the air force picked the YF-16; that is, the YF-17 in the long run would have posed a greater threat to the favorite.

Services Also Need Numbers

The air force leadership accepted the F-16 because it was promised to regain its former force structure of 26 wings; since the old force structure had been cast in terms of number of wings, rather than budget, there was a tremendous incentive to buy the most expensive and advanced plane available without any thought of the cost. Secretary of Defense Schlesinger changed that in his first budget, prepared in the fall of 1973. The reason why the navy refused for so long to choose a less expensive complement to the F-14 Tomcat is that the navy believed it could get away with all 780 Tomcats originally scheduled. It was only because the navy was forced to embark upon an actual source-selection process in the summer of 1974 that the moment of truth came nearer. Although the navy refused to be ready with its selection when the air force was ready in January 1975, the Secretary and Deputy Secretary of Defense in fact ordered the navy to pick one of the YF-16 and YF-17 derivatives in May of that year. Since it was obvious that the F-14 production run would be shortened, since both the Defense Department leadership and Congress had ordered it to make a choice, and since the research and development (R&D) money for an alternative to the F-14 might otherwise be taken out of its budget, the navy reluctantly picked the YF-17 in May 1975. It then proceeded to try to kill the airplane during every budget cycle until 1978, while adding F-14 Tomcats to the inventory at the same time; since the R&D money invested in the F-18 (as the old YF-17 now is called) has increased every year, however, the effort has become more difficult and is probably now impossible.

The Demand for Different Airplanes

In September 1974, the Senate Appropriations Committee stated that

$20,000,000 was provided for Navy Air Combat Fighter rather than VFAX. Adaptation of Air Force Air Combat Fighter... is the prerequisite for use of the funds provided future funding is to be contingent upon capability of the Navy to produce a derivative of the selected Air Force Air Combat Fighter design.[12]

On January 13, 1975 the air force announced the selection of the F-16 as its air-combat fighter. On May 2, the navy announced the selection of the F-18. The Comptroller General's Office rejected the protest of the losing Ling Temco Vought (LTV) Aerospace Corporation that the navy had violated the guidelines of Congress. The political efforts of LTV and parts of the Texas delegation in Congress to kill the winning F-18 design, in order to either have another round of evaluation or to continue with the old Grumman F-14 and LTV A-7 production runs, were also defeated.

The story is an old one. In 1962, Secretary of Defense Robert McNamara had tried in vain to force the navy to select the F-111 airplane after the air force had selected it, and in 1973 Deputy Secretary of Defense Clements had tried to order a fly-off between the F-14 and the F-15. Despite guidance from Congress to make the air force and the navy air-combat fighters a common development effort, both services in fact tried to avoid selection of the same aircraft. The air force did not want the navy plane because it had already been forced to pick two navy planes in the last decade (the F-4 and A-7). Moreover, it included features that were unnecessary and hence expensive for the air force plane; the navy, as always, claimed that to be carrier-capable, an aircraft needs special features such as robustness and resistance to sea-water corrosion that are unnecessary in an air force plane.

In this the air force has a constant disadvantage since it always can be claimed that carrier-specific capabilities are necessary for the navy, whereas there are no air force specific capabilities. The F-4 Phantom in 1965 and the A-7 Corsair II in 1969 were thus two navy planes that had to be adopted by the air force. Since both are essentially attack aircraft and this was the primary mission of the air force in Vietnam, the adoption went more smoothly than otherwise. In 1974, the air force saw the navy selection of a common aircraft as another threat; hence, air force personnel deliberately and repeatedly briefed high Defense Department officials on air-force-designed navy planes in order to prevent the navy from briefing the department on navy-designed air force planes. Each service kept officers in the other camp, ostensibly to coordinate the selection process of the same aircraft, but, in fact, to make sure that this would *not* happen.

Just as it is important within one service, timing is important between the services. The air force was anxious to go ahead and select its own plane in January 1975, knowing that if the navy caught up the navy's plane might be selected for both; the navy, at the time, was happy to let the air force go it alone. But the air force was also eager to seek outside hostages for the plane selected, and the European nations were ideal for the purpose since the standardization argument could be used; this turned out to be a shrewd calculation on the part of the air force. When the navy was about to announce its decision to pick the YF-17, fourteen weeks later, high officials in DDR&E (Directorate of Defense Research and Engineering) tried to have the air force evaluate its own decision once more to see if commonality could not be achieved after all, that is, reversing the air force decision and selecting the navy plane. The air force then could point to the negotiations almost completed in Europe as an impossible obstacle to such a move. In this perspective the "arms deal of the century" can be seen as a Washington air force/navy game—with the outside world as a side show—providing bindings, deadlines, and hostages. A final factor supporting service pride is the effort of military and political leaders to keep production options open, thereby keeping a certain number of aerospace firms, including military jet-engine firms, in business; several planes achieve that purpose better than one. Several airplane developments at one time also are in tacit competition to keep the services themselves in check. Should the F-15 grow too much or become too expensive, the F-16 would become a threat, exactly as the F-18 is a threat to the F-14. But the landbased version of the F-18, the F-18L, also forms a corrective system against which the development of the F-16 can be measured. In this way the various systems can keep each other in check and the production lines in business.

THE UNITED STATES AS PROVIDER: CORPORATIONS

Corporations Want to Stay in Business

In an unconventional piece of analysis, Jim Kurth predicted six years ago which major aerospace companies would get which contracts in the mid-1970s.[13] Although he was right only in 50 percent of the cases, the two concepts he formulated—the "follow-on imperative" and the "bail-out imperative"—have been useful for this kind of prediction. He was right, for instance, in awarding the lightweight fighter contract to General Dynamics' plant at Fort Worth, Texas; his seven big air frame contractors also remained prominent in fiscal 1975 with defense sales ranging from 2 billion to 370 million dollars: Lockheed, Boeing, McDonnell-Douglas, Grumman, General Dynamics, Rockwell International, and LTV. Not included in Kurth's list are the two major military jet-engine companies, United Technologies (Pratt & Whitney) and General Electric. Nor is Northrop included, although it ranked above LTV with military sales of $600 million in 1975. The exclusion of Northrop in Kurth's article goes to prove one of the points to be made here. Most U.S. corporations in the armaments field are U.S.-oriented with the U.S. armed services as their main customers.

Northrop is different, however, being a very cosmopolitan corporation with major sales abroad and having little recent experience with the U.S. Air Force as a customer for major weapons systems, with the exception of the T-38 trainer. Some companies (e.g., Grumman and LTV) are traditionally navy companies, while others (General Dynamics and Boeing) are air force companies. Very few, such as Northrop, are neither, and in the past to be neither has often been proven harmful to competition in the U.S. market. This is an area where economics helps to explain some of the outcomes of various weapons-systems awards, but also an area where anthropological studies of tribal societies go a long way to explain the rest.

Corporations Have a Home Base

Fighter planes are not made in heaven, but in Congress. Large defense contracts provide jobs, taxes, and R&D resources to states and urban centers. It is no coincidence, as the Soviets put it, that the two companies competing for the air combat fighter contract were based in the two major aerospace centers of the nation: General Dynamics of Dallas-Fort Worth and Northrop of Los Angeles. In each year's appropriations cycle, from these and other states, Congressmen make sure that the bounty is evenly split and, clearly, in this game some states and corporations do better than others. For the time being the champion of political clout is General Dynamics with headquarters in traditionally strongly air-power-oriented St. Louis—home of McDonnell-Douglas Corporation, and former Senator Stuart Syming-ton—with several divisions in California, one division each in Texas, Florida, and Massachusetts, and with the ownership controlled by the Crown family of Cook County, Illinois.* Despite the greater power of some states to secure aerospace contracts, largesse is also frowned upon. It would have taken tremendous political doing to award the navy air-combat fighter to LTV and Texas in 1975 only four months after the Dallas-Fort Worth area already had won the air force contract through General Dynamics. This is one but not the only, explanation why Congress had not succeeded in killing the F-18, even though the navy was only lukewarm.

Aerospace Corporations Have Different Marketing Skills

Of the four major aerospace firms competing in the arms deal in question, two—Northrop and Dassault of France—were cosmopolitan, worldly, and sophisticated, with excellent information about the outside world. General Dynamics and Saab (Sweden) had little of this. Yet General

---

*The Trident submarine is produced by the Electric Boat Division of General Dynamics in Groton, Connecticut. As the main symbol of the future U.S. strategic deterrent it would go ahead, even if its local power base were in Idaho or Iowa.

Dynamics landed the contract and opened the door to a long series of exports that eventually might lead to 2000 F-16s in foreign inventories.*

Clearly this does not fit the stereotype image of clever arms merchants selling their products in competition with equally clever foreigners. The reason for the outcome is simple: the Europeans, this time around, wanted the same aircraft as the U.S. Air Force and were willing to wait for the United States decision before they committed themselves. The strategies of the two U.S. aerospace firms were different, but were the only ones each could pursue given their traditions. Whereas Northrop tried to conquer the foreign market independently of Washington and got into the lightweight-fighter competition indirectly, the only option open to Genral Dynamics was to win at home, with the U.S. Air Force. The air force, realizing that the Europeans were about to go ahead and pick the Northrop F-18L Cobra, agreed to accelerate its own decision, in order to prevent the Europeans from preempting the decision and selecting the Cobra, thereby forcing it upon the air force for the sake of standardization. Hence, the lack of marketing skill that General Dynamics showed in the beginning did not matter for the signing of the Memorandum of Understanding since most of the negotiating was between governments and in order to make sure that the Europeans would pick its plane, the air force did most of the negotiating on behalf of the U.S. government. General Dynamics' inexperience *did* matter when it came time to work out the specifics of the deal, since there was more to it than was initially perceived by the United States and European negotiators; the management of the project, the choice of the co-producers, and the fulfillment of offset agreements turned out to be much more complex than anticipated.

NATIONS AS CUSTOMERS

The United States, then, is not a monolithic unit when it comes to the selling and buying of arms; nor are other states. The difference is one of scale and thus, perhaps by definition, one of asymmetry; that is, the President of the United States very rarely acts as a salesperson for weapons systems (but does sometimes take the role of arbitrator through the National Security Council), while the French president, the British prime minister, and (a little more discreetly) the German chancellor do so quite often. In these and smaller nations, weapons systems are definitely too important to be left to the "soldiers"; the cabinets make the decisions both when it comes to selling

---

*Admittedly General Dynamics was helped by the F-16 engine company, United Technologies, which has vast international experience and a share of the continental Fokker-VFW stock. Note that, in contrast to the F-18 Hornet and F-18L Cobra, no name has been found for the F-16 even now.

and buying. Despite this, the institutional players are the same, but asymmetry, however, makes them behave differently.

Services Want New Weapons Systems

Weapons systens in European armed forces grow old, too, and although the number of aircraft in each European air force is much smaller, there is often the same type of airplane in several air forces, making a coordinated purchasing effort feasible. The sale of 348 F-16 air-combat fighters to Norway, Denmark, Belgium, and the Netherlands has, for instance, been named a Starfighter (F-104) replacement. What was really to be replaced initially in these air forces was 220 F-104 Starfighters in Belgium and the Netherlands, 75 F-5 Freedom Fighters in Norway, and 50 F-100 Super Sabres in Denmark—a total of 345 aircraft. After the delivery the inventory of the four air forces would be composed of: Belgium, F-16s and Mirage Vs; Netherlands, F-16s and NF-5 Freedom Fighters; Norway, F-16s, F-104 Starfighters, and RF-5A Freedom Fighters; and Denmark, F-16s, F-104 Starfighters, and J-35 Draken. So much for standardization.

Should the four nations all replace their remaining combat aircraft with the F-16, they will all be standardized around 1988, sixteen years after the Netherlands began her search for a Starfighter successor. This goes to show the large time span of not only the development and production of combat aircraft, but also the time purchase from abroad takes. Even more, it shows how inexorably the inventory of an air force is linked to time. Different types of aircraft have entered in different years, and they will become obsolete at different times; although many air forces keep obsolete airplanes too long, and although airplanes considered obsolete can be serviceable, metal fatigue, if nothing else, sets a time limit.

Different-aged inventories and her own development of the Multi-Role Combat Aircraft (MRCA) was the reason why Germany was not involved with the other European nations in choosing the F-16. Since Germany is likely to want a two-engine aircraft (the F-16 has one) and since the German Air Force provides most of the aircraft in the 2nd Allied Tactical Air Force to which both the Netherlands and Belgium belong, little standardization will be achieved between the air forces on this part of the central front. European air forces want new airplanes because the old ones got too old. NATO studies of specialization have done little more than confirm national political facts of life, for instance, formulated in the Hague, as was the case with the NATO study eliminating the deep penetration and high altitude air defense role for the Dutch Air Force in 1973[14] Many European air forces will find missions to fit the aircraft they buy in the following sequence: by observing approaching obsolescence and finding missions for a new plane; by buying a new plane; or if the mission does not fit the new plane, by redefining the mission.

Some Europeans Want Standardization

In 1974–75, General John Vogt, commander of U.S. air forces in Europe and all NATO air forces in central Europe, fought a vigorous campaign against the acquisition of the weather-limited F-16 by the four European nations. Why did they all buy the very plane he did not want, despite his being the field commander? One reason was the elevation of the F-16's status upon its acceptance by U.S. forces.*

Another reason for the European acceptance of the F-16 was that the decisions in Europe were made in Oslo, Copenhagen, the Hague, and Brussels, and not within the NATO structure which has no power. These small European states that have no development capability in the field of aeronautics want standardization, and by that they mean standardization with the major NATO nations; in aircraft that is often the United States. In 1974 these nations, above all, did not want to repeat the Starfighter situation of 1958 when European air forces bought Starfighters while the U.S. Air Force in the end bought very few.[16] Hence, one of the demands of the four F-16 nations was the procurement and deployment by the U.S. Air Force of substantial numbers of the F-16, including the deployment of at least two wings to Europe. The cabinets, if not the parliaments, of the smaller NATO nations were anxious to preserve the U.S. commitment in the 1970s, and buying the same plane as the U.S. Air Force was one way of doing so.

The European services, being shrewd players too, were invited to observe the proceedings of the Source Selection Acquisition Council selecting the winner at Wright Patterson Field in Dayton, Ohio. The services would tell European political leaders that they had an input into the selection, while Congress was assured that they had been observers only, with no say whatsoever. Since the Europeans, for various reasons, did want a U.S. plane they even managed to switch their allegiance from the F-17 (Cobra derivative) to the F-16, as did the Dutch when they understood which way the U.S. Air Force was tilting. Although they had worked with Northrop for six years in designing the Cobra, being on the right side in the United States is what eventually mattered.

In the face of standardization, the mission orientation of the European services had to give. Given the different geographical situations of the four

---

*An increase in the production run of the F-16 served two purposes: it decreased the unit cost of the aircraft and also provided a larger production quantity of F-100 engines. One of the major factors in the selection of the F-16 had been the fact that it shares the F-100 engine with the F-15. Problems in performance and cost of the F-100 engine had already surfaced in air force testimony in 1975, and thus, the selection of the F-16 and the production increase offered by the sale to the Europeans provided an outlet for rectifying these problems. The subsequent announcement by the U.S. Air Force of plans to buy a total of 1388 F-16s further diluted the engine problem.[15]

F-16 nations it was impossible to formulate a common mission for the planes to be acquired, much to the irritation of Dassault and Saab-Scania who were used to selling aircraft specified to a mission at home and abroad. But since, for instance, Norway and Denmark needed air-to-sea capability and Belgium and Holland, relying on the U.S. F-15s needed no all-weather capability, such a task became impossible. In the choice between a missionized aircraft, such as the F-5E Tiger, and a more advanced fighter, such as the F-16, the Dutch Air Force was bound to choose the latter. They wanted the F-16 because it was the more advanced plane from a technical point of view, whereas the politicians chose it because it meant standardization with the United States and it also seemed to be the least expensive.

European Corporations Exist Too

In Western Europe only Great Britain, France, Germany, Italy, and Sweden have full-fledged aircraft industries with indigenous R&D capability. Since at least the first three nations make a conscious effort to maintain that capability, preaching the marvels of standardization and, hence, U.S. combat aircraft to them will remain a waste of time. Political developments are, of course, mirrored in this process; 13 years ago the British aircraft industry was dealt a blow through the canceling of the TSR2, whereas the then tiny German air-frame industry, once satisfied with Starfighter construction under license, is now turning out MRCAs and Airbus 300s. It is virtually impossible to sell fighter planes to nations with their own aircraft industries without going into co-production or licensing schemes.* Here the various corporations do not have to compete for the overall contract as in the United States; rather, their opinion about the foreign corporations trying to sell a nation combat aircraft and the arrangements they can offer the host companies are sought by their respective governments. Since the European armaments industry has been so split this has traditionally not helped any particular company but, with the European integration now underway, efforts have been made to consolidate the aircraft industries also. In the case of the F-16 choice, both the aircraft industries of the Netherlands (Fokker-VFW) and Belgium (SABCA, Fairey, Fabrique National) were in the beginning strongly in favor of the Mirage. The chairman of Fokker-VFW tried to use the occasion for closer cooperation and eventual merger between the Dutch-German Fokker-VFW, the Belgian SABCA, and the French Dassault. The French, knowing their advantage in playing the

---

*According to the Memorandum of Understanding, 40 percent of the procurement value of the 348 European aircraft will be produced in Europe; 10 percent of the procurement value of the 650 U.S. aircraft will also be produced in Europe as well as 15 percent of all third-country sales. The minimum co-production of the first 348 European aircraft is, therefore, 58 percent $(40\% \times 348 + 10\% \times 650 = 204)$.

European card, tried to use the same argument vis-à-vis the four potential customers, but too heavily in Denmark as it turned out, and without success in Norway, which does not belong to the Common Market.

In the end the opinions and lobbying of the corporations neutralized each other because they were split on the issue, because they were competing for the co-production offered by the winning U.S. companies, and because the decision ultimately was a political one. In the end it was also a triumph for the services, of the air forces over the corporations. Neither the Dutch Air Force nor the Flemish part of the Belgian Air Force wanted a French plane and managed to neutralize their opponents in business and government by giving the winning Americans local information and their own political leaders U.S. information—an unusual application of the "two-way street." To Norway and Denmark, the corporate game on the continent proved the irony of entanglement. Since both nations lack an aircraft industry, buying the F-16 off the shelf would have saved them over $1 million per aircraft. But since they bought the F-16 in a package deal that enabled them to buy a plane at a time when many politicians were against further defense expenditures, the glories of offset and co-production were also preached in Scandinavia.

CONCLUSION: POLITICIANS WANT DIFFERENT THINGS

In 1975 five capitals announced that they would acquire the General Dynamics F-16 Air Combat Fighter. The reasons in the various cases were the following:

January 13   United States   650 aircraft

● A less expensive complement to the F-15 Eagle leading to force structure growth to meet a perceived Soviet threat.
● A fighter suitable to allied needs, advancing commonality and leading to U.S. revenue in exports.
● Air Force favorite (symbolized in flight test results) compared to less service oriented Northrop F-17 prototype.
● Need for follow-on production at almost empty production line at Fort Worth, thereby keeping the future aerospace options of the nation more open.

March 21   Norway   72 aircraft

● Replacing obsolete combat aircraft and strengthening defense in the North.

- Symbolizing American commitment to Norway in a worsening national security situation.
- F-16 more advanced and less expensive than French and Swedish competitors.
- Norway an overt example for other three consortium nations to follow.

May 24 Netherlands 102 aircraft

- Replacing obsolete aircraft.
- Showing NATO solidarity.
- F-16 more advanced and only aircraft within budget already allocated to this particular purpose.
- Offering good co-production and off-set agreements with seller, to be negotiated in detail.

May 28 Denmark 58 aircraft

- Replacing obsolete aircraft.
- Showing NATO solidarity in a situation when things have gone too far and backing out will look bad.
- F-16 more advanced and less expensive than competitors.

June 7 Belgium 116 aircraft

- Replacing obsolete aircraft.
- Offering good co-production and off-set agreements with seller.
- Avoiding 1968 situation when Belgium and the Netherlands chose different aircraft, and also avoiding breakup of consortium.

The complexity of this, or any other, arms transaction shows that arms deals usually are not deals at all. Rather they form a web of negotiations between service, corporate, and political interests with numerous players whose stakes sometimes coincide, but quite often are detrimental to each other. If the timing is right something can be accomplished, if not, a nation might end up strengthening its cavalry instead of buying fighter jets.[17]

Clearly, it is impossible to analyze such situations with simplistic slogans, or to prescribe simple solutions when there is no consensus on the nature of the problem (or whether there is a problem in the first place). Some of the recent scholarly literature in international relations has stressed the importance of low politics, of economic and social affairs, rather than the traditional high politics of military security and diplomacy.[18] Should the low politics advocates be right, arms deals are, indeed, exactly that, a frivolous expenditure of the taxpayers' money to no other purpose than to please the military and enrich the military-industrial complex. But if the cabinets of small, peaceful European democracies refuse to believe that and buy arms for other reasons, as they did in 1975, the low politics theorists are either wrong, or out of touch with what is called, for lack of better terminology, political reality.

NOTES

1. Leslie H. Gelb: "Arms Sales," *Foreign Policy* 25 (1976–77): p.5.

2. One of the few exceptions has been the refusal to sell LTV A-7 Corsair II attack planes to Pakistan, an example Gelb uses to illustrate a potentially harmful arms transfer; see Gelb, "Arms Sales," pp. 12–13.

3. Andrew Pierre, "International Restraints on Conventional Arms Transfers," in Jane O. Sharpe, ed., *Opportunities for Disarmament* (Washington, D.C.: Carnegie Endowment for International Peace, 1978) pp. 47–60; and consistently all publications of the Stockholm International Peace Research Institute (SIPRI). Much more reasonable but still on the prescriptive side is Anne H. Cahn, Joseph J. Kruzel, Peter Dawkins, Jacques Huntzinger: *Controlling Future Arms Trade* (New York: McGraw-Hill, Council on Foreign Relations, 1977).

4. Tom Gervasi, *Arsenal of Democracy: American Arms Available for Export* (New York: Grove Press 1978), p. 9; his introductory chapter is the best published overview of U.S. sales procedures.

5. In fiscal 1977, 75 percent ($8.4 billion out of a total of $11.2 billion) worth of military sales agreements went to the Middle East; only $1.3 billion or 12 percent went to advanced industrial nations. Clearly this is a temporary phenomenon that is bound to change. See U.S. Congress, House, Committee on International Relations, Subcommittee on International Security and Scientific Affairs, *Conventional Arms Transfer Policy: Background Information*, 95th Cong., 2d sess., February 1, 1978, pp. 157–58.

6. Graham Allison has this to say about the information cost: "Some observers (particularly players in the game) rely on a version of Model III [organizational politics] for their own government's behavior, while retreating to Model I [rational actor] analyses of other nations." See Graham T. Allison, *Essence of Decision—Explaining the Cuban Missile Crisis* (Boston: Little, Brown, 1971), p. 251.

7. Richard E. Neustadt, *Alliance Politics* (New York: Columbia University Press, 1970). p. 76.

8. The important role of the services is confirmed by Graham T. Allison and Frederick A. Morris in "Armaments and Arms Control: Exploring the Determinants of Military Weapons," vol. 104 *Daedalus* (1975): 99–129.

9. Neustadt, *Alliance Politics.*

10. See Robert J. Art, *The TFX Decision: McNamara and the Military* (Boston: Little, Brown 1968), and "TFX: The Commonality Decision," Kennedy School of Government (Cambridge, Mass. 1974).

11. USAF, SAR Summary for Aircraft Systems, USAF fact sheet, December 31, 1977.

12. U.S. Congress, Senate, Committee on Appropriations, *Lightweight Fighter Aircraft Program*, 93d Cong., 2d sess., September 18, 1974.

13. James R. Kurth, "Why We Buy the Weapons We Do," *Foreign Policy* 11 (1973):33–56.

14. The Dutch Yellow Book explaining the Dutch F-16 decision notes the 300-million-guilder ($130 million) saving achieved through the omission of these missions. See *De keuze van een opvolger voor de F-104G voor de Koniklijke Luchtmacht* (The Hague: Ministry of Defense, 1975), p. 4.

15. *Status of the F-16 Aircraft Program*, PSAD-77-41, and *Status of the Air Force's F-16 Program*, PSAD-78-36 (Washington, D.C.: Government Printing Office, 1977 and 1978); and "Pratt and Whitney's Engine Problem," *Fortune*, November 6, 1978.

16. Of 2,872 Starfighters built, 100 served with the U.S. Air National Guard in 1963–66 and 19 are still in service with the Guard. All others form the backbone of 15 allied air forces, including those in the F-16 consortium. See Gervasi, *Arsenal of Democracy*, pp. 72–75.

17. Sepp Moser, *Operation Null: Die Schweitz Sucht Ein Kampfflugzeug* (Zurich: Flamberg Verlag, 1972).

18. An excellent and skeptical exposition of the high-low politics theme is John J. Weltman, "On the Obsolescence of War: An Essay in Policy and Theory," vol. 18 *International Studies Quarterly*, December 1974: 395–416.

PART FOUR

THE NATION STATE
LEVEL II—
RECIPIENT STATES

13 ARMS TRANSFERS AND ECONOMIC DEVELOPMENT: SOME RESEARCH AND POLICY ISSUES

Stephanie G. Neuman

INTRODUCTION

In recent years, the international trade in arms has taken on increasing military, political, and economic importance. Total arms sales have risen to over $20 billion per year, the United States accounting for more than 50 percent of this amount.[1] Front-line sophisticated military technology is diffusing at a rapid pace throughout the world.

For policy makers who must make decisions regarding these transfers of technology, the ramifications of these developments are not well understood. For example, they do not know what long-run impacts particular military-transfer programs have upon social, economic, and political developments within recipient states or how they affect the supplier's security interests in the region. They are undecided whether military assistance and sales programs act to promote socioeconomic development, or to hinder it, and how the socioeconomic consequences of these programs affect the internal stability of the recipients and the long-term policy interests of the United States. They are also divided by the moral imperative to seek arms controls and the strategic and economic benefits which make arms transfers attractive to seller and buyer alike.

Curiously, despite the importance of the issue, there has been little empirical research on the connection between economic development and arms transfers. The result has been that policy makers, academics, and various interested publics have been engaged in emotional arguments, enlightened by few facts, which have become increasingly heated over the years.

The Debate: The Positive versus Negative Effects of Military Technological Transfers

What little research does exist on the subject is, for the most part, a collection of unexamined intuitive impressions published primarily in policy papers and media reports. A majority of policy makers, academics, journalists, and the U.S. public hold that defense expenditures are inherently wasteful and, at best, a necessary evil.[2] The "guns vs. butter" analogy is used in the economic context of scarcity of resources and opportunity costs.[3] These analysts maintain that the buying of arms utilizes scarce foreign exchange and resources that could be used for more constructive developmental purposes in the Third World.

Even military grant aid programs, unlike economic assistance, require expenditures for building infrastructure, the diversion of skilled personnel from the civilian sector, and operation and maintenance costs not covered by military programs. Whatever spin-off effects military expenditures may have, these observers argue, they cannot be as productive as direct investment in development. Furthermore, they contend, large-scale arms transfers provoke regional arms races which precipitate wars, instability, and conflicts—all of which negatively affect not only the developing countries' economic capabilities and growth, but the national interests of the United States as well.

On the other hand, recent research indicates that the relationship between economic growth and military expenditures may not be totally negative. Emile Benoit's study concludes that defense expenditures may have a favorable influence on economic development (as measured by gross domestic product [GDP]).[4] Luigi Einaudi et al. also found that higher defense expenditures were not associated with lower growth rates.[5] But because these findings are based on macrostatistical comparisons of a large number of countries they are neither definitive nor explanatory. Why there should be a relationship between defense expenditures and economic growth and what that relationship is can be explained only intuitively by the authors.

To a minority in the academic and policy-making communities arms-transfer programs have obvious positive effects on the developmental prospects of developing countries. These analysts believe that critics of the arms trade overlook the possible long-term dynamic consequences that military transfers may have for nonindustrial societies.[6] It is necessary, they maintain, to take a long-range view in order to perceive developmental progress. Arms-transfer programs are geared to improving technical proficiencies, whereas economic-assistance programs may have tended to take the economic situation in developing nations as static, gearing projects and plants to, and thereby perpetuating, existing technical levels.[7]

Furthermore, according to these analysts, possession of weapons does not necessarily cause wars. They point to examples illustrating both sides of the argument (e.g., Turkey and Greece and Pakistan and India, on the one hand; Iran and Iraq and the United States and the Soviet Union, on the other), which suggest that arms transfers may reflect rather than create interstate hostilities;[8] besides, deterrence, rather than war, is the name of the diplomatic game in the twentieth century, they claim. Conventional-arms transfers may, in fact, generate stability rather than war.

The debate continues, and while there is still no consensus, even critics of the arms trade concede that military technological transfers are of some benefit to the civilian economy. The challenging, and as yet unanswered, question is whether they make a net favorable contribution to development.

Research Constraints

One reason for the dearth of research is the interdisciplinary nature of the problem. Academics and policy makers are trained in a particular discipline, methodology, and vocabulary. Given the paper explosion of the twentieth century, most can barely keep up with developments in their own specialty, let alone another. Little wonder then that questions which require a broader expertise receive little systematic attention.

Much of the academic and policy-making literature relating to the effects of arms transfers on socioeconomic development is divided between two main disciplines: economic development theory—which concerns itself with growth in the civilian sector—formulated by economists, and descriptive (and often normative) analyses of who buys which arms where, why, and for how much—written by political scientists and security-studies analysts.

These two fields are subdivided still further. For example, some economists have developed the transfer of technology into a distinct specialty, with its own extensive literature. Within security studies, arms-transfer specialists are distinguished from strategic and policy theorists; often arms-transfer analysts further segregate themselves into conventional and nuclear weapons specialists. And if one wishes to accurately define the state of the field, one must subdivide again into methodological preference groups—those using quantitative and those using qualitative approaches to their subject. Each subdivision creates its own vocabulary and produces publications understood and read primarily by others within the same field.

Each discipline is like a discrete set of Chinese puzzle boxes. There is little communication between parts, but even less between the two wholes. The debate, thus far, is being carried on between people who neither speak, read, nor understand each other's language.

A second reason for the lack of empirical research is the intractable nature of the problem. Finding a causal relationship between two discrete variables is challenging enough for the hard sciences when laboratory conditions can be created to block out extraneous "noise" from the environment. But social scientists rarely find such conditions in the real world. Unlike laboratory procedures, social processes cannot be held constant while other factors are allowed to vary for the benefit of the observer.

For example, in order to determine how arms affect development, not only must relevant variables somehow be identified in a dynamic, changing, multivariate society, but their cause-and-effect relationships must be established. This has proven to be very difficult. The rise in GNP observed by Benoit, for instance, may have had only a coincidental relationship to defense expenditures; some other totally unidentified factor may have linked the two in an as yet not understood relationship.[9] Norwood Russell Hanson's use of the variables clock winding and sleep in his discussion of causality succinctly defines the problem.

There is no causal relation between my winding the clock and then going to sleep, though no two events occur with more monotonous regularity. One could predict my going to sleep from watching me wind the clock, or retrodict my having wound the clock from observing me asleep. But this is risky, like amateur weather forecasting or angling advice.[10]

To date, it is not clear whether the observed connections between arms and development are causal sequences or mere coincidence.

Assumptions and Premises

Like many political scientists and sociologists trained in the 1960s, the present author conceives of states as integrated systems; the implicit model assumes that what takes place in one sector of society affects other sectors of society as well, very much the way the parts of the human body are interrelated. A corollary to this assumption suggests that, because systems are interdependent, the planned actions of individuals and organizations set into motion a host of intended and unintended forces which in the long run transform society in ways unforeseen by either the actors or planners involved.[11] The analogy of the human body may clarify matters. Modern cancer therapies, for example, are designed to destroy malignant tumors in one part of the body in order to permit the system to prosper and develop. These therapies, however, also produce unintended side effects in other parts of the body which can themselves lead to illness and death. Scientists today are trying to sort out which of the various therapies are *least dysfunctional* to the desired end—a healthy system.

Therefore, the assumption is brought to this chapter that if states are interrelated systems they will respond to external stimuli in ways similar to that of a human system. The decision to modernize the military sector of society by importing military technology will have many unanticipated effects on other sectors of society, triggering a spiral of societal changes which will, in turn, have other unintended consequences for the evolution of the system. It seems to follow, then, that any discussion of development strategies for developing nations must also include the foreign military assistance they receive. Although it may not be possible to predict social evolution, it may be possible, by systematically studying the unanticipated consequences of the past, to reduce the negative costs of future development.

Second, the present study questions an implicit assumption which seems to characterize both sides of the debate. In most analyses, developing countries are discussed as if, by virtue of their lack of industrialization, they are the same. They are thought to have similar development problems which require similar development strategies. The different socioeconomic characteristics of these countries, their varying strategic situations, and their perceived security needs, are not considered part of the development equation. But for an area-studies specialist, discussing Iran and Bangladesh in the same context is as theoretically fruitful as equating the economic and security situations of Italy and the United States. Rather than assuming similarity, it might be more useful to assume uniqueness, unless proven otherwise. Searching for recurring patterns is different from assuming them, and for area specialists there are many other factors, besides the level of industrialization, which determine a country's developmental future.

Third, one wonders about the implicit paternalistic assumption which pervades much of the U.S. discussion on arms transfers: that although the United States and other Western powers are armed with the most lethal weapons produced, it is a United States (and Western) *moral* responsibility to limit the flow of arms to other regions of the world. The corollary assumption is that the West is more responsible, stable, and less emotional and, therefore, can be trusted to use military technology more responsibly than Third World countries. Furthermore, there is the added implication that the Western powers know better than the developing nations what is best for them—at least in the area of economic development and national security. Clearly, a rational foreign-assistance policy must serve U.S. national-security interests first, but where there is no conflict, it should also serve the economic *and* security needs of recipient states, as *they* perceive them.

These then are the assumptions, biases, and premises upon which this chapter is based. Using them as a conceptual foundation, the author will, in the following pages, attempt to link the Chinese puzzle boxes of economic development and security studies in order to analyze and identify the main theoretical questions at issue between them. It is hoped that an exercise of this kind will shed some light on the relationship between arms and development by first providing new and more systematic ways of thinking about the subject and, second, suggesting hypotheses and some direction for further research. Last, but not least, it is hoped that this chapter will offer some support to the biases and intuitive judgments which partially motivated it in the first place.

ECONOMIC DEVELOPMENT: DEFINITIONS AND STRATEGIES

Economic Growth versus Social Welfare

There is little consensus among economists as to what development is or how it works. In the 1960s, the classical "trickle-down" economists dominated the development field.[12] They conceived of economic growth as a long-term, incremental process in which the economic well-being of the state must be established before the quality of life of individuals can be improved. In this model (adapted from thinking about the history of Western development), development occurs by saving and capital investment. Savings are invested in capital, and productive capital produces both more productive capital and more consumption goods, which ultimately improve the quality of life for individuals. In this view, the process can be speeded up for developing countries by rich states giving assistance to help provide the massive increase in capital and technological "know-how" needed to move toward "takeoff" into sustained growth.[13] Development aid is to be focused on the small "modern" sectors of society which can then, through a similar diffusion process, help to develop the more traditional sectors through a gradual expansion of modern institutions and ideas and an eventual "trickle-down" of economic benefits.

But as the gap between rich and poor countries grows wider and the disparities between rich and poor within Third World states increases, the classical trickle-down model of development is being challenged by many developmental economists and leaders of developing countries. They believe that growth, as measured by increases in GNP, at the expense of employment levels and an equitable distribution of wealth is no longer an acceptable definition of development and they question whether the structure of development is necessarily predetermined.[14] The results of the development process are considered by this school of thought to be the product of man-made policy decisions, the consequences of which may be intended or unintended, but are not necessarily inevitable. They insist that attention should be directed toward finding alternate growth paths without sacrificing the important things people care about; this has come to be known as the "human-needs" approach to development. These political leaders and development theorists define "the important things people care about" in terms of economic benefits derived from a more equitable distribution of income.

Ironically, by late 1977 still another group of theorists began to question the human-needs approach. Development, they maintain, should include the concept of independence—cultural and economic independence from one or more of the great powers. As Dudley Seers observes,

. . . "development plans" would henceforward not put the main emphasis on overall growth rates, or even on new patterns of distribution. The crucial targets would be for (i) ownership as well as output in the leading economic sectors; (ii) consumption patterns that economise on foreign exchange (including imports, such as cereals and oil); (iii) institutional capacity for research and negotiation; (iv) cultural goals like those suggested above, depending on the country concerned.[15]

The conceptual confusion and the absence of a precise, to say nothing of an operational, definition of development makes research on the consequences of arms transfers for economic development difficult at best. Without definitional guidance, researchers are at a loss as to which sectors in society will best reflect "development" and how "progress" can be measured. Although vague dependent and independent variables are not uncommon in the social sciences, they represent serious obstacles to any kind of systematic and empirical research.

The "Engines of Development": Technology versus Human Resources

Out of the debate over definitions and strategies of development have come several conceptual advances and some consensus as to what factors are related to the "development" process. First, there is a more relativistic conception of development evolving in the field, one which recognizes the typological differences between countries (e.g., size, availability of resources, and structural characteristics—such as land versus labor surpluses, etc.) as well as their divergent developmental needs. The old assumption that a general theory of development can be applicable to countries as diverse, for example, as Japan, Iran, and Bangladesh is no longer considered acceptable. [16]

Hypothesis 1: If the socioeconomic characteristics of states determine their path and rate of developmental progress, then intensive case studies rather than macrostatistical analyses are a necessary first step to understanding the connections between arms and economic development.

Second, some developmental specialists today believe that "appropriate"[17] technology transfers (and the way recipients adapt them for domestic purposes) may represent the single most important element affecting the reduction and possible elimination of any trade-off between growth, employment, and income objectives.[18] They suggest that techonological transfers need not be made only to the modern industrial sector of society, but to other sectors as well.

The new wisdom claims there are alternative growth paths and alternate technological choices which can render growth, employment, income distribution, and, presumably, "independence" more compatible. Flexibility exists not only in initial choice of technology from abroad, but also in the domestic adaptative potential on top of such imported technology.[19] The trick is, of course, in learning what mix of technology is best suited to the developmental needs of societies with different socioeconomic characteristics and how they should institutionally organize themselves to get the best out of indigenous and imported resources (both physical and human) over time.

But, if technology is essential to the development process, why would only civilian technology qualify? And if "appropriate" technology transfers to various sectors of society promote development, then why exclude the military sector from the process? Clearly, in situations where military technology makes up a substantial portion of the technology imports for an industrializing country, the same new "wisdom" holds true.

Hypothesis 2: If the transfer of technology is an important factor in the development process, and if there is flexibility between sectors, then transfers of military technology, like civilian technology transfers, can play an important positive role in the socioeconomic growth of a country.

The third conceptual advance that has shifted thinking about growth and development is closely related to the second. It stresses the importance of human resources in the development process. For this school, the fundamental problem is not the creation of wealth but rather the capacity to create wealth. The capacity to create wealth resides in the people of the country—the trained manpower, the skilled personnel who apply minds to research and innovative change, to problems of production, and to the organization and management of the economic institutions of the country. In the view of these theorists, only a minor part of economic progress is attributed to the traditional economic factors of production (such as capital and labor).[20] Education and those social services (such as better housing, nutrition, health care, etc.) which enable people to apply their talents to technological innovation and organizational change are investments in human resources which are the engines of economic growth and development.

In this conceptualization—sometimes called the "human-investment model" of development—improvement in the quality of human life is both the means by which production is increased and the objective of the developmental process itself.[21]

Wealth and power are no longer measured in material terms. They are not gifts. They are not gifts of nature or of chance like oil or gold or even population. Rather they are victories won by the human spirit; the ability to transform an idea into reality through the industrial process: the talent for coordinating skills making rigid organizations susceptible to change....Modern power is based on the capacity for innovation, which is research, and the capacity to transform inventions into finished products, which is technology....Training, development, and exploitation of human intelligence—these are the real resources, and there are no others....Education is the driving force behind technological innovation.[22]

Although this approach was developed by economists concerned with the civilian sector of society, their observations are equally relevant for the military sector. What many observers overlook is the scale of training, construction, and industrial demand generated by the transfer of military technology. In the military sector, during the long period between the approval of a request for military equipment and the actual delivery of military technology, often five to seven years, large amounts of training and construction prepare the military in recipient countries to operate and maintain the equipment. The Iranian military, for example, during the reign of the Shah, bought training for thousands of young people in mechanical, technical, language, and management skills. From 1964, under foreign military sales (FMS) and the military assistance program (MAP), approximately 21,500 passed through U.S. military training centers,[23] and thousands more were trained in Iran. Many of the high-level skills that are taught to trainees from developing countries such as electronics and management are transferrable into the rest of society; other military personnel are trained in transferrable skills such as driving, mechanics, the English language, and medical aid. In addition, these defense programs foster the development of new communities in sparsely populated areas of the country. Roads, water supply, ports, housing, electricity, and communications add not only to the basic infrastructure of the country, but create, as well, conditions in which human resources can be developed and utilized.

Out of each dollar spent on military technology, between 35 percent and 40 percent is for the purchase of hardware. The other 60–65 percent is for support, training, and construction.[24] This means that in countries such as Iran, where orders for military hardware between 1973 and 1977 averaged over $2.5 billion annually, about $1.5 billion each year went into these activities. Thus, although they have never been systematically studied, the spinoff effects of military technology transfers are potentially large, and their impact cannot be left out of the development equation.

In sum, the new thinking about development has both enriched and complicated our understanding of how the process works and the possible role military technology can play in it. Feedback and spinoffs are now considered essential parts of development; it is no longer pictured as a monocausal, deterministic progression of events. Instead development is seen as a complex, untidy series of circles whereby improved levels of living and knowledge lead to higher productivity, and high productivity in turn leads to higher levels of living. Change comes about not just through a modern industrial sector, but through other sectors as well; however, distinguishing between cause and effect in this conceptualization remains a problem. Where these circles begin and how positive socioeconomic development (however defined) is fostered, is only dimly understood.

Although the field is still trying to solve the development puzzle, there is general consensus that transfers of technology and training are crucial ingredients in the process.[25] These conceptual advances pave the way for new, more innovative thinking about development and security.

Hypothesis 3: Levels of socioeconomic development co-vary with the importation of military technology over time.

Hypothesis 4: The number of weapons systems imported and their level of technological sophistication determine the quality and quantity of spinoffs into the civilian sector of society.

Hypothesis 5: The availability of skilled personnel, the infrastructure base, and the level of industrial productivity are related to the pace of socio-economic development.

NATIONAL SECURITY AND DEVELOPMENT

National Security versus Economic Growth in Developing Countries: Conflicting Perspectives

Generally, little attention has been paid to the relationship between the national security goals and the economic development objectives of developing nations; both the academic literature and policy-making debates tend to treat them as separate and unrelated issues. Perhaps this is because analysts tend to generalize from their own experiences, and development experts and policy makers are no exception. Extrapolating from the nineteenth century American experience, for example, when the United States was able to isolate itself from the conflicts of Europe and concentrate on its own internal development and expansion, analysts assume that the developing countries should and can do the same (if they were only willing). In the opinion of many, military expenditures are a waste of energies and resources for developing countries.

Only recently has the international environment in which a country lives and grows been considered as of major import to the structure of its economic growth, and, to the best of this author's knowledge, only one economist has developed this point. Simon Kuznets has observed that the international environment has changed considerably from the one in which the United States found itself in the nineteenth century; in the interdependent twentieth century, states can no longer isolate themselves from one another. Furthermore, the greater danger of war-induced devastation—precipitated, in part, from the spread of high-technology weapons throughout the world—gives decision makers few options with regard to defense expenditures.[26]

In fact, a cursory reading of the daily newspapers suggests that non-Western leaders, unlike policy makers in the West, do not make a clear distinction between development and national-security objectives. Expenditures on armaments and expenditures for economic development are not seen as mutually exclusive policy alternatives, but as mutually complementary political necessities. Iran, for instance, during the Shah's reign, regarded its national security interests in terms of guarding the sea lanes in the Persian Gulf, the Gulf of Oman, the Arabian Sea, and the northwestern quadrant of the Indian Ocean to protect the flow of oil (and oil receipts) essential for the nation's development. The behavior of neighbors or internal opposition groups was often interpreted as threatening to stability and, hence, developmental goals. Therefore, investments in defense were not regarded as antithetical to development, but as insurance safeguarding the nation's independence, wealth, and development. Security was seen as a prerequisite for development. Although all industrializing states may not view their situation in this way, security and economic development are, judging from recent history, considered equally pressing national priorities in a majority of countries.[27]

As long as Third World leaders view their situation in this way, they will continue to purchase weapons, if not from the United States then from other willing suppliers. There is a widely held assumption in the Third World that the West tends to apply a double standard to the nonindustrial states.[28] As one Iranian has put it: "It is not easily understood for example, why France and Germany (with populations of 53 and 63 millions), covered by security guarantees and nuclear weapons, are cautioned against arms *cuts* when they already possess some 500 combat aircraft in their inventories. Nevertheless, when Iran, a growing power, strategically exposed and essentially self reliant for defense, seeks to augment and modernize its aircraft inventory (of 300) over the course of the next decade, it is criticized for doing so."[29]

In recent years, leaders in developing nations have begun to insist upon their right to organize and manage their own resources and bring an end to the double standard. Proposals to reduce military expenditures must convincingly demonstrate to individual states that such reductions are not only being asked of the developing countries, and that such reductions will not make the external environment more dangerous.

Hypothesis 6: Given the present level of military technological invention and the structure of the international system, leaders of the developing states will continue to obtain weapons. The level of worldwide arms transfer and production in the Third World will increase, not decrease.

Hypothesis 7: In an interdependent environment in which (for various reasons) military technology has taken on an increasingly important role in the economies of all states, learning how to utilize this technology for the dual purpose of development and security can make an important contribution not only to development theory and strategy but to the stability of the less industrialized regions of the world.

Economic Assistance, Arms Transfers, and Arms Control: A Non-Debate

Recently, Congress and the press have expressed concern over the worldwide increase in arms transfers and the nature, scope, and purposes of U.S. arms-transfer programs, particularly when judged by their potential threat to other U.S. objectives and world peace. After lengthy hearings in 1976, Congress inserted a strong arms-control flavor into legislative policy guidance governing arms transfers.[30] In May 1977 President Carter announced new controls on arms transfers and a general policy of restraint for his administration. The across-the-board planned reduction in the dollar value of U.S. military-hardware sales for subsequent years is considered the most restrictive of the controls.[31]

These policy directives come at a time when U.S. options in this area are diminishing. First, the United States is militarily retrenching abroad, relying on states which seem capable of becoming "regional centers of power" to sustain local stability and safeguard U.S. overseas interests without U.S. involvement. To many Third World countries, this policy implies a more equal partnership with the United States, based on common strategic interests. Previously under the U.S. security umbrella and now forced to seek and pay for their own means of self-defense, the leaders of many of these nations find the arms-control flavor of U.S. foreign policy puzzling indeed. With more and more Third World leaders increasingly sensitive to signs of neocolonialism, the price of retrenchment may be the fact that the United States can no longer prescribe for the defense and development needs of recipients of U.S. military technology.

Second, mitigating the world's arms trade requires not only stemming the flow of U.S. arms but controlling the actions of other seller nations also.[32] Other suppliers, however, are less willing to sacrifice the substantial economic advantages accruing from arms sales.[33] From the perspective of the military and related U.S. industries, the new policy neither controls arms sales to the Third World nor serves the U.S. economy well. In the near future, they can be expected to challenge Congress and the administration to explain how arms-control policies are in the U.S. national interest.

Third, even if the United States is willing and able to implement a policy unilaterally reducing arms sales to developing nations, using cuts in the dollar value of military expenditures or sales as the sole criterion will not control the level of destructiveness which is being exported worldwide. The qualitative changes in the arms trade have made it possible for states to simultaneously increase their destructive power while decreasing their military expenditures;[34] thus the calculation of arms-control in terms of dollar value in view of the qualitative differences in weapons systems transferred may prove to be a nonproductive exercise. As pressure mounts, the problem for Congress and the administration will be how to justify U.S. arms-transfer and control policies to the many interested U.S. publics, to allies and friends abroad, and to the various bureaucratic, political, and business groups in Washington.

Curiously, little attention has been paid to the possibility that military technological transfers may be a means of not only fostering economic development, but of implementing arms restraints as well. Although Third World leaders may not be willing to curtail their purchases to conform with the political purposes of a particular U.S. leader, they might be willing to tailor their purchases to suit their socioeconomic needs—or at least organize their defense procurements so as to give the greatest benefit to their own civilian sectors. This assumes, of course, that a relationship between arms transfers and development can be established and that there is a general understanding of how the process works. It is also curious that Third World leaders are not consulted on their views about the relationship between arms transfers, arms control, and development, since security and development are probably their two main concerns.

In the field of development assistance, U.S. policy has lent lip service to the idea that development planning is now the responsibility of the recipient: "United States assistance should be administered in a collaborative style to support the developmental goals chosen by each country receiving assistance."[35]

Unfortunately, despite the hopeful designation of "New Directions in Development Assistance,"[36] both the legislation and policy implementation have reflected ambivalence rather than change in this area. For example, on the one hand section 102(b) of the Foreign Assistance Act of 1961— amended to the FAAct in 1973—requires that "the development goals [be] chosen by each country receiving aid"; on the other hand, section 102(d) establishes specific criteria which, in effect, direct U.S. assistance to some sectors while neglecting others, apparently regardless of the preferred development goals of recipient states.* A similar contradiction exists in the "human rights" amendments to the FAAct of 1975; † section 116 not only unilaterally defines "human rights," but prescribes them as universal criteria for determining which recipients will and will not receive U.S. development assistance. From the point of view of the recipients, unilateral legislation of goals contradicts the rhetoric of a "collaborative style" of development assistance, masking what Denis Goulet has called a "partnership among unequals."[37]

In the area of arms-control policy, the ambivalence has been less, and the lack of communication between U.S. and Third World policy makers even greater. Arms-control agreements have gained the support of specialists in the United States because they can relate it to a perceived national interest—making deterrence more stable;[38] but there has been no comparable arms-control theory which relates to the perceived national interests of developing countries. No theory of regional, conventional stability which is comparable to the theory of deterrence has been developed,[39] nor, as discussed above, do theories exist about the trade-offs between military technology and development. The result has been little corresponding support in developing countries for the idea of arms control.

Yet some local military thinkers and bureaucrats are quite knowledgeable about the tactical implications of different varieties of military equipment[40] and the various ways they interact with the civilian economy, ‡ but relatively few of the U.S. policy makers who are interested in restraining the trade in conventional arms draw on this body of knowledge. Perhaps the potential of harnessing this military and economic expertise to the question of arms limitation and economic development should not be overlooked by

---

*Section 102(d) enumerates specific criteria for development aid programs. They should "(1) increase agricultural productivity per unit of land through small-farm, labor-intensive agriculture; (2) reduce infant mortality; (3) control population growth; (4) promote greater equality of income distribution, including measures such as more progressive taxation and more equitable returns to small farmers; and (5) reduce rates of unemployment and underemployment."

† Section 116 reads: "(a) No assistance may be provided under this part to the government of any country which engages in a consistent pattern of gross violations of internationally recognized human rights, including torture or cruel, inhuman, or degrading treatment or punishment, prolonged detention without charges, or other flagrant denial of the right to life, liberty, and the security of person, unless such assistance will directly benefit the needy people in such country."

‡ On a recent three-week trip to Iran, the author collected a surprising amount of information about possible connections between military technology and development from members of both the military and the bureaucracy. The military, because of infrastructure and industrial capability problems, have become increasingly involved in quasi-civilian socioeconomic ventures. Because of the size of Iran's military imports few Iranian civilian economists and development specialists have no involvement in questions of military significance.

U.S. policy makers, since the two issues may not be unrelated. If support for arms control in the United States has come about because it was seen as a way to provide equivalent or better defense more safely (and some say more cheaply), then generating arms-control theories related to the national interests of developing nations should accomplish the same thing. A careful assessment of local conventional balances, along with a definition of the possible economic spinoffs to be derived from certain types of hardware purchases, might add the support of Third World military thinkers and economic development specialists to that of U.S. arms controllers for some sort of restraint in the transfer of arms. An alliance between these groups, in a true collaborative style which reflects the national interests of both recipients and suppliers, may help obtain arms-limitation agreements which are in the interests of all concerned.

Hypothesis 8: Arms control, arms transfers and economic development issues are not unrelated. Learning how transferred military technologies can be used for the dual purpose of security and development can lead to a more balanced procurement policy on the part of the recipient and a more rational transfer policy on the part of the supplier.

CONCEPTUAL AND METHODOLOGICAL ISSUES

A Preliminary Framework: A Sectoral Approach to Arms and Development.

Earlier in this chapter some conceptual advances in the field of economic development were noted; this new, more flexible approach conceives of development as a total process. It is visualized as a series of interlocking circles in which all social sectors are connected to each other by a network of functional and structural relationships. This model suggests that inputs at one point in the network will have important effects elsewhere; it also implies that there is no one priority sector, or one development strategy. Catalysts in development can be found in numerous sectors, sometimes simultaneously, and may differ from country to country.

Richard Ward, for example, develops the health sector concept in his *Development Issues for the 1970s.*[41] Focusing on health services, he demonstrates (conceptually) how they can act as an agent for change in other parts of society as well. He discusses how health services affect the physical and intellectual capacities of the labor force—which in turn influence labor productivity—and how building, operating, and maintaining a health sector in various regions of the country can mobilize the housing, communication, food, and other industries in the economy. These spinoffs have further spinoffs, until the whole economy is affected by activities which originated in the health sector.

A similar model—one using the military instead of health as the nucleus development sector, and arms transfers instead of medical services as the major catalyst—might be an interesting heuristic device for research on arms and development. The assumptions and hypotheses discussed earlier in this chapter could form the foundation upon which the model rests. These are expanded and listed below in a more systematic fashion.

1. Development is an untidy, complex process. It can be thought of as a series of circles in which improved levels of living and knowledge lead to higher productivity, and high productivity in turn leads to higher levels of living. A stable internal and external environment is necessary at key stages in the process for positive, rather than negative, growth to occur.

2. Catalysts for change come from many sectors of society, not just the modern industrial sector.

3. Employment, economic trade activity, and GNP per capita are indicators of regional and national socioeconomic growth.

4. Skilled manpower, infrastructure, and industrial productivity are closely related to the development process. Changes in these factors will be reflected in the socioeconomic indicators of growth (see no. 3).

5. In the long run, regardless of sector, development strategies which produce skilled manpower, build infrastructure, and create demand for domestic industrial products will generate positive growth consequences for the society as a whole.

6. The technological sophistication of arms transfers determines the impact they have on society. The particular socioeconomic system determines the absorptive capacity of the military. Over time, societal feedback into the military sector determines the dollar value and technological sophistication of future arms procurements.

7. Arms-transfer activities can, if rationally planned, contribute to the economic growth and productivity of developing countries.

8. Learning what mix of military technology is best suited to the developmental needs of different societies, and how they can make the best developmental use of it, may help Third World leaders establish rational policy and procurement priorities, aid U.S. policy makers to formulate consistent arms-transfer programs, and, in the long run, contribute to a pragmatic and receptive arms-control climate in the Third World.

Figure 13.1 represents a hypothetical model of how military imports connect with the rest of society. The following is a description of how it might work in a hypothetical Third World society. The process begins when Third World policy makers decide on the basis of their available resources, and security and development goals, to obtain arms abroad. After negotiations with the supplier state are complete and the "shopping list" established, the formal mechanics of the arms transfer begin.[42] Even before deliveries are made, the military derives benefits from the arms transfer:

FIGURE 13.1: A Preliminary Model of Military Technological
Transfers and Their Effects on the Civilian Sectors of Society at $t_1 - t_n$

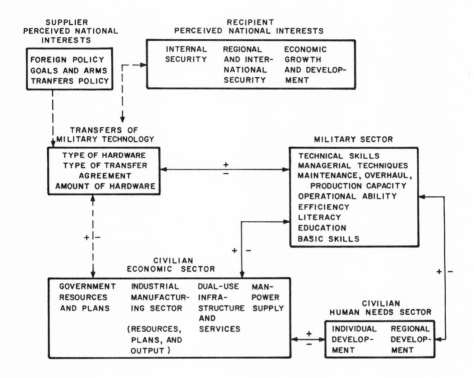

Note: The direction of any particular arrow and the value of its net flow (positive or negative) may change from time period to time period.

Source: Constructed by the author. This chart has benefited from research conducted for the Department of State.

increased technical, management, and language training; perhaps higher morale; travel abroad; larger budget outlays; and so on.

As the weapons begin to arrive, however, the picture becomes more complicated. Negative spinoffs affect some parts of society, although this can vary with the amount and kind of military technology received. For example, increased military demand may create a drain on already scarce human and natural resources, disrupt civilian services, and overload insufficient communications networks and infrastructure facilities. On the other hand, some civilian sectors may derive many unanticipated benefits from these military activities; the housing, communications, transportation, educational, and health sectors are often the first to be mobilized to meet military requests associated with imported military technology. Bases must be built to store, operate, and maintain new weapons. Housing, roads, railroads, ports, telephones, electricity, water supplies, schools, and hospitals must be established to service them. In turn, these bases, often located in remote regions of the country, stimulate the growth of satellite cities which leads to still further change. Facilities, designed for military purposes, perform dual functions for surrounding villages and cities, improving living conditions in once isolated areas of the country as well. And this is but the beginning of the spreading process.

Soon the industrial sector becomes involved too. A larger, better educated military creates a larger, more sophisticated domestic market. In addition, more food, uniforms, medicines, supplies, and technical equipment (ranging from batteries to buses) must be purchased by the military from the civilian economy. In this way, not only profits, but large amounts of technical and management know-how, are transferred into the civilian industrial sector, since U.S. specifications and quality-control standards are often made part of the procurement contracts. Thus, local manufacturers gear up their production lines for a bigger market and are, at the same time, encouraged to produce a better product.

With time, perhaps five to ten years, positive spinoffs to other sectors of society increase as the linkages between sectors become more intertwined. More employment and trade opportunities are created, and the standard of living of certain groups rises. Over the long run (perhaps fifteen to twenty years) the circles widen still further, until most groups in society and most sectors of the economy are affected by the processes now in motion. Then, as the capabilities of the country increase, feedback from the civilian sector influences arms-procurement policies. Security and development goals change as the country grows; competing pressure groups vie for foreign-exchange resources; domestic industries and educational institutions provide more of the needed resources so that foreign military equipment and training become less necessary, and the circle is complete.

This, then, is how the military-nucleus strategy of development might work. The approach is not envisaged as either a panacea for development problems, nor as relevant to the development process in all countries. Rather it is introduced here as a heuristic device to encourage further research and thought about a sector of activity which, until now, has been left out of development-planning strategies. As an intellectual exercise, thinking about arms transfers as a catalyst, rather than as a hindrance to the process of human development, might be a self-fulfilling prophecy; it could conceivably lead to creative solutions for some of the policy problems now facing decision makers in supplier and recipient countries throughout the world.

A Methodological Postscript

Now that a preliminary conceptual framework has been outlined, what research strategy is best suited to a "military-nucleus approach" to development? The author has argued elsewhere that one reason why so little progress has been made toward an understanding of the socioeconomic consequences of military-technology transfers is the field's obsessive focus on macrostatistical analyses which use defense expenditures as an indicator of the economic impact arms have on society; an attempt was made to show why these studies are misleading, inaccurate, and prone to the kind of ideological misinterpretation that has confused rather than illuminated the field to date.[43] After over a decade and a half, quantitative experimentation has indicated that the questions asked as well as the problems studied often dictate the kind of methodology called for. In the case of the military-nucleus approach, relevant empirical data have simply not been collected or are not available for quantification; they must be generated. In addition, in a study on arms and development, many of the variables are "soft" and do not lend themselves to counting. For instance, how does one quantitatively define the value of security? Is it a positive or negative input to society? And, is more security better or worse for the economic future of a country? Conditions which affect the development process, such as inefficiencies, bottlenecks, level of organizational and management skills, cultural attitudes toward work and time, and infrastructure inadequacies, are equally difficult to count. The trouble various U.S. agencies had with the "absorptive-capacity" studies they were asked to produce on Iran and Saudi Arabia illustrates this problem.

The difficulties associated with macrostatistical techniques are not limited to the arms-and-development question. Gradually, other empirically oriented social scientists have come to believe that the thousands of cases usually associated with macrostatistical analyses are not a necessary prerequisite for empirical research.[44] It is the comparability of cases, not their number, which provides evidence for theory and policy. If the same variables and interrelationships are measured by the same method in each country studied, then the number of cases need not be large in order to establish patterns of similarity and difference between them. For example, investigating only one society over time can suggest probable effects in other countries as well. By comparing the impact of arms transfers on development in states with different socioeconomic structures (perhaps by classifying them into resource-versus-labor-abundant economies), even a few examples can indicate whether the effects are similar or not and can suggest which foreign military-assistance and sales programs are most likely to meet the needs of different recipients.

In an area of research where there is little or no theoretical literature for guidance and where data sources are either nonexistent or scarce, an empirical but, perhaps, not completely quantitative approach may be necessary. In such a situation, a comparative case study method may be the best way of generating theory and information simultaneously.

Barney G. Glaser and Anselm Strauss have made a strong case in favor of such a method.[45] They argue that by following what they refer to as "the constant comparative method" even a single case example can generate relevant theory for further testing and comparison. They advocate starting with one case, taking slices of the available data by analyzing them in different time periods with a view to establishing conceptual categories, a list of conditions necessary for these categories, and hypotheses about their interrelationships. The approach is both comparative and historical, qualitative and quantitative; material from the past and present is constantly compared, and conceptual categories and hypotheses as they emerge from the research are reevaluated in the light of new data.

There is, then, developing in the field a more relaxed attitude about methodology which is admirably suited to the question of arms and development. What can be counted should be counted, but not for its own sake. Case studies, even single case examples in which systematic comparative methods are followed, are now felt to be as empirical as other quantitative techniques. There is the optimistic feeling—at least this author feels it—that with a more flexible methodological approach the pitfalls of much of the social science research of the past can be avoided. Information should not be forced—often at the expense of other relevant data—to fit a preexisting deductively derived theory, and data should not be collected in the hope that when the project is finished relevant propositions will emerge.

Given the primitive state of research on the linkage between arms transfers and development, and the need to generate both theory and data, the case-study method seems admirably suited for the job. Although it is probably true that, regardless of methodology, all significant theorizing in the social sciences is the product, for the most part, of the intuitive insights of the sensitive researcher, in areas where so little conceptualization and data gathering has been attempted, models and theoretical analyses must be developed simultaneously with data sources if any progress is to be made toward solving the arms and development dilemma in the foreseeable future.

CONCLUSION

In conclusion, this chapter has tried to suggest new ways of thinking about arms transfers and development and to indicate ways in which this kind of research might be conducted. In an international climate in which sophisticated military technology threatens the security of all countries, it is unlikely that supplier states, particularly well-armed supplier states, will successfully persuade recipient states not to obtain arms. Although it may seem paradoxical to associate positive consequences with lethal weapons, helping the developing world to achieve positive economic and security benefits from their weaponry may be more moral and realistic than legislating arms restraints for nations that will not comply.

POSTSCRIPT

This chapter was written before the 1978–79 Iranian political turmoil and the subsequent overthrow of the Shah's regime. Since then, various postmortems have analyzed what happened in Iran, many suggesting that U.S. arms transfers played an important role in bringing about the "debacle."[46] George Ball, for example, has put forth the thesis that arms purchases, by diverting funds from the civilian sector (combined with the Shah's corrupt and repressive regime) were responsible for the revolution.[47] George Lenczowski, on the other hand, rejects this conclusion: "Considering the impressively high level of Iran's oil revenue (roughly $20 billion a year...) and the fact that annual arms spending never exceeded some $6 billion—thus leaving a husky $14 billion or so for development— this argument does not seem very persuasive. Iran was in the fortunate position to afford both guns and butter."[48]

As the debate continues, it underscores the importance of questions raised in this chapter. There is little disagreement among analysts, regardless of their position on either arms or the Shah, that the development process itself somehow contributed to political instability in Iran. And if, as this chapter has tried to demonstrate, arms transfers have important consequences for development, and the issue for the United States is no longer *whether* to sell weapons to reliable allies, but *what* to sell them, then understanding how certain types of military technology affect countries at different levels of development has become an ever more pressing policy priority.[49] Although the Iranian experience has raised many interesting questions about U.S. arms transfer decisions, it has thrown into sharpest relief the necessity for learning more about the socioeconomic and strategic consequences of our policies.

NOTES

1. *Report to Congress on Arms Transfer Policy pursuant to sections 202(b) and 213 of the International Security Assistance and Arms Export Control Act of 1976.* Report to Congress for use by The Committee on Foreign Relations, U.S. Senate, July 1977. The $20 billion figure refers to the value of contracts signed between buyers and sellers. Actual deliveries of military hardware amount to significantly less. In 1973 worldwide exports were valued (in constant dollars) at $10.5 billion, in 1974 at $9.3 billion, and in 1975 at $8.9 billion. The United States accounts for about one-half of world deliveries. *World Military Expenditures and Arms Transfers, 1966–1975* (Washington, D.C.: p. 56); also Library of Congress, Congressional Research Service, "Implications of President Carter's Conventional Arms Transfer Policy," September 22, 1977, p. 8

2. The various United Nations documents on the economic and social consequences of the arms race and disarmament develop this point of view. See particularly *Economic and Social Consequences of the Armaments Race and its Extremely Harmful Effects on World Peace and Security,* Report to the Secretary General, August 12, 1977; Barry Blechman and Edward R. Fried, *Disarmament and Development: An Analytical Survey and Pointers for Action,* Report for the Committee for Development Planning, United Nations Economic and Social Council, January 26, 1977; *Economic and Social Consequences of the Arms Race and of Military Expenditures,* Report of the Secretary General, 1972. Also, Emma Rothschild, "Carter and Arms: No Sale," *New York Review of Books,* September 15, 1977, p. 10.

3. "Opportunity costs" refers to the economic argument that if resources (such as labor or capital) are scarce, then an increase in the production of one commodity (e.g., guns) requires a reduction in the output of some other commodity (butter). The amount of butter which must be "foregone" is the opportunity cost of the additional guns. See Stephen P. Dresch, "Disarmament: Economic Consequences and Developmental Potential," paper submitted to Center for Development Planning, Projects and Policies, Department of Economic and Social Affairs, United Nations, New York, December 1972.

4. Emile Benoit, *Defense and Economic Growth in Developing Countries* (Lexington: Lexington Books, D.C. Heath and Co., 1973). Benoit found "that the average 1950–1965 defense burdens (defense as a percent of national product) of 44 developing countries were positively, not inversely, correlated with their growth rates over comparable time periods: i.e., the more they spent on defense, in relation to the size of their economies, the faster they grew—and vice versa." (p. xix).

5. Luigi Einaudi et al., *Arms Transfers to Latin America: Toward a Policy of Mutual Respect,*Rand Corporation, R-1173-DOS, Santa Monica, Calif., June 1973. Using a "crude model" to calculate what would "be the effect on overall economic growth if funds currently devoted to 'unproductive' military end items were allocated instead to civilian investment," the authors found that"the amount spent on advanced weapons is so small that its reallocation would have little effect on productivity even when we assume that it would be invested rationally" (pp. 34–35).

6. Testimony of Lt. Gen. H. M. Fish, Director, Defense Security Assistance Agency; U.S. Congress, Senate, Committee on Foreign Relations, Subcommittee on Foreign Assistance, *Foreign Assistance Authorization: Arms Sales Issues,* 94th Cong., 1st sess., June 18, 1975.

7. Daniel L. Spencer, "An External Military Presence, Technological Transfer, and Structural Change," *Kyklos* 19 (1965): 451–73.

8. The May 19, 1977 policy statement by President Carter on conventional-arms transfers

reflects the lack of certainty among policy makers on this issues. The president stated that "the virtually unrestrained spread of conventional weaponry threatens stability in every region of the world." This assertion, which set the tone for the entire statement, appears to presume that arms transfers, in general, are destabilizing. But within the same policy paper, President Carter also declared, "We will continue to utilize arms transfers to promote our security and the security of our close friends." Thus, for the United States, somewhat contradictorily, arms transfers to the seventeen states specifically exempted from U.S. controls policy (Japan, New Zealand, Australia, and fourteen NATO allies) and to "countries friendly to the United States [who] must depend on advanced weaponry to offset quantitative and other disadvantages in order to maintain a regional balance" are not destabilizing. This leaves few regions of the world where U.S. arms are not being transferred for *stabilizing* purposes.

The ambivalence regarding the role of arms transfers in the international arena extends to academic research as well. Quincy Wright (*A Study of War*, Chicago University Press, 1964, pp. 167–68) reports a positive correlation between the relative military power of a state and its warlikeness. Others, such as M. Small and J. D. Singer ("Patterns in International Warfare, 1816–1965," *Annals* 391, (1970): 151), came up with analogous findings, i.e., that major powers have been the most likely states to engage in war. However, Rudolph Rummel finds little relationship between military power and foreign conflict behavior for 77 states in 1955-57; see his "Relationship Between National Attributes and Foreign Conflict Behavior," in J. D. Singer (ed.) *Quantitative International Politics*, (New York: Free Press, 1968), pp. 204–13. And E. Weede, reworking Singer's data, found an inverse relationship—with more powerful states tending to be involved in *less* violent conflict activity ("Conflict Behavior of Nation-States," *Journal of Peace Research* 7 (1970): 230).

9. For a more detailed critique of the macrostatistical approach to development and defense see Stephanie G. Neuman, "Security, Military Expenditures, and Socioeconomic Development," *Orbis* 22 (1978).

10. Norwood Russell Hanson, *Patterns of Discovery* (London: Cambridge University Press, 1965), p. 64.

11. Robert K. Merton, "The Unanticipated Consequences of Purposive Social Action," *The American Sociological Review* 1 (1936). As this seminal article points out, the concept of "unanticipated consequences" has been treated by "virtually every substantial contributor to the long history of social thought," although in a diversity of contexts and using a variety of terms. It was, however, Professor Merton who, in 1936, first attempted to systematically analyze the concept.

12. The "trickle-down" model is presented in the following works: Benjamin Higgins, *Economic Development: Principles, Problems and Policies* (New York: W.W. Norton & Company, 1959); and P.N. Rosenstein-Rodan, "Notes on the Theory of the 'Big Push'," MIT Center for International Studies, Cambridge, Mass., March, 1957.

13. W. W. Rostow, *The Stages of Economic Growth* (London: Cambridge University Press, 1965).

14. Irma Adelman and Cynthia Morris, *Economic Growth and Social Equity in Developing Countries* (Stanford, Calif.: Stanford University Press, 1973).

15. Dudley Seers, "The New Meaning of Development," *International Development Review* (1977) 19: 5. The cultural goals he refers to are reducing cultural dependence on the great powers—i.e., increasing the use of national languages in schools, for allotting more t.v. time to programs produced locally (or in neighboring countries), raising the proportion of higher degrees obtained at home, etc." This approach attempts to integrate *dependencia* theory (also known as dependency theory) into development strategies. Because it is so new, however, it is difficult to assess its impact on the field in general. Johan Galtung has predicted that the impact of this new school of thought will be great. He recently warned the development community that there is "a rather important political conflict shaping up between the two new Grand

Designs in development theory and practice, the New International Economic Order (NIEO) and the Basic Needs approaches (BN)." See Johan Galtung, "Grand Designs on a Collision Course," *Development* 20 (1978): 43-47.

16. Gustav Ranis, "Development Theory at Three Quarters Century," *Economic Development and Cultural Change* 25 (1977) supp.

17. In practice, the term "appropriate technology" has empirical meaning. Its definition differs from group to group and changes from situation to situation. It derives empirical content only from the specific criteria or objectives provided by those who use the term. As Hawthorne has pointed out, a group of Algerian planning advisors recommended a massive emphasis on capital-intensive industry and a U.N. advisory group recommended a labor-intensive technology when both groups were asked to come up with "appropriate technologies." Because the field is still uncertain about what development is or how it works, making judgments about the "appropriateness" of technology often boils down to a value judgment. See Edward P. Hawthorne, *The Transfer of Technology* (Paris: U.N. Organization for Economic Cooperation and Development, 1971), pp. 22–23. The same, as we have seen can be said of the term "economic development."

18. E. F. Schumacher, *Small is Beautiful: Economics as if People Mattered* (New York: Harper & Row, 1973).

19. Ranis, "Development Theory," p. 261.

20. Harry Gideonse, "Economic Growth and Educational Development," *College and University*, Summer, 1968; and Richard Ward, *Development Issues for the 1970s* (New York: Dunellen, 1973).

21. Hans Singer, "The Notion of Human Investment," *Review of Social Economy* 24 (1966).

22. J. J. Servan-Schreiber, *The American Challenge* (New York: Atheneum, 1968), pp. 45, 81, 83, 46.

23. These figures are derived from the U.S. Department of Defense, *Foreign Military Sales and Military Assistance Facts*, December 1977, and from data supplied by various departments in the Pentagon concerned with security assistance.

24. Report to Congress for use of Committee on Foreign Relations, U. S. Senate, *Arms Transfer Policy*, July 1977, p. 5. "FMS orders, which make up more than 85 percent of the value of total U.S. arms transfers, have for the past several years consisted of about 40% weapons and ammunition, 25% support equipment and spare parts, and 35% training, construction, and other services." Support items include general-purpose vehicles like trucks and tractors, communications equipment, and so on.

25. Simon Kuznets, in "Two Centuries of Economic Growth: Reflection on U.S. Experience," *American Economic Review* 67 (1977): 1–14, reevaluates the determinants of America's economic growth experience. Aside from geographic size and immigration, which made an economy of wider scale possible, Kuznets isolates the transfer of technology and the international climate as decisive elements in the process. According to Kuznets, the lateness of American entry into modern economic growth and its ability to capitalize on the technological advances of European countries worked in the United States' developmental favor. Throughout the nineteenth century the United States was a follower nation technologically, adapting and modifying technological imports from abroad. It was not until the end of that century that it began contributing technological innovations of its own.

Nathan Rosenberg, "American Technology: Imported or Indigenous?" *American Economic Review* 67 (February 1977): 21–26, also emphasizes the historical importance of technology transfer to the U.S. development process. He, however, stresses the role knowledge and technical training, which the settlers brought with them from Europe, played in promoting U.S. growth. These skills, he believes, made it possible for the settlers to innovate and adapt a European-specific technology to the environment and resource base of America (e.g., adapting an iron-based technology imported from Great Britain to a wood-surplus environment in the United States).

26. Simon Kuznets discusses the nineteenth century international environment as the fourth element determining the U.S. development pattern (ibid.).

27. There may be other, less rational reasons for large military expenditures—regional or international prestige, bureaucratic politics—but it is the perception of security risks which is generally dominant. For example, Israel's and the Arab states' defense expenditures grew 18 and 16 percent a year, respectively, in the five years before the 1973 Middle East war. (Together Egypt, Israel, Jordan, and Syria now spend about $8 billion—at U.S. 1976 prices—on defense each year.) China's defense expenditures grew 7 percent a year during the five years prior to the 1971 break with the USSR *(Baltimore Sun,* November 28, 1977).

28. Shahram Chubin, "Iran's Security in the 1980s," paper presented at the International Studies Association Annual Meeting, March 1977, p. 9. Dr. Chubin was an outspoken critic of many of the Shah's programs, including exorbitant military expenditures. In this instance, he was speaking out, as an Iranian nationalist, against Western interference in the decision-making process of developing states.

29. Ibid., p. 10.

30. U. S. Congress, House, Committee on International Relations, *The Arms Export Control Act,* 9th Cong., 2d Sess., August 25, 1976.

31. Statement on conventional-arms transfer policy issued by President Carter on May 19, 1977. Included in *Report to Congress on Arms Transfer Policy,* op. cit. He listed six specific controls to be implemented during his administration:

1. The dollar volume (in constant fiscal 1976 dollars) of new commitments under the Foreign Military Sales and Military Assistance Programs for weapons and weapons-related items in fiscal 1978 will be reduced from the fiscal 1977 total.

2. The United States will not be the first supplier to introduce advanced weapons systems into a region. Sales or coproduction of weapons not deployed with U.S. forces will not be permitted.

3. Development or significant modification of advanced weapons systems for export only will not be permitted.

4. Co-production agreements for significant weapons, equipment, and major components are prohibited.

5. The United States will further discourage retransfers of equipment.

6. Increased regulations to prevent the promotion of arms sales abroad by private or government agents.

The following year, President Carter reasserted this policy in a news conference: "I have pledged myself to cut down on the volume of weapons each succeeding year as long as I'm in office, barring some unpredictable worldwide military outbreak." *New York Times,* February 18, 1978. See also Chapter 11 in this volume by William Lewis for an analysis of the Carter administration's policy.

32. Communist states account for 18 percent of the worldwide arms transfers; non-Communist states, 26 percent; and the United States for the rest *(Report to Congress on Arms Transfer Policy,* op. cit., p. 4).

Lucy Wilson Benson, Undersecretary of State for Security Assistance, Science, and Technology, cited the task of persuading other major suppliers not to fill the voids created by U.S. restraint as "the second big problem" inherent in the new U.S. arms-transfer policy ("Controlling Arms Transfers: An Instrument of U.S. Foreign Policy," speech before the Women's National Democratic Club, Washington, D.C., June 27, 1977, quoted in the Library of Congress Congressional Research Service Report, "Implications of President Carter's Conventional Arms Transfer Policy," p. 60. For a full discussion of why multilateral restraints are unlikely, see ibid., Ch. 4, "Prospects for a Multilateral Approach," pp. 60–73.

33. The Carter administration's efforts to gain the cooperation of other supplier states has been less than successful. France's defense minister stated that his country is not a large supplier of other nations, and that it will not follow President Carter's lead in trying to slow

foreign arms sales: "We believe this is a problem that must receive a global solution. We supply weapons to some countries which asked for them in a spirit of cooperation and are for their security. We are a modest supplier of arms" *(Aerospace Daily,* November 23, 1977, p. 27). The response of the Soviet Union has been more oblique. Although negotiations between the Soviet Union and the United States on the limitation of conventional weapons sales began in mid-1978, prospects for their success are not promising. The *New York Times* reported on December 1 1977, that Soviet weapons sales are increasing and are expected to "more than double" the $2.5 billion figure for 1976: "The view of one experienced source is that the Russians will be willing to talk 'interminably' on the subject, but that it is highly unlikely that they will agree to any restrictions." Hard currency deficits are cited as the primary factor motivating Soviet sales; as of mid-1979, little substantive progress has been reported, although it is sometimes difficult to determine whether it is the United States or the Soviet Union that is dragging its feet the hardest. See "Feud in Administration said to Endanger Talks on Arms Sales Pact," *New York Times,* December 20, 1978.

34. For a discussion of this issue, see S. J. Dudzinsky, Jr. and James Digby, "Qualitative Constraints on Conventional Armaments: An Emerging Issue," Rand Corporation, Santa Monica, Calif., July 1976.

35. Section 2(2) (B) of the Foreign Assistance Act (FAA) of 1973.

36. See U. S. Agency for International Development, House of Representatives, "Implementation of Legislative Reforms in the Foreign Assistance Act of 1973," July 22, 1975.

37. Denis Goulet and Michael Hudson, *The Myth of Aid: The Hidden Agenda of the Development Reports,* prepared by the Center for the Study of Development and Social Change (New York: IDOC North America, 1971).

38. John H. Barton, "The Developing Nations and Arms Control," *Studies in Comparative International Development* 10 (1975): 79.

39. Ibid.

40. Ibid.

41. Ward, *Development Issues for the 1970s,* op. cit., pp. 249–6l.

42. For a detailed description of how the supplier state's decision-making process affects what recipients eventually buy, see "How the U.S. Makes Foreign Military Sales" by Jo Husbands, Chapter 9 in this volume.

43. Neuman, "Security, Military Expenditures, and Socioeconomic Development."

44. James N. Rosenau, "International Studies in a Transnational World," *Journal of International Studies* 5 (1976): 8. Rosenau cites other social scientists who believe that comparability can be achieved without excessive quantification through the analysis of "crucial" cases: Harry Eckstein, "Case Study and Theory in Political Science" in Fred I. Greenstein and Nelson W. Polsby, *Handbook of Political Science* (Reading, Mass.: Addison-Wesley, 1975) vol. 7, pp. 79–137; and P. G. Herbst, *Behavioral Worlds: The Study of Single Cases* (London: Tavistock Publications, 1970).

45. Barney G. Glaser and Anselm Strauss, *The Discovery of Ground Theory: Strategies for Qualitative Research* (Chicago: Aldine Publishing Co., 1976). Others who advocate a more inductive, configurative and comparative approach to research are Clifford Geertz, *Peddlers and Princes* (Chicago: University of Chicago Press, 1963); Sidney Verba, "Some Dilemmas in Comparative Research," *World Politics* 20 (1967); E. E. Evans-Pritchard, *Witchcraft, Oracles and Magic among the Azande* (New York: Oxford University Press, 1937); and Eckstein, "Case Study and Theory."

46. Among others see: "Iranian Debacle Shows Need for Caution in Selling Arms," *Louisville Courier-Journal* (February 20, 1979); David Schoenbaum, "Passing the Buck(s)," *Foreign Policy* 34 (Spring 1979): 20–23; Cynthia Arnson, Stephen Daggett and Michael Klare, *Background Information on the Crisis in Iran* (Washington, D.C.: Institute for Policy Analysis,

1978); George Ball, "Letter to the Editor," *The Economist*, reprinted in the *Baltimore Sun,* February 26, 1979, p. 13; Anthony Lewis, "Who Lost Iran?" *New York Times,* January 1, 1979.

47. Ball, *op. cit.* "This costly burden (military hardware) resulted not only in precipitating a financial squeeze that compelled cut-backs on construction, with resulting unemployment and disaffection, it also led the Shah to megalomania..."

48. George Lenczowski, "The Arc of Crisis: Its Central Sector," *Foreign Affairs* 57, no. 4 (Spring 1979): 812.

49. As Richard Burt observed, one unresolved question facing the Carter administration is "whether the decision to allow Shah Mohammed Reza Pahlevi to purchase almost $20 billion in American arms over the last decade contributed to the social and economic instability that led to the ruler's departure last month." "Iranian Turmoil Impels U. S. Aides to Question Effects of Arms Sales," *New York Times,* February 6, 1979.

14 DEPENDENT MILITARISM IN THE PERIPHERY AND POSSIBLE ALTERNATIVE CONCEPTS

Herbert Wulf

If one examines the declared political aims of practically all governments in the periphery* to increase and strengthen their political independence by building up powerful armed forces, one must conclude that the periphery is far from achieving this goal. In addition to economic influence it is the military sector of the central capitalist countries which has shaped the path of development of the periphery. Importing sophisticated arms from industrialized countries is by no means a panacea for the defense of a nation's sovereignty against outside aggression. On the contrary, the importation of modern arms allows for an intensified penetration by metropolitan countries into societies in the underdeveloped world. Instead of the establishment of political and military independence, new forms of dominance and dependence are created.

This chapter begins with the presentation of evidence that intensified dependency is a logical consequence of the diffusion of modern weapons technology. Second, questions are addressed about the function of the military in controlling internal conflicts and on its "semi-client" status. An

---

*The terms periphery and underdeveloped countries rather than developing or Third World countries are used to stress the dependence of that part of the world on the center countries. The center-periphery theorem has been brought forward particularly in the dependencia literature.

attempt is then made to describe a few principles essential for an alternative military concept based on self-reliance. Lastly, two strands of thought which have so far been unrelated are drawn together; it is argued first that self-reliance cannot be reduced to the formula of economic self-reliance alone, and second, that economic self-reliance is dependent on a convincing, self-reliant defense concept.

ARMS TRANSFER AND ARMS PRODUCTION: DEPENDENCE OF PERIPHERY

Countries

An analysis of the transfer of military technology—including the import and production of modern, sophisticated, and, therefore, highly complex weapons systems designed in industrialized countries requires and absorbs resources which are scarce in underdeveloped countries.[1] Moreover, the ongoing modernization of arms in the East-West confrontation or competition results in perennial obsolescence of weapons, and this modernization process imposes a burden on the resources available. Only a few peripheral countries are in a position to raise enough funds to import the latest equipment, while there is virtually no country in the periphery able to keep up the pace of modernization in local arms production. Despite considerable effort, in India and Israel, for example, to pursue a strict policy of import substitution in the field of military procurement, in more than a decade neither country has approached self-sufficiency in the production of major arms. All major arms-production programs depend on the import of high-technology components, technical assistance, and quite often licenses from industrialized countries. It is particularly onerous and often impossible for peripheral countries to allocate the resources required: research and development facilities, qualified and experienced personnel, government funds (local as well as foreign currency), industrial and infrastructure facilities. The unimpeded flow of arms technology into the periphery, therefore, has substantial negative effects on the development process.

Rapidly increasing prices for new weapon systems—increases way above average inflation rates—have initiated and enhanced efforts in capitalist countries to substitute capital for labor in the production, operation, maintenance, and repair of arms. The intention was to save funds in limited military budgets for the procurement of new weapon systems, but the increasing capital intensity and, concomitantly, the expansion of production facilities, constitute insuperable difficulties for underdeveloped countries. Not only is more scarce capital required, but also the existing gap between large arms-production facilities and small markets (the demand of the armed forces and limited government funds) is enlarged. To use the available resources optimally, an entirely different, even contrary, development in the arms sector is necessary; one which saves capital, emphasizes the use of labor, and thus reduces the size of the production facilities and their volume (if the production of arms is considered essential).*

In comparison to civil production, larger numbers of qualified personnel are absorbed in the production, operation, and maintenance of arms. Since qualified labor is generally a scarce factor in peripheral countries, the importation or local production of modern weapons necessarily intensifies existing bottlenecks in civilian sectors. On the other side, the military and arms sector absorbs relatively few unqualified or semiskilled personnel who are available in abundance and are therefore under- or unemployed. The reason for the low demand for unqualified personnel in arms production is the great complexity of weapons and the constant introduction of new types. Arms never "mature" and reach a significant stage of standardization in production; maturity and standardization in production, however, is a condition for the absorption of unskilled labor in the production process. Consequently, the underdeveloped countries are likely to suffer from a double disadvantage if arms-production programs are initiated locally or modern equipment is procured by the armed forces; the scarcity of skilled personnel raises the cost of technology transfer and, subsequently, production and maintenance costs. Arms production, therefore, is not suitable to alleviate unemployment problems, as is often claimed by governments in peripheral countries. On the contrary, the allocation of insufficient financial resources to purchase or produce weapons reduces the potential for the promotion of development through labor-intensive technologies in civilian sectors of the economy. The argument of creating employment opportunities by producing arms is a rather paltry one and obfuscates the development issue. This is particularly true since the qualifications acquired in arms production or in the military services are only of limited value and only occasionally applicable in civil production.[2]

Dramatically increased imports and greater production of modern military equipment in the periphery were necessarily based on a multiplication of the number of technicians, engineers, and scientists from industrial countries working there. Without their services, it is impossible to keep the

---

*We abstain from raising, at this point, the question whether the import of arms or its local production is required at all, but try instead to elaborate the economic and technological rationality of arms production and its consequences for peripheral countries importing these arms or its production technology.

equipment operational according to the pattern of industrialized countries. The independent decision-making in the military sector which is hoped for, and expected through indigenous arms production, cannot be attained since local production is crucially reliant on the delivery of technology and personnel from abroad.

Besides the fact that modern equipment often lies rusting in ports or stores since it cannot be maintained in actual fighting between peripheral countries, sophisticated carrier systems like fighter-bombers and main battle tanks have often proved a handicap. Because of poor logistics (like shortage of munition supplies), lack of special military infrastructures (like airfields and fortified bridges) and inferior training of soldiers, the modern equipment can be used only marginally or even not at all. Furthermore, once a decision to produce a particular weapon has been taken, further production is predetermined, since arms production requires substantial investment which cannot be simply written off after the first production run. Relatively diversified arms-production programs (as, for example, in India) especially illustrate the constraints imposed on the range of choice for procurement. Alternative (e.g., labor-intensive) production techniques cannot be chosen once a capital-intensive technology has been imported to produce a particular weapon system, nor can the production facilities be easily and quickly converted for the production of a different weapon system. Thus, long-term decisions are made when modern arms are imported. Technology is not freely available, but is the monopoly of those organizations which developed it. Consequently, long-term relations have to be established with suppliers, which might be inopportune and hampering, since political priorities may change even after a short period.

There are obvious parallels between indigenous weapons production and industrialization for import substitution in underdeveloped countries. Like industrialization, the indigenous production of arms suits nationalistic ambitions to reduce the dominance of the metropolitan countries. Empirical results prove, however, that because of dependency on technology transfers from industrial countries, expectations have not been met and additional aims of both industrialization and indigenous arms production, like saving hard currency, enlarging the qualified work force, creating new jobs, and spinoff effects, were likewise unattainable. Instead, difficulties in utilizing installed production capacities emerged.

We can conclude that, as long as there continue to be large disparities in the level of industrialization between underdeveloped and industrialized countries, the production of arms in the periphery according to the standards of industrial countries is impossible; however, despite the failure (in both economic and political terms) of many arms-production programs in the periphery, projects are continued with substantial public subsidies, either because of political prestige or to grant local capitalists a source for accumulation.

The common practice among private firms in industrialized countries of contracting out to producers or installing their own production facilities in the periphery can also be observed, with some time lag, in the field of arms production; arms producers also apply strategies to expand markets or utilize cost differentials in production. For economic reasons, firms in metropolitan countries are willing to satisfy some illusory and unrealistic demands (like developing or producing the most sophisticated fighter bomber) of governments and capitalists in the periphery. This tendency leads to an integration of underdeveloped countries as "suppliers" into the arms transfer system. This incorporation will necessarily be intensifed since indigenous arms production is hampered by insurmountable difficulties and since producers in the periphery adjust to the export-oriented, international division of labor, but without abandoning the formal pretension to accomplish self-reliance. In practice the two types of arms production—indigenous, self-reliant and export-oriented—are not so different as the protagonists of the indigenous production claim, since substantial cooperation of industrialized countries is required in either case.

Numerous examples show that small weapons, light fighting ships and planes, more complex carrier systems (occasionally) and, particularly, components of arms are exported by peripheral countries. Producers in underdeveloped countries are entirely dependent, however, on licenses and technology imports whenever technologically complex arms are to be produced and exported. The two most ambitious arms-production programs in the periphery, those of India and Israel, prove that either intensive government subsidies and incentives for foreign investments have to be made (with all the negative side effects on the whole economy) or exports remain negligible. One can safely predict that, on the basis of far-reaching production plans, arms production in the periphery will expand both quantitatively and qualitatively; the burden placed on the societies will, however, hardly be compensated by aggressive export strategies and internal conflicts will instead be exacerbated. For example, the import of military oriented technology absorbs a large proportion of the import capacity of peripheral countries. In a number of cases (Egypt, Israel, Iraq, Syria, South Korea, Turkey, Libya), a substantial portion of total technology imports are directly related to military activities.[3] Once modern equipment is imported, a chain of supplementary demands is induced, often with a high import content, and with detrimental effects on the balance of payments.

Similar long-term effects are felt in the industrial sector. Capital-intensive arms technology has a locomotive function insofar as the pattern of industrialization is structured according to the needs of the arms sector. By backward and forward linkages, arms-production technology imposes its capital intensity on previous and subsequent production stages. Therefore, local arms production based on the mode of production of industrialized countries is a hindrance for alternative, labor-intensive strategies of development. As the industrial structure is conditioned by the production of arms, so is the infrastructure in the periphery, which develops according to the need to keep modern weapon systems operational. Measured against the basic needs of the majority of the population, such special military infrastructures are, at least, expensive and suboptimal; often, however, they are pacemakers for world market integration and destroy viable subsistence societies.

THE ROLE OF THE ARMED FORCES

The term "arms transfer" is usually associated with the export of tanks, fighter planes, missiles, ships, and other military equipment. But not only is military hardware transferred to the periphery, but "software," including military doctrines and ideologies, are also explicitly exported to influence the armed forces of the periphery. Miles Wolpin states that "Western nations, and particularly the United States, have gradually incorporated political indoctrination into the technical training programs for officers from the Middle East, Africa and Latin America."[4] Moreover, concepts about the development of the societies of the underdeveloped world, such as those of the noncapitalist development path, are transferred together with military concepts from socialist countries.*

Since the military in peripheral countries is oriented to the standards of the armed forces in industrialized countries, and since they experienced a push for modernization immediately after World War II due to the expansion of the U.S. Military Assistance Program, high hopes were placed on the role of the military as an agent of economic, social and political change. These ideas have been formulated most prominently by Lucian Pye.

Above all else...the revolution in military technology has caused the army leaders of the newly emergent countries to be extremely sensitive to the extent to which their countries are economically and technologically underdeveloped. Called upon to perform roles basic to advanced societies, the more politically conscious officers can hardly avoid being aware of the need for substantial changes in their own societies.

Furthermore, "The solder...is constantly called upon to look abroad and to compare his organizations with foreign ones. He thus has a greater awareness of international standards and a greater sensitivity to weaknesses in his own society."[5]

---

*In legitimizing military assistance programs, it is a normal procedure in the United States and in the Soviet Union to point out that the assistance is given to "anticommunist" forces to strengthen the "free world" and to "anti-imperialist" forces building a "socialist" society, respectively.

The external organization described by Pye is still valid in the 1970s;[6] the positive role ascribed to the military in the periphery, however, has not been performed. The functions of the armed forces were permanently expanded and in many countries the army is the political power center. The armed forces as organizations—as well as the political system—were streamlined during the process of decolonization according to the ideology of capitalist countries: parliaments were formed according to the Westminster model, and the armed forces were institutionalized in conformity with the ideas of military academies like Sandhurst, St. Cyr, and, later, West Point. While the Westminster model failed and the state apparatus remained weak, the military prospered and gained in influence, even in those countries where they did not formally assume governmental power. "But training in the use of sophisticated weapons," it is pointed out by Robin Luckham,

does not mean that army officers are more skilled or progressive in their attitudes than any other elite groups. The military has a special place in Third World societies not because its technology is "modern," but because it is a particular kind of technology, that of force. And force is never used in the abstract, but in the struggle between different classes and groups.[7]

The military in the periphery is not only entrusted with the defense of the country against outside aggression (which is the function of the military according to the concept of the liberal state), its internal role is even more essential. The effectiveness of the military in controlling internal conflict and planning and promoting a particular economic model guarantees international cooperation and is the basis for foreign capital investment. Crisis situations in the periphery and the process of underdevelopment can often only be managed with military intervention—that is, internal repression and external aggression. The role of the military is based on a constellation of contradictory international and national interests, or as Irving L. Horowitz put it, "by tacit agreement between a nervous bourgeoisie and a nationalistic military caste."[8]

Even though the military in the periphery is oriented toward the military concepts and doctrines of metropolitan countries, and despite the large amounts of weapons imported from industrial countries, their relationship to the metropoles cannot be characterized as a simple and direct dominance-dependence structure. As a consequence of internal and external threats and hostilities, the doctrine of national security and development emerged, first in Latin America, and then in other underdeveloped areas as well. In this concept, the military is entrusted with the task of maintaining law and order—"a euphemism accepted the world over, for keeping the ruling party or group in power "[9]—and promoting a path of development which permits a certain degree of national autonomy against the penetration of multinational companies. These duties of the armed forces and its contradictions are pertinently described by Robin Luckham as on the one hand, military nationalism directed towards the creation of an internationally effective nation-state supported by a well developed conventional army, increasingly linked through its arms purchases to the international economy; on the other, international pressure for political "stability" at the periphery, requiring an internally powerful state machinery and enlisting military commitment to doctrines of "national security" legitimizing its role in internal repression.[10]

Equally contradictory is the unprecedented accumulation of sophisticated weapon systems in the periphery. This is of direct interest to arms producers in industrialized countries, and it is indirectly essential for capital accumulation since the peripheral economies must be oriented toward export to the world market in order to earn the hard currency to pay for arms imports. On the other side, the allotment of resources for the military and arms restricts the proportion of GNP available for public consumption and national development (social surplus); in a number of peripheral societies (particularly in South Africa and Rhodesia, but also in Chile and other Latin American countries), military activities and the resources allocated for this purpose are so voluminous that the social surplus is totally wasted. The long-term development of these societies is therefore in danger, and the political system that it fought for is jeopardized.

The importation of major weapon systems is contradictory also insofar as this equipment is only of limited value for mastering internal conflicts. Modern fighting ships, fighter planes, or battle tanks are not the equipment used in putting down strikes or crushing a peasant revolt. And, as argued above, this equipment is also only marginally useful for defending the country against outside aggression. Nevertheless, the import of modern weapons from industrial countries is not only of interest to producers in the metropoles or their coproducers in the periphery, but the armed forces are also keen to be equipped with the latest gadgets from the research and development laboratories of industrialized countries. Opposition to importing modern equipment would be inconsistent with the ideology that most militaries have been importing and incompatible with their professionalism. Hence, the demand for arms and the requirement for foreign collaboration reinforce each other; by importing military doctrines and military technology, not only is the mode of production of the supplying country imported (as argued in the previous section), the dependency of the military in the periphery is perpetuated simultaneously.

AN ALTERNATIVE MILITARY CONCEPT

The military posture in the periphery, the doctrines adopted, and the military equipment are not appropriate to resist political pressure from outside, to defend the country, and to make independent decisions in the international arena. Thus, the question arises whether viable alternatives exist to change the asymmetric relations between periphery and metropole. This section spells out a few principles of a possible alternative; naturally, the model must remain somewhat theoretical as almost all peripheral countries at the moment are trying to form their armed forces and military doctrines according to notions from industrialized countries. Practically no peripheral country is seriously attempting to set up a self-reliant defense system, one which depends as little as possible on external assistance in matters of national defense.* The model described here emphasizes reliance on a nation's own efforts instead of imitating industrialized countries or trying to catch up with them by importing doctrines and equipment. The basic idea is to reduce the links to the metropoles as far as possible, to opt out of the periphery-metropole structure, and to develop military concepts, armed forces, and arms suitable to the situation in the particular periphery country. It is obvious that such a defense model is a system of securing peace which includes military power. In view of existing international and internal conflicts, it would be unrealistic and illusionary to suggest the adoption of a strictly nonviolent attitude. This would certainly be understood in the periphery as neocolonial, since existing dominance structures could be enforced by the concentration of military might in the metropoles.

What alternatives exist for a peripheral country to defend itself against an attack or against occupation? What are the means of defense against an enemy using modern arms? If an industrial country, or a peripheral country assisted by a militarily powerful nation, attacks a small country, it will use the means advantageous to it—sophisticated technology; at the same time, however, it will try to limit its military operations so that they cannot be misunderstood by other great powers as an aggression against them. Since peripheral countries are always at a technological disadvantage, the *first principle* of an alternative military concept is that under *no* circumstances should the aggression be countered by using modern, *sophisticated major weapon systems.*[11] The permanently increasing flow of arms into the periphery proves, however, that peripheral countries are attempting to build up their armed forces with equipment of doubtful value. The endeavor to fight with conventional, major weapon systems, despite the technological handicaps and disadvantages, must lead to defeat. "Unconventional" behavior, however, might bring success; peripheral countries have to realize their limited potential for fighting with modern carrier systems and have, therefore, to make a virtue of necessity.[12] From the impossibility of appropriately utilizing modern imported weapon systems, one can delineate the necessity to rely on one's own resources; that is, to stress as

---

*As one possible exception, Yugoslavia might be mentioned; but in Yugoslavia, as well as in the People's Republic of China, during the past few years arms are increasingly produced on the basis of sophisticated military technology from Western countries.

primary the abundant labor available in the periphery. Not only should it be a rule in arms production to limit the use of capital-intensive techniques, but strategic arguments also emphasize the priority of labor intensity.

The substitution of labor by technology, the technique chosen in the industrial countries, appears to be unsuitable to gain increasing self-reliance in the periphery. Equally unrealistic as a viable defense system is a pure form of civil resistance. As an alternative, there remains a type of militia or "people's army" defense system to deter potential aggressors from initiating a war. The *second principle* of an alternative defense system is to guarantee the effectiveness of a labor-intensive defense system through a *high degree of participation by the population.*

A potential aggressor might expect to be able to occupy part or the whole of a territory of a country, but it can be sure to be fought by the active and passive resistance of the whole population. Since the defenders are not dependent on external assistance, the aggressor cannot hope to blackmail the defenders into surrender by cutting off international relations or the supply of weapons and spare parts. On the contrary, the invaders are permanently harassed and attacked by a large number of lightly armed combatants with the intention not necessarily of defending the territory or the border of the country, but of ultimately forcing the aggressors to surrender.

There will be sabotage and petty irritations at many places instead of big battles along front lines. It is part of the attitude and ideology of the population to refuse to do the invaders any service and to resist authority. The mighty U.S. military has recognized that a defense system based on the whole population could even resist U.S. interventions, Brig. Gen. Edward B. Atkeson wrote:

> There is little question that the United States maintains the physical capability to project forces into almost any member state or combination of members of the Organization of Petroleum Exporting Countries. This assessment, however, relates to our ability to overcome or to suppress either a conventional military or guerrilla type of resistance...but they [the U.S. forces] have no comparable background for coping with CBD [civilian based defense].[13]

The intentional lack of emphasis on the use of large carrier systems and a stress on the utilization of labor limits enemies' possibilities for concentrated attacks. Practically no military targets can be hit by an attacker since there are hardly any strictly military targets. Improvements in the accuracy and destructiveness of munitions, improved target-acquisition techniques, and so on, have increased the vulnerability of carrier systems like fighter planes, tanks, and ships. Because the relative immobility of major weapon systems (lack of logistics and infrastructure), they are particularly inappropriate in peripheral countries. The more concentrated such major arms are, and the fewer facilities that are available to move them, the easier a well-equipped aggressor can knock them out. These arguments lead to two conclusions: first, refraining from using sophisticated weapons systems makes the dispersal and decentralization of military units possible, thus giving an aggressor fewer attack options, and the battle can therefore be taken up where the invader shows weakness;[14] second, the application of such a strategy transforms the technological advantages of an invader into a burden. The equipment can only be operated as long as there is some payoff; the longer a military operation in a foreign country lasts, the costlier and less likely is victory.

An additional positive condition, our *third principle*, for an alternative military concept which could be called the militia's independence of special military logistics, is related to the aforementioned: to abstain from using modern, complex weapon systems and to rely on dispersed military units reduces the necessity to move troops and equipment and diminishes logistics problems. The lack of a special military infrastructure decreases the dependence on imports for the installation of infrastructures and also limits the mobility of an invader using complex weapon systems. This situation again strengthens the effectiveness of self-reliant, nontechnical alternative defense systems.

The *fourth principle* is the *decentralization of forces*, but not only because an invader is refused large military targets, and because logistics problems are mounting for an aggressor. When people are trained to fight in the area where they live and work, they can take up military positions at a moment's notice and be mobilized immediately.[15] To mobilize a professional army and to move it to a certain battlefield or front requires much longer periods and is easily detectable by a well-equipped enemy. Also, scarce qualified personnel are recruited for professional armies and are not available for the production of goods and services. In a militia defense system, tasks in production and in defense are basically synchronized.

What kind of weapons are then required for such a defense system stressing self-reliance? The *fifth principle* concerns military units, which, to be compatible with the above principles are, first of all, *lightly armed infantry units*; tanks, fighter planes with a large tactical radius or seagoing ships are not required. In addition to these infantry units, equipped with simple wire-guided antitank missiles, mines, and antiaircraft equipment, a small navy for coastal protection is occasionally required, whereas the protection against possible air attacks lies in the hands of the decentralized infantry units. The weapons will be produced locally as far as possible; should imports be required, supplier relationships will have to be diversified to forestall possible one-sided dependencies.

This defense system is, according to our *sixth principle, defensive in nature and totally unsuitable to attack* a neighboring country. No weapon and no military system can be called purely defensive by definition; however, decentralized military units with their limited radius of movement and the lack of a special military infrastructure, attack ships, and military air-transport capacity can be complemented by a declared policy of non-aggression and the will to avoid offensive operations. This defense system requires only limited funds during peacetime, while in crisis situations immediate and effective reaction is possible because of the high mobilization potential. It guarantees, on the other hand, readiness for defense without unbearable costs, and on the other, signals peaceful intentions towards neighboring countries. Such a system deters would-be aggressors not because they have to fear retaliation, but because the possibilities for a successful invasion are low and occupation of the territory would be highly expensive. The absence of a threat potential could, however, initiate disarmament steps in the region and thus set free resources for social and economic development. Table 14.1 summarizes the basic characteristics of a conventional, highly technocratic army oriented towards the methods of industrialized countries and the alternative of a self-reliant military system dissociated from the industrialized model.

Obviously, the self-reliant military model, if institutionalized, affects not just the military, but it has consequences for the whole society. One of the basic conditions for putting this defense system into practice is the willingness of the majority of the population to participate. This raises the question of whether the society is worthy of defense. Often, only the question of how, but not what, to defend is posed. The people can be motivated to take their share in defending a country when they attach a value to it; that this is not the case in the periphery is not surprising, given the conditions of underdevelopment and the parallel existence of the wealth of a few and the poverty of the masses.

For the rulers in the periphery the self-reliant defense system implies, of course, a danger. Decentralization of military power and participation of the majority of the population requires the breakdown of traditional military hierarchies and a democratization of decision making; it also results in giving up the state monopoly of force. Well-drilled masses, trained in techniques of resistance to authority, would pose a threat against the ruling elite, and military power could not be used for internal repression to maintain the status quo.[16] The establishment of a professional army instead of a people's army to defend the privileges of the ruling class therefore seems natural. In a country, however, where the political system and military power, as well as the economy, is decentralized and self-reliant, "there is little or no domino effect to be obtained by knocking out the centre."[17] Adam Roberts draws attention to the fact that the military seizure of power might not altogether be impossible, but would be less likely.

If military power is the monopoly of a few professionals, it is urged, a military take-over is always politically probable and technically feasible. If, on the other hand,

TABLE 14.1: Characteristics of Alternative Military Concepts in the Periphery

Criteria of the Military and Arms Sector	Technocratic Army (conventional, oriented toward industrial countries)	Militia/Peoples' Army (self-reliant, dissociated from industrial countries)
Budget	High, hard currency required in large quantities	Small, few hard currency requirements
Infrastructure	Diversified and specialized	No special military infra-structure, little logistic system necessary
Weapons and equipment	Capital-intensive modern carrier systems: tanks, aircraft, and fighting ships with large tactical radius, mobile tank divisions; partly locally built and assembled, occasionally exported	Simple: antiaircraft and anti-tank missiles, light infantry weapons; mainly local production; diversified supply lines; marine equipment for coastal protection
Specialists from industrialized countries	Numerous	None
Alliances	Membership; bilateral agreements; often no formal alliance, but neutral with the expectation of receiving external assistance during crises	Principally neutral; nonaggression agreements
Armed forces	Professional army: specialized troops in army, navy, air force	Militia system; personnel-intensive, not organized according to traditional force structure; primarily oriented not according to military but economic functions
Mobilization	Permanent mobilization of the professionals, limited reserves; movement of troops to fronts and battlefields	During times of peace limited degree of mobilization; total mobilization of the population in case of war; mobilization of people in areas where they work and live

TABLE 14.1 *(continued)*

Command structure	Hierarchical, centralized	Democratic, decentralized
Strategy	Defensive and offensive, including potential of preemptive strikes	Defensive, reactive, territorial defense to prevent occupations
Importance of militarism	Expansion of the military's role	Almost the total society participating

Source: Compiled by the author.

the army and the nation are, thanks to a citizen army system, one and the same, then there can be no motive for a coup d'état. Even if some standing forces remain, but the citizenry at large is also armed, then there is a countervailing force which would challenge and defeat any attempt at a coup by the professional soldiers.[18]

The present status of the military, and particularly the strengthening of military postures in the periphery, has recently been described in numerous articles as "militarization." While this militarization is centered around the military and the political and economic elite (not without, of course, tremendous effects on the majority of the people in the underdeveloped world), the self-reliant military concept embraces the whole society. A demilitarization, aimed at for sound humanitarian, ethical, political and economic reasons, is something entirely different from what has been outlined in this section. This "militarism," however, develops in a different direction. Its characteristic is not the expansion of the armed forces' role, but rather the expansion of military functions for the majority of the population. Even if this is carried out in democratic form, the danger exists that this self-reliant military concept could create something like a "war mentality." On the other side, as has been pointed out, great chances exist to initiate a process of disarmament which might eventually lead to the demilitarization of whole regions of the world.

SELF-RELIANT DEVELOPMENT—SELF-RELIANT DEFENSE

Like those contrary military concepts of a technocratic and a self-reliant army, we can observe two opposite concepts in the development debate:

industrialization based on international division of labor and development based on self-reliance. Most development strategies are based on the implicit assumption that development and industrialization in the periphery can best be promoted by an international division of labor, taking into account the different factor endowment of industrialized and underdeveloped countries. International specialization rules are straightforward: industrial countries which are relatively well endowed with capital will export capital-intensive goods; underdeveloped countries with capital scarcity, but an abundance of labor, will import the capital-intensive goods and exchange them against the labor-intensive goods they produce.* By strictly observing the rules of comparative advantage, the export position of peripheral countries is the basic criterion for development policy.

The model of self-reliant development stands in contrast to this trade theory.[19] The historical experience of the peripheral economies proves, according to protagonists of the self-reliance concept, that the international division of labor, world market integration, is asymmetric. The periphery has a structurally disadvantageous position in the international trade system; comparative advantage is the exception rather than the rule, whereas advantages usually exist for the metropoles. Typical of dependent reproduction in the periphery is the economic concentration on export production and luxury consumption, while industrialization has been based historically on stressing the connection of agriculture, goods for mass consumption, and capital goods. To overcome dependent reproduction, the establishment of basic industries and capital-goods industries (particularly for the agricultural sector) is suggested to improve agricultural production quickly, enabling self-reliance in this sector. Marginalized labor, it is urged, should be used in public works in the infrastructure; the increased mass income will increase the internal demand for simple products. Industrial production is to be concentrated on relatively simple and labor-intensive goods, which are protected against world market competition. Through increasing productivity in the agricultural sector, a redistribution of the social surplus, and the utilization of local factors, a self-reliant process of accumulation is initiated which is as far as possible dissociated from the world market.

Economic considerations led to the formulation of the concept of self-reliant development; the analysis of the military-strategic situation in the

---

* This model, explained in numerous economics textbooks (based on the works of Ricardo, Heckscher, and Ohlin), is refined in the so-called product-cycle theory which takes into account that labor can be skilled and unskilled. The theory further takes into account that products that are manufactured pass through certain production cycles, from the stage of experimentation, research, and development to standardization and maturity. Since standardized and matured goods need only little skilled labor, peripheral countries ought to specialize in their production.

periphery, particularly the dependence on arms produced in industrial countries, has led for similar normative reason, to the design of a self-reliant military concept. Johan Galtung pointed to the parallels between economic development and military concepts.

Just as there is a basic compatibility between capitalistic growth and modern, hierarchical, technocratic military organisation, there is also a basic compatibility between self-reliance as the basic mode of production and paramilitary/guerrilla/satyagraha forms for defense whereby the civilian population is mobilised and becomes less vulnerable and less clientelised through dependence on vertical military organizations that in turn depend on Centre countries for supplies of military hardware and software through hierarchical 'alliance' systems.[20]

From the analysis of the periphery-metropole system, one can delineate the essential role of the periphery for the international capitalist system. If the assumptions of the self-reliance theorists are correct, self-reliance will obviously reach its limits where the capitalist system is affected. Self-reliance, if practiced, will therefore probably be fought with sanctions, political vetoes, and military actions by the metropoles. Hence, a basic condition for a self-reliant society is the existence of a credible and viable defense system to guarantee the process of dissociation against outside aggression and threats. Economic dissociation can only be accomplished by previously or simultaneously opting out of the international arms trade and military system.

NOTES

1. The first section of this chapter is based on detailed empirical research by the Institute for Peace Research and Security Policy (IFSH) Study Group on Armaments and Underdevelopment at Hamburg University. For some of the findings, see Ulrich Albrecht, Dieter Ernst, Peter Lock, Herbert Wulf, *Rustung and Unterentwicklung,* Reinbek 1976. See also the article by the same authors, "Armaments and Underdevelopment," *Bulletin of Peace Proposals* 5 (1974): 173–86; and Peter Lock and Herbert Wulf, "Register of Arms Production in Developing Countries," Hamburg, March 1977, mimeo; as well as Peter Lock and Herbert Wulf, "Consequences of the Transfer of Military-Oriented Technology on the Development Process," *Bulletin of Peace Proposals* 8 (1977): 127–36.

2. Arguments—such as those of Emile Benoit—that claim positive effects resulting from the application of qualifications received in the armed forces (among other reasons) should be refuted rather than taken seriously. See his *Defense and Economic Growth in Developing Countries* (Lexington, Mass.: Lexington Books, 1973).

3. For details, see Lock and Wulf, "Consequences of the Transfer of Military-Oriented Technology," p. 129.

4. Miles D. Wolpin, "External Political Socialization as a Source of Conservative Military Behavior in the Third World," *Studies in Comparative International Development* 1 (1973): 3.

5. Lucian W. Pye, "Armies in the Process of Political Modernization," in John J. Johnson ed. *The Role of the Military in Underdeveloped Countries* (Princeton, N.J., Princeton University Press, 1962), pp. 78 and 79.

6. Two examples of the many studies on the subject are Robert M. Price, "A Theoretical Approach to Military Rule in New States," *World Politics* 23 (1971): 399–430; and Uma O. Eleazu, "The Role of the Army in African Politics," *Journal of Developing Areas* (1973): 265–86.

7. Robin Luckham, "Militarism: Arms and the Internationalisation of Capital," Institute for Development Studies, *IDS Bulletin*, 8 (1977): 40.

8. Irving L. Horowitz, "Military Origins of the Cuban Revolution," *Armed Forces and Society* No. 4 (1975), p. 41

9. "Political Growing Power," *Economic and Political Weekly* 9 (1974): 846.

10. Robin Luckham, "Militarism: Force, Class and International Conflict," *IDS Bulletin* 9 (1977): 23.

11. Emil Spannocchi, "Verteidigung ohne Selbstzerstörung," in G. Broosolet and E. Spannocchi, *Verteidigung ohne Sclacht* Munich: Hansen, 1976. Spannocchi, chief of staff of the Austrian armed forces, concluded with respect to the Austrian situation: "Woe to the attacked small country which would try to start a reverse on the same level with mini forces downgraded to its own proportions. The permanently increasing technological hiatus would choke it within days."

12. The lack of economic and military resources forced leaders like Mao, Giap, and Tito to develop "unconventional" military strategies which finally proved to be superior to technologically advanced enemies. Over several decades, even the United States armed forces had to recognize that the practice of loading the armed forces of the periphery with modern equipment was only of limited value. The "Nixon Doctrine" is an expression of this experience: "Total-force planning is ... of questionable utility for shaping our military relations with developing nations that lack technological skills and an indigenous industrial base." (G. J. Parker, S. Canby, R. R. Johnson, and W. B. Quandt, "In Search of Self-Reliance: U.S. Security Assistance to the Third World Under the Nixon Doctrine," R-1092-ARPA, Rand Corporation, Santa Monica, Calif., June 1973, p. 16. Furthermore, with respect to Yugoslavia's military concept, "A modern conventional army is ill-equipped to control territory." (ibid.).

13. Edward B. Atkeson, "The Relevance of Civilian-Based Defense to U. S. Security Interests," *Military Review*, June 1976, p. 52.

14. This strategy, used by Mao, Giap, Che Guevara and others, is currently being discussed by strategists in Europe with respect to European theaters. See, for example, Spannocchi, "Verteidigung ohne Selbstzerstörung"; Guy Brossollet, "Das Ende der Schlact," same volume; Horst Afheldt, *Verteidigung und Frieden, Politik mit militärischen Mitteln* (Munich, Hansen, 1976); and with different conclusions, Adam Roberts, *Nations in Arms* (London: Chatto and Windus, 1976).

15. For this argument, see Roberts, *Nations in Arms,* p. 229.

16. Socialists like Marx, Engels, Lenin, Liebknecht, Bebel, Lasalle, and others have extensively dealt with the question of democratizing the armed forces and creating a state of armed workers. A discussion of this literature is in Roberts, *Nations in Arms,* Ch. 1. See also Wolfram Wette, *Kriegstheorien Deutscher Sozialisten* (Stuttgart, 1971). It should also be noticed that liberation armies (like those in Algeria and Indonesia) at least came close to the above described defense system. They were, however, after the successful decolonization, streamlined according to the principles of industrial countries of the West.

17. Johan Galtung, "Trade or Development: Some Reflections on Self-Reliance," *Economic and Political Weekly,* February 1976, p. 215.

18. Roberts is not totally convinced by the arguments he quotes and gives possible divergent examples (Greece and Algeria): see *Nations in Arms,* p. 242.

19. See, particularly, Samir Amin, *Accumulation on a World Scale: A Critique of the Theory of Underdevelopment,* 2 vols., and *Unequal Development: An Essay on the Social Formations of Peripheral Capitalism* (New York: Monthly Review Press, 1974 and 1976).

20. Galtung, "Trade or Development," p. 215. Galtung appears to be the only advocate of the self-reliance model who has mentioned the necessity to include the military sector—theoretically as well as practically—in the transformation process necessary to achieve self-reliance.

15 ARMS TRANSFERS AND THE "BACK-END" PROBLEM IN DEVELOPING COUNTRIES

Geoffrey Kemp

INTRODUCTION

The Vietnam and 1973 Arab-Israeli wars demonstrated that modern nonnuclear weapons systems can perform remarkable tasks, owing to the revolution in microelectronics and parallel increases in lethality due to improvements in accuracy and guidance systems. Furthermore, in some cases, new generations of weapons, because of microelectronics and modular replacement techniques, have made routine operation and maintenance tasks easier than in the past. It might be assumed, therefore, that the capability of developing countries to operate and maintain modern armed forces is to be enhanced as they are sold or given more and more weapons. It is the aim of this chapter to suggest that this may not, in fact, be the case and that most developing nations are becoming more dependent upon the supplier countries as they modernize their armed forces. This is resulting in a growing discrepancy between *static* indicators of a local military balance—which are usually expressed in terms of nominal weapons inventories in publications such as the International Institute for Strategic Studies' (IISS) annual publication, *The Military Balance*—and more *dynamic* indicators—which take into account the operational status, deployment patterns, mission characteristics, and support infrastructure of military forces, as well as estimates of military doctrine and fighting capabilities of local forces.

In view of the great political significance attached to "raw" numbers, whether in the context of debates on arms-transfer policy or in assessments of regional power relationships, it is important to pursue this question further. In addition, since the United States under the legacy of the "Nixon Doctrine" is coming to rely more and more on local friendly countries to play an active role in regional defense, a clearer understanding of the relationship between arms transfers and military capabilities is essential. This is especially valid in view of the collapse of the Shah's regime in Iran and the unanswered questions this crisis has posed for U.S. arms-transfer policies.

The military force structures which many developing countries are buying require very sophisticated management and, despite new-found wealth and large defense budgets, rich recipient countries lack the basic skills and infrastructure to support military forces without considerable outside help. For instance, although countries such as Iran and Saudi Arabia have paid cash for sophisticated weapons, they have also had to buy the services of U.S. and European personnel, both civilian and military, to manage many of them. This ongoing and symbiotic relationship between the suppliers and the rich recipients has already led to political complications resulting from the large number of foreign technicians and their families that have to reside in these countries. For instance, the presence of Soviet military advisors in Egypt created enormous discontent within Egyptian society, as did the burgeoning American presence in Iran before the fall of the Shah. It must be considered that the U.S. presence in Saudi Arabia might also create difficulties—if, for example, there were to be a major breakdown in law and order in that country, the United States would have to mount a major evacuation effort. We also have to acknowledge, however, that this presence gives the supplier considerable leverage over the recipient. In the event that the United States were to withdraw its presence and cut off spare parts, then, as in the case of the Soviet withdrawal from Egypt, the level of preparedness of the local armed forces would decline precipitously.

These issues are part of a set of political, logistical, and support problems—so-called back-end problems—that were less apparent in the past, when the recipients of sophisticated U.S. and Soviet arms were either capable of operating and maintaining the weapons themselves, or were recipients of U.S. and Soviet arms aid and were, therefore, under the direct control of both superpowers. This chapter will focus upon the back-end phenomenon, a factor that is rarely considered in most arms-transfer literature, yet is the key to understanding the practical implications of arms transfers to major recipients in developing countries.

In this context, back-end operations refer to those activities that take place once an arms-transfer agreement has been reached and these activities can continue for many years, for they include not only the initial support for a new program (training, infrastructure, etc.) but follow-on support, including maintenance and logistics. "Front-end" operations refer to the decisions and activities that take place before a transfer is made and, since the nature and extent of back-end operations will be dependent upon the front-end decisions, control of the front-end decisions is a critical element in any arms-transfer relationship. Most writing and official pronouncements about arms sales to developing countries concern front-end decisions—who buys and sells what types of weapons and why—rather than back-end operations. In part, this reluctance to take notice of back-end operations stems from ignorance. It also results, however, from the fact that the front-end process tends to be more stimulating; it is more exciting to debate whether country X should receive weapons system Y than whether country X has the trained personnel to operate and maintain weapons system Y.

A good example of the need for back-end analysis is the case of the Indonesian arms buildup in the late 1950s and early 1960s. The Soviet Union, eager to assist the far-reaching ambitions of President Sukarno, provided Indonesia with lavish amounts of military equipment, and by 1965 the nominal inventory of major Soviet weapons in the Indonesian navy and air force consisted of the following: Navy—1 heavy cruiser, 5 destroyers, 12 submarines; and Air Force—18 Mig-21s, 42-plus Mig-17/19s, 25 Tu-16s, 25 IL-28s.

By all accounts this was an impressive list for a less industrial country at that time and, on paper, it helped to make Indonesia by far the largest military power in Southeast Asia.* Yet when Sukarno was overthrown in 1965, it was discovered that virtually none of the Soviet-supplied jet aircraft and warships were operable. The reasons for this extraordinary discrepancy between the *nominal* and *operational* inventories were simple: the Indonesians were not capable of operating and maintaining such sophisticated weapons, and the Soviets were quite willing to provide weapons they knew would never be used. The point is that no country can support a modern armed force unless it has a well-established infrastructure. Furthermore, it is not enough for a country merely to have an industrial base, although this naturally helps. It will be recalled that West Germany had great problems

---

*At the time Indonesia was engaged in the "confrontation" with Britain and Malaysia, and there were ongoing skirmishes between British and Indonesian forces in North Borneo. Despite the fact that the fighting never escalated beyond company-level encounters in the jungle, there was considerable concern in Britain and Malaysia that Indonesia might use its Soviet weapons, so much so that at one point an RAF V-bomber squadron was rotated out of Singapore to act as a deterrent against an Indonesian escalation of the conflict. In retrospect, it is clear that Great Britain had little to fear from these weapons.

with the F-104G program in the early 1960s because, among other things, it attempted to absorb the weapon too quickly*.

Throughout the 1950s and 1960s U.S. arms-transfer policy reflected a sensitivity to the support requirements for developing nations and, in this respect, there is no equivalent in the U.S. record of the Soviet arms transfers to Indonesia. The reason for this is that in the days when the vast bulk of U.S. arms transfers to developing countries were funded under the Military Assistance Program (MAP) the executive and legislative branches were able to exercise considerable control over the types of force structures with which these countries were provided. There were numerous occasions during this period when requests for MAP arms were turned down on the grounds that a certain weapon was too sophisticated for the recipient; so long as U.S. taxpayers were footing the bill, such control was possible.

This began to change in the 1970s. Congress became increasingly disillusioned with the Military Assistance Program, in part as a result of the experience of the Vietnam war, which some felt was, among other things, an outgrowth of early involvement with MAP in that country. In addition, the ability of many recipients of MAP to pay for their own arms was increasing during this period and, naturally, there was no inclination in Congress to subsidize countries who could pay cash for arms, and the shift from MAP to foreign military sales (FMS) began in the late 1960s, when countries such as Iran and Japan began to pay for U.S. weapons. The trend was dramatically accelerated after the 1973 oil-price hike. This meant that former MAP recipients such as Iran and Saudi Arabia could now afford to buy on the world arms market most of the weapons they wanted.

In very simple terms what happened was that the constraints on the procurement of advanced weapons were removed overnight, and as a result of the ensuing financial bonanza, it became increasingly difficult for the United States and other suppliers to turn down requests for advanced arms, especially when several of the richest purchasers were also important suppliers of oil to the United States. There were also good incentives for the oil-rich buyers to order large quantities of arms. Some of them, especially Iran, had a backlog of deferred demand from the more restrictive period in the late 1960s and early 1970s; also, the new wealth of the Persian Gulf states brought with it a new sense of insecurity and thereby added to the pressures for a rapid improvement in military capabilities. There was a further

---

*The F-104G Starfighter became known as the "Widow Maker" in Germany because of the high number of pilot deaths in the early years of its service. Since many other countries operated a similar but not as sophisticated version of the F-104, the crashes were put down to German inexperience with advanced airplanes, rather than because of any fundamental defect in design.

assumption that the future reliability of the suppliers could not be guaranteed unless orders were firmly placed; hence, there were incentives to order today, in large quantities, arms that were needed tomorrow. Furthermore, since the demand for advanced arms has grown, the timetable for supplying modern weapons has slipped unless recipients were placed high in the "queue" for deliveries. This, together with the clear interest of Western arms sales personnel to secure orders for their countries and companies, has led to what can only be described as an overload on the market. In virtually all cases, a good *strategic* argument could be made to justify a particular sale; just as frequently, however, the preparations for absorbing the weapons were woefully inadequate.

In sum, once economic and political factors began to influence major front-end decisions on arms transfers, it was inevitable that the back-end would become strained, especially in the short run. This is the situation found today in most well-armed developing countries and it has had particular relevance in Iran, which under the Shah tried to meet the threats to its security by purchasing large quantities of foreign weapons and foreign technical personnel to help operate and maintain them.

SUPPORT REQUIREMENTS FOR A MODERN MILITARY FORCE

In the days prior to the industrial revolution, an army marched on its stomach, and the major constraint on a navy's mobility was access to fresh-water supplies. Napoleon's Grande Armée had much the same support requirements as Caesar's legions; that is to say, the most important constraint on fighting mobility was access to "food and fodder." The English navy at the time of Trafalgar fought in ships not much larger than Roman galleys, though having different armament. In contrast, a modern military force depends upon a different set of support priorities to that found in the preindustrial era. Today, fuel and ammunition account for the bulk of logistic requirements in wartime and, in peacetime, fuel and spare parts are the most critical factors; food is only a minor item in terms of budgets and transportation. In addition to these basics, to deploy and operate effectively, armies need barracks and an adequate road system; an air force must have air bases with protection and maintenance for its aircraft; a navy needs a port and supply ships. All three services must have adequate command, control, and communications (CCC), which include land, air, and sea communications, early-warning radar capabilities, and standard operating procedures to follow in event of crisis or war.*

---

*Before the introduction of the telegraph in the mid-nineteenth century, communications between military units were either visual or hand-carried. Improvement in communication made it possible to control larger, more complicated military formations over longer distances, thereby centralizing command systems and radically altering the nature and uses of military forces.

Once the broad requirements for peacetime deployment are met, the next need is for routine day-to-day support. Modern land, air, and sea equipment will not function unless it is serviced properly. Heavy items such as tanks break down with predictable frequency; a modern combat aircraft wears out tires very quickly, quite apart from more complicated items of equipment; a warship operating on routine training missions requires around-the-clock maintenance to insure that its boilers and pumps are working and that its electrical system is operational. These routine tasks pose little problem for an industrial country that has experience and a pool of trained personnel, but for less industrialized countries, such routine tasks can become extreme burdens.

If a modern military force has to fight, the tasks become far more difficult, and things can go seriously wrong even for an industrial country. Once weapons begin to be used in combat, the demands on the support services increase geometrically. The fuel requirements may triple or quadruple because the force is on the move; this means that fuel transportation and the availability of the correct types of petrol, oil, and lubricants (POL) loom large as constraints which are less apparent in peacetime conditions. If fighting occurs, the demand for ammunition and its transportation rises from virtually zero to potentially high levels, depending upon the intensity of combat. At this stage routine maintenance is not enough; crews must be trained to repair damaged equipment under fire or on the move. It is one thing to repair a tank that has lost a track in a training area, and quite another to repair it along a muddy ditch with shells exploding all around. Similarly, the wear and tear on aircraft and ships expands exponentially once high-intensity operations begin. After two or three days of sustained combat, the actual inventories of weapons capable of being used may decline precipitously. After several weeks of combat, the critical constraints will now come to include the repair and replacement of major items such as engines, transmitters, and electronics. By the end of a week or so of high-intensity combat, the divergence between military capabilities as indicated by nominal peacetime inventories and the in-commission wartime forces—including, in the case of aircraft, the numbers of sorties that can be generated daily—will be very great.

The impact of these constraints over the operational effectiveness of developing-country military forces has been amply demonstrated in several conflicts fought over the past 15 years. In 1965, India and Pakistan fought a short, but high-intensity war in the Punjab, using modern tanks and aircraft. The war was abruptly terminated after a couple of weeks' fighting, in part because of the arms embargo imposed upon both sides by Britain and the United States. Although the embargo hurt Pakistan more, even India would have found it difficult to conduct such operations for much longer without external support. The brief war between El Salvador and Honduras in 1971 literally ground to a halt after one week of fighting because the United States refused to resupply basic materiel, including ammunition. The nature and course of the 1973 Arab-Israeli war were, after the first weeks, greatly influenced by the respective resupply policies of the Soviet Union and the United States. In fact, it is difficult to think of an example of protracted, high-intensity war in less industrialized regions that has not ultimately been dependent upon the industrial powers to sustain it, and such dependencies may be growing, rather than diminishing, despite the so-called "diffusion of power."

SELF-SUFFICIENCY FOR DEVELOPING NATIONS?

To what extent can developing countries, over time, develop the infrastructure and skills necessary to become more self-reliant in force management and, therefore, more capable of conducting large-scale military operations independent of the industrial powers? The answer will depend upon the country in question, the types of weapons involved, and the level of autarky desired.

Although most recipients of modern weapons wish to maximize their self-sufficiency for reasons of national control, a majority also want to have the most up-to-date weapons. This can lead to a vicious circle; as a country reaches the point of becoming relatively self-sufficient in operating a given weapons system, a more modern weapon is procured which requires a new series of dependencies upon the supplier. To illustrate the point, consider the case of Israel, perhaps the most sophisticated of all industrializing nations in the field of weapons management, and certainly a country capable of effectively operating weapons in combat. Israel has had strong reasons to develop its own armaments industry in view of the perfidious nature of its previous arms suppliers, especially France. As a result, Israel now has a flourishing aircraft, tank, missile, and patrol-boat industry which produces excellent sophisticated equipment for its own forces and for the export market. Israel must buy from the United States, however, the latest military technology to keep ahead of the Arab countries in the "qualitative" balance. Thus, at the same time that Israel is trying to market the sophisticated Kfir Mach 2.0 jet fighter, it is coming to rely even more on the United States for its next generation of sophisticated aircraft (the F-15 and F-16).*

---

*Israel's performance in weapon design and production is remarkable for a country so small. One indicator of its export capabilities in this field is found in a special advertising supplement on the Israel Air Industry found in *Aviation Week & Space Technology,* which lists 20 pages of export products ranging from highly sophisticated electronic equipment to the Kfir fighter (which to Israel's chagrin still has U.S. engines) and air-to-air systems.

Although the goal of self-sufficiency is usually sought, in reality there can be costs in seeking too much autarky from military, economic, and political standpoints. Developing countries have these initial alternatives when seeking to build up a modern military force. They can seek autarky or accept dependency on one supplier, or they can opt to receive their arms from multiple suppliers. Each of these options has drawbacks as well as benefits.

With the autarky option, it is assumed that the country decides to rely almost entirely on its own resources for the implementation and support of weapons procured or received by grant aid from external sources. The benefits of this are considerable: first, a state is able to use weapons when and where it pleases and not operate under the fear of cutoffs, embargoes, or slowdowns in spare parts and additional arms; secondly and more from a military point of view, if one relies on one's own labor to undertake basic maintenance and repair operations, there will be greater control over combat operations. For instance, during the hostilities with the United States, North Vietnam opted for a policy of comparative autarky; that is to say, while it relied on the Soviet Union and the People's Republic of China for weapons, it was careful not to have to rely on Soviet or Chinese advisers to operate and service these weapons. There are suggestions that the North Vietnamese never accepted the more sophisticated Soviet surface-to-air missile (SAM-3), but instead relied on the old-fashioned SAM-2 because they made a trade-off between the costs of bringing in Soviets to run SAM-3 and the benefits of keeping SAM-2 under their own control. Certainly North Vietnam would have benefited from the SAM-3 in any campaign analysis of the air war, yet it would have been dependent upon the Soviet Union to control the operation; the cost of going it alone, then, was that the North Vietnamese forewent better weapons. This type of trade-off is a difficult one for a small country at war to make; the introduction of new weapons may make all the difference between victory and defeat, yet the price of dependency may be to compromise sovereignty during and after a conflict.

India is another example of a country that has made every effort to rely as little as possible on external suppliers beyond the purchase of initial equipment and blueprints for co-production. In the process, however, India's overall defense preparedness has suffered; the weapons in the inventories of the Indian armed forces are not very modern, even by less industrial standards, and Indian defense planners constantly have to worry that their potential adversaries would be able to outclass their forces if they received large quantities of new equipment from Western countries. Despite these risks, however, India has saved foreign exchange and has built up an impressive support infrastructure which makes it far less susceptible to arms embargoes than was the case in 1965.

The second option open to the recipient, dependency on a sole supplier, has many benefits. First and foremost, it is the most efficient way to procure and operate a modern military force; if a developing country's air force operates only U.S. airplanes that are in the current inventory of the U.S. Air Force or U.S. Navy, logistical support and routine maintenance are much simpler than buying several different types of airplanes from different foreign air forces. Similarly, if a country has a sole-supplier relationship with the producer, it may well get preferential treatment in the queue of customers who are seeking to buy weapons. However, the costs of this dependency are considerable. The supplier has enormous leverage over the recipient and can at any time slow down or cut off the flow of spare parts. This has been done by the Soviet Union, United States, Great Britain, and France and, in almost all circumstances, the recipients have taken steps to avoid future sole dependency. The few important developing countries who presently have sole-dependency relationships are those who have no other options; that is, they cannot buy their sophisticated arms elsewhere for political reasons, such as South Korea, Taiwan, and Cuba. It should be remembered, however, that the reference here is to *sophisticated* weapons; virtually any country in the world, including pariah states, can gain access to small arms and less sophisticated heavy weapons, owing to the diversity of suppliers and a flourishing private arms trade.

The third option is to rely on multiple suppliers, and this has almost opposite costs and benefits to those of sole dependency. The benefits are the avoidance of decisive leverage and an embargo by one supplier. The costs can be measured in terms of inefficiency since the multiplication of different systems increases the logistical-support requirements. In reality, those countries who rely on multiple suppliers face various costs and benefits, depending upon the actual status of their inventories.

An interesting example of this type of relationship is Iran. Under the Shah, the Iranian armed forces embarked upon a massive and costly rearmament program involving the very latest nonnuclear technology. Although the Iranian air force had an all-American inventory of weapons, there was a deliberate policy of diversification for other services. The navy had large numbers of European ships and the army had British tanks and even some Russian equipment. Iran has no capacity to build or fabricate most of the spare parts required for its inventories, which currently include the F-14/Phoenix missile system. Although the new regime has cancelled many of the orders placed by the Shah for future systems, such as the F-16 combat aircraft and the ultrasophisticated airborne warning and control systems (AWACS), the remaining Iranian inventory is still very large and still very dependent upon foreign suppliers. Herein lies the dilemma for the regime which, on the one hand, professes to wish to expunge all foreign, and especially U.S. influence, and yet, on the other hand, can only do so at great cost to its armed forces. For instance, spare parts for Iran's air force must either come from stockpiles in Iran or U.S. logistical support facilities in the United States and Europe. So long as the United States and Iran maintained very close relations, this was an efficient way to build up a modern air force and Iran avoided many of the problems of developing a comprehensive support infrastructure, which it would have to do if it wished to be self-sufficient in all components. The price Iran paid, however, was dependency on the United States. It can be argued that the United States will never deny the present regime spare parts, provided U.S. technology is not further compromised, but there are circumstances under which the Iranian use of its air force would not be approved by the United States; for instance, the use of Iranian forces against Israel would automatically result in an arms embargo.

If the latter two options are unsatisfactory and the first unattainable, developing countries can switch suppliers. This can have long-run benefits if newer and better equipment is procured from a different source. The costs are primarily of the short term, but they may be serious, especially if the recipient faces the prospect of actually having to fight a war. It is not easy to switch suppliers if you have a relatively large infrastructure and inventory. Egypt's attempts to switch to Western suppliers, as a result of its dissatisfaction with the Soviet Union, illustrate the point; it will be five or more years before the Egyptian air force can be fully equipped and operational with Western airplanes, and in the meantime Egypt is at a serious disadvantage in event of renewed hostilities with Israel. Therefore, in the process of switching suppliers, countries may be vulnerable to attack or, alternatively, may have to forego the option of using military force.

BACK-END PROBLEMS AND U.S. ARMS SALES POLICY

To what extent should back-end considerations influence U.S. arms-transfer policies? Obviously, this is an important question in view of the large number of developing countries that want to purchase U.S. weapons and the pressures on the United States government to balance the perceived benefits and costs of selling arms. Back-end arguments can be used by both supporters and detractors of U.S. arms sales. Supporters can point to the fact that unless back-end problems are solved, the military effectiveness of arms transfers will be diminished and, therefore, the capacity of the recipients to fight in the event of war will be weakened. Detractors can argue that, because of the inherent difficulty of maintaining a modern military force without outside help, the back-end phenomenon should be used as an argument for limiting the sale of advanced arms to developing nations.

Unfortunately, there is no easy answer as to what the optimum U.S. policy should be, for, as always, there are trade-offs between short- and long-term costs and benefits no matter what perspective one takes. Again, the example of past U.S. arms-sale policy to Iran is illustrative. From the perspective of those who believed that Iran, under the Shah, was an important pro-Western country that should receive U.S. military support, there were difficulties in determining what the arms-transfer policy should be; while supporters of a pro-Iran policy agreed that arms should be sold, not everybody agreed on the types, quantities, and delivery schedules. The short-term benefits of selling Iran large numbers of sophisticated aircraft were primarily political and economic; the short-term costs were that Iran would be unable to fight with the weapons because of training and support deficiencies. Furthermore, in the short run, the level of effort required to implement new programs actually downgraded existing military capabilities by "poaching" on skilled personnel reserves. There is evidence, for instance, that while Iran was giving priority to implementing the F-14 program, air and ground crews from the F-4 were denuded, thus compromising the operational effectiveness of the F-4 squadrons.*

The fact that Iran under the Shah required an open-ended U.S. back-end commitment was seen by some as a plus because it supposedly gave the United States some control over the overall nature and direction of Iranian military policy. However, as events turned out, such control was insufficient to save the Shah; though it must be added that if the United States had been prepared to intervene more determinedly the military connection would have been invaluable.

The Iranian example is perhaps the most visible of the various policy dilemmas the United States has had to face, but it is only one of many. In other cases, such as Saudi Arabia, the United States also has back-end commitments that are likely to continue into the indefinite future provided the current regime remains in power. Beyond a certain level of involvement, the questions raised by back-end operations transcend the narrow calculations of benefits and costs in the context of arms-transfer policy. For instance, the large numbers of U.S. personnel hired to look after U.S. weapons and support systems, and the families who accompany them, raise sociological questions that can complicate relations between the United States and the recipient country, as the Iranian example demonstrates.

Most important, though, are the emerging political relationships between the United States and developing countries who buy large quantities of arms. In the past, the United States had direct control over most of its well-armed clients and was therefore able to influence the overall nature and direction of their foreign and domestic policies. In short, the

---

*For more details on this and other problems of Iranian military programs, see Geoffrey Kemp and Robert Mantel, "U.S. Military Sales to Iran," Staff Report to the Subcommittee on Foreign Assistance of the Committee on Foreign Relations, U.S. Senate, U.S. Government Printing Office, July 1976.

United States was able to control or influence many of their "front-end" operations. The new wealth of many developing nations has increased their importance to the United States, while at the same time their independence in terms of "front-end" operations has dramatically improved. The United States and other industrial powers still have implicit control over their back-end operations, but the implications of this new set of power relationships are not yet clear. On the surface, a more equal partnership between the industrial and developing world has emerged but, in reality, basic asymmetries remain; in the last resort, the only protection for many of the new emerging countries is the military power of the United States. Yet, because the day-to-day nature of political relationships has become more diffused, there is no consensus in the United States as to what sort of relationship should ultimately be pursued with these countries. One thing is certain, though; because of back-end commitments it simply will not be possible for the United States to isolate itself from the inevitable turmoil that will continue to accompany rapid modernization in important strategic areas such as the Middle East. It is in this context that the seeds of confusion, drama, and crisis lie.

16 ARMS TRANSFERS, MILITARY TRAINING, AND DOMESTIC POLITICS

Ernest W. Lefever

This chapter is based on the premise that arms transfers and associated training and advice constitute a single instrument of U.S. foreign policy. The basic purpose of this or any other U.S. foreign-policy instrument is to influence the foreign policy of other governments, rather than their domestic policies or institutions, at least to the extent that the two arenas of decision can be separated. This point was made clearly by President Richard Nixon at the U.S. Naval Academy in 1974.

Our primary concern in foreign policy must be to help influence the international conduct of nations in the world arena. We would not welcome the intervention of other countries in our domestic affairs and we cannot expect them to be cooperative when we seek to intervene directly in theirs. We cannot gear our foreign policy to transform other societies....Peace between nations with totally different systems is also a high moral objective.[1]

It is further assumed here that the primary goal of U.S. policy toward the Third World has been and is to maintain and strengthen regional stability (i.e., a non-war-prone condition) that encourages mutually beneficial political, economic, and cultural relations between the United States and other countries.[2]

In the real world of politics, foreign and domestic policies cannot be neatly separated since each realm necesssarily impinges on the other. This is

276

true for the United States as well as for the smaller countries of the Third World which have received military assistance from Washington. The assessment of the domestic effects of military aid is further complicated by the ever-present reality of multiple causation and by the several, though not fully identifiable, connections between regional stability and the internal stability of the states in the region. Generally, U.S. policy-makers have assumed there is a high positive correlation between internal and interstate stability. This assumption is not without plausibility; it is virtually self-evident that a country living at peace and having a government with broadly-based consent is less likely to make trouble for its neighbors than a country that is turbulent or on the brink of civil war.

The ideological factor should also be noted. Messianic regimes that seek to impose their ideology on other peoples, whether such regimes are of the extreme left or right, whether they are internally orderly or turbulent, tend to be destabilizing forces in world politics because their doctrine requires them to be. Constrained only by limited resources and available opportunities, they are compelled to seek by subversion or attack the overthrow of unfriendly regimes; recently, Castro's Cuba, Neto's Angola, and Kim Il Sung's North Korea have pursued this course. Democratic governments, almost by definition, tend to favor internal order and stability in other states because conditions are seen as prerequisites to constructive and peaceful change and development.

In assessing the impact of any foreign-policy program, it is important to distinguish between intention and consequences, between desired effects and collateral and unintended effects. Any U.S. policy designed to enhance regional stability by strengthening one state against the threat of attack or subversion from another, may well have the unintended side effect of bolstering, at least temporarily, the regime of the former, which may be repressive or liberal, authoritarian or democratic, popular or unpopular, strong or weak. It is also important to distinguish military aid from CIA activities, a point elaborated later in this chapter.

With these caveats in mind, this study examines the official U.S. program of arms transfers to more than 70 friendly and allied countries since the end of World War II, focusing on Third World states. These transfers have always been accompanied by U.S. training and advice for officers and men of the recipient's armed services. The objectives, significance and political consequences of military deliveries, whether provided by grant, loan, or sale, cannot be understood apart from the training and advice associated with the arms and equipment. It is primarily through direct and varied contacts between personnel of the U.S. armed services and their counterparts in the cooperating country that the presumed interests of the two parties are served.

Since the Military Assistance Training Program got underway in

1950, more than 488,000 officers and troops from Europe, Asia, Africa, and Latin America have been trained in more than 175 facilities in the United States, the Panama Canal Zone, and elsewhere in more than 2,000 different skills, ranging from auto mechanics and bookkeeping to computer sciences and command and staff procedures.[3] Hardware transfers and training programs have both been facilitated by U.S. military advisory missions in the host countries; these groups have ranged from one officer to 2000 troops and officers. By mid-1970, some 3264 foreign officers had received high-level instruction in these command courses in the same classes with their U.S. counterparts.[4] Many of these officers from Asia, Africa, and Latin America have held or now hold high political positions in their respective countries.

In attempting to ascertain the nature of U.S. training and advice and the effect of this program on the armed services, economy, internal politics, and foreign policy of recipient countries, interviews were conducted at more than 20 military training facilities in the United States, including the army, navy, marine, and air force command colleges.[5] The curriculums of the army and air force schools in the Panama Canal Zone for Latin Americans were also examined. Visits were made to Panama, El Salvador, Guatemala, Liberia, Morocco, Iran, Thailand, Taiwan, and Japan to interview U.S. embassy and military personnel and host-country military and civilian officials. English-language textbooks used by foreign trainees, as well as material prepared for the official information program which introduces them to U.S. life and institutions, were also analyzed.

IMPACT ON DOMESTIC POLITICS

The U.S. military-aid effort has had and continues to have an inevitable, diverse, and largely unintended influence on domestic political development. The impact is unintended because the program does not seek to reform the domestic policies of recipient regimes or alter domestic political or social institutions; its political influence is inevitable because the program is addressed to the military establishment which plays a significant political role in the great majority of Third World states. The impact is diverse because the societies involved are diverse and because their military elites have widely differing views on and roles in basic constitutional and political questions, and military leaders within one country often differ in their political outlook; they tend to be security-oriented, but espouse political views ranging from authoritarian to democratic and economic views from feudal to socialist. Consequently, to the extent that external military aid strengthens a given armed service having two or more factions, it tends to reinforce the political potential of each. U.S.-trained officers have initiated and resisted coups, advocated the nationalization of U.S. corporations and resisted nationalization. In the dramatic but unsuccessful F-5 air assassination attempt against King Hassan of Morocco in 1972, both rebel and loyalist pilots were trained in the United States.[6] This does not mean military aid has had no influence on domestic politics; it does mean that its influence may be felt in several directions at the same time.

The impact of the U.S. military-aid program on internal developments is severely limited because political decisions are largely determined by domestic social, economic, cultural, religious, ethnic, and military factors. Even in situations where internal military forces may be decisive, the political role of the military will be determined far more by other domestic factors than by a necessarily superficial exposure to U.S. ideas or values in a brief training experience abroad; moreover, it is certain that the acquisition of hardware as such is largely a politically neutral factor, the significance and impact of which are determined by the purposes to which it is put.

The world views and characters of military men are the products of their total experiences. Six or nine months in the United States is a tiny portion of an individual's life, which moreover, has already been preceded by maturation in another environment and with a different history. Brief contacts in the United States, even in repeated tours, are less important than lifelong family and class connections, religious outlook, economic orientation, secondary schooling, and daily associations with fellow officers.

Even though the political impact of a U.S. training experience on a foreign officer may be slight, it is important to note the nature of that influence. The author's earlier study went to great lengths to ascertain the "political content" of the training experience, including the voluntary information program made available to those on longer tours. Repeatedly, two questions were asked of trainees and instructors, with regard to training manuals: (1) Was there any attempt at political indoctrination, and if so what kind? and (2) Do the political values and attitudes of a trainee undergo a significant change as a result of a U.S. training tour?

Addressing the second question first, available evidence indicated that the great majority of trainees underwent no basic political change during or immediately after their training period. A tiny minority—perhaps 1 percent—of trainees may have become "anti-American," and at the other extreme, an equally insignificant group who experienced a kind of "love affair" with the United States or the U.S. military service that hosted them may have become uncritically "pro-American." But the great bulk returned from their experience with their own political values intact, though probably with a slightly better understanding of U.S. foreign-policy goals and how U.S. democracy works in practice.

This conclusion is not surprising in view of the objectives and actual practices of the training program, which is strongly geared to transmitting a great variety of technical and managerial skills and is only peripherally interested in political matters. Most foreign military personnel attended the same classes with U.S. trainees, learning the same skills in the same language. The higher officers who attended nine-month command and staff colleges were exposed to foreign-policy lectures which presented the official U.S. position along with dissenting views. A careful examination of the "political" content of the textbooks and lectures at the U.S. Army Command and General Staff College at Fort Leavenworth, Kansas, revealed a diversity of views that would have done credit to any contemporary political science faculty in a U.S. university. In fact, some foreign officers who went to Fort Leavenworth were critical of the college for permitting academic speakers to denounce so brazenly U.S. foreign policy; one officer called the practice of presenting opposing views an example of "extreme democracy." In the noncompulsory information program, an explicit effort was made to develop an understanding of U.S. democratic institutions through lectures, films, and field trips to farms, local courts, state legislatures,factories, and private homes, but as far as could be ascertained, the program did not assert or imply that trainees and their countries should adopt U.S. ways, much less be made over in the U.S. image.

This is not to say that either the training program proper or the information program are politically neutral. Obviously, they advance U.S. values, including the idea of tolerating diversity; but the trainees are not "indoctrinated" as are foreign military trainees who go to the Soviet Union, East Germany, or Cuba. The training program is simply not concerned with reforming domestic practices or institutions in the trainee's home country, nor with developing strategy or tactics for overthrowing regimes of any kind.

CRITERIA FOR PROVIDING MILITARY ASSISTANCE

Fundamental to understanding the multiple effects of military transfers or training is the recognition that any bilateral agreement for these purposes between Washington and the recipient regime is regarded as a foreign-policy instrument by both governments. The agreement is not entered into in the first place unless there exists a perceived degree of mutual interests that can sustain a working relationship. Governments that receive U.S. arms, particularly those getting large deliveries, usually have a similar appreciation of external threat and a similar interest in maintaining regional stability. Certainly, the United States and Iran, for example, share a common interest in preserving the territorial integrity of Iran. The same is true of other countries exposed to powerful Soviet or Chinese pressures, such as Greece, Turkey, and South Korea. In short, U.S. military aid and the size of the program is more a reflection of an existing compatibility of interests than a lever to induce a reluctant regime to alter drastically its foreign policy stance, though there have been cases where U.S. assistance was offered as an inducement to modify the external policy of the recipient. The Middle East is a prime example where Washington has provided arms to Israel and Arab states to induce moderation on both sides.

To put it another way, there have been three chief foreign-policy reasons for extending U.S. military aid and sales. The principal one is to help buttress the defenses of countries directly exposed to Soviet expansionist pressures—hence U.S. aid to NATO members, Yugoslavia, Spain, Iran, Thailand, South Korea, and Japan. The second reason is to pay for the right to locate U.S. communication, military, or other facilities on the soil of the state concerned, such as in Japan, the Philippines, Turkey, and in the nearest past in Iran and Ethiopia. The third is to encourage regional stability by helping governments to maintain better trained and disciplined military services capable of defending themselves against aggression or subversion; virtually all Third World regimes fail in this category. There is a fourth and more general reason: to provide an additional link of official communication between the two governments, a military channel which supplements the other instruments of diplomacy; this applies to all assisted states. It is readily apparent that these different objectives are not mutually exclusive and that both parties believe their security and foreign-policy interests are served by military-assistance agreements negotiated between legally sovereign states.

Some Marxist and other writers have charged that U.S. military aid is given to buttress dictatorial, repressive or, reactionary regimes. One such author asserts that the goal of the program in the host country is to (1) develop a propensity to solicit and/or acquiesce in American policy suggestions; (2) structure a definition of national interests which precludes non-alignment; and (3) inculcate an ideology of development which stresses subsidies and hospitality to transnational corporations.[7] These allegations are simply not supported by empirical evidence. Of course, Washington prefers allies to adversaries, but for at least fifteen years, U.S. advice has not urged aid recipients to become allies. In fact, Washington has encouraged genuine nonalignment. Washington has, for example, no allies in Africa and has sought none, but it has occasionally pursued policies to discourage African regimes from becoming allies of the Soviet Union. In late 1975, the U.S. Senate prevented President Ford from taking modest military measures in Angola designed to keep the Soviet Union from installing, by the use of Cuban troops, a Marxist regime in Luanda. Washington would have been quite content with a neutralist regime, but Moscow wanted an ally and was prepared to pay the price.

The allegation that the United States favors "reactionary" regimes is refuted by the great variety of governments that have received or are receiving military assistance, ranging from Franco's Spain to Tito's Yugoslavia. Successive U.S. administrations have not only given aid to many types of regimes, but have usually continued it when the government was significantly altered by a scheduled or unscheduled change of leadership. Authoritarian and democratic, feudal and socialist regimes have received military assistance, not because the United States approved or disapproved of their internal policies, but because Washington believed that the aid served U.S. foreign-policy interests.

There have been, however, two kinds of regimes that have been barred from substantial military assistance, though in some cases a token program of training has been continued: regimes that pursued foreign policies judged to be seriously inimical to U.S. interests, such as Castro's Cuba, Sukarno's Indonesia in 1964, Nasser's Egypt, Al-Bakr's Iraq, and Qaddafi's Libya, and regimes that became so repressive, weak, or corrupt that they could not be depended upon, including at different times, Haiti, Batista's Cuba, and Paraguay. It is interesting to note that U.S. military training and advice continued uninterrupted in Chile during the last three governments, including the Marxist regime of Salvador Allende and the military regime that replaced it in 1973, though hardware transfers were reduced significantly during the Allende period.

POLITICAL STABILITY AND PEACEFUL DEVELOPMENT

Attempting to identify and assess the significance of the effects of military assistance on internal political developments is difficult because such aid is one factor among many and, equally important, it is one of the least influential factors. Dramatic events like coups and revolutions are plain to see, but their multiple causes and long-range political import defy easy analysis. Quiet and gradual changes in the breadth of political participation or in the modes of political competition are difficult to discern, though they may be more significant than the dramatic events.

The chief political problem of most Third World states is to develop a central government with sufficient authority to impose law and order throughout their territory and sufficient consent to permit peaceful adaptation, change and development. U.S. aid is designed to help strengthen the armed forces in their primary task of maintaining security from external threats, and their secondary task of maintaining internal order by countering subversive challenges from left or right. National security is seen as a necessary but not sufficient condition for constructive political development.

The effects of all U.S. aid on political development vary. As noted earlier, the immediate result is to help strengthen the current government, whether it is civilian or military, effective or ineffective, authoritarian or democratic, relatively corrupt or relatively honest. Such aid also tends to reinforce the existing political system. Most regimes in the Third World are authoritarian, with various combinations of left and right politics. Whether the immediate stabilizing effect of military aid will lead to development in a particular political direction depends upon the balance of internal forces and interests, including the political orientation of the military elite. In the short run, the program tends to reinforce the status quo, but things are always changing and in the longer term its impact—however slight—is in the direction of moderate government. There are three reasons for this.

First, and most important, the net impact of the program in the great majority of cases has been to enhance the capability of the assisted government to maintain internal stability and, if the absence of turbulence is generally conducive to constructive change as Western democratic theory suggests, the program will have helped to facilitate nonviolent political adjustment and adaptation. While there are philosophical differences on the question of the relative merits of revolutionary and peaceful change, it is self-evident that enhanced stability increases the probability of peaceful change and thus keeps open those political options that are foreclosed by chaos, civil strife, or revolutionary violence. Third World societies usually offer several political alternatives in times of relative stability, but these options are almost always reduced or narrowed when serious violence erupts. Under the pressure of civil war or revolutionary violence, the political situation tends to polarize and the moderate options of the middle give way to extreme alternatives of the left and right.

Second, since military officers are active politically, any democratic ideas they may have gained during a U.S. training tour can have a small positive effect as they become advisors or participants in the top policy-making elite. One should not expect too much, because a trainee's political outlook is well formed before he comes under American influence, which at most is a brief period in his life and hence has limited impact.

Third, moderate politics have also been encouraged because U.S. training and advice has generally reinforced the disposition of Third World militaries to approach problems pragmatically rather than ideologically. Traditionally, military personnel distrust ideology; some even distrust politicians. They look upon themselves as practical individuals who address and solve practical problems, and regard themselves as more rational, stable, and enduring than politicians. Further, Third World militaries tend to embrace members of the most modernized elite and they have had more contact with modern technology and management techniques. All this has encouraged a kind of pragmatism as opposed to ideology. This was found to be the case in Ghana, the Congo (Zaire), and Ethiopia in another study.[8] U.S. training, especially in advanced professional courses, emphasizes the problem-solving approach that respects practical expertise, is skeptical of abstract theory and political dogma, and emphasizes the marshaling of available resources to get the objective at hand accomplished efficiently. U.S.-trained personnel are probably more inclined to reject the doctrinaire approaches of the ideological system builders, be they Marxist or of the extreme right, than those with no U.S. training. Their professionalism and their recognition of the need for specialists and for planning tend to have a spillover effect on the administration of government. Orderly government tends to reinforce moderate policies rather than extreme measures, although some orderly governments are repressive.

General Suharto's Indonesia illustrates this point. His government, in effect, has been run by a number of Leavenworth graduates who, during their command and general staff courses, had instilled into them the virtues of the pragmatic, problem-solving approach. Observers insist that this influenced the character of their management and planning.[9] The Leavenworth experience reinforced, though it did not create, their deep suspicion of and growing hostility toward former President Sukarno, who constantly injected ideology and doctrinaire slogans into his government as he moved closer to a communist position. Leavenworth also deepened their respect for experts and their recognition of the limitations of military personnel. They knew, for example, they were not qualified to run the Indonesian economy, so they turned the complicated task of national resource and investment planning over to professional economists, many of whom, incidentally, were trained in American universities.

POLITICAL CRISES AND MILITARY INTERVENTION

The political role of Third World military leaders ranges from active support of the existing regime to active efforts to replace it with military rule. Miles Wolpin and other U.S. foreign-policy critics have alleged that U.S. military aid has been designed to encourage, or has had the effect of encouraging, military coups, especially coups that have resulted in "right-wing military dictatorships." In each country visited for this study this charge was carefully examined and the resulting evidence does not support the allegation. On the contrary, overwhelming evidence points to the conclusion that there is no discernible relationship between U.S. military assistance and the character or frequency of military takeovers. In answering questions about possible connections between the two, every respondent—U.S. training officials, resident U.S. advisors, former trainees, Third World defense officials, and knowledgeable civilian observers—replied either that the program had no effect on the nature or frequency of military intervention in crises, or that it may have had an insignificant effect in certain circumstances.[10] This assessment is corroborated by an independent study of the Latin American situation which concludes that U.S. military aid "neither contributes to nor detracts from the propensity for military interventions," although it appears that the larger the aid program, the less likely the military is to intervene.[11]

In his elaborate statistical analysis of the level of Latin American defense spending and the volume of U.S. military aid, Charles Wolf, Jr., comes to the same conclusion. He found no correlation between either defense expenditures or military assistance and "movements toward more authoritarian political institutions," adding that these conclusions hold true, "whether we consider the total quantity of military aid or defense outlays, or the per capita quantities;" he insists that domestic forces are determinative in political-military phenomena as complex and profoundly indigenous as military coups.[12] Another study likewise found no correlation between U.S. aid and the political behavior of the officer corps.[13] Evidence gathered in interviews in Africa and Asia suggests that Mr. Wolf's findings in Latin America are largely applicable to countries in those areas, primarily because the same basic relationship between indigenous and external influence prevails. Ironically, Mr. Wolf found evidence to suggest "a *positive* relationship between the level of democracy and either total or per capita domestic defense programs," indicating that "both per capita defense outlays and level of democracy may be positively correlated with per capita income in Latin America."[14]

In response to congressional allegations that military assistance leads to or encourages coups, the U.S. State Department in 1969 offered data demonstrating that the frequency of unscheduled changes of government in Latin America has been decreasing: in the decade of the 1930s there were 35 coups, compared to 28 for the 1940s and 29 for the 1950s. In the most recent decade, "There have been 18 or almost exactly half of those suffered from 1930–1940."[15] General Robert H. Warren, then military aid director, elaborated this point by relating 50 successful and 28 abortive military coups worldwide (exclusive of Indochina) to the volume of U.S. military aid to the country (Table 16.1).

In statistical terms, there were fewer than half as many coups or attempted coups in countries with moderate or large U.S. programs than in those with very small or no programs. This strong positive correlation between U.S. assistance and nonintervention does not necessarily prove a causal relationship. The data, however, virtually disprove the charge that U.S. military training, advice, and hardware cause or encourage coups of any kind; no study of the period since 1969 that refutes this conclusion has come to the attention of the present writer. Hence, this study concludes that no causal connection has been established between U.S. military training and military coups. This does not rule out the possibility of some U.S. influence,

TABLE 16.1: Military Coups and U.S. Military Aid (numbers of states)

Size of U.S. Program	1961	1962	1963	1964	1965	1966	1967	1968	1969	Totals
				Successful Coups						
Moderate or large*	2	3	3	2	3	1	1	1	0	16
Small or none	2	1	7	2	2	9	5	5	1	34
Total	4	4	10	4	5	10	6	6	1	50
				Attempted Coups						
Moderate or large	0	3	3	0	0	0	1	1	0	8
Small or none	2	3	1	3	2	3	2	4	0	20
Total	2	6	4	3	2	3	3	5	0	28

Source: U.S. Congress, House Committee on Appropriations, Subcommittee on Foreign Operations and Related Agencies, *Foreign Assistance and Related Appropriations for 1970,* 91st Cong, 1st sess., 1969, p. 667.

*Greater than $1 million annually.

however small, on the frequency or character of military intervention.

On the question of frequency, only attempted coups, both abortive and successful, can be taken into account because statistical data on plans for intervention that never materialized are unavailable. For every attempted coup, there probably has been at least one contemplated coup, whether limited to vague conversation between a few officers or developed to the latter stages of planning. When intervention is contemplated, the local officers involved have on occasion approached trusted U.S. military advisers for their informal views. Since U.S. advisers are under instructions to remain aloof from internal politics, any such approach must be reported to the ambassador and be dealt with according to his instructions. The U.S. ambassador may instruct a military adviser who is approached to drop the matter or inform the local officer who contacted him that the U.S. government wishes to remain neutral.

Although U.S. military aid has had no discernible impact on the propensity of Third World military personnel for direct intervention in the political sphere, in some cases the U.S. military missions associated with such aid may have had the effect of discouraging some contemplated coups. A U.S. military officer assigned to a Latin American capital spoke to this point in an interview with the author. Making a distinction between constructive coups (those with some chance of correcting gross corruption or subversion), and nonconstructive coups (those that seemed to be only a changing of the guard or seemed likely to develop subversive external contacts), he said that the very presence of a U.S. military mission, with its prudent day-by-day advice and emphasis on professionalism, had the effect of helping to prevent some contemplated military interventions, particularly badly planned ones. In the very rare cases where U.S. advisers were approached, the general response (again after consultation with the ambassador, who would in turn consult with Washington) was to caution restraint within the larger context of the adviser's role, which, he said, was not to encourage, discourage, or prevent coups, but to improve the quality of the armed forces. In such situations, U.S. advice probably has had the effect of reducing the number of coups, particularly those that would have been abortive rather than successful. Referring to the abortive 1960 coup in Ethiopia, the U.S. ambassador who was there says that no U.S. military officers had been consulted by the plotters, adding that "the coup might not have been attempted had any American advisers been consulted."[16]

On the subtle question of the character, substance, and political consequences of coups, the program has had no discernible effect, apart from the possibility that U.S. advice has deterred more nonconstructive interventions than constructive ones. No responsible U.S. civilian or military officer would encourage a contemplated coup that Washington thought would have an adverse effect on regional stability. If Washington believed the proposed action would enhance the long-range chances of stable and just governments, the U.S. ambassador could authorize his military advisers to give technical advice designed to carry it off efficiently and with minimum violence. This may well have happened in the bloodless coup that brought General Joseph Mobutu to power in the Congo (Zaire) on November 25, 1965. If Washington's judgment were sound, the advice would have the effect not only of increasing the chances of immediate success, but also of creating a situation conducive to better government and interstate stability.

The difficult role of U.S. military advisers during periods of political turmoil and confusion is well illustrated by the Bolivian coup of August 1971. Shortly after President Juan José Torres was ousted, the *Washington Post* ran the headline "U.S. Major had Role in Bolivian Coup," but acknowledged that "it was not possible to determine whether this role was actually important to the coup's success."[17] Specifically, the *Post* said Major Robert J. Lundin, USAF, the sole military adviser at the Bolivian air force training school in Santa Cruz, "had been in touch with the plotters" for six months and had permitted them to use his short-wave radio. A qualified Defense Department official called the *Post* story by Lewis H. Diuguid "a total fabrication based on hearsay from people who had axes to grind."[18]

The State Department denied any U.S. involvement in the coup, but acknowledged that Bolivian officials in Santa Cruz did use Major Lundin's radio.[19] The stories in the *Post* and *New York Times* did not mention that Major Lundin's radio was located in the Bolivian air force school and it was normally used by the Bolivian government and military for official communications. Before, during, and after the August coup, it was so used, and Major Lundin was not in a position to deny it to some officers and make it available to others, even if he had been so inclined. Further, he was under standing orders to remain neutral, which were reinforced in this case by specific instructions from Washington. There is no evidence that Major Lundin took sides. The case was carefully investigated by U.S. authorities, but was not pursued by Bolivian authorities.

This incident demonstrates that the presence of U.S. military advisers in a Third World country inevitably makes them a potential target for U.S. or foreign critics, regardless of how correctly they behave. In the Bolivian case, resident U.S. civilian and military officials were approached before and during the coup by various Bolivian factions seeking U.S. support or understanding. The case also illustrates a point made in numerous interviews in a dozen countries: despite opportunities to become involved in internal politics, the U.S. military advisors rarely, if ever, succumbed to the temptation. On the contrary, they maintained their professional integrity and remained aloof from domestic conflict. Although reliable information is difficult to obtain, exceptions could have occurred if a U.S. officer had been instructed to provide specific forms of assistance to support a CIA effort that was approved by Washington and designed to change or modify an existing regime for foreign-policy, not domestic, reasons. Such collaboration between the CIA and U.S. military advisors is highly unlikely because the former operates covertly while the latter operates openly.

THE NATURE OF CIA INTERVENTION

In the 1950s, the U.S. government assisted internal groups in three countries to oust a regime whose foreign policy Washington regarded as inimical to peace and security. In each case the target regime or official was working with external Communist governments. U.S. covert action in Iran in 1953 and Guatemala in 1954 was successful, but the U.S.-assisted effort to topple President Sukarno in Indonesia in 1958 was not. The essence of the two successful efforts can be summarized briefly.[20]

In Iran in 1953 Premier Mossadegh, with the covert support of the Soviet Union and the Communist Party of Iran, seized Britain's oil properties in that country and attempted to threaten the United States. In a letter received by President Eisenhower on May 28, 1953, Mossadegh warned that he would turn to Moscow if he did not get more financial aid from Washington. The president authorized the CIA to assist in staging an anti-Mossadegh demonstration in Teheran which resulted in the Premier's arrest and the installation in his place of General Zahedi, who was committed to a moderate foreign policy.

The Guatemalan situation in 1954 was similar. The National Security Council concluded that the 2,000 tons of small arms, ammunition, and light artillery pieces from Czechoslovakia which had arrived in unmarked cases in Guatemala City would be used by the near-communist Arbenz regime to take over El Salvador and Honduras, and thus establish a Soviet foothold in Central America. The president authorized the CIA to oust Arbenz. This was accomplished by arming Colonel Castillo Armas and his band of lightly armed Guatemalan refugees who marched across the border into Guatemala, supported by three P-47 fighter planes flown by CIA-recruited soldiers of fortune. Arbenz's forces refused to fight; he fled, and an anticommunist regime took over.

In each case, the U.S. intervened to replace a regime which was working very closely with the Soviet Union and which was considered a threat to regional security. In neither case was the action designed to modify basic domestic institutions or policies. In both, the CIA was the chosen instrument of action, and in neither did prior U.S. military assistance or the U.S. resident military mission have anything to do with the operation. The decisions were made by the National Security Council, approved by the president, and carried out by the Central Intelligence Agency. The same is true of the abortive effort to oust Sukarno in 1958.

It may be noted in passing that there were two later presidentially approved covert actions, both in Latin America, both carried out by the CIA and both unsuccessful: the highly publicized Bay of Pigs invasion to overthrow Castro in 1961 and efforts to prevent Allende's Marxist regime from coming to power in 1970. According to ranking U.S. officials in Chile at the time, the U.S. government had nothing to do with the overthrow of Allende on September 11, 1973. The two abortive efforts had no connection with U.S. military assistance.

SUMMARY AND CONCLUSIONS

U.S. military training and advice have had a small, unquantifiable, and unpredictable impact upon the internal political developments of the recipient Third World countries. This is true because the primary political determinants are indigenous social, cultural, and economic factors. One of these determinants is the military establishment, but even in countries where many officers have had substantial contact with U.S. training and advisory efforts, this experience has had little impact on their subsequent political behavior.

The insignificant portion of U.S. training and advice that relates to politics broadly defined is devoted to foreign policy—perceptions of external threat and the requirements of regional stability. Since the program is regarded as a foreign-policy instrument both by Washington and the recipient government, it is simply not concerned with the domestic politics of the cooperating state. Consequently, training in the United States, including the official but voluntary information program, has not significantly altered the domestic political orientation or behavior of the foreign students. Much less has it tampered with their political loyalties. The U.S. resident military missions have with extremely rare, if any, exceptions remained neutral toward internal conflicts on domestic issues. The basic neutrality of the program on such issues is attested to by its acceptability to many kinds of regimes and its continuation in the face of abrupt and sometimes drastic changes in government. The neutrality is also evidenced by the diverse political behavior of Third World officers who have had years of experience with various facets of the program.

What limited influence the program may have had on a particular Third World regime has probably been in the direction of a less corrupt administration, respect for the rule of law and human rights, and measured efforts to move toward competitive politics. To the extent that former trainees are active in politics, their influence tends to be in the direction of moderate, as opposed to extremist, political decisions, reflecting the U.S. preference for pragmatic rather than ideological approaches to problem solving.

If one assumes that regional and internal stability are conducive to constructive political change, the chief contribution of U.S. military aid toward the development of moderate and more representative government derives from the enhanced stability attributable to the program. Stability cannot cause movement toward competitive politics, a broader franchise, or respect for human rights, but it can help keep open the political options that would be foreclosed by subversion, infiltration, revolutionary violence, civil strife, or anarchy.

A distinction should be made between the short-term and long-term political influence of the human contacts in military-assistance programs. Training is a short-range investment in military skills; if the officers involved are in a position of political influence, it is possible that their experience with the program might have a small impact. But the program is also a long-range investment in many persons, some of whom may later play a significant political role. Even if a small number of these attempt to emulate the democratic values and practices they heard about and saw in the United States, the net, long-term effect, however modest, would be in the direction of a more representative and responsive government than most Third World countries now enjoy.

Third World military coups have varied widely in motivation, character, and consequences. Some have led to repressive and arbitrary rule; others have installed regimes that are less corrupt and less arbitrary than the deposed regimes and thus improved the chance for peaceful and constructive political development. This study concludes that U.S. military assistance has had no discernible effect on the frequency or character of unscheduled changes in government in which the military have played a key role. No evidence was found to indicate that U.S. military advisers encouraged or supported coups or took actions in times of political crises contrary to explicit instructions from Washington. In fact, the professional and prudent character of U.S. training and advice may have had the effect of decreasing the number of coup attempts, especially those that were ill-conceived or had little chance of arresting chaos, corruption, or subversion; this, however, is difficult to prove.

Regardless of how correct and neutral U.S. military advisers may be, they are always a potential scapegoat in a turbulent political crisis in which two or more factions seek direct or indirect U.S. support. Like any other U.S. officials, they can become targets of official displeasure or of opposition abuse in a world where anti-Americanism is often a popular strategem in the internal struggle for power. Available evidence suggests, however, that military advisory personnel have been less frequently singled out for such negative attention than civilian representatives of the official American presence: ambassadors, AID officials, and Peace Corps volunteers.[21] A small military mission is less conspicuous than the embassy compound and the U.S. Information Service libraries in urban centers, and less intrusive than many AID and Peace Corps projects; moreover, military missions have seldom, if ever, been accused by host governments of meddling in domestic affairs. In contrast, Peace Corps volunteers have been asked to leave a half dozen countries for interfering in internal affairs or taking sides on domestic issues.

NOTES

1. *New York Times*, June 6, 1974.
2. The Carter administration's use of foreign aid as an instrument to alter the domestic policies in other nations under the rubric of "human rights" represents a departure from traditional U.S. foreign policy. See Ernest W. Lefever, "The Trivialization of Human Rights," *Policy Review*, No. 3 (Winter 1978), 11–26.
3. See Department of Defense, Security Assistance Agency, "Foreign Military Sales and Military Assistance Facts," Washington, D.C., December 1977, page 31.
4. These statistics were provided to the author by the U.S. Army Command and General Staff College, Fort Leavenworth, Kansas; Air University, Maxwell Air Force Base, Alabama; U.S. Naval War College, Newport, Rhode Island; and Marine Corps Command and Staff College, Quantico, Virginia. The Air Force Command and Staff Course started in 1945 and the Naval Command Course began in 1957.
5. The analysis and conclusions of this chapter are drawn from a larger, unpublished study by the present writer, "U.S. Military Training and Advice in the Third World," 1974, undertaken at the Brookings Institution in the early 1970s, which focused on U.S. military training for Third World regimes and on U.S. advisory missions in their capitals.
6. *Washington Post*, August 17 and 18, 1972.
7. Miles D. Wolpin, *Military Aid and Counterrevolution in the Third World* (New York: D.C. Heath, 1973), p. 11.
8. See Ernest W. Lefever, *Spear and Scepter: Army, Police, and Politics in Tropical Africa* (Washington, D.C.: Brookings Institution, 1970), pp. 187–91.
9. Author interviews with U.S. diplomatic and military personnel and Indonesian officials, Jakarta, August 23–28, 1970.
10. This conclusion is based on extensive interviewing by the author in Ecuador and the Panama Canal Zone, July 1968; Panama, El Salvador, and Guatemala, May 1970; Morocco, Liberia, Iran, Indonesia, and Taiwan, August 1970; and Japan, September 1970.
11. Barry J. Roller, "Military Intervention in Latin America, 1955–1970: A Bi-Variant Analysis," n.d., p. 3, and letter from Mr. Roller to the author, January 7, 1972.
12. Charles Wolf, Jr., *United States Policy in the Third World* (Little, Brown and Co., 1967), p. 109.
13. Philip B. Springer, "Social Sources of Political Behavior of Venezuelan Military Officers: An Exploratory Analysis," *El Politico* (1965), pp. 348–55.
14. Wolf, *United States Policy and the Third World*, p. 111.
15. U.S. Congress, Senate, Committee on Foreign Relations, Subcommittee on Western Hemisphere Affairs, U.S. Military Aid Hearings, 90th Cong., 2d Sess., June 24 and July 8, 1969, p. 68.
16. Arthur L. Richards, letter to author, August 17, 1971.

17. *Washington Post*, August 29, 1971.

18. Author's interview, May 8, 1972.

19. *New York Times*, August 30, 1971; *Washington Post*, September 3, 1971.

20. The basic facts in the Iran, Guatemala, and Indonesian cases are reliably summarized in Ray S. Cline, *Secrets, Spies and Scholars: Blueprint of the Essential CIA* (Washington, D.C.: Acropolis Books, 1976), pp. 131–33 and 181–82. Dr. Cline served for 30 years in the U.S. government, most of the time with the CIA. Further details of the Iran and Guatemala cases can be found in Andrew Tully, *CIA: The Inside Story* (New York: Fawcett Publications, 1962), pp. 54–60 and 78–84; and David Wise and Thomas B. Ross, *The Invisible Government* (New York: Random House, 1964), pp. 110–14 and 165–83.

21. Statistics were gathered by the author from relevant offices in the Defense Department, State Department, Agency for International Development, and the Peace Corps.

17 DEFENSE INDUSTRIES IN THE THIRD WORLD: PROBLEMS AND PROMISES

Michael Moodie

In the last thirty years, the world has experienced an unprecedented militarization; greater numbers of increasingly sophisticated weapons systems have entered the arsenals of more countries than ever before. An important, yet relatively neglected, trend associated with this process has been the emergence of a class of secondary arms-producing states in the nonindustrialized regions of the world which are not only arming themselves with modern weapons, but exporting arms to other countries as well. Israel, India, Brazil, Argentina, South Africa, South Korea, Taiwan, Australia, and Iran have developed, or have the potential to develop, significant national arms industries and become important regional arms merchants.

These countries have been the leaders of a remarkable growth in the production capabilities of national arms industries throughout the Third World;* today, more than 30 developing countries produce weapons of one kind or another.[1] To be sure, most arms industries in the Third World are limited to production of small arms, ammunition, or small naval vessels, but even this limited capability represents a vastly different situation than that which existed in the mid-1960s (Table 17.1), when indigenous defense

---

*The Third World comprises here non-European and, for the most part, nonaligned developing nations. It does not include the People's Republic of China, however, which by virtue of its proven nuclear weapons capability, is classified here as a great power.

production in Third World states, with a few exceptions, was rare. Moreover, the trend toward greater indigenous defense production appears to be intensifying; new members are joining the club, and Third World states with established defense industries are expanding the variety of weapons and military hardware produced. In addition, the export of arms by Third World states is growing rapidly in volume and value.

Despite the impressive expansion of defense industries in the developing world, no Third World arms producer is yet in a position to challenge those industrial states that have been traditional arms manufacturers and exporters. It is for this reason, perhaps, that the issue of indigenous defense production in the Third World has received such scant attention, particularly in terms of its implications for regional and international stability or for efforts to control the transfer of conventional arms. The greater emphasis that Third World countries themselves are placing on indigenous defense production capabilities, however, portends increasingly serious problems associated with it. This chapter examines some of the basic issues related to this dimension of the arms-transfer problem. It will concentrate specifically on the defense-production capabilities of the more advanced Third World arms producers. It is not a catalog of what military hardware those states are producing, however, as that has been done elsewhere.[2] Rather, this study is intended to raise questions about defense production in the Third World as a potential regional-security problem and as an issue for U.S. policy.

DEVELOPMENT OF DEFENSE INDUSTRIES IN THE THIRD WORLD

The origins of arms industries in some Third World countries can be traced to World War II or even earlier. Argentina's Fabrica Militar de Aviones, for example, has a history dating back to 1927.[3] Arms-production facilities and maintenance workshops were established in India by the British with help from the United States during World War II to support the Allied war effort.[4] The boom in the growth of arms industries in the developing world, however, did not begin until the 1960s. India's experience in the 1962 war with China, for example, "moved official Indian thinking away from benign neglect in defense matters toward a conscious and deliberate armaments programme."[5] Although Brazil had experience in the production of light aircraft for more than twenty years, it was not until the Empresa Brasileria de Aeronautica (Embraer) was founded in 1969 that Brazil began to be noticed as a potentially important aircraft manufacturer.[6] The Israel Aircraft Industry (IAI) was not even created until 1953, and it was the 1958 agreement for licensed production of the French Magister— the first copy of which rolled off Israeli production lines in 1960—that sparked IAI's rapid development.[7] Today, Israel's aircraft industry is the most advanced in the Third World.

TABLE 17.1: Domestic Defense Production in Developing Countries, 1965 and 1975

	Aircraft		Missiles		Armored fighting vehicles		Warships		Small arms		Electronics		Aircraft engines	
	'65	'75	'65	'75	'65	'75	'65	'75	'65	'75	'65	'75	'65	'75
India	x	x		x	x	x	x	x	x	x	x	x	x	x
Israel	x	x		x		x		x	x	x	x	x		x
S. Africa	x	x		x		x		x	x	x		x	x	x
Brazil	x	x		x		x		x	x	x		x	x	x
Argentina	x	x				x	x	x	x	x			x	x
Pakistan		x	x				x	x	x	x		x		
Chile		x					x	x	x	x				
Egypt	x^a	x^b	x^c	x^d					(x)	x				
Iran		x								x		x		
Indonesia	x	x						x		x				
N. Korea		x						x	x	x				
S. Korea		x						x		x				
Philippines		x						x		x				
Singapore								x		x		x		
Taiwan		x		x				x		x	x	x		
S. Vietnam							x		(x)					
N. Vietnam		x						x		x				
Colombia		x					x	x	(x)	x				
Dominican Republic							x	x	(x)	x				
Mexico							x	x	(x)	x				

296

Rhodesia				
Thailand	x			x
Guyana			x	
Peru		x	x	
Saudi Arabia				x
Gabon			x	
Bangladesh			x	
Burma		x	x	
Nepal				x
Malaysia				x

Source: International Institute for Strategic Studies, *Strategic Survey, 1976* (London: IISS, 1976), p. 22.

x = domestic defense production underway either as indigenous development or under license; (x) = no definite information available on whether production underway; a. Production of aircraft terminated in mid-1960s; b. Advanced plans to start aircraft production under license within the framework of AMIO; c. Production of missiles terminated in 1965; d. Advanced plans to start missile production under license within the framework of AMIO.

The incentives generating the drive toward increased domestic defense production in the Third World include security and economic and political concerns. Underlying all other motives, however, is the desire to eliminate, or at least greatly reduce, dependence on industrial countries for arms deemed vital for national security. Indigenous defense production is an expression of self-reliance, and thus, it is a means of reducing a state's vulnerability to military and political pressures during times of crisis. This sentiment was clearly articulated by an Israeli official in 1977: when asked what Israel needed to sustain itself in a crisis, he noted, "...arms, food and energy.... We have to be independent in the sphere of defense production to as great a degree as possible."[8] His attitude was echoed by Brazilian Air Force Minister Joelmir Campos de Araripe Macedo, in December 1977 when he told a Chilean audience, "The time has come to free ourselves from the United States and the countries of Europe. It is a condition of security that each nation manufacture its own armaments."[9]

The drive for self-reliance through domestic defense production may result from several factors. Some states have no other choice; in the case of South Africa and Taiwan, for example, growing isolation in the international community has forced them to depend on no one but themselves for preservation of their national security. Israel today is also something of an international "pariah." Despite the acquisition of massive amounts of arms from the United States, however, the leadership of Israel has been oriented toward self-sufficiency since the birth of the state. The historic experience of the Jewish people, together with an immediate and potentially over-whelming threat at the time of independence and today, has engendered strong "go-it-alone" sentiments, not only in the leadership, but in the population as a whole.

For some countries the drive toward self-reliance is generated by other factors. Growth of the Brazilian arms industry, for example, is seen to complement that nation's long-term policy goal of maintaining dominance in Latin America and exerting greater influence in sub-Saharan Africa and the Third World in general. Australia's motivation stems from its physical isolation, occasional perceived threats, and the demands of normal indus-trial growth. India's status as the dominant nonaligned state of the Indian Ocean basin—a region of increasingly strategic importance—has combined with its experience of three postindependence wars (during which it felt the constraint of an arms embargo) to stimulate the desire for more sophisti-cated, domestic defense industries.

Economic incentives also play a role; that is, national arms industries are often considered potential leading sectors in a state's modernization process by providing the initial elements of an industrial base from which further industrialization can proceed. It is argued that the domestic manufacture of weapons systems forces Third World states to develop important skills, creates foreign-exchange savings, and helps a nation keep abreast of current technology. Whether these arguments are correct is another matter; what is important to note here is that in the Third World economic incentives combine with security and political concerns to form a complex matrix of motivations for the development of domestic arms industries. Understanding these factors must be the first step in the formulation of a coherent U.S. policy on this issue.

Most Third World states have followed a step-by-step process to develop their domestic defense industries, using the infrastructure and experience acquired at one stage as a building block from which to move on to the next.[10] First, maintenance and overhaul facilities are established for the service and repair of imported arms. Second, licenses are negotiated for the domestic assembly of a particular system, and unassembled kits are put together. Third, simple components are domestically fabricated under license while sophisticated components, such as engines and electronics, continue to be imported. At this stage, the Third World producer can begin to earn some foreign exchange by selling components or finished systems back to the licensor or elsewhere. Fourth, the developing country decreases the number of components for a given system that must be imported and a point is then reached when the Third World state can be said to be producing the entire system under license. Fifth, components for weapons systems are designed locally and incorporated into existing systems. Sixth, production of domestically designed systems is begun, initially using some imported components embodying more sophisticated technologies beyond the capability of the Third World producers. Finally, indigenously designed systems incorporating no imported components are manufactured. Although it is the expressed goal of almost every arms producer in the developing world, very few Third World states have reached this final stage, and these with very few systems. The extent to which this situation will change, and the rate at which it will change over the next few decades, obviously cannot be determined. That it will change, however, cannot be doubted.

THIRD WORLD ARMS PRODUCTION: IMPLICATIONS FOR REGIONAL SECURITY AND ARMS CONTROL

In general, the problems associated with local defense production in Third World states coalesce around four major issues: the impact of indigenous defense production within the country engaged in the process; its implications for the stability of the arms producer's region; the impact of arms exports by Third World producers to areas of potential conflict; and implications for efforts designed to achieve arms control at the conventional level.

The Domestic Impact

The primary purpose of a Third World arms industry is enhanced national security. As mentioned earlier, it is often argued that indigenous defense-production facilities reduce the vulnerability of a state to political and military pressures that flow from dependence on external sources of arms. The argument is also heard that, by using systems designed and manufactured specifically to meet their requirements, the military forces of a Third World arms producer will perform more effectively in responding to external and internal threats to national security. Are these arguments correct? Is dependence on industrialized countries for arms really reduced? Do armed forces of Third World states operate better with domestically produced weapons? Evidence suggests that the arguments of Third World producers must, at least, be modified.

In order to answer the question of reduced dependence, the definition of "dependence" and the nature of the arms must be specified. If dependence is defined in terms of the importation of assembled, finished weapons systems, then those countries that assemble arms or use imported components could be considered self-sufficient. This definition, however, is obviously too narrow to reflect accurately the reality of the current arms-transfer relationship between industrialized and developing countries. The transfer of finished weapons systems is a diminishing part of the arms trade. As the International Institute for Strategic Studies (IISS) has noted, "The transfer of technology for producing weapons is...as important a phenomenon as the transfer of weapons themselves."[11] The dependence of Third World countries on industrialized states for weapons has evolved into a dependence on those states for the technology to build weapons.

Dependence of major Third World arms producers on imported technology is most evident in the developing countries' production of highly sophisticated systems, such as tanks and jet aircraft. In May 1977, for example, Israel announced that it had started production of the Chariot, a new 56-ton tank of indigenous Israeli design.[12] Although Israel indicated that it expected to be soon producing 60 to 80 percent of the new tank's components locally, it must continue to import a crucial component, the engine, from the United States. India's Vijayanta tank is a similar example. Based on the British Chieftain, the first Vijayanta rolled off Indian assembly lines in 1965; thirteen years later, the tank's powerplant is still imported from Britain.[13]

India has now decided on a successor to the Vijayanta, and while a local design was certainly preferred,[14] the government has apparently decided to purchase Soviet tanks.[15] This comes as somewhat of a surprise, however, since New Delhi has had past difficulties with the Soviet Union, which has not shown a great willingness to share its manufacturing know-how.[16]

An analysis of local Third World production of sophisticated aircraft throws the problem of dependence on imported technologies into even sharper relief. India, for example, is looking for a new deep penetration aircraft, which it feels it requires to counter Pakistan's Mirage Vs. Although its aircraft industry is well advanced by Third World standards, India has no intention of developing a new system indigenously. The best it can hope for is licensed production. Initially, the major contenders were the Swedish Viggen, the Anglo-French Jaguar, and the French Mirage F-1. President Carter's refusal to allow Sweden to sell the Viggen—based on the incorporation in the Viggen of the Pratt and Whitney JT8D engine—eliminated it from the competition, and the Jaguar now has been selected. According to some reports, New Delhi has required Britain to buy back spare parts made in India.[17] While this deal demonstrates how far India's aircraft industry has come in thirty years, it also shows that it remains far from self- sufficient.

The Republic of China finds itself in a similar situation; Taiwan is concerned that efforts to modernize its air force through new arrangements with the United States will be jeopardized by the latter's normalization of relations with the People's Republic of China. Its own aerospace industry, however, has neither the avionics or engine technology nor the manufacturing capability to produce a sophisticated design of its own.[18] General Wu Yeh, commander of Taiwan's air force, has succinctly stated the ROC's dilemma: "It will be many years before we can build our own fighter, so we still need the support and assistance from the United States. We can wait, but I am not sure our enemy will."[19]

In contrast, Israel is domestically designing an advanced fighter which, if given government go-ahead, will mark a large step forward toward that country's self-sufficiency in aircraft production. The Aryeh (Lion) was originally conceived as an alternative to the U.S. F-16. A major attraction of the plane is that it could be powered by a European engine. Defense Minister Weizman has said that Israel would insist on a guarantee of "no strings attached" from the European country whose engine was selected.[20] Even this project, however, is not without its problems. The Israelis could experience major difficulties in developing the plane independently of U.S. technology, especially in terms of its avionics. Advanced fire control and terrain-following radar of the kind needed in the plane have not yet been developed by Israel; without them, the plane would be no match for fighters whose acquisition is being planned by other countries.

Third World dependence associated with arms imports from industrial countries does not disappear, then, with the creation of local defense industries; the form of the dependence is changed. Technological innovation will continue to be led by the industrialized countries. Developing states cannot match their vast sums spent on general research and development, and Third World states will find themselves constantly in the position of being outpaced and trying to catch up in many areas of advanced technology. Of course, by concentrating funds and R&D efforts in one specific area of advanced technology, a Third World state can make significant advances and even achieve a level of sophistication not matched by a country like the United States. Israel's electronics industry is a case in point.[21] No Third World country, however, can match the across-the-board technological developments generated by traditional arms manufacturers of the industrialized world. Given the variety of technologies demanded by the modernized military in the contemporary international environment, the dependence of Third World arms producers on imports of advanced technologies is likely to continue for some time to come.

The attempt by Third World arms producers to achieve self-sufficiency might even accentuate dependence, at least in the short term. After the U.S. arms embargo of 1974, for example, Turkey sought to expand her defense industrial base. To do so, however, the government had to maximize funds for industrial investment, which meant seeking favorable credit terms and sustaining arms imports.[22] Similarly, as part of Iran's drive for autonomy in defense production, the Shah concluded a number of co-production agreements with the United States and European countries that would have kept Iran dependent on their technology and skilled labor for some time to come.[23] It is highly doubtful, however, that the new government will implement these plans.

Iran's experience reflects another dimension of the dependence problem of Third World arms producers—the requirement for assistance in training and support. Imported personnel have been vital to the success of indigenous arms industries from the outset. Brazil, India, and Israel, for example, all depended heavily on foreigners in the early years of their aircraft industries.[24] Another element in recent deals has been concerned with infrastructure. These elements often are difficult to quantify and are neglected in many assessments of the problem, but, as Sir Ronald Ellis, head of Britain's Defence Sales Organization, has said, "The really big money is coming from military projects—runways, hangars, laboratories, hospitals, arms factories and repair shops."[25]

What are the implications of continued dependence on imported military technologies for Third World states' vulnerability to pressure from their sources of supply? As Third World military imports shift increasingly from finished weapons systems to military technology and infrastructure, one could well find a change in the nature of Third World susceptibility. In simple terms, short-term vulnerability to external pressure during times of crisis or actual hostilities could decrease, while sensitivity to influence over the long term might grow. In the first case, defense-production facilities in a Third World state—using imported technologies or producing under license—could continue to manufacture arms and military equipment during hostilities, making that state less susceptible to an actual or threatened embargo by an industrial supplier intent on inducing a change of behavior. Of course, the greater the percentage of components produced domestically by the Third World, the greater will be its freedom to maneuver. In addition, there is no guarantee that indigenous defense industries will be able to produce new material at the level at which it is consumed during hostilities, as Israel discovered during the October War of 1973.

In the long term and in noncrisis situations, however, the agreements with industrialized states on which Third World states are basing the development of their arms industries could heighten their susceptibility to external pressures. The widespread presence of foreigners in a Third World state, for example, will continually generate interest by suppliers in both internal and external developments affecting the safety of their nationals. Similarly, although co-production arrangements allow Third World producers to tailor a system to its particular needs, the joint companies that are created—such as Irano-British Dynamics, created to produce the British Aerospace Corporation (BAC) Rapier in Iran—also give a vested interest to the state whose company has joined a Third World producer. With heightened interests many states also often try to exert greater influence and control.

Most Third World states accept the fact that some degree of dependence on imported technology will be required. On the other hand, their national industries have developed in response to a perceived need for self-reliance. Therefore, they will minimize the degree of their dependence by making the deal that allows them the greatest degree of flexibility. Moreover, as Egypt, Somalia, Israel, and Turkey have shown, many countries will pay a heavy price to avoid letting their dependence on others for arms or technology strongly influence their foreign policies.

Imports of military technology by Third World states is, in part, a function of the kinds of weapons developing nations feel they must produce; these requirements stem, in turn, from the operational requirements of their armed forces. It is sometimes argued that the domestic production of weapons enhances operational efficiency because those weapons will be more suitable for the environment. A weapons system imported by a Third World country, the argument continues, is often not really suited for that country's operational requirements; rather, it reflects the requirements of the industrialized country from whom the system is purchased. Consequently, it also reflects the strategy and tactics adopted by the industrial producer to fight the kind of conflict with which it is potentially confronted. It is not necessarily the most appropriate system for the Third World state which faces conflicts of a different type. While some industrial countries are building weapons systems to respond to the unique defense needs of Third World states, from the perspective of developing countries the best remedy is local design and production of needed systems.

Theoretically, indigenous design and production allows a developing country greater opportunity to match weapons specifications and operational requirements, and sometimes theory is borne out in reality. The success achieved by the Indian air force's Gnat during the 1965 and 1971 wars with Pakistan is one example. Although the Gnat's ancestor was designed in Britain, RAF interest in the plane was sidetracked, and Hindustan Aircraft Limited (HAL)—India's national aircraft company—refined it. In 1965, the lightweight fighter was India's primary air-defense weapon, and it enjoyed considerable success against Pakistan's F-86s and F-104s. According to *Air International*, "India was in a mood to acclaim the Gnat as the hero of the 1965 conflict."[26] Once war had erupted in 1971, the PAF was reportedly so concerned about the Gnat that it issued a directive to its pilots to avoid dogfights with it. The lightweight frame of the Gnat made it extremely effective for the environment in which it had to operate and for the pilots who had to fly it. The Indians have been so pleased that they have moved on to a second version of the plane, christened the Ajeet, which will be an entirely HAL effort conforming to IAF specifications.[27]

A less dramatic but no less telling example is Israel's experience in 1967 when it found the Cyrano radar installed in its Mirages was not designed to acquire and track a target at low altitude with ground-clutter background. Israel's experience in the war showed that such a capability was necessary for the type of air-to-air combat that occurred in the Middle East. This prompted the Israeli air force to seek a simpler radar designed to detect low-flying targets and the result was the new Elta 2001 radar, which is said to have no competitor in the West.[28]

Several vehicles for land warfare produced in the Third World are also adapted to their operating environments. The armor of Argentina's new tank, for example, is not as thick as that in the new tanks being designed for Europe, since it is expected to function in conflicts likely to be less dense with antitank guided weapons. South Africa's Ratel—an infantry fighting vehicle—and Brazil's armored Urutu are also highly regarded for Third World contingencies.

Numerous other systems could be added to this list to bear out the argument, but it is not universally true. Some weapons systems produced by Third World states are no more, and sometimes less, appropriate for a Third World environment than weapons systems that can be bought off the shelf, and there are several reasons for this. First, the range of systems being produced by traditional arms manufacturers has expanded because those producers, especially in Europe, must export to maintain the health of their own defense industries. The Third World is a most attractive export market, and systems are now being designed for it by the Europeans. Second, prestige considerations have sometimes pushed a Third World state beyond its capabilities and the resulting system has proven inadequate. Prestige has also made Third World states develop systems indigenously when equally good, if not better, systems were available elsewhere. Brazil's development of a maritime version of the Bandeirante reconnaissance aircraft, when several systems were already being produced in Europe to perform the same function, is an excellent example. Finally, Third World states with relatively more advanced arms industries are approaching a stage at which the industry tail wags the security dog, when the nature of weapons produced strongly influences precepts of national security. If a country is intent upon using weapons systems it produces, it has two choices: build weapons appropriate to military needs or modify its doctrines to accommodate the kinds of weapons that can be produced. This choice is familiar to most industrial arms producers where the dynamics of arms production has become grounded in the need to create new concepts and produce at the frontier of technological development. Consequently, their experience has shown that changes in doctrine are made to respond to new weapons systems that are introduced. Although the technological frontiers of Third World states may not be so extended the more sophisticated Third World producers are beginning to experience similar pressures and the impact on their military doctrines is also likely to be similar.

Regional Stability

The major Third World arms producers—present and potential—are all important, if not key, actors in their respective regions. It is striking that many of them are also traditional rivals: Brazil and Argentina, India and Pakistan, Israel and Egypt. Other important or potentially important arms producers among developing countries are located in areas considered highly volatile; South Africa and South Korea, for example, face difficult security problems in regions of possible conflict. Given these conditions, are local arms industries destabilizing factors in regions of potential interstate conflict in the Third World?

Regional instability occurs when a key actor in an area, perceiving an unacceptable balance between itself and a state in the region that is considered a possible threat, undertakes to rectify that perceived imbalance. Balance in this case does not mean numbers of soldiers and weapons, but roughly equivalent "national power," broadly defined to include money, territory, population, industrial capacity, and armaments. Samuel P. Huntington has argued that "in the past century the relative importance of the internal means of balancing power has tended to increase."[29] States have increasingly sought to counter potential threats by developing their indigenous capabilities rather than seeking external assistance through an alliance or foreign military aid.

A successful, indigenous arms industry is certainly perceived as one component of national power; a regional actor whose defense-production capabilities lag behind those of a rival, then, could well feel pressure to improve its own capability. Such thinking might be at least part of the reason behind the decision of Egypt, Saudi Arabia and some smaller Persian Gulf states to create the Arab Organization for Industrialization (AOI). The AOI is intended to provide a military and civil industrial base that will give the Arab world some measure of independence from industrialized nations.[30] There can also be no doubt that the countries engaged in this enterprise hope the AOI will in the future offset to some degree—if not match—Israel's defense industries, although for each of these countries Israel is not their only, and in some cases not their primary, security concern. At the present time, the Arab states cannot consider the AOI anything but a small addition to the "balance of power" between the two sides. Their willingness to go to war with Israel does not hinge on their success in building up the organization. Whether this will be true in twenty years, however, when national arms industries have matured and become more sophisticated, must be considered.

In regions of the developing world where arms producers are also traditional rivals, the buildup of indigenous defense-production capabilities might be viewed as a novel dimension of their arms races. Even in an area where an arms producer has no specific rival, however, local arms production is the product of political conflicts that generate a perceived need to enhance national security. In either case, it is not the existence of defense industries that fuel political disputes; rather, defense industries are kept alive by potential or active conflicts, since regional disputes define the threats to national security that locally produced arms are intended to counter. In some cases, the existence of a local arms industry might exacerbate a conflict by contributing to an overbearing confidence on the part of one side or another, but as only one component of national power, and usually a small one in the Third World, it cannot necessarily be considered a destabilizing factor in a region of potential interstate conflict.

A further point must be briefly noted: not all threats to regional stability in the Third World—perhaps the minority—stem from disputes between governments. Unrest within a key developing country can easily spill over to affect the power balance of an entire area. In situations of violent domestic challenges to sitting governments, the quality of arms held by the contestants often makes little difference, as the war in Vietnam highlighted; whether or not the arms used are locally manufactured is not of extreme importance. Certainly, if a local arms plant is destroyed or captured by insurgents, they would profit, at least psychologically, but so many factors will determine the ultimate consequences of political violence in a developing country that the existence of local defense-production capabilities has little impact one way or the other.

Third World Arms Exports

The export of arms by Third World producers is a third major issue related to indigenous defense production in developing countries. According to U.S. Arms Control and Disarmament Agency (ACDA) figures, in 1968 Israel exported approximately $10 million worth of weapons, and in 1976 that figure had risen to $102 million.[31] Among its best sellers are the Gabriel missile, the Arava Short-Takeoff and Landing (STOL) air transport, Galil rifles, and Reshef patrol boats.

Brazil, too, has initiated an extensive export drive. Although it began exporting arms as recently as 1975, some estimates indicate that by the 1980s Brazil may be marketing $500 million of military hardware annually.[32] It has already made important deals to sell its Cascavel armored reconnaissance vehicle to Libya and Qatar, and there is substantial interest in the Cascavel in other Third World countries. The Brazilian state-controlled aircraft company is also making a concerted effort to sell its Bandeirante and Xavante aircraft. Several Latin American   countries, including Uruguay and Chile, have agreed to purchase the former while Togo has concluded a deal for the latter.[33]

Most Third World arms producers share the opinion of an Israeli Defense Ministry spokesman, who argued that it is "impossible for a small country...to maintain an economically viable arms industry without exports."[34] The domestic market in these countries is not large enough to support an arms industry on its own, and to achieve the economies of scale Third World producers must go overseas.

The need to export arms abroad has several important implications. First, it can create difficulties between the Third World producer and the industrial producer who supplies it sophisticated technological components. Israel discovered the extent of the problem when the United States refused to allow it to sell the Kfir to Ecuador; the U.S. right to veto the sale derived from the Kfir's use of the General Electric J 79-17 engine. Washington did so on the grounds that it did not want to introduce advanced aircraft into Latin America; but there was some speculation in Israel that the United States was merely trying to eliminate competition in the region. For its part, the United States has been concerned over Israeli use of foreign military sales credits, not only to obtain U.S. weapons, but also to import technical-data packages that eventually may be exported in competition with U.S. products.[35] In some cases, Israel makes minor modifications in a system it receives from the United States, then claims it is not a U.S.

system and sells it overseas without U.S. approval. The use of U.S. funds and technology to foster an arms industry runs counter to the Carter administration's efforts to control the flow of conventional arms around the world and, in the long run, such practices could cause a strain in bilateral relations.

Second, Third World arms producers will eventually encounter competition from traditional arms manufacturers. Most European countries must also export to maintain the health of their defense industries; for these countries, new arms exporters will increase competition in an already crowded market. The impact of that competition, while not likely to be debilitating in the short run, could have an adverse long-term impact on the European industries. At the same time, providing support and technical assistance to new Third World industries—as the British and French are giving the new Arab enterprise—gives industrial countries additional opportunities to improve the state of their own defense industries. It may be that in the future industrialized states will be replaced by some Third World arms producers as exporters of hardware, while they provide arms-related services—a sort of "postindustrial" phase of their arms industry. Britain is already heavily engaged with service agreements such as the reported $500 million deal for maintenance and support of the Royal Saudi Air Force.

Third, industrialized arms producers have had in the past some measure of control over regional conflicts in the Third World by virtue of their ability to regulate the arms pipeline. It may become increasingly difficult to exert this control as regional arms-production capabilities expand. In addition, dependence of developing countries on arms from the developed world has given the industrialized nations a certain amount of political leverage in pursuit of their own foreign-policy goals. Whether that leverage would be diluted as a consequence of increased arms exports by alternative suppliers in the Third World must be seriously considered.

Finally, just as industrial arms exporters have found themselves involved in the regional disputes of their clients, Third World exporters are likely to become engaged more deeply in international affairs beyond their immediate regions. An Israeli spokesman has commented, for example, that through Brazil's arms sales to Arab countries, that country will de facto enter the arms race in the Middle East "and may even exert influence on the armament balance of the region."[36] Israeli experts consider that Brazilian participation in the Middle East arms race will become an additional concern for Israel, and the prospects of this are intriguing. So are several other questions: How will Israel's exports to, and cooperation with, South Africa affect the course of events in southern Africa? To what extent do arms exports reflect a growing cooperation among states considered "pariahs" in the present international system?

Conventional-Arms Control

A final set of issues related to Third World defense production addresses the prospects for arms control. As a candidate, Jimmy Carter assailed previous U.S. administrations for their efforts to sell arms abroad, and as president he has sought to limit the international transfer of conventional arms, albeit without much success. The existence of Third World arms producers who must also export adds an additional dimension to President Carter's dilemma. In an effort to assert some control over this problem, the Carter administration announced as part of its formal arms-transfers policy that co-production agreements for significant systems would be prohibited. It added that as a condition of sale for certain systems, the U.S. may stipulate that it will not entertain *any* requests for retransfer.[37]

From the administration's perspective these prohibitions may compromise other goals, particularly in Europe.[38] From the viewpoint of Third World producers, restrictions such as these can only be seen as another attempt by the United States to impose its view of the world on others and to prevent them from achieving what industrialized states have already gained. As mentioned previously, Third World arms producers insist that they must export if they are to maintain viable industries, and they are intent on doing just that. It is highly doubtful, therefore, that they will be persuaded by the administration's position, especially since the United States is seen as making so many exceptions to its own rules.

Third World emphasis on production and export of arms is helping to fuel a proliferation of conventional arms that would be difficult for anyone to control. Arms are perceived as lending legitimacy, power, and prestige to developing countries. Just as industrialized nations, Third World states want arms, and Third World producers want to sell them; restrictions on those sales that are in any way perceived as imposed are likely to be counterproductive. If any success is to be achieved, Third World arms exporters must be consulted and made part of the decision-making process.

CONCLUSION

The impact of the expansion of defense industries in developing countries is potentially far-reaching. It could influence not only relations among Third World states themselves, but also those between the industrialized and developing worlds; it may also affect the outcome of regional conflicts and create additional problems in arms-control forums. Admittedly, Third World arms industries are in their early stages, and their influence will not be strongly felt for some time. This does not permit, however, the luxury of ignoring potential problems. U.S. decision makers too often wait until problems have reached crisis proportions, and they must start thinking now about what their response will be as defense industries in the Third World continue to grow and mature.

NOTES

1. A number of publications have provided inventories of the scope of weapons production by Third World states. In 1971, the Stockholm International Peace Research Institute (SIPRI) published *The Arms Trade With the Third World* (New York: Humanities Press). A chapter of this book, "Domestic Defense Production in Third World Countries," presents a roster of developing countries and the scope of their domestic armaments programs, as well as case studies of the arms industries of India, Argentina, and Israel. SIPRI also publishes "Registers of Indigenous and Licensed Production of Major Weapons and Small Arms in Third World Countries" in its annual publication, *World Armaments and Disarmament* (Cambridge: Massachusetts Institute of Technology Press, yearly). Other sources providing general information on Third World defense industries include International Institute for Strategic Studies, *Strategic Survey* (London: IISS, 1976), pp. 20–23; and Peter Lock and Herbert Wulf, "Register of Arms Production in Developing Countries," Study Group on Armaments and Underdevelopment, University of Hamburg, March 1977. For more detail on the companies involved in Third World arms production, see the annual *Defense and Foreign Affairs Handbook* (Washington, D.C.: Copley and Associates). Despite these sources, there are still some data problems with respect to this topic, particularly the lack of complete data on the numbers of countries producing arms and the quantities of arms—especially small arms and electronic equipment—that are manufactured.

2. For a brief review of the current status of arms-production programs in the major Third World states, for example, see Gregory R. Copley, Michael Moodie, and David Harvey, "Third World Arms Production: An End to Embargoes?" *Defense and Foreign Affairs Digest,* No. 8 (1978) and Gregory R. Copley, "Third World Arms Production," *Defense and Foreign Affairs Digest,* no. 9 (1978).

3. SIPRI, "Domestic Defense Production in Third World Countries," in *The Arms Trade With the Third World,* op. cit., p. 761.

4. Peter Lock and Herbert Wulf, "Consequences of the Transfer of Military-Oriented Technology on the Development Process," *Bulletin of Peace Proposals,* no. 2 (1977), p. 127.

5. Frank Bray and Alvin Cottrell, "The Armed Forces of India, Iran and Pakistan: A Comparative Assessment," in Royal United Services Institute for Defence Studies, ed., *Defence Yearbook 1977/78* (London: Brassey's Publishers Ltd., 1978), p. 34.

6. Roberto Pereira de Andrade, "Bandeirante: A Brazilian Breakthrough," *Air Enthusiast International* (June 1974), p. 284.

7. SIPRI, "Domestic Defense Production in the Third World Countries," op. cit., p. 773.

8. Broadcast by Jerusalem Domestic News Service, cited by Foreign Broadcast Information Service, *Middle East and North Africa,* April 18, 1977, p. N6.

9. *Washington Post,* December 18, 1977, p. 1.

10. This process has been particularly evident in Third World aircraft industries. See "Aircraft Manufacturing in the Developing Nations," *Interavia* no. 12 (1977), p. 1156.

11. IISS, *Strategic Survey,* p. 21.

12. *The Times* (London), May 16, 1977.

13. Lock and Wulf, *Register of Arms Production,* p. 95.

14. India began a design for a main battle tank at its Avadi research and development department in 1970. It is planned to have the tank in production by 1980 (ibid.).

15. The Soviets have reportedly agreed at least to the transfer of seventy T-72 tanks to India. See Copley, "Third World Arms Production," op. cit., p. 41.

16. For example, difficulties in obtaining design plans prevented India from making desired modifications to the MiG-21. See SIPRI, "Domestic Defense Production in Third World Countries," p. 730.

17. Defense Publications, *Defense and Foreign Affairs Daily*, vol. 6, 355, (1978).

18. For a review of the current status of Taiwan's civil and military aviation, see Donald E. Fink, "Nationalists Update Fighter Force," *Aviation Week and Space Technology* (May 29, 1978); and "Center Designs Two Aircraft," *Aviation Week and Space Technology* (June 5, 1978).

19. *Aviation Week and Space Technology*, May 29, 1978, p. 16.

20. *Washington Post*, April 21, 1978.

21. For an evaluation of the current status of the Israeli avionics industry, see Philip J. Klass, "New Capabilities Building Rapidly," *Aviation Week and Space Technology* (April 10, 1978); "Three Firms Dominate Output," *Aviation Week and Space Technology* (April 17, 1978); and "Tadiran Enters Airborne Avionics Field," *Aviation Week and Space Technology* (April 24, 1978).

22. IISS, *Strategic Survey*, p. 23.

23. Shahram Chubin, "Iran's Security in the 1980's," *International Security* 2 (1978): 66–68.

24. For background on India's and Israel's respective aircraft industries, see Pushpindar Chopra, "Spinal Cord of Indian Air Defense," *Air International*, January 1975, and Irving J. Cohen, "Arava: Israel's First-Born Bid for World Market," *Air Enthusiast International*, February 1974.

25. Quoted in Lawrence Freedman, "Britain and the Arms Trade," *International Affairs* 54 (1978): 385.

26. Pushpindar Chopra, "Fly with a Sting," *Air International*, August 1977, p. 73.

27. See Pushpindar Chopra, "Ajeet," *Air International*, June 1977, pp. 284–290.

28. Philip Klass, "New Capabilities Building Rapidly," *Aviation Week and Space Technology*, April 17, 1978, p. 32.

29. Samuel P. Huntington, "Arms Races: Prerequisites and Results," in Robert J. Art and Kenneth N. Waltz, eds., *The Use of Force: International Politics and Foreign Policy* (Boston: Little, Brown and Co., 1971), p. 369.

30. For details, see Robert R. Ropelewski, "Arabs Seek Arms Sufficiency," *Aviation Week and Space Technology*, May 15, 1978, pp. 14–16.

31. U.S. Arms Control and Disarmament Agency, *World Military Expenditures and Arms Transfers, 1967–1976* (Washington: ACDA, 1978), p. 135.

32. "Brazil: A Major Contender in the Arms Business," *Business Week*, July 31, 1978.

33. Ibid.

34. Broadcast by Jerusalem Domestic Service, cited by Foreign Broadcast Information Service, *Middle East and North Africa*, January 26, 1977, p. N5. For example in an interview in *Jornal de Brasil*, General Arnaldo Carderari, Chief of the Brazilian Army's Material Department echoed this sentiment in saying that Brasilia must concentrate its military hardware production efforts on foreign markets as a way of insuring its domestic military industry's viability and development (cited in *Latin American Affairs Weekly*, January 13, 1978).

35. Clarence A. Robinson, Jr., "Israel Arms Exports Spur Concern," *Aviation Week and Space Technology*, December 13, 1976.

36. Quoted in the Brazilian newspaper *O Estad de Sao Paulo*, cited by Foreign Broadcast Information Service, *Latin America*, April 15, 1977, p. D5.

37. Statement by the president on conventional arms transfer policy, Office of the White House Press Secretary, May 19, 1977.

38. For a discussion of these problems, see David J. Louscher, "Continuity and Change in American Arms Sales Policies," in *Ohio Arms Control Seminar: Workshop II—Selected Papers*,

Mershon Center of the Ohio State University, June 18, 1977, pp. 41–42; and Seymour Weiss, *President Carter's Arms Transfer Policy: A Critical Assessment* (Washington, D.C.: Advanced International Studies Institute in association with the University of Miami, 1978), monograph, pp. 13–14.

PART FIVE

CONCLUSION

18 THE ROAD TO FURTHER RESEARCH AND THEORY IN ARMS TRANSFERS

– the editors

The preceding panoply of contributions on arms transfers was intended by the book's editors to provide relatively broad coverage of an issue area which has come to occupy a very central position in international diplomacy. It was further intended to provide an overall analytical framework which, through a "levels of analysis" organization, could incorporate contributions dealing with theory and measurement, with substantive issues at the foreign policy level (suppliers and recipients), and with various kinds of relationships at the international systems level.

No explicit attempt was here made to uncover a "theory" of arms transfers. The subject is quite probably of a complexity well beyond the level where one might contemplate tight causal models, and explicitly set forth formal relationships between sets of dependent and independent variables. Besides, it would presumably be neither possible nor wise to attempt to isolate the arms transfer phenomenon from its surrounding context. Indeed, one major purpose of this volume was to demonstrate the extent to which the arms trade is located in a vortex of important interrelationships involving, among other things, oil diplomacy, balance of payments, technology transfer, alliances, nuclear proliferation, the competition for overseas bases, and so forth.

At least one of the chapters, however, that by Edward Kolodziej, does assay a very broad analytical framework—a "pre-theory"—which involves the use of the "national," "sub-national," "transnational," and "international" levels. As such, it has provided a framework which might prove useful in a number of related issue areas or "regimes," for instance, that of nuclear technology transfers. Here one sees a fruitful attempt at integrating the now conflicting emphases in international relations scholarship between the traditional state-centric perspective and the more recent vogue of "transnational" relations, which focus respectively on inter-state relationships and a mixture of those and other sub-state and non-state actors.

In choosing a selection of essays to depict the scope of arms transfer issues, the editors were well aware that some aspects of the subject—even important ones—would have to be left unexplored (although they might be cursorily touched upon in essays primarily devoted to related subjects). Three definable areas have been neglected: (1) certain substantive topics and issues; (2) historical or longitudinal analyses; and (3) systematic comparative studies. This volume, particularly on the supplier side, is weighted heavily toward a U.S. perspective and basis for analysis. It is a comment on the state of the field, that although the editors consciously tried to avoid this bias, they were unable to do so. The following paragraphs detail some of these research needs. They are merely indicative of the gaps and are by no means exhaustive.

On the supplier side, in addition to those essays provided here on economic impacts and rationales (Anne Cahn), bureaucratic politics (Jo Husbands), and rivalries amid the military-industrial complex (Ingemar Dörfer), there is considerable room for more research in what is still a relatively unexplored area of foreign/domestic policy linkages. For instance, there has been little depth analysis on the impact of public opinion on arms transfer policies (in the United States and elsewhere) at a time when some of the polls appear to demonstrate a rather surprising American public opposition to arms transfers. Whether public response is in full understanding of what is involved is not clear, nor is the origin of public opinion understood. Is it reflective of or reactive to official rhetoric? These and other such questions deserve further investigation.

Then too, some recent events have highlighted the impact of ethnic politics on U.S. arms supply decision making, and here there has also been little adequate empirical analysis. Although Dörfer's contribution provides one case study on the impingement of interest group politics on arms transfer decisions, there is need for a more comprehensive analysis of this subject. Research might encompass the roles and perspectives of labor unions, a broader group of military contractors and industrial corporations, "public interest" organizations, religious groups, and other interested parties. Such research could usefully extend the observations of Cahn and Husbands and provide, for the United States at least, a comprehensive picture of the overall domestic/foreign policy linkages involved.

The need for comparative studies along the lines described above is obvious. None such now exist. Furthermore, on the supplier side, the extant literature is lacking in broad comparative analyses of how and to what extent the major suppliers have utilized arms transfers to extend their military power and security overseas, a matter that encompasses not only formal alliances such as NATO, but also the use of "surrogate" forces in regional conflicts. The now quietly lapsed "Nixon Doctrine," for example, which expressed an earlier U.S. strategy along such lines, might be compared with the Soviet arming and backstopping of Cuban forces in Africa, or the kind of dual control over weapons exercised by the Soviets in Libya, designed to give the USSR strategic flexibility along the Mediterranean. This subject is related to, but somewhat distinct from, that of the relationship between arms and overseas bases discussed by Robert Harkavy in this volume.

On the recipient side, this volume has provided chapters on the important relationships of arms transfers to political and economic development (Ernest W. Lefever and Stephanie Neuman), to "back-end" logistics and maintenance problems (Geoffrey Kemp), to the dependency relationships inherent in the assymetries between suppliers and recipients (Herbert Wulf), and to indigenous arms development and production programs (Michael Moodie). But further attention needs to be directed at how dependent nations choose the sources, amounts, and types of arms they acquire, in the context of external threat assessments, security strategies, and related force planning. Here, as on the supplier side, attention might be directed to various aspects of domestic politics (interest groups, bureaucratic politics, etc.), and to analyses of the comparative significance of "push" (from suppliers) and "pull" (from domestic) factors. Although some research has been done, further comparative studies might be conducted on the nature of correlations between levels of arms acquisitions, GNPs, defense expenditures, etc.; on acquisitions as a function of regime types (pro-West or pro-Soviet, military and nonmilitary), and on measurable mixes of security and prestige rationales for arms acquisitions.

It is apparent that making a clear demarcation between relationships and transactions at the international systems level and the national policy-making level is not a simple matter. Hardly lamentable, that difficulty merely demonstrates the necessity for greater attention to the linkages between levels. With that caveat, contributions were sought for this volume that focus primarily on the role arms transfers play on the global or regional level, for example, patterns of donor-recipient acquisitions (Michael Mihalka), reciprocal lines of influence and leverage between suppliers and recipients (William Lewis), the impact of new weaponry on arms supply relationships (Steven Rosen and C.I. Hudson), and the nexus between conventional arms transfers and nuclear proliferation (Richard Burt).

Though this would appear a fairly comprehensive catalog of important issue areas, perhaps above all, further analysis is still necessary on the interrelationships between global patterns and other political and economic phenomena. To what extent, for example, have arms transfers been congruent with overall trade relationships, economic aid flows, direct investment, raw material flows, base acquisitions, educational exchanges, and the like? And what has tended to precede, drive, or follow what? Have arms transfers normally constituted an opening wedge leading to other, broader relationships, or have they tended to follow upon preceding forms of political and economic alignment? The scholarly jury is still out.

Two other topics at the systemic level not treated in this volume bear mention here: first the possibilities for multilateral controls arrangements, and second, the "two-way street" problem[1] within NATO, which is subtly connected to the former issue. The chapters by Lewis, Husbands, and Wilcox, primarily concerned with other questions, have provided some analyses related to controls, but largely from the perspective of Washington and in the context of the Carter administration's new directions based on PD Presidential Directive) 13. The recent CAT (Conventional Arms Transfer) talks with the Soviets, which may adumbrate multilateral controls in some form, suggest that further consideration is needed of various possible frameworks or alternate arrangements—formal or informal, regional or global, by suppliers, recipients or both, involving quantitative and/or qualitative restraints. Why arms control transfer efforts have borne so little fruit since they began in the 1890s, is still another fertile ground for investigation.

Regarding arms transfers within the NATO alliance (and those within the Warsaw Pact), the editors are aware that with the exception of the chapter by Dörfer, the book's focus is primarily on arms relationships between the major supplier states and developing country recipients. Such a focus might admittedly serve to obscure the continuing importance of arms relationships among the advanced nations. Though often less interesting and controversial, transactions among the major powers continue to constitute a large fraction of the global arms trade. Here, of course, further analysis is needed on the impact such transfers have on alliance maintenance and coordinated defense planning, balances of payments, industrial competition and technology transfer, third-party transfer dilemmas, and perhaps nuclear proliferation, among other things.

Two chapters were provided in this volume (Richard Wilcox and Edward Fei) on definitions and measurement in arms transfers. Together, they may have moved the state of knowledge in these much argued and important areas to new levels. In relation to other writings, however, and in connection with Mihalka's technique of measuring acquisition patterns, they appear to point to the necessity for some kind of overall, aggregate value measurement which might somehow combine or integrate the imputed monetary value of transfers with the counting of discrete weapons systems. The resolution of this central methodological conundrum remains elusive.

As noted, the contributions to this volume have primarily been devoted to current problems and recent trends, raising all manner of questions about their durability and viability in a longer-range historical context, a problem by no means specific to arms transfers. Unavoidably, there may be dangers in extrapolating to the future from the recent past, or in perceiving trends from not-so-distant earlier base-lines. The recent literature on arms transfers is heavily larded with dire lamentations about its allegedly unprecedented nature and volume, about its "getting out of hand," about "revolutionary" new weapons, etc. And yet, a scanning of the earlier arms trade literature—in the 1930s or the 1890s—reveals surprisingly similar rhetoric leading one to question seriously the extent to which one is really now dealing with something new under the sun.

A review of the earlier literature raises questions, for instance, about the real mix of "irreversible" changes, cyclical ebbs and flows, and periodic reversals which may have characterized various aspects of arms transfer practices and diplomacy.[2] Have, for example, the numbers of significant suppliers expanded continuously with the entry of ever-new indigenous weapons production programs (and hence dependency gradually lessened), or might cyclical swings in overall independence and autarky be discerned over a long period? To what extent have arms transfer relationships in different periods been determined by ideological ties or been correlated with or related to basing diplomacy, raw materials access, etc.? Are there systemic factors, alternating in time, that have determined the influence/leverage relationships between suppliers and recipients, that go beyond specific dyadic circumstances? Clearly, systematic historical research on these issues would add depth to our understanding of the arms trade.

A final set of summary comments has to do with the obvious truism that the arms transfers literature has long been characterized by furious ideological polemics. What has been involved, of course, is a mere subset of widely differing assumptions and emotions about the very essence of world politics and the conduct of diplomacy, often characterized as Lockean and Hobbesian polar opposites. The reader will have noted that such polemics are not absent from this volume, though they are often subtle and not usually explicit. The editors recognized that the inclusion of widely varying viewpoints was both unavoidable and to be encouraged. They consciously strove for a combination of political viewpoints on the arms trade that spans the political spectrum. Because of space restrictions (combined with the editors' desire to include as wide a variety of related topics as possible), it was not possible to present the differing views within a debate format. Instead, "representative" political beliefs are scattered among the different issue areas.

At the risk of some disagreement, it might be claimed that heretofore the arms transfer literature has been somewhat dominated by a "reformist" or "utopian" perspective.[3] It is true that in between historical bursts of reformism, the literature has been relatively sparse, less argumentative, mostly descriptive, and an appendage to national security studies. But few scholars or publicists have at any time argued the "goodness" of arms transfers or urged its expansion. Rather, debates over the arms trade have normally been between the majority who would curb or reform it, and those "cynics" who resignedly accept it as part of the natural order in an assumed relentlessly Hobbesian world.

If one were to venture a slightly broader typology, three perceptual paradigms begin to emerge from the above dichotomy as characteristic of the arms transfer literature. They might be described as (1) power/ "realist"/geopolitical; (2) arms control; and (3) dependency perspectives. The power/"realist"/geopolitical paradigm tends to assume that arms supply competition among the major suppliers (and the maximizing of power through acquisitions on the part of recipients) is endemic and ineradicable. It is one aspect of overall political and military competition, subject to limitations only to the extent that international rivalries and enmities can themselves be resolved or moderated. The emphasis then is on arms transfers as an accepted instrument for achieving political influence, allies, money, strategic access, etc. It is an instrument of grand strategy by both supplier and recipient, and its importance is measured by the extent to which the arms trade affects the balance of power between states. Arms control advocates, of course, perceive this viewpoint as callous, while critics from the dependency school reject what they consider to be a cynical justification of the global power status quo.

Arms controllers constitute the second group. As modern Wilsonians, they look, if not to a cessation, then to a mitigation of the arms trade as an assumed curable evil, which allegedly contributes mightily to war and to economic misallocation of resources. Their emphasis is on a quantitative reduction of the arms trade and a stanching of the spread of still more sophisticated weapons technology. Curiously, arms control perspectives are often resented by those in dependent nations (and by some dependency theorists in the West) as paternalistic, aimed at perpetuating unbalanced global assymetries of power, and hypocritical in the light of the ongoing "vertical" proliferation of weapons in the supplier states.

The third group, the dependency theorists, are not normally open advocates of arms transfers, but see their essential significance in a manner distinct from the power/"realist"/geopolitical and arms control schools. To dependency theorists, the patterns of arms transfers reflect and reinforce a structured and highly unequal global social system, which demands change. Such theorists look to a "new world military order" as a complement to a "new world economic order," with an emphasis either on forced, "deserved" arms transfers or on bootstrap indigenous production efforts.

And so the debate goes on. As we have demonstrated, it is by no means a new one. It is hoped that this volume, which reflects the unresolved nature of the debate, will have shed some light on its current nature and progress. Thomas S. Kuhn, in *The Structure of Scientific Revolutions*,[4] argues that in the natural sciences, periods of "normal science" alternate with periods of "scientific revolutions"—the latter characterized by competing models, old and new, struggling for ascendency. Normal science is guided by a generally accepted paradigm, which serves as a foundation for research and the cumulative growth of scientific knowledge. It is distinguished by a general acceptance of an approach or theory within the scientific/scholarly community. The field of arms transfers and controls still awaits that agreement. The editors hope that this collection of essays has, at least, elucidated some of the competing models, and perhaps, in some small way has paved the way toward conceptual maturity and more systematic research in the future.

NOTES

1. This refers to the European view that there should be reciprocity in the purchase of arms between the United States and Western Europe.

2. For further discussion see Robert E. Harkavy, *The Arms Trade and International Systems* (Cambridge, Mass.: Ballinger, 1975).

3. The utopian perspective has been partly a reflection of two identifiable historical junctures: the late 1920s and early 1930s, and then during the contemporary period. The first of these junctures occurred in the aftermath of World War I, during the heyday of the League and Wilsonian idealism, and was related to the "merchants of death" controversies which peaked at the time of the Nye Committee hearings. The second has been one aspect of the post-Vietnam mood in America, characterized by, among other things, a denunciation of military-industrial complexes and cold-war diplomacy. Both periods have been characterized by heightened interest in achieving controls on the arms trade.

4. Thomas S. Kuhn, *The Structure of Scientific Revolutions* (Chicago: University of Chicago Press, 1970).

THE ARMS TRADE:
A SELECTED BIBLIOGRAPHY

Compiled by Nicole Ball

CONTENTS

BIBLIOGRAPHY

In general, newspapers and news magazines (such as *Newsweek* or *The Economist*) have not been surveyed although a few longer articles from sources of this nature have been included.

I. POST-1945 ARMS TRADE
A. General

Books and Monographs
Albrecht, Ulrich, *Der Handel mit Waffen* (Munich: Carl Hanser Verlag, 1971).
———, *Politik und Waffengeschäfte; Rüstungsexporte in der BRD* (Munich: Carl Hanser Verlag, 1972).
Beaton, Leonard, Geoffrey Kemp, and Uri Ra'anan, "Arms Trade and International Politics," Occasional Paper 13, Carleton University School of International Affairs, Ottawa, August 1971.
Burt, Richard, "Nuclear Proliferation and Conventional Arms Transfers: The Missing Link," Discussion Paper no. 76, California Seminar on Arms Control and Foreign Policy, Santa Monica, Calif., September 1977.
Fox, W. T. R.; Anglin, D. G. and Gellner, John, *Working Papers: Conference on Arms Trade and International Politics,* Occasional Paper 12, Carleton University School of International Affairs, Ottawa, May 1971.
Frank, Lewis A., *The Arms Trade in International Relations* (New York: Praeger, 1969).
Harkavy, Robert E., *The Arms Trade and International Systems* (Cambridge, Mass.: Ballinger, 1975).

We wish to thank Dr. Richard D. Burns of the Center for the Study of Armament and Disarmament, California State University, Los Angeles, for permission to reprint portions of Arthur Gillingham, *Arms Traffic: An Introduction and Bibliography;* and Milton Leitenberg, Peace Studies Program, Center for International Studies, Cornell University, for making his files on arms trade available.

Hoagland, J. H. and Clapp, P. A., "Notes on Small Arms Traffic," Center for International Studies, Massachusetts Institute of Technology, Cambridge, 1970.

Johnson, George E., *International Armament*, 2 vols. (Cologne: International Small Arms Publishing, 1965).

Leiss, Amelia C., "Changing Patterns of Arms Transfers: Implications for Arms Transfer Policies," Cambridge, Mass.: Center for International Studies, Institute of Technology, 1970.

Menahem, Georges, *La Science et le Militaire* (Paris: Seuil, 1976).

Owens, Joe S. *The Arms Merchants—Who's Number One*, AD-771 529. Carlisle Barracks, Pa., distributed for the Army War College by National Technical Information Services (NTIS), U.S. Department of Commerce, February 1972.

Ronfeldt, David F., "Superclients and Superpowers," Report P-5945, Rand Corporation, Santa Monica, Calif., April 1978.

Sampson, Anthony, *The Arms Bazaar: From Lebanon to Lockheed* (New York: Viking Press, 1977).

Secretary-General of the United Nations, *Economic and Social Consequences of the Armaments Race and Its Extremely Harmful Effects on World Peace and Security*, A/32/88, New York, August 12, 1977. [Addendum, September 12, 1977].

Stanley, John and Pearton, Maurice, *The International Trade in Arms* (London: Chatto & Windus, 1972).

"The Arms Pushers: Booming World Arms Trade," *SANE WORLD*, Washington, D.C.: August-September 1974.

Vayrynen, Raimo, *Arms Trade, Military Aid and Arms Production* (Basel: Herder Verlag, 1973).

Articles and Pamphlets

Albrecht, Ulrich, "On the Internationalization of the Arms Business," *Instant Research on Peace and Violence* 4 (1973): 205–07.

_____, "The Study of International Trade in Arms and Peace Research," *Journal of Peace Research* 9:2 (1972): 165–78.

_____, Ernest, D., Lock, P., and Wulf, H., "Militarization, Arms Transfer and Arms Production in Peripheral Countries," *Journal of Peace Research* 12:3 (1975): 195–212.

"Anatomy of the Arms Trade," *Newsweek*, September 6, 1976, pp. 39–42.

Bader, William B., "The Proliferation of Conventional Weapons," in Cyril E. Black and Richard A. Falk, eds., *The Future of the International Legal Order, Vol. 3: Conflict Management*, pp. 210–223 (Princeton, N.J.: Princeton University Press, 1971).

Baker, Steven, "Arms Transfers and Nuclear Proliferation," *Arms Control Today* 7 (April 1977).

Balz, Daniel J., Corrigan, Richard, and Samuelson, Robert J., "Muffling the Arms Explosion," *National Journal*, April 2, 1977, pp. 496–513.

Cahn, Anne Hessing, "Have Arms, Will Sell," *Arms Control Today* 4 (October 1974): 1–3.

"Chucking Guns Around," *The Economist*, July 8, 1967.

Gray, Colin S., "The Arms Phenomenon: Definitions and Functions." *World Politics* 24 (October 1971): 39–79.

Haftendorn, Helga, "Der Internationale Waffentransfer und die Bemuhungen um seine Einschrankung," *Europa-Archiv* 26 (January 25, 1971): 25–74.

Harkavy, Robert E., "Comparison of the International Arms Trade in the Interwar and Postwar Periods," *Michigan Academician* 4 (1972): 445–60.

_____, "The Pariah State Syndrome," *Orbis* 21 (Fall 1977): 623–49.

Karnow, Stanley, "Weapons for Sale: No Recession in the Arms Business," *The New Republic*, March 23, 1974, pp. 21–23.

Kemp, Geoffrey, "Dilemmas of the Arms Traffic," *Foreign Affairs* 48 (January 1970): 274–84.

_____, "The International Arms Trade: Supplier, Recipient and Arms Control Perspectives," *Political Quarterly* 42 (October-December 1971): 379–89.

Klare, Michael T., "The Political Economy of Arms Sales," *Society* 11 (September-October 1974): 41–49.

Klein, Jean, "Commerce des Armes et Désarmement," *Politique Etrangère* 33:4 (1968): 351–59.

Kuebler, Jeanne, "Traffic in Arms," *Editorial Research Reports* April 28, 1965, pp. 303–19.

Leiss, Amelia C., "Comments on 'The Study of International Trade in Arms and Peace Research' by Ulrich Albrecht," *Journal of Peace Research* 9:2 (1972): 179–82.

Lock, Peter and Wulf, Herbert, "New Trends and Actors in the Arms Transfer Process to Peripheral Countries: A Preliminary Assessment of Peace Research, Some Hypotheses and Research Proposals," *Instant Research on Peace and Violence* 5 (1975): 185–96.

Luck, Edward C., "The Arms Trade," in David A. Kay, ed., *The Changing United Nations: Options for the United States*, pp. 170–83 (New York: Academy of Political Science, 1977).

Miksche, Ferdinand O., "Auswirkungen des Waffenhandels auf die Weltpolitik," *Wehr und Wirtschaft* 12 (October 20, 1968): 494–95.

"Now: A Worldwide Boom in Sales of Arms," *U.S. News & World Report*, January 22, 1973, pp. 50–53.

Rothschild,Emma,"The Boom in the Death Business," *New York Review of Books*, October 2, 1975, pp. 7–12.

_____, "The Arms Boom and How to Stop It," *New York Review of Books*, January 20, 1977.

Sivard, Ruth L., "Let Them Eat Bullets," *Bulletin of the Atomic Scientists* 31 (March 1975): 6–10.

Stone, William T., "International Arms Deals," *Editorial Research Reports*, November 16, 1955, pp. 791–808.

"The Arms Dealers: Guns for All." *Time*, March 3, 1975.

"Towards Collision: World Military Spending Takes Off," *To the Point*, November 3, 1978, pp. 8–11.

B. Control of Arms Trade

Bailey, Sydney D., "Can the Booming Arms Trade be Halted?" *Christian Century* 89, February 23, 1972, pp. 220–22.

Ball, Nicole and Leitenberg, Milton, "The Foreign Arms Sales Policy of the Carter Administration," *Bulletin of the Atomic Scientists* 35 (February 1979): 31–36.

_____, "The Foreign Arms Sales Policy of the Carter Administration," *Alternatives* 4:4 (1979).

Barton, John H., "The Developing Nations and Arms Control," *Studies in Comparative International Development* 10 (Spring 1975).

Benson, Lucy Wilson, "Controlling Arms Transfers: An Instrument of U.S. Foreign Policy," speech to Women's National Democratic Club, Washington, D.C., June 27, 1977.

Blechman, Barry and Fried, Edward R., "Disarmament and Development: An Analytical Survey and Pointers for Action," Committee for Development Planning, United Nations Economic and Social Council, New York, January 26, 1977.

Bloomfield, Lincoln P. and Leiss, Amelia C., "Arms Transfer and Arms Control," *Proceedings of Academy of Political Science* 29 (March 1969): 37–54.

_____, *Controlling Small Wars: A Strategy for the 1970's*, (New York: Knopf, 1969).

_____, "Arms Control and the Developing Countries," *World Politics* 18 (October 1965): 1–19.

Burt, Richard R., "Developments in Arms Transfers: Implications for Supplier Control and Recipient Autonomy," P-5991, Rand Corporation, Santa Monica, Calif., September 1977.

Cahn, Anne Hessing, Kruzel, J., Dawkins, P., and Huntzinger, J., *Controlling Future Arms Trade* (New York: McGraw-Hill Book Co., Council on Foreign Relations, 1977).

Culver, Sen. John C., "Need for an International Conference on Arms Sales," *Congressional Record*, September 23, 1975, p. S16510.

_____, "Prospects for International Limits on Arms Sales," *Congressional Record* September 27, 1976.

Evron, Yair, "The Role of Arms Control in the Middle East," Adelphi Papers, No. 138 (London: International Institute for Strategic Studies, Autumn 1977).

Gardner, Judy, "Congress Weighs New Controls on Arms Sales," *Congressional Quarterly Weekly Report*, December 20, 1975, pp. 2817–2819.

Gray, Colin S., "Traffic Control for the Arms Trade?" *Foreign Policy* no. 6 (Spring 1972): 153–69.

Hansen, Erland B. and Ulrich, Jorgen W., "A Weapons Transfer System for Inter-Nation Conflict Regulation: A Proposal," in Bengt Hoglund and J. W. Ulrich, eds., *Conflict Control and Conflict Resolution*, pp. 156–73. (Copenhagen: Munksgaard, 1972).

Johnson, William, "U.S. Military Aid Programs and Conventional Arms Control," California Arms Control and Foreign Policy Seminar, Santa Monica, Calif., January 1973.

Kemp, Geoffrey, "Regulating the Arms Trade," *Disarmament* 16 (December 1967): 11–15.

Klein, Jean, "Les Aspects Actuels de la Reglementation du Commerce des Armes," *Politique Estrangère* 34:2 (1969): 161–89.

Leonard, James F., "U.S. States View on Conventional Arms Restraints," *U.S. Department of State Bulletin* 65 (September 20, 1971): 309–15.

Pierre, Andrew, "International Restraints on Conventional Arms Transfers," in Jane M. O. Sharp, ed., *Opportunities for Disarmament*, pp. 47–60 (Washington, D.C.: Carnegie Endowment for International Peace, 1978).

Pomeroy, L. H., "The International Trade and Traffic in Arms: Its Supervision and Control," *U.S. Department of State Bulletin* 22 (March 6, 1950): 357–64; 507–515; 520.

Rothschild, Emma, "Carter and Arms: No Sale," *New York Review of Books*, September 15, 1977, pp. 10.

Simpson, John, ed., "The Control of Arms Transfers," Report of an FCO/FISA Seminar, Arms Control and Disarmament Research Unit, Foreign and Commonwealth Office, London, September 23, 1977.

"Sondernummer Wehrbereitschaft, Rüstungproduktion und Waffenausfuhr," *Allgemeine Schweizerische Militärzeitschrift*, no. 138 (1972), pp. 297–352.

Stanley, John, "The International Arms Trade: Controlled or Uncontrolled?" *Political Quarterly* 43:2 (1972): 155–68.

Stubbs, Comm. G. D., "The International Arms Trade and Its Control," *Army Quarterly and Defence Journal* [UK], No. 103 (1973), pp. 202–10.

Taylor, Trevor, "The Control of the Arms Trade," *International Relations* 3 (May 1971): 903–12.

United Nations Association of the United States of America, National Policy Panel on Conventional Arms Control, "Controlling the Conventional Arms Race," New York, November 1976.

U.S. General Accounting Office, *Arms Sales Ceiling Based on Inconsistent and Erroneous Data*, FGMSD-78-30, April 12, 1978.

Weiss, Seymour, *President Carter's Arms Transfer Policy: A Critical Assessment* (Washington, D.C.: Advanced International Studies Institute, University of Miami, 1978).

C. The Arms Manufacturers

"Another Scandal at SCECE," *Canard Enchaîné*, January 11, 1967.

Berkeley, George E., "The Myth of War Profiteering," *The New Republic*, December 20, 1968, pp. 15–18.

Boulding, Kenneth, "The Role of the War Industry in International Conflict," *Journal of Social Issues*, vol. 23 (1967): 47–61.

Copley and Associates, *Defense and Foreign Affairs Handbook*. (Washington, D.C.: Copley and Associates, annually).

Engelmann, Bernt, *The Weapons Merchants*, trans. E. Detto (New York: Crown, 1968).

Ferrell, Robert H., "The Merchants of Death: Then and Now," *Journal of International Affairs* 26 (Spring 1972): 29–39.

Fletcher, Raymond, "Where are the Merchants of Death?" *Twentieth Century* 171 (Spring 1963), pp. 89–96.

Gray, Colin, S., "What is Good for General Motors . . ." *Royal United Services Institution Journal* 117 (June 1972), pp. 36–43.

Hutton, J. Bernard, *The Traitor Trade* (New York: Obounsky, 1963).

Itskov, Igor M., *Kontrakundisty vo Vrakakh* (Moscow: Znanie, 1964).

Klare, Michael, "Le Multinationalisation des Industries de Guerre," *Le Monde Diplomatique*, February 1977.

Manchester, William, *The Arms of Krupp, 1587–1968* (Boston: Little, Brown, 1969).

"Now a Worldwide Boom in Sales of Arms," *U.S. News & World Report*, January 22, 1973, pp. 50–53.

Perlo, Victor, *Militarism and Industry: Arms Profiteering in the Missile Age* (New York: International Publishers, 1963).

Sherman, George, "The Pentagon's Merchants of Death," *Progressive*, November 1967, pp. 30–33.

Szulc, Tad, "Kickback: Corruption in U.S. Arms Sales," *The New Republic*, April 17, 1976, pp. 8–11.

Thayer, George, *The War Business: The International Trade in Armaments* (New York: Simon & Schuster, 1969).

Wells, C. A., "Krupps Again," *Between the Lines*, February 1, 1964.

D. Arms-Transfer Data

Benoit, Emile, *Defense and Economic Growth in Developing Countries* (Lexington, Mass.: Lexington Books, 1973).

Blumenfeld, York, "International Arms Sales," *Editorial Research Reports*, September 2, 1970, pp. 649–66.

Browne & Shaw Research Corporation, "The Diffusion of Combat Aircraft, Missiles, and their Supporting Technologies," Waltham, Mass., 1966.

Gervasi, Tom, *Arsenal of Democracy: American Arms Available for Export* (New York: Grove Press, 1978).

Hoagland, J. H., "World Combat Aircraft Inventories and Production, 1970–1975: Implications for Arms Transfer Policies," Massachusetts Institute of Technology, Center for International Studies, Cambridge, Mass., 1970.

International Institute for Strategic Studies, *The Military Balance* (London: IISS, annually).

Loftus, J., "Latin American Defense Expenditures, 1938–1965," Rand Corporation, Santa Monica, Calif., 1968.

Lydenberg, Steven, *Weapons for the World. Update: The U.S. Corporate Role in International Arms Transfers*, CEP Report (New York: Council on Economic Priorities, 1977).

Miller, Lynn H., "Security Studies Project. Vol. 5: The Reporting of International Arms Transfers," WEC-126, University of California Arms Control Special Studies Program, Los Angeles, 1968.

Stockholm International Peace Research Institute, *Arms Trade Registers: The Arms Trade With the Third World* (Cambridge, Mass.: MIT Press, 1975).

————, *SIPRI Yearbook of World Armament and Disarmament, 1968/1969*. New York: Humanities Press, 1969. [This is an annual yearbook. Since 1972, the title has read: *World Armaments and Disarmament: SIPRI Yearbook, 19——*.]

U.S. Agency for International Development, Statistics and Reports Division, Office of Financial Management, *Report Required by Section 657, Foreign Assistance Act, FY 1972*, 1972.

U.S. Arms Control and Disarmament Agency, *World Military Expenditures and Arms Trade, 1963-1974*, ACDA Publication 74 (Washington, D.C.: U.S. Government Printing Office, 1975). This publication is updated from time to time.

U.S. Department of Defense (DOD), *Military Assistance and Foreign Military Sales Facts (1950-1970)* (Washington, D.C.: U.S. Government Printing Office, 1970). There are also single-year issues for 1971, 1972, and 1973.

_____, Defense Security Assistance Agency (DSAA), *Foreign Military Sales and Military Assistance Facts,* Washington, D.C.: DOD/DSAA 1974. [Annual publication superseding above entry.]

Volman, Daniel and Klare, Michael, comp., *Arms Trade Data* (Washington, D.C.: Institute for Policy Studies, 1978).

"World Helicopter Market." *Flight International* [UK], July 14, 1966 and July 13, 1967.

II. SUPPLIERS

Articles on suppliers frequently discuss recipients while those on recipients often deal with major suppliers. Therefore, readers interested in particular recipients, suppliers, or arms trade cases should consult both this and the following sections.

A. General

Becker, Abraham S., "Arms Transfers, Great-Power Intervention and Settlement of the Arab-Israeli Conflict," in Milton Leitenberg and Gabriel Sheffer, eds., *Great-Power Intervention in the Middle East* (New York: Pergamon Press, 1979).

Harkavy, Robert, "Strategic Access, Bases, and Arms Transfers: The Major Powers' Evolving Geopolitical Competition in the Middle East," in Milton Leitenberg and Gabriel Sheffer, eds., *Great-Power Intervention in the Middle East* (New York: Pergamon Press, 1979).

Kaldor, Mary, "Economic Aspects of Arms Supply Policies to the Middle East," in Milton Leitenberg and Gabriel Sheffer, eds., *Great-Power Intervention in the Middle East* (New York: Pergamon Press, 1979).

Pajak, Roger F., "West European and Soviet Arms Transfer Policies in the Middle East," in Milton Leitenberg and Gabriel Sheffer, eds., *Great-Power Intervention in the Middle East* (New York: Pergamon Press, 1979).

B. United States

General

Benson, J. W., Dunleavy, J. G., Minckler, R. D., and Widder, R. I., "Potential Criteria for the Determination of Items on the U.S. Munitions List," Research Report, Battelle Columbus Laboratories, Washington, D.C., June 1974.

Bryan, B. O., "Today's Pattern for Munitions Control," *U.S. Department of State Bulletin* 32 (May 30, 1955): 884–89.

Hout, Marvin J., "Munitions Export Control Policies and Procedures," *Defense Management Journal* 8 (July 1972): 49–52.

Truman, Pres. Harry S., "Control of Exportation and Importation of Arms, Ammunition and Implements of War," *U.S. Department of State Bulletin* 16 (April 27, 1947): 750–57.

U.S. Arms Control and Disarmament Agency, *Compendium of U.S. Laws on Controlling Arms Exports*, Research report 66-2 (Washington, D.C.: U.S. Government Printing Office, May 1966).

U.S. Department of State, *International Traffic in Arms: Laws and Regulations Administered by the Secretary of State Governing the International Traffic in Arms, Ammunition, and Implements of War*, Publ. No 6587, llth ed. (Washington, D.C.: U.S. Government Printing Office, March 1958). This is revised frequently.

Arms Sales and Military Assistance

Books and Monographs

Barber, W. F. and Ronning, C. N., *International Security and Military Power* (Columbus: Ohio State University Press, 1966).

Barny, S., "The Arms Trade and Underdeveloped Areas, Center for International Studies, Massachusetts Institute of Technology, Cambridge, April 1964.

Brown, William A., Jr. and Opie, Redvers, *American Foreign Assistance* (Washington, D.C.: Brookings Institution, 1953).

Catledge, Capt. Morris B. and Knudsen, Capt. Larrie F., "Foreign Military Sales: United States Involvement in Coproduction and Trends toward Codevelopment," M.A. thesis, Air Institute of Technology, Air University, 1969.

Clay, Lucius, "Report to the President of the United States from the Committee to Strengthen the Free World: Scope and Distribution of United States Military and Economic Assistance Programs," Washington, D.C., March 1963.

Cleveland, Harlan, Mangone, Gerald J., and Adams, John Clarke, *The Overseas Americans* (New York: McGraw-Hill, 1960).

Cullin, William H., *How to Conduct Foreign Military Sales* (Washington, D.C.: American Defense Preparedness Association, 1977).

Draper Committee, *Report of the President's Committee to Study the Military Assistance Program* (Washington, D.C.: U.S. Government Printing Office, 1959).

Farley, Philip J., Kaplan, Stephen S., and Lewis, William H., *Arms Across the Sea* (Washington, D.C.: The Brookings Institution, 1978).

Furniss, Edgar C., *Some Perspectives on American Military Assistance* (Princeton, N.J.: Princeton University Press, 1957).

Holcombe, John L. and Berg, Alan, *MAP for Security* (Columbia: University of South Carolina Press, 1957).

Hovey, Harold A., *United States Military Assistance: A Study of Policies and Practices* (New York: Praeger, 1965).

Institute of International Education, *Military Assistance Training Programs* (New York: IIE, 1964).

Klare, Michael T., *Supplying Repression* (New York: The Field Foundation, 1977).
_____, and Holland, Max, "Conventional Arms Restraint: An Unfulfilled Promise," Special Report, Coalition for a New Foreign and Military Policy, The Institute for Policy Studies, and The Center for International Policy, Washington, D.C., 1977.

Lefever, Ernest W., "U.S. Military Training Programs for Developing Countries," Brookings Institution, Washington, D.C., n.d.

Lockwood, David E., *"International Security Assistance: An Analysis of Recent Developments in U.S. Government Organization and Management,"* JX 1435 U.S. Gen., 73-18 F, Congressional Research Service, Library of Congress, Washington, D.C., January 9, 1973.

Louscher, Daniel J., "Foreign Military Sales: An Analysis of a Foreign Affairs Undertaking," Ph.D diss., University of Wisconsin, 1972.

Nanes, Allan S., "Some Current Limitations and Restrictions on Economic and Military Assistance to Foreign Countries," JX 1435 U.S. Gen., 69-219 F, Legislative Reference Service, Library of Congress, Washington, D.C., October 20, 1969.

North American Congress on Latin America, *AID Police Programs for Asia & Africa, 1971-72* (supplement to NACLA Newsletter, special issue, July–August 1971), New York and Berkeley, Calif., n.d.

Pauker, Guy J., Canby, S., Johnson, A. R., and Quandt, W. B., "In Search of Self-Reliant U.S. Security Assistance to the Third World Under the Nixon Doctrine," R-1092-ARPA, Rand Corporation, Santa Monica, Calif., June 1973.

Pranger, Robert J. and Tahtinen, Dale R., "Toward a Realistic Military Assistance Program," Foreign Affairs Study no. 15., American Enterprise Institute for Public Policy Research, Washington, D.C., December 1974.

Pregelj, Vladimir N., "The Impact of Foreign Assistance and Defense Transactions on U.S. Balance of Payments: Summary of Statistical Data, 1960–1973," HF 1014, 74-112 E, Congressional Research Service, Library of Congress, Washington, D.C., May 28, 1974.

Refson, J. S., *U.S. Military Training and Advice: Implications for Arms Transfer Policies* (Cambridge, Mass.: MIT Press, 1970).

Schandler, Herbert Y., "Summary of U.S. Arms Transfer and Security Assistance Programs," TX 1435 U.S. Gen., 75-198 FA, Congressional Research Service, Library of Congress, Washington, D.C., September 1975.

Stamey, Roderick A., Jr., "The Origin of the U.S. Military Assistance Program," Ph.D. diss., University of North Carolina–Chapel Hill, 1972.

Tahtinen, Dale R., with the assistance of Lenczowski, John, *Arms in the Indian Ocean: Interests and Challenges*, Studies in Defense Policy (Washington, D.C.: American Enterprise Institute for Public Policy Research, 1977).

U.S. Arms Control and Disarmament Agency, "The Control of Local Conflict," Massachusetts Institute of Technology Center for International Studies, Cambridge, Mass., 1967.

U.S. Congress, Congressional Budget Office, "Budgetary Cost Savings to the Department of Defense Resulting from Foreign Military Sales," Staff Working Paper, May 14, 1976.

———, "The Effect of Foreign Military Sales on the U.S. Economy," Staff Working Paper, July 23, 1976.

———, "Foreign Military Sales and U.S. Weapons Costs," Staff Working Paper, May 5, 1976.

U.S. Department of State, *The Military Assistance Program*, Publ. no. 3563 (Washington, D.C.: U.S. Government Printing Office, 1949).

U.S. General Accounting Office, *Reorganization Proposals Relative to Foreign Aid and Foreign Military Sales Programs*, B-172311, November 24, 1971.

————, *Use of Excess Defense Articles and Other Resources to Supplement the Military Assistance Program*, B-163742, March 21, 1973.

————, *How Ship Transfers to Other Countries are Financed*, B-163742, June 25, 1974.

————, *Excess Defense Articles Provision in Proposed Foreign Assistance Legislation*, B-163742, July 15, 1974.

————, *Reimbursements from Foreign Governments for Military Personnel Services, Provided Under the Foreign Military Assistance Act*, B-180633, August 16, 1974.

————, *Excess Defense Article Valuation and Transfers of War Reserve Materials to Allies*, ID-75-69, June 10, 1975.

————, *U.S. Monitoring of Defense Articles Provided to Foreign Countries*, ID-76-9, August 15, 1975.

————, *Issues and Observations on the Purposes of Special Security Supporting Assistance Programs*, ID-76-11, September 12, 1975.

————, *Use and Future Availability of Excess Defense Articles in the Military Assistance Program*, ID-76-8, September 12, 1975.

————, *U.S. Logistical Support of Major Military Equipment Provided to Foreign Countries*, ID-76-22, October 21, 1975.

————, *Assessment of Overseas Advisory Efforts of the U.S. Security Assistance Program*, ID-76-1, October 31, 1975.

————, *Coproduction Programs and Licensing Arrangements in Foreign Countries*, ID-76-23, December 2, 1975.

————, *Stopping U.S. Assistance to Foreign Police and Prisons*, ID-76-5, February 19, 1976.

————, *Foreign Military Sales—A Growing Concern*, ID-76-51, June 1, 1976.

————, *Defense Action to Reduce Charges for Foreign Military Training Will Result in the Loss of Millions of Dollars*, FGMSD-77-17, February 23, 1977.

————, *A Potential Drain on the U.S. Defense Posture*, [unclassified version]. LDC-77-440, September 2, 1977.

————, *Military Sales—An Increasing U.S. Role in Africa*, ID-77-61, April 4, 1978.

————, *The Department of Defense's Continued Failure to Charge for Using Government-Owned Plant and Equipment for Foreign Military Sales Costs Millions*, FGMSD-77-20, April 11, 1978.

————, *Management of Security Assistance Programs Overseas Needs to be Improved*, ID-78-27, April 21, 1978.

————, *Budget Authority for Foreign Military Sales is Substantially Understated*, PAD-78-72, July 27, 1978.

————, *Profiles of Military Assistance Advisory Groups in 15 Countries*, ID-78-51, September 1, 1978.

————, *Cost Waivers Under the Foreign Military Sales Program: More Attention and Control Needed*, FGMSD-78-48A, September 26, 1978.

Wolf, Charles, Jr., "Some Connections Between Economic and Military Assistance Programs in Underdeveloped Areas," P-2389, Rand Corporation, Santa Monica, Calif., August 1961.

————, "Methods for Improving Coordination Between Economic and Military Aid Programs," RM-3449-ISA, Rand Corporation, Santa Monica, Calif., March 1963.

————, "Military Assistance Programs," P-3240, Rand Corporation, Santa Monica, Calif., 1965.

_____, *United States Policy and the Third World* (Boston: Little, Brown and Company, 1967).

_____, "Economic Impacts of Military Assistance," P-4578, Rand Corporation, Santa Monica, Calif., February 1971.

Wolpin, Miles D., *Military Aid and Counterrevolution in the Third World* (Lexington, Mass.: D.C. Heath and Co., Lexington Books, 1972).

Articles and Pamphlets

"Aiming at the Arms Market Overseas: Technology and Lucrative Licensing Abroad Put U.S. Ahead in Weapon Sales," *Business Week*, December 3, 1966, p. 66.

"America on Top Among World's Arms Peddlers," *U.S. News & World Report*, January 13, 1975. pp. 24–25.

American Defense Preparedness Association, "Meeting Report, Third Annual Executive Seminar on Foreign Military Sales and International Logistics Support," Washington, D.C., November 28–29, 1977.

"American Weapons Abroad: Sales Instead of Giveaways..." *U.S. News & World Report*, July 27, 1970, pp. 52–53.

Anderson, Sally, "U.S. Military Assistance and Sales (U.S. Is Number One!)," *Defense Monitor* 3 (May 1974): 1–12.

"Arms Sales: Nixon Doctrine May Boost U.S. Arms Sales Abroad," *Congressional Quarterly Weekly Report*, March 6, 1970, pp. 698–701.

"Arms Sales and Foreign Policy," *Bulletin of the Atomic Scientists*. no. 23 (1967): 44–48.

Foreign Relations Committee, U.S. Senate, "Arms Sales and U.S. Foreign Policy." *Current* no. 86 (August 1967): 33–41.

Atlantic News (Brussels), no. 772 (October 31, 1975).

Baker, Marshall E., "The Case for Military Assistance," *Armed Forces Management* 5 (June 1959): 13–15.

Blake, Gen. Donald F., "A Realistic Look at USAF Military Assistance and Foreign Military Sales," *Air University Review* 22 (November-December 1970): 35–44.

Brownlow, Cecil, "Arms Exports Curbs Expected to Bend," *Aviation Week & Space Technology* 106 (June 6, 1977), pp. 85, 87.

Burbank, John, "Foreign Military Transfers—Credit Arrangements and Sales to the Third World: Methods, Loopholes and Circumventions," Military Audit Project, Washington, D.C., November 1977.

Cahn, Anne Hessing, "America the Arsenal: What Should U.S. Arms Policy Be?" *Harvard Magazine*, June 1976.

_____, "US Arms to the Middle East 1967-1976: A Critical Examination." in Milton Leitenberg and Gabriel Sheffer, eds., *Great-Power Intervention in the Middle East* (New York: Pergamon Press, 1979).

Center for Defense Information, "Military Assistance: Arsenal for Democracy?" *Defense Monitor* 1 (September 8, 1972).

_____, "U.S. Weapons Exports: Can We Cut the Arms Connection?" *Defense Monitor* 7 (February 1978).

Connery, R. H. and David, Paul T., "The Mutual Defense Assistance Program." *American Political Science Review* 45 (June 1951): 321–47.

"Counter-insurgency in the Third World." *Ploughshares Monitor* (Canada) 1 (February 1978): 1–2.

"DOD Organizes to Meet New Challenges of Security Assistance Program," *Defense Management Journal* 8 (April 1972): 55–59.

Eaker, Gen. Ira C., "Arms Sales Policies Hurt U.S. Interests," *Air Force Times* 31 (February 10, 1971): 13.

"Export Policies Relaxed on Technology," *Aviation Week & Space Technology*, 102 (January 27, 1975): 78–87.

Fish, Lt. Gen. H. M., USAF, "Foreign Military Sales." *Commanders Digest* 17 (May 29, 1975): 2–8.

———, "MAP and FMS Aid Prospects for Greater Stability and More Durable World Peace," *Commanders Digest* 18 (September 4, 1975): 2–8.

Ganguly, Shivaji, "U.S. Military Assistance to India 1962–63: A Study in Decision-Making," *India Quarterly* 28 (July-September 1972): 216–226.

Gelb, Leslie H., "Arms Sales," *Foreign Policy* no. 25 (Winter 1976–77): 3–23.

Gibert, Stephen P., "Implications of the Nixon Doctrine for Military Aid Policy," *Orbis* 16 (Fall 1972): 660–81.

Government Business Worldwide Reports, "U.S. Foreign Military Sales," *International Defense Business*, June 23, 1975, pp. 2679–82.

"Growing Export Markets: Weapons," *Forbes Magazine*, February 1, 1966, pp. 15–16.

Hamilton, A., "Antimissile Missile for Export?" *The New Republic*, December 10, 1966, pp. 14–17.

Harlamor, Slava W., "Future of Arms Sales Policy Questioned," *Aviation Week & Space Technology* 108 (January 16, 1978), pp. 26–29.

Heymont, Irving, "U.S. Military Assistance Programs," *Military Review* 48 (January 1968): 89–95.

Hughes, Col. David R., "The Myth of Military Coups and Military Assistance." *Military Review* 47 (December 1967): 3–10.

Irwin, John N., "New Approaches in International Security Assistance," *U.S. Department of State Bulletin* 64 (February 22, 1971): 221–27.

Johnson, Katherine, "State Dept. Doubts Arms Limit Success," *Aviation Week & Space Technology* 105 (October 4, 1976), p. 16.

Jones, Capt. Douglas N., "Economic Aspects of Military Assistance," *Air University Review* 16 (November-December 1964): 42–46.

Jordan, Amos A., Jr., "Military Assistance and National Policy," *Orbis* 2 (Summer 1958): 236–51.

Kaplan, Fred, "Still the Merchants of Death," *The Progressive*, March 1976, pp. 22–23.

Kaplan, Stephen S., "U.S. Arms Transfers to Latin America, 1945-1974," *International Studies Quarterly* 19 (December 1975): 399–431.

Katzenbach, Nicholas deB., "U.S. Arms for the Developing World: Dilemmas of Foreign Policy," *U.S. Department of State Bulletin* 57 (December 1967): 794–98.

Kemp, Geoffrey, "U.S. Military Policy: Dilemmas of the Arms Traffic," *Foreign Affairs* 48 (January 1970): 274–84; reprinted in *Military Review* 50 (July 1970): 2–31.

Kintner, W., "The Role of Military Assistance," *U.S. Naval Institute Proceedings* 87 (March 1961): 76–84.

Kissinger, Henry A., testimony: U.S. Congress, House, Committee on International Relations, *Hearings: Security Assistance Program*, 94th Cong., 1st sess., November 6, 1975.

————, testimony: U.S. Congress, Senate, Committee on Foreign Relations, Subcommittee on Foreign Assistance, *Hearings: FY 1977 Security Assistance Program*, 94th Cong., 2d sess., March 26, 1976.

————, "Security Assistance and Foreign Policy," *Department of State Bulletin*, April 19, 1976, pp. 501–5.

Klare, Michael T., "How We Practice 'Arms Restraint,'" *The Nation* September 24, 1977, pp. 268–73.

————, "The Political Economy of Arms Sales," *Bulletin of the Atomic Scientists* 32 (November 1976): 11–18.

Kozicharow, Eugene, "Hearings Set on Arms Sales Financing," *Aviation Week & Space Technology*, 108 January 16, 1978, pp. 24–25.

Lefever, Ernest W., "The Military Assistance Training Program," *Annals of the American Political and Social Sciences* no. 424 (1976): 85–95.

Lemnitzer, Gen. Lyman L., "The Foreign Military Aid Program," *Academy of Political Science Proceedings* 23 (1948–50): 436–42.

Ligon, Walter B., "Foreign Military Sales," *National Defense* 60 (July-August 1975): 30–32.

Lincoln, George A., "Forces Determining Arms Aid," *Academy of Political Science Proceedings* 25 (May 1953): 263–72.

Loomba, Joanne F., "U.S. Aid to India 1951–1976: A Study in Decision-Making," *India Quarterly* 28 (October-December 1972): 304–31.

Louscher, David J., "Continuity and Change in American Arms Sales Policies," in *Ohio Arms Control Seminar: Workshop II—Selected Papers*, The Mershon Center of the Ohio State University, June 1977.

————, "The Rise of Military Sales as a U.S. Foreign Assistance Instrument," *Orbis* 20 (Winter 1977): 933–62.

Luck, Edward C., "Does the U.S. Have a Conventional Arms Sales Policy?" *Arms Control Today* 6 (May 1976): 1–4.

"MAP Orientation," *Marine Corps Gazette*, February 1965.

McCarthy, Sen. Eugene J., "Arms and the Man Who Sells Them," *Atlantic*, October 1967, pp. 82–86.

————, "The U.S. Supplier of Weapons to the World," *Saturday Review*, July 9, 1966, pp. 13–15.

McNamara, Robert S., "Military Trade: A Two-Way Street," *Aerospace International* 3 (April 1967): 21–23.

Meyer, C. A., "U.S. Military Activities in Latin America," *InterAmerican Economic Affairs* 23 (Autumn 1969): 89–94.

"Military Sales Bolster Free World Defenses," *Armed Forces Management* 15 (January 1969): 55–57.

Moench, Maj. Gen. John O., USAF, "Military Security Assistance," *Ordnance* 58 (July-August 1973): 38–41.

Mondale, Vice-Pres. Walter F., "Excessive U.S. Arms Sales Must Stop," *World Issues* (Center for the Study of Democratic Institutions), December 1976-January 1977, pp. 22–24.

Moran, Theodore., "A Primer on U.S. Arms Sales Around the World," *Ripon Forum* 5 (July 1969): 15–18.

Morse, Lt. Col. David L., "Foreign Arms Sales: Two Sides to the Coin," *Army* 26 (January 1976): 16–21.

Mott, Comm. William C., USN, "Mutual Defense Insurance," *United States Naval Institute Proceedings* 76 (November 1950): 1187–95.

Netherland, Robert., "A Challenge in Teaching the Foreign Military Student," *United States Naval Institute Proceedings* 86 (March 1960): 78–85.

Nihart, Brooke, "Increased Foreign Military Sales Inescapable Under Nixon Doctrine," *Armed Forces Journal* 108 (November 2, 1970): 22.

_____, "A New Approach to an Old Problem," *Armed Forces Journal* 109 (November 1971): 44–47. [Deals with the Security Assistance Program.]

Nitze, Paul H., "The Policy Background of Military Assistance," in *International Stability and Progress* (New York: The American Assembly, 1957).

North American Congress on Latin America, "U.S. Arms Sales to the Third World: Arm Now—Pay Later," *NACLA's Latin America & Empire Report* 6 (January 1972): 1–3.

Pancake, Col. Frank R., "Why Military Assistance for Latin America?" *Air University Review* 18 (November-December 1966): 3–12.

Perlo, Victor, "Alliance of Militarists and Arms Manufacturers," *International Affairs* (Moscow) 15 (September 1969): 19–25.

Powell, Craig, "Arms Sales is More Than Just a Military Question," *Armed Forces Management* 14 (January 1968): 72.

Raymond, Daniel A., "Reflections on Mutual Defense Assistance Program," *Military Review* 35 (August 1955): 31–44.

"Reduction of the Military Assistance Program." Message from the President of the United States, January 20, 1976.

Rogers, Gen. F. Michael, USAF, "The Impact of Foreign Military Sales on the National Industrial Base," *Strategic Review*, 5 (Spring 1977): 15–21.

Schemmer, Benjamin F., "Pentagon Reevaluates Carter Arms Transfer Policy," *Armed Forces Journal International* 114 (August 1977): 12–14.

"Security Assistance," GIST [US Department of State], December 1975.

Stein, Nancy and Klare, Michael, "Merchants of Repression: U.S. Police Exports to the Third World," *NACLA's Latin America Report*, July-August 1976.

Taylor, Trevor, "President Nixon's Arms Supply Policies," *Year Book of World Affairs* 26 (1972): 65–80.

Teplinsky, B., "US Military Programme," *International Affairs* (Moscow) 8 (1967): 46–51.

"The Arms Sales Number Game," *The New Republic*, February 18, 1978, pp. 5–6. [Deals with Carter's "arms-sale ceiling."]

U.S. Department of Defense, *Military Assistance and Foreign Military Sales Facts* (Washington, D.C.: U.S. Government Printing Office, 1967).

_____, *Military Assistance Facts* (Washington, D.C.: U.S. Government Printing Office, March 1966).

U.S. General Accounting Office, "Letter Report: Unclassified Version of GAO Report Concerning Controls on Major US Equipment Transferred to Republic of Vietnam Armed Forces," LCD-75-227, April 1, 1975.

_____, "Letter Report: Two Basic Types of Sales to Non-United States Government Buyers," PSAD-76-61, December 18, 1975.

————, "Letter Report: Payment for Training and Technical Assistance Services Rendered by the US Department of Defense to Foreign Countries," FGMSD-76-64, July 13, 1976.

————, "Letter Report: Foreign Military Sales Credits," B-115398, September 24, 1976.

————, "Letter Report: Reimbursement to the US Department of Defense for Activities Which Support Foreign Military Sales," FGMSD-77-40, May 6, 1977.

————, "Letter Report: Impact of Foreign Military Sales on Supply Operations Within the Department of Defense," LCD-77-222, May 27, 1977.

————, "Letter Report: Reimbursement of Department of Defense for Sale of Defense Articles to Foreign Governments," FGMSD-77-43 (90353), September 8, 1977.

————, "Letter Report: Security Assistance Accounting Center," FGMSD-77-46 (90346), September 16, 1977.

U.S. Department of State, Bureau of Public Affairs, "U.S. Foreign Military Sales," *Current Policy*, no. 4 (July 1975).

Vance, Cyrus R., "An Overview of Foreign Military Assistance." Statement before the House Foreign Operations Subcommittee, March 2, 1977.

————, "U.S. Foreign Assistance Programs." Statement before the Senate Foreign Operations Committee, February 24, 1977.

Victor, A. H., "Military Aid and Comfort to Dictatorships," *United States Naval Institute Proceedings* 95 (March 1969): 42–47.

Warren, Robert H., "Military Assistance Program: Foreign Military Sales," *Vital Speeches* 34 (1969): 601-603.

"Where Arms Ban Backfired on U.S.," *U.S. News & World Report*, January 22, 1973, pp. 53–54.

"Why Carter Will Have a Tough Time Trying to Curb Arms Sales," *U.S. News & World Report*, August 1, 1977, pp. 39–40.

"Why Didn't We?" *Armed Forces Journal*, 107 (1970), pp. 16–17.

"Why the U.S. Is Pushing the Sale of Weapons," *U.S. News & World Report*, October 11, 1965, p. 122.

Windle, C. and Vallance, T. "Optimizing Military Assistance Training," *World Politics* 15 (October 1962): 91–107.

Winston, Donald C., "DOD Plan Would Separate Civil, Military Aid Requests," *Aviation Week & Space Technology* 87 (December 25, 1967): 17-18.

Wood, Gen. Robert J., "Military Assistance Program," *Armed Forces Management* 11 (1964): 105–06.

————, "Military Assistance and the Nixon Doctrine," *Orbis* 15 (1971): 247–74.

Congressional Material

Aspin, Rep. Les, "To Establish an Annual Foreign Military Arms Sales Budget," *Congressional Record*, June 12, 1975, pp. H3116–17.

Dupont, Rep. Pierre, "U.S. Arms Sales Policy: It's Time to Develop One," *Congressional Record*, June 12, 1975, pp. H5409–11.

"Eight Democratic Senators See Our Latin American Arms Program as a Menace to Security," *I. F. Stone's Weekly*, December 11, 1963.

Hamilton, Rep. Lee, "Foreign Military Sales," *Congressional Record*, September 10, 1973, pp. H7704–6.

Harrison, Stanley, "Congress and Foreign Military Sales," *Military Review* 51 (October 1971): 79–87.

"House Votes $9-Billion Ceiling on Annual U.S. Arms Sales," *Aviation Week & Space Technology*, March 8, 1976, p. 19.

Humphrey, Sen. Hubert, "International Security Assistance and Arms Export Control Act of 1975," *Congressional Record*, November 13, 1975, pp. S19880–90.

"International Security Assistance Act of 1976," *Congressional Record*, March 3, 1976, pp. H1506–80.

"International Security Assistance and Arms Export Control Act of 1976," *Congressional Record*, February 17, 1976, pp. S1737–60, February 18, 1976, pp. S1875–1917.

Johnson, Katherine, "Congress to Expand Arms Sales Monitoring," *Aviation Week & Space Technology*, 109 (August 14, 1978): 14–15.

_____, "Foreign Arms Sales Spur Congressional Surveillance," *Aviation Week & Space Technology* 102 (June 23, 1975): 14–15.

Kennedy, Sen. Edward, "Arms and Men in the Persian Gulf," *Congressional Record*, July 9, 1975, pp. S12120–23.

"Liberals Join Southerners in Attacking Arms for Military Dictators," *I. F. Stone's Weekly*, September 7, 1964.

"Massive Congressional Review Could Cause Arms Exports Cuts," *Aviation Week & Space Technology* 87 (July 31, 1967): 22.

Mondale, Sen. Walter, "Senate Resolution 296—Submission of a Resolution Relating to Arms Sales," *Congressional Record*, November 6, 1975, pp. S19396–99.

Nelson, Sen. Gaylord, "S.854—Amendment for Foreign Military Arms Sales Act," *Congressional Record*, February 26, 1975, pp. S2653–59.

_____, "U.S. Arms Sales and the National Interest," *Congressional Record*, September 23, 1975, pp. S16507–10.

"New Arms Sale Battle Looms in Congress: Congress Restricts Arms Sale to Developing Nations," *Congressional Quarterly Weekly Report*, March 22, 1968, pp. 596–600.

Pell, Sen. Claiborne, "The International Weapons Trade," *Congressional Record*, June 12, 1969, pp. S6419–21.

Proxmire, Sen. William, "Department of Defense Role in Foreign Arms Sales and Its Consequences," News Release, February 14, 1976.

Ribicoff, Sen. Abraham, "The Export of Military Technology—Unanswered Questions," *Congressional Record*, March 6, 1973, pp. S3077–90.

Shuman, William, "Tighter Foreign Sales Controls Studied," *Aviation Week & Space Technology* 102 (June 16, 1975): 20–21.

"Statements on Introduced Bills and Joint Resolutions. S.1443: A Bill to Revise the Foreign Military Aid and Sales Program," *Congressional Record*, April 3, 1973, pp. S6420–32.

U.S. Arms Control and Disarmament Agency, *The International Transfer of Conventional Arms*, Report to Congress, April 12, 1974.

U.S. Congress, House, *Foreign Aid, Message from the President of the United States Transmitting Proposals to Redirect Our Efforts in Foreign Aid.* 91st Cong., lst sess., May 28, 1968.

U.S. Congess, House, Committee on Appropriations, Subcommittee on Foreign Operations and Related Agencies, *Foreign Assistance and Related Agencies Appropriations for 1970. Part I.* 90th Cong., lst sess., 1969.

U.S. Congress, House, Committee on Armed Services, *Report by the Special Subcommittee on Transfer of Naval Vessels to Foreign Countries,* 92nd Cong., 2d sess., October 10, 1972.

U.S. Congress, House, Committee on Banking and Currency, *Export-Import Bank and Credit Sales of Defense Articles,* 90th Cong., lst sess., July 17, 1967.

U.S. Congress, House, Committee on Foreign Affairs, *The Foreign Military Sales Act,* 90th Cong., 2d sess., June 26–27, 1968.

————, *Foreign Assistance Act of 1969,* 91st Cong., lst sess., June-August 1961.

————, *Foreign Assistance Act of 1971,* 92nd Cong., 1st sess., April-June 1971.

————, *International Transfer of Conventional Arms; Report to Congress from U.S. Arms Control and Disarmament Agency Pursuant to Sec. 302 of Foreign Relations Authorization Act of 1972,* 93rd Cong., 2d sess., April 12, 1974.

————, *Military Assistance Training,* 91st Cong., 2d sess., 1970.

————, *To Amend the Foreign Military Sales Act,* 91st Cong., 2d sess., February 5, 17, 1970.

————, *Amending the Foreign Military Sales Act,* 91st Cong., 2d sess., 1970.

————, *Background Material: Foreign Assistance Act. Fiscal Year 1970,* 91st Cong., 1st sess., 1969.

————, *Conference Report on Foreign Assistance Act of 1968,* 90th Cong., 2d sess., 1968.

————, *Conference Report on Foreign Assistance Act of 1969.* 91st Cong., 1st sess., 1969.

————, *Military Assistance Training,* 92nd Cong., 1st sess., 1971.

————, *Staff Memorandum on the Foreign Assistance Program, Authorizations and Appropriations for Fiscal Year 1969,* 90th Cong., 2d sess., 1968.

————, Subcommittee on Africa, *Implementation of the U.S. Arms Embargo (Against Portugal and South Africa) and Related Issues,* 93rd Cong., 1st sess., March–April 1973.

U.S. Congress, House, Committee on International Relations, *The Arms Export Control Act,* 94th Cong., 2d sess., August 25, 1976.

————, *International Security Assistance Act of 1976,* 94th Cong., November, December 1975, and January, February 1976.

————, *International Security Assistance Act of 1976,* 94th Cong., 2d sess., February 24, 1976.

————, *International Security Assistance and Arms Export Control Act of 1976,* 94th Cong., 2d sess., November, December 1975, March, April 1976.

————, *Human Rights Practices in Countries Receiving U.S. Security Assistance,* 95th Cong., 1st sess., April 25, 1977.

————, Subcommittee on International Economic Policy, *The Activities of American Multinational Corporations Abroad,* 94th Cong., 1st sess., June, July, September 1975.

————, Subcommittee on International Political and Military Affairs, *U.S. Defense*

Contractor's Training of Foreign Military Forces, 94th Cong., 1st sess., March 20, 1975.

———, Subcommittee on International Security and Scientific Affairs, *Conventional Arms Transfer Policy. Background Information*, 95th Cong., 2d sess., February 1, 1978.

———, Subcommittee on International Security and Scientific Affairs, *Foreign Assistance Legislation for Fiscal Year 1979. Part 2: Policies on Security Supporting Assistance and Arms Transfers Worldwide*, 95th Cong., 2d sess., March-April 1978.

———, Subcommittee on International Security and Scientific Affairs, *Review of the President's Conventional Arms Transfer Policy*, 95th Cong., 2d sess., February 1–2, 1978.

———, Subcommittee on International Trade and Commerce, *Export Licensing of Advanced Technology: A Review*, 94th Cong., 2d sess., March 1976.

U.S. Congress, Joint Economic Committee, *Economic Issues in Military Assistance*, 92nd Cong., 1st sess., January, February 1971.

U.S. President, *U.S. Foreign Assistance in the 1970's: A New Approach*. Report from Task Force on International Development. Washington, D.C.: U.S. Government Printing Office, 1970.

U.S. Congress, Senate, Committee on Appropriations, *United States Military Operations and Mutual Security Programs Overseas*, 86th Cong., 2d sess., 1960.

U.S. Congress, Senate, Committee on Armed Services, *Department of Defense Appropriations Authorization for Fiscal Year 1977*, 94th Cong., 2d sess., 1976.

U.S. Congress, Senate, Committee on Banking and Currency, *Export-Import Bank Participation and Financing in Credit Sales of Defense Articles*, 90th Cong., 1st sess., July 25, 1967.

———, *Export-Import Act Amendments of 1967*, 90th Cong., 1st sess., 1967.

U.S. Congress, Senate, Committee on Foreign Relations, *Section-by-Section Analysis of the Proposed Foreign Military Sales and Assistance Act*, 93rd Cong., 2d sess., April 24, 1974.

———, *United States Economic and Military Foreign Assistance Programs. Compilation of General Accounting Office. Report, Findings and Recommendations*, 92nd Cong., 1st sess., March 29, 1971.

———, *Foreign Assistance Act of 1968*, 90th Cong., 2d sess., March 13–14, 1968.

———, *Foreign Assistance Act, 1969*, 91st Cong., 1st sess., July 14–18, and August 6, 1969.

———, *Foreign Assistance Authorization*, 93rd Cong., 2d sess., June–July 1974.

———, *Foreign Assistance Authorization: Arms Sales Issues*, 94th Cong., 1st sess., June 18, 1975.

———, *Foreign Military Sales*, 90th Cong., 2d sess., June 20, 1968.

———, *Foreign Military Sales Act Amendment, 1970, 1971*. 91st Cong., 2d sess., March 24, and May 11, 1970.

———, *Foreign Military Sales and Assistance Act, 1973*, 93rd Cong., 1st sess., May 2–8, 1973.

———, *Middle East Arms Sales Proposals*, 95th Cong., 2d sess., May 3–8, 1978.

———, *Amending the Foreign Military Sales Act*, 91st Cong., 2d sess., 1970.

———, *Arms Transfer Policy*, 95th Cong., 1st sess., July 1977.

———, *Foreign Assistance Act of 1965*, 89th Cong., 1st sess., April 29, 1965.

_____, *Foreign Assistance Act of 1967*, 90th Cong., 1st sess., August 9, 1967.

_____, *Foreign Assistance Act of 1968*, 90th Cong., 1st sess., 1968.

_____, *Foreign Assistance Act of 1969*, 91st Cong., 1st sess., 1969.

_____, *Foreign Assistance Act of 1973*, 93rd Cong., 1st sess., August 2, 1973.

_____, *International Security Assistance and Arms Export Control Act of 1976*, 94th Cong., 1st sess., 1976.

_____, *The Mutual Security Act of 1959*, 86th Cong., 1st sess., June 22, 1959.

_____, Subcommittee on Foreign Assistance, *Foreign Assistance Authorization: Arms Sales Issues*, 94th Cong., 1st sess., July, November, December 1975.

_____, Subcommittee on Foreign Assistance, *International Security Assistance,*, 94th Cong., 2d sess., March, April 1976.

_____, *Implications of President Carter's Conventional Arms Transfer Policy*, 95th Cong., 1st sess., December 1977. [Also published as U.S. Library of Congress, Congressional Research Service, Foreign Affairs and National Division, *Implications of President Carter's Conventional Arms Transfer Policy*, 77-223 F (Washington, D.C.: U.S. Government Printing Office, 1977).]

U.S. Congress, Senate, Joint Committee on Foreign Relations and Committee on Armed Services, *Military Assistance Program, 1949*. 81st Cong., 1st sess., July, August, September 1949.

U.S. Congress, Senate, Staff Study: *Arms Sales and Foreign Policy*, 90th Cong., 1st sess., January 25, 1967.

U.S. Congress, Senate, Special Committee to Study the Foreign Aid Program, *Compilation of Studies and Surveys*, 85th Cong., 1st sess., 1957.

Winston, Donald C., "White House Battles to Block Export Ban," *Aviation Week & Space Technology* 87 (August 21, 1967): 21.

C. Soviet Union

Alexandros, L., "Sowjetische Rakentenschiffe im Mettelmeerraum," *Wehr und Wirtschaft* 10 (April 15, 1966): 257–59.

Atkinson, James D., "Arms for the Third World," *Ordnance* 54 (May-June 1972): 622–23.

Atlantic Research Corporation, Georgetown Research Project, *The Soviet Military Aid Program as a Reflection of Soviet Objectives*, Contract no. AF-49 (638) 1412, June 24, 1965.

Baker, Ross K., "Soviet Military Assistance to Tropical Africa," *Military Review* 48 (July 1968): 76–81.

Einbeck, Eberhardt, "Moscaus Militärhilfe an die Dritte Welt," *Aussenpolitik* 22 (May 1971): 300–13.

Gail, Bridget, "'The Fine Old Game of Killing': Comparing U.S. and Soviet Arms Sales," *Armed Forces Journal*, 116 (September 1978): 16–20.

_____, "'The Fine Old Game of Killing': Part Two," *Armed Forces Journal*, 116 (November 1978): 37.

Gasteyger, Curt, "Moscow and the Mediterranean," *Foreign Affairs* 46 (July 1968): 476–87.

Gibert, Stephen P., "Wars of Liberation and Soviet Military Aid Policy," *Orbis* 10 (Fall 1966): 839–58.

_____, "Soviet-American Military Aid Competition in the Third World," *Orbis* 13 (Winter 1970): 1117–37.

_____, *Guns and Rubles: Soviet Aid Diplomacy in Neutral Asia* (New York: American-Asian Educational Exchange, 1970).

_____, and Joshua, Wynfred, *Arms for the Third World: Soviet Military Aid Diplomacy* (Baltimore: Johns Hopkins Press, 1969).

Glassman, Jon D., *Arms for the Arabs. The Soviet Union and War in the Middle East* (Baltimore, Md.: Johns Hopkins Press, 1975).

Hahn, Walter F. and Cottrell, Alvin J., *Soviet Shadow over Africa*, Monographs in International Affairs (Miami, Fla.: Center for Advanced International Studies, University of Miami, 1976).

Halperin, M. H., "Sino-Soviet Relations and Arms Control: An Introduction," *China Quarterly* no. 26 (April-June 1966): 118–22.

Heinman, L., "Moscow's Export Arsenal," *East Europe* 13 (May 1964): 2–10.

Hinterhoff, Capt. E., "The Soviet Military Aid and Its Implications," *NATO's Fifteen Nations* 6 (February-March 1962): 80–87.

Holst, J. J., "Soviet International Conduct and the Prospects of Arms Control," *Cooperation and Conflict*, no. 1 (1965), pp. 53–64.

Pajak, Roger F., "Soviet Arms and Egypt," *Survival* 17 (July-August 1975): 165–73.

_____, "Soviet Aid to Iraq and Syria," *Strategic Review* 4 (Winter 1976): 51–59.

_____, "Soviet Arms Aid to Libya," *Military Review* 56 (July 1976): 82–87.

Pye, Lucian, "Soviet and American Styles in Foreign Aid," *Orbis* 9 (Summer 1960): 159–73.

Ramazani, R. K., "Soviet Military Assistance to the Uncommitted Countries," *Midwest Journal of Political Science* 6 (November 1959): 356–73.

Ra'anan, Uri, *The USSR Arms the Third World: Case Studies in Soviet Foreign Policy* (Cambridge, Mass.: MIT Press, 1969).

"Soviet Military Aid, Source of International Conflicts," *Military Review* 42 (February 1962): 33–41.

"Syria and the Soviet Union," in Anne Sinai and Allen Pollack, eds., *The Syrian Arab Republic. A Handbook*, pp. 93–108 (New York: American Academic Association for Peace in the Middle East, 1976).

Szulc, Tad, "Russia Arms Peru," *New Republic*, February 19, 1977, p. 18–19.

D. Great Britain

Berry, Clifton, Jr. and Schemmer, Benjamin F., "How Europe Sells," *Armed Forces Journal International*, 114 (August 1977): 15, 18.

Brown, David A., "British Order Nimrod AEW Development," *Aviation Week & Space Technology* 106 (April 4, 1977): 15.

_____, "Nimrod Early Warning Version Pushed," *Aviation Week & Space Technology* 106 (March 14, 1977): 47,50.

Freedman, Lawrence, "Britain and the Arms Trade," *International Affairs* 54 (July 1978).

Great Britain, *Parliamentary Papers, Export of Surplus War Material*, Cmd. 9676, 1956.

_____, Select Committee on Estimates, *Sale of Military Equipment Abroad*, Second Report, Session 1959.

Hickmott, J. R., "We Must Have Conventional British Weapons," *Contemporary Review*, 210 (April 1967): 171–72.

"If We Don't Sell Those Arms," *The Economist*, November 21, 1970, pp. 13–14.

Keith-Lucas, David, "The British Aircraft Industry and Its Future," *Royal United Services Institute Journal* 112 (May 1967): 120–31.

McDougall, D., "Wilson Government and the British Defense Commitment in Malaya-Singapore," *Journal of South Eastern Asian Studies* 4 (September 1973): 229–40.

Ramsden, J. M., "EEC and British Aerospace," *Flight International* (UK) (January 20, 1972): 89–92.

Watt, D. C., "Britain Stirs It Up," *Spectator*, September 16, 1966, pp. 339–40.

E. France

Alia, Josette, "Les Marchands de Mort," *Nouvel Observateur*, November 19, 1970, pp. 24–25.

Crocker, C. A., "France's Changing Military Interests," *Africa Review* 13 (June 1968): 16–24.

Dévolvé, Pierre, "A Propos d'une Décision d'Embargo: Le Régime Juridique Français de l'Exportation des Materiels Militaires," *Actualité Juridique de Droit Administratif* 1 (October 1969): 528.

"Die Franzosiche Heereswaffenschau 1971: In Satory standen Panzerfahrzeuge und Raketenwerfer im Vordergrund," *Soldat und Technik* 14 (September 1971): 498–505.

Dubos, Jean-François, *La Politique d'Exportation des Armes* (Paris: Université de Paris, 1973).

───────, *Ventes d'Armes: Une Politique* (Paris: Gallimard, 1974). [This also contains two chapters dealing with the United States, the Soviet Union, and other arms exporters.]

Erven, L., "France in the Mediterranean," *Review of International Affairs* 21 (March 5, 1970): 10–13.

France. *Livre Blanc sur la Défense Nationale*. I. 1972.

"France Woos Libyans With Aid," *Africa Report* 15 (June 1970): 20–21.

"France's Aircraft Industry," *Flight International* [UK] 86 (July 16, 1964): 101–15.

"French Aircraft and Missile Activities," *Interavia* 22 (May 1967): 652–54.

Gallois, P. M., "French Aerospace Industry To-Day," *NATO's Fifteen Nations* 9 (February-March 1965).

Grapin, Jacqueline, "Arms Exports: When Means Become an End," *The Guardian*, November 28, 1976. [Reprinted from *Le Monde*, November 9, 1976.]

Isnard, Jacques, "French Arms Exports," *Survival* 13 (1971): 134–35.

Klein, Jean, "Commerce des Armes et Politique: Le Cas Français," *Politique Étrangère*, 41:5 (1976): 563–86.

Kowitt, Sylvia, "The Politics of a Tacit Alliance: France-Israel Relations, 1956–1967," Ph.D. diss., Columbia University, 1970.

Lamarché, René, "Death at Any Price—France: The Hard Sell," *Agenor*, October 1974, pp. 22–25.

Le Centre Local d'Information et de Coordination de l'Action Non-Violente, *La France et le Commerce des Armes*, Toulon, January 3, 1973.

Leprêtre, Comm., "Assistance Militaire Technique," *Revue Militaire d'Information*, no. 345 (January 1963), pp. 57–63.

_____, "Coopération Militaire Outre-Mer," *Revue Militaire d'Information*, no. 344 (December 1962), pp. 41–47.

Leroy, Daniel, "La France Exportatrice de Missiles," *Science et Vie* 120 (November 1971): 112–19.

Manor, Yohanan, "Does France Have an Arms Export Policy?" *Res Publica* 16:5 (1974): 645–62.

Ramsden, J. M., "France's Aircraft Industry," *Flight International* [UK] (October 28, 1971): 685–700.

"Record French Exports in 1970," *International Defense Review* 4 (April 1971): 113–14.

Sirjacques, Françoise, *Determinanten der Französichen Rüstungs-Politik* (Frankfurt: Peter Land, 1977).

de Virieu, François-Henri and Thibau, Paul, "Le Vingt-Troisième Client," *Nouvel Observateur*, August 18, 1975, pp. 21–22.

F. Other Suppliers

Battistelli, Fabrizio and Devoto, Gianluca, "Italian Military Policy and the Arms Industry," *Lo Spettatore Internazionale* 9 (July-December 1974): 197–221.

Baur, E. "New Horizons for the Czech Aircraft Industry," *Interavia* 22 (May 1967): 714–17.

Borgström, Henric, "Argentina får Bantam-robot; Luftvärnskanoner till Iran," *Dagens Nyheter* [Stockholm], February 5, 1978, p. 28.

"Brazil: Reversing the Arms Flow," *Latin America*, October 18, 1974, pp. 322–23.

Cahn, Anne Hessing, "Have Arms, Will Sell," *Bulletin of the Atomic Scientists* 31 (April 1975): 10–12.

Cobban, William, "Dealing Out Death Discreetly: The Traffic in Canadian Arms," *Saturday Night* no. 86 (November 1971): 23–26.

Coleman, Herbert J., "Paris Show Springboard for Israeli Sales," *Aviation Week & Space Technology* 102 (June 23, 1975): 45.

Daniels, Jeff, "Swedish Strike Power From SAAB," *Flight International* [UK] 10 (March 9, 1972): 360–62.

"Die Illegale Waffenausfuhr aus der Schweiz," *Flugwehr und Technik* 31 (January-February 1969): 15–18.

"Germany's Aerospace Industry," *Interavia* 19 (April 1964): 469–80; 21 (May 1966): 685–90.

Haftendorn, Helga, *Militärhilfe und Rüstungsexporte der BRD* (Dusseldorf: Bertleman Universitätsverlag, 1971).

Heinman, L., "Military Assistance by Small Nations," *Military Review* 44 (March 1964): 14–18.

Jacob, A., "Israel's Military Aid to Africa, 1960–1966." *Journal of Modern African Studies* 9 (1971): 165–87.

Kurz, H. R. "Die Durch-und Ausfuhr von Kriegsmaterial aus der Schweiz," *Osterreische Militärische Zeitschrift* 2 (March-April 1966): 109–16.

Latour, Charles, "Armament Sales," *NATO's Fifteen Nations* 18 (April-May 1973): 74–76.

Lock, Peter and Wulf, Herbert, "Rüstungsexporte und Ihre Volkswirtschaftlichen Auswirkungen für die Bundesrepublik," *Vorgänge: Zeitschrifte für Gesellschaftspolitik*, no. 22 (1976): 77–85.

Militärpolitik Dokumentationsdienst, *Rüstungswirtschaft und Dritte Welt* (Stuttgart: ESG-Geschäftsstelle, 1976).

Parlement Belge, Bibliothèque, *Dossiers Documentaires. No. 7: Le Commerce des Armes.* Bruxelles: 1973. [This contains information on other European suppliers as well as on Belgium.]

Port, A. Tyler, "Co-operation on Arms Production: The Task Ahead," *NATO Review* 21 (May-June 1973): 13–17.

Regehr, Ernie, *Making a Killing: Canada's Arms Industry* (Toronto: McClelland and Stewart, Ltd., 1975).

Robinson, Clarence A., "Israel Arms Exports Spur Concern," *Aviation Week & Space Technology,* 105 (December 13, 1976): 14–17.

Schneyder, Philippe, "Pékin à l'Assaut du Tiers Monde," *Revue Militaire d'Information,* no. 315 (April 1960): 17–26.

"Schweiz: Rüstungsproduktion und Waffenausfuhr," *Wehrkunde* 19 (February 1970): 104–05.

"Sweden's Arms Export Policy: Tight but Easing," *Armed Forces Journal,* 110 (February 1973): 56.

"Who Has Been Arming the Middle East?" *Business Week,* July 18, 1970, pp. 72–73.

Yefimov, S., "The Struggle of Monopolies on European Arms Market," *International Affairs* (Moscow) 7 (July 1961): 37–43.

Zartman, Lt. (jg) I. William, USNR, "Communist China and the Arab-African Area," *United States Naval Institute Proceedings* 86 (1960): 23–30.

III. RECIPIENTS

A. Europe/NATO

Ashcroft, G., *Military Logistic Systems in NATO: The Goal of Integration,* Adelphi Papers nos. 62 and 68 (London: Institute for Strategic Studies, 1969, 1970).

Beer, F. A., *Integration and Disintegration in NATO* (Columbus: Ohio State University Press, 1969).

Dubrovin, V., "Atlantic Fights on Arms Market," *International Affairs* (Moscow) 11 (September 1965): 78–83.

Edmonds, M., "International Collaboration in Weapons Procurement: The Implications of the Anglo-French Case," *International Affairs* (London) 43 (April 1967): 252–64.

Ford, Pres. Gerald, "Assistance to Greece," House document 94-317, 94th Cong., 1st sess., December 8, 1975.

———, "Security Assistance to Spain," House Document No. 94-549, 94th Cong., 2d sess., July 19, 1976.

———, "Military Sales to Turkey," House Document No. 94-590, 94th cong., 2d sess., August 30, 1976.

Hovey, Harold A., *United States Military Assistance: A Study of Politics and Practices* (New York: Praeger, 1965). [See esp. pp. 75–90.]

"Reduction in US Arms Dominance Urged," *Aviation Week & Space Technology* 109 (July 3, 1978): 15.

Schutze, W., *European Defense Cooperation and NATO* (Paris: Atlantic Institute, 1969).

Simpson, John and Gregory, Frank, "West European Collaboration in Weapons Procurement," *Orbis* 16 (Summer 1972): 435–61.

Sisco, Joseph J., "U.S. Military Assistance and Sales to Turkey," Department of State News Release, July 10, 1975.

"Spanish Treaty Contains Terms for F-16 Sales," *Aviation Week & Space Technology* 105 (July 5, 1976): 69–70.

U.S. Congress, House, Committee on International Relations, *Supplemental Military Assistance for Portugal for Fiscal Year 1977* 95th Cong., 1st sess., March 15, 1977.

U.S. Congress, House, Committee on International Relations, *Sale of AWACs to NATO,* 94th Cong., 2d sess., March 19, 1976.

_____, *Suspension of Prohibitions Against Military Assistance to Turkey,* 94th cong., 1st sess., July 10, 1975.

_____, Subcommittee on Europe and the Middle East, *Foreign Assistance Legislation for Fiscal Year 1979. Part 5: Economic and Military Aid Programs in Europe and the Middle East,* 95th Cong., 2d sess., 1978.

_____, Subcommittee on International Political and Military Affairs, *Proposed Sale of Airborne Warning and Control System Aircraft (AWACs) to NATO,* 94th Cong., 2d sess., March 11, 1976.

U.S. Congress, Senate, Committee on Foreign Relations, *Supplemental Military Assistance to Portugal,* 95th Cong., 1st sess., March 9, 1977.

_____, Subcommittee on Foreign Assistance, *Military and Economic Assistance to Portugal,* 95th Cong., 1st sess., February 25, 1977.

_____, Subcommittee on Foreign Assistance, *Proposed Sale of AWACs to NATO,* 94th Cong., 2d sess., March 12, 1976.

Vandevanter, Gen. E., Jr., "Coordinated Weapons Production in NATO: A Study of Alliance Processes," RN-5282-PR, Rand Corporation, Santa Monica, Calif., 1967.

Watson, William, "25 Years of US Military Involvement in Spain, 1951–1975," North American Congress on Latin America, 1975. [Available through NACLA, P.O. Box 226, Berkeley, California.]

Zwissler, Tilbert, "Probleme der Wehrwirtschaft und Rüstung," *Wehrkunde* 20 (1971): 231–36.

B. General Third World

Albrecht, Ulrich and Sommer, Brigit A., "Deutsche Waffen für die Dritte Welt," in *Militärhilfe und Entwicklungspolitik* (Hamburg: Rowohlt Verlag, 1972).

_____, et al. "Armaments and Underdevelopment," *Bulletin of Peace Proposals* 5:2 (1974): 173–85.

_____, Ernst, D., Lock, P., and Wulf, H., *Rüstung und Unterentwicklung. Iran, Indien, Griechenland/Türkei: Die Verschärfte Militarisierung* (Hamburg: Rororo Aktuell, Reinbek, 1976). [English-language version by MIT Press, forthcoming, 1979.]

"Arms Trade and Transfer of Military Technology," *Bulletin of Peace Proposals* 8:2 (1977). [Special issue.]

Barrett, Raymond J., "Arms Dilemma for the Developing World," *Military Review* 50 (April 1970): 28–35.

Bova, Sergio, "Il Commercio Della Armi E I Paesi del Terzo Mondo," *Quaderni di Sociologia* 21: 2 (1972): 217–26.

Chaudhuri, Gen. J. N., "International Arms Trade: The Recipient's Problem," *Political Quarterly* 43 (July-September 1972): 261–69.

Cook, Fred J., "Deadly Contagion: Arms Sales to the Third World," *The Nation*, January 24, 1972, pp. 106–09.

Copley, Gregory, "Third World Arms Production," *Defense and Foreign Affairs Digest*, no. 9 (forthcoming).

_____, Moodie, Michael, and Harvey, David, "Third World Arms Production: An End to Embargoes?" *Defense and Foreign Affairs Digest*, no. 8 (1978).

Davinic, Prvoslav, "Basic Characteristics of Arms Trade with Developing Countries," *Medunarodni Problemi* 23: 3 (1970): 55–92.

Dudzinsky, S. J. and Digby, James, *Qualitative Constraints on Conventional Armaments: An Emerging Issue*, Rand Corporation, Santa Monica, Calif., July 1976.

Hanning, Hugh, "Lessons from the Arms Race," *Africa Report* 13 (February 1968): 42–47.

Hoagland, John H., "Arms in the Developing World," *Orbis* 12 (Spring 968): 167–84.

_____, "Arms in the Third World," *Orbis* 14 (Summer 1970): 500–504. [Review article.]

"Increasing Weaponry Sales Struggle Seen," *Aviation Week & Space Technology* 85 (October 24, 1966).

Kemp, Geoffrey, "Arms Sales and Arms Control in the Developing Countries," *World Today* 22 (September1966): 386–95. [Reprinted as "Arms in Developing Countries," *Military Review* 47 (May 1967): 58–65.]

_____, "Arms Traffic and Third World Conflicts," *International Conciliation*, no. 577 (March 1970): 1–80.

_____, "Classification of Weapons Systems and Force Designs in Less Developed Country Environments: Implications for Arms Transfer Policies," Massachusetts Institute of Technology, Center for International Studies, Cambridge, 1970.

_____, "Strategy, Arms and the Third World," *Orbis* 16 (Fall 1972): 809–15.

Kennedy, Gavin, *The Military in the Third World* (New York: Scribner's, 1974).

Leiss, A. C. and Kemp, G., "Arms Transfers to Less Developed Countries," Report C/70–1, Massachusetts Institute of Technology, Center for International Studies, Cambridge, February 1970.

Lock, Peter and Wulf, Herbert, "Register of Arms Production in Developing Countries," Study Group on Armaments and Underdevelopment, University of Hamburg, March 1977.

Luckham, Robin, "Militarism: Arms and the Internationalisation of Capital," *IDS Bulletin* [UK] 8 (1977).

Mallman, Wolfgang, "Der Transfer von Marinegerät an Entwicklungsländer," in Dieter Mahncke and Hans-Peter Schwarz, eds., *Seemacht und Aussenpolitik*, pp. 476–93 (Frankfurt-am-Main: Alfred Metzner Verlag Gmbh., 1974).

Martin, Laurence, "The Arms Trade with the Third World," in his *Arms and Strategy*, pp. 253–67 (New York: David McKay, 1973).

Massachusetts Institute of Technology, Center for International Studies, "Regional Arms Control Arrangements for Developing Nations: Arms and Arms Control in Latin America, the Middle East and Africa," Cambridge, Mass., September 1964.

Menges, Constantine C., "Military Aspects of International Relations in Developing Areas," P-3480, Rand Corporation, Santa Monica, Calif., 1966.

Mihalka, Michael, "Arms to the Third World: 1967–76," P-6207, Rand Corporation, Santa Monica, Calif., 1978.

Miksche, Ferdinand O., "The Arms Race in the Third World," *Orbis* 13 (1968): 161–66.

_____, "Rüstungsgeschaft des Ostblocks mit der Dritten Welt," *Wehr und Wirtschaft* 15 (September 1971): 438–39.

Neuman, Stephanie G., "Security, Military Expenditures, and Socioeconomic Development," *Orbis* 22 (1978).

Øberg, Jan, "Arms Trade with the Third World as an Aspect of Imperialism," *Journal of Peace Research* 12: 3 (1975): 213–34.

_____, "Third World Armament: Domestic Arms Production in Israel, South Africa, Brazil, Argentina and India from 1950–65," Department of Peace and Conflict Research, Lund University, 1975, mimeo.

Peleg, Ilan, "Arms Supply to the Third World—Models and Explanations," *Journal of Modern African Studies* 5:1 (1977).

Ra'anan, Uri, Pfaltzgraff, Robert L., Jr.; and Kemp, Geoffrey, eds., *Arms Transfers to the Third World* (Boulder, Colo.: Westview Press, 1978).

Sutton, John L. and Kemp, Geoffrey, *Arms to Developing Countries, 1945–1965*, Adelphi Papers no. 28 (London: Institute for Strategic Studies, October 1966).

Stockholm International Peace Research Institute, *The Arms Trade with the Third World* (New York: Humanities Press, 1971).

U.S. Congress, House, Committee on International Relations, Subcommittee on International Organizations, *Foreign Assistance Legislation for Fiscal Year 1979. Part 4: U.S. Policy on Human Rights in Indonesia, Nicaragua, Philippines, Thailand and Iran*, 95th Cong., 2d sess., 1978.

Whitaker, P. M., "Arms and the Nationalists," *Africa Review* 15 (May 1970): 12–14.

Wolf, Charles, Jr., "The Political Effects of Military Programs: Some Indications from Latin America," *Orbis* 8 (Winter 1965): 871–93.

C. Africa

South Africa

African National Congress, South Africa, *Conspiracy to Arm Apartheid Continues: FRG-SA Collaboration* (Bonn: Progress Dritte Welt Verlag-Verleih-Agentur, n.d.).

"Arms to Dr. V.," *The Observer*, November 29, 1964.

Klare, Michael T. and Prokosch, Eric, "Getting Arms to South Africa: The U.N. Embargo Evaded," *The Nation*, July 8–15, 1978, pp. 49–50.

_____, "How the United States is Helping Equip South Africa's Military," *The Sun* (Baltimore), February 19, 1978.

Legum, Colin, "West Cuts Arms to Verwoerd," *The Observer*, June 9, 1963.

Lipton, Merle, "British Arms for South Africa," *The World Today* [UK] 26 (October 1970): 427–34.

Minty, Abdul S., *South Africa's Defense Strategy* (London: Anti-Apartheid Movement, 1969).

Rippon, Geoffrey, "South Africa and Naval Strategy: The Importance of South Africa," *Round Table* 60 (July 1970): 303–09.

"South Africans Shopping in France," *The Observer*, June 20, 1965.

Stockholm International Peace Research Institute, *Southern Africa: The Escalation of a Conflict* (Stockholm: Almqvist & Wiksell, 1976). [Relevant chapters are 6.III, 7.III, and Appendix I.]

United Nations, Office of Public Information, Press Section, "Committee Against Apartheid Opens Meetings on South African Military Build-up," GA/AP/857, May 30, 1978.

U.S. Congress, House, Committee on International Relations, Subcommittee on Africa [See especially testimony by Sean Gervasi.] *The Breakdown of the Arms Embargo Against South Africa*, 95th Cong., 1st sess., July 14, 1977.

Other Africa

Akehurst, Frederick S., ed., *Arms and African Development* (New York: Praeger, 1972).

"Arms for Lagos," *West Africa*, no. 2620 (August 19, 1967).

Bell, M. J. V., *Military Assistance to Independent African States*, Adelphi Papers no. 15 (London: Institute for Strategic Studies, 1964).

Cervenka, Zdenek, "The Arms Trade in Africa," *Africa* 7 (March 1972): 14–17.

Cooley, John K., "From Mau Mau to Missiles," *African Forum* 2 (Summer 1966): 42–56.

Edmonds, Martin, "Civil War and Arms Sales: The Nigerian-Biafran War and Other Cases," in Robin Higham, ed., *Civil Wars in the Twentieth Century* (Lexington: University of Kentucky Press, 1972).

Gutteridge, William F., "The Political Role of African Armed Forces: The Impact of Foreign Military Assistance," *African Affairs* 66 (April 1967): 93–101.

Jacob, A., "Israel's Military Aid to Africa, 1960-1966," *Journal of Modern African Studies* 9 (August 1971): 165–87.

Mazrui, Ali A., "African Radicalism and Arms Policy," *African Scholar* 1: 4 (1970): 3–4.

Shaw, Lt. Bryant P., "Military Assistance to Black Africa: Blessing or Curse?" *Air University Review* 23 (May-June 1972): 72–78.

Short, Philip, "Army Still Takes Biggest Slice of Uganda's Budget," *African Development* 6 (1972): 15–16.

"Somali Arms: East Africa's Fears," *African Review* 11 (1966).

U.S. Congress, House, Committee on Foreign Affairs, Subcommittee on International Political and Military Affairs, *U.S. Policy and Request for Sale of Arms to Ethiopia*, 94th Cong., 1st sess., March 5, 1975.

U.S. Congress, House, Committee on International Relations, Subcommittee on Africa, statement by John J. Gilligan, "U.S. Economic and Military Assistance to Africa," 95th Cong., 1st sess., March 25, 29, 1977.

_____, Subcommittee on Africa, *Foreign Assistance Legislation for Fiscal Year 1979. Part 3: Economic and Military Assistance Programs in Africa.* 95th Cong., 2d sess., 1978.

U.S. Congress, Senate, Committee on Foreign Relations, Subcommittees on African Affairs and Foreign Assistance, *Security Supporting Assistance for Zaire*, 94th Cong., 1st sess., October 24, 1975.

D. Asia

India and Pakistan

Brodkin, E. I., "United States Aid to India and Pakistan: The Attitudes of the Fifties," *International Affairs* (Moscow) 43 (1967): 4.

Cohen, Stephen P., "U.S. Weapons and South Asia: A Policy Analysis," *Pacific Affairs* 49:1 (1976): 49–69.

"Friends Have Their Uses," *The Economist*, August 5, 1967, pp. 487–88.

Graham, I. C. C., "The Indian MiG Deal and Its International Repercussions," P-2842, Rand Corporation, Santa Monica, Calif., January 1964.

Guha, S. B., "Pakistan's Air Power," *Institute for Defence Studies and Analysis* [New Delhi] 2 (October 1969): 124–49.

Hasan, K. Sarwar, "The Background of American Aid to Pakistan," *Pakistan Horizon* 20:2 (1967): 120–26.

———, "United States Arms Policy to South Asia, 1965–1967," *Pakistan Horizon* 20:2 (1967): 127–36.

Nihart, Brooke, "Who Armed Pakistan?" *Armed Forces Journal* 109 (November 1971): 50–52.

Qureshi, Khalida. "Arms Aid to India and Pakistan," *Pakistan Horizon* 20:2 (1967): 137–50.

Rajasekhariah, A. M. and Patil, V. T., "Soviet Arms Supply to Pakistan: Motives and Implications," *Modern Review* (October 1968); pp. 706–10.

Rao, R. Rama, "Pakistan Re-Arms," *India Quarterly* 27 (April-June 1971): 140–48.

Rizvi, Absar Hussain, "Lifting of the U.S. Arms Embargo," *Pakistan Pictorial* 14 (March-April 1975), pp. 38–40.

Sharma, B. L., "Soviet Arms for Pakistan," *United Service Institution of India Journal* 98 (July-September 1968): 223–38.

"Soviet Aid to India: Indian Views on Soviet Aid to India," *East-West Relations* 7 (May 1973). [Special issue.]

Spain, James W., "Military Assistance for Pakistan," *American Political Science Review* 48 (September 1954): 738–51.

U.S. Congress, Senate, Committee on Foreign Relations, *Arms Sales to Near East and South Asian Countries*, 90th Cong., 1st sess., March, April, June 1967.

Zubeida, H., "US Arms Policy in South Asia, 1965-67," *Pakistan Horizon* 20:2 (1967).

Other Asia

Center for International Policy, "Human Rights and the US Foreign Assistance Program: Fiscal Year 1978. Part II—East Asia," Washington, D.C., 1977.

Hovey, Harold A., *United States Military Assistance* (New York: Praeger, 1965). [See pp. 17–43.]

Jordan, Amos A., Jr., *Foreign Aid and the Defense of Southeast Asia* (New York: Praeger, 1962).

Marsot, Alain G., "China's Aid to Cambodia," *Pacific Affairs* 43 (Summer 1969): 189–98.

Nagashima, Shusuke, "Japan's Defense Rests on U.S. Technology," *Technology Week* 19 (December 6, 1966): 32–33.

National Coordinating Committee of the Anti-Martial Law [Philippines] Movement, "The Logistics of Repression. A Report on the Volume, Forms & Functions of US Military Assistance to the Martial Law Regime in the Philippines," 1975. [Available through North American Congress on Latin America, P.O. Box 226, Berkeley, Calif. 94701]

Parry, A., "Soviet Aid to Vietnam," *Reporter*, March 1967.

Polsky, Anthony, "Asia's Little Israel," *Far Eastern Economic Review*, September 11, 1969, pp. 655–57. [Singapore.]

Siegel, Lenny, "Arming Indonesia," *Pacific Research and World Empire Telegram* 7 (November–December 1975): 1–6.

Smith, Alphonso, "Military Assistance in the Far East," *United States Naval Institute Proceedings* 86 (December 1960): 40–48.

U.S. General Accounting Office, "Unclassified Digests of Progress and Outlook for U.S. Security Assistance to the Republic of Korea," ID-76-28, June 18, 1976.

U.S. Congress, House, Committee on International Relations, Subcommittee on Asian and Pacific Affairs, statement by Richard C. Holbrooke, "U.S. Economic and Security Assistance in East Asia," 95th Cong., 1st sess., March 1977.

_____, Subcommittee on Asian and Pacific Affairs, *Foreign Assistance Legislation for Fiscal Year 1979. Part 6: Economic and Security Assistance in Asia and the Pacific*. 95th Cong., 2d sess., 1978.

Warner, D., "Will Indonesia Become a Second Cuba?" *Reporter*, December 1961.

Wolf, Charles, Jr., *Foreign Aid: Theory and Practice in Southern Asia* (Princeton, N.J.: Princeton University Press, 1960).

Wurfel, David, "Foreign Aid and Social Reform in Political Development: A Philippine Case Study," *American Political Science Review* 53 (June 1959): 456–82.

E. Latin America

Arnson, Cynthia and Klare, Michael, "Law or No Law, The Arms Flow: Pipeline to Pinochet," *The Nation*, April 29, 1978, pp. 502–05.

Avery, William P., "Domestic Influences on Latin American Importation of U.S. Armaments," *International Studies Quarterly* 22 (March 1978): 121–42.

Baines, John M. "U.S. Military Assistance to Latin America: An Assessment." *Journal of Inter-American Studies and World Affairs* 14 (November 1972): 469–87.

Brownlow, Cecil, "Brazil Looks Again to U.S. for Weapons," *Aviation Week & Space Technology* (December 9, 1974) pp. 21–22.

_____, "Peru Military Build-up Worries Neighbors," *Aviation Week & Space Technology*, 101 (December 2, 1974) pp. 21–22.

_____, "U.S., Europe Vie for Latin Fighter Order," *Aviation Week & Space Technology*, 84 (May 31, 1960): pp. 26–27.

Dame, H., "*United States Military Assistance and Latin American Relations*," Center for Research in Social Systems, American University, 1962.

Einaudi, Luigi, et al., "Arms Transfers to Latin America: Toward a Policy of Mutual Respect," R-1173-DOS, Rand Corporation, Santa Monica, Calif. June 1973.

Estep, Raymond, "United States Military Aid to Latin America," Documentary Research Division, Air University, Maxwell AFB, Ala., 1966.

Fitch, John Samuel, "The Political Consequences of U.S. Military Assistance to Latin America," University of Florida, n.d.

Gailer, Col. Frank, Jr., "Air Force Missions in Latin America," *Air University Quarterly Review* 13 (Fall 1961): 45–58.

Gebhardt, Herman P., "Komplexe Rüstungsprobleme in Latinamerika," *Aussenpolitik* 19 (April 1968): 220–29.

Government Business Worldwide Reports, "Defense and Market Developments in Latin America," *International Defense Business*, May 1973.

⸻, "Arms Sales to Latin America," *International Defense Business*, August 26, 1974.

Grant, Zalin B., "Alliance Against Revolution: Training, Equipping the Latin American Military," *New Republic*, December 16, 1967, pp. 13–14.

Gruening, Sen. Ernest, "Export Trouble," *The Nation*, October 6, 1962, pp. 194–96.

Haahr, John C., "Military Assistance to Latin America," *Military Review* 46 (May 1966): 12–21.

Kemp, Geoffrey, "Rearmament in Latin America," *World Today* 23 (September 1967): 375–84.

⸻, "Some Relationships Between U.S. Military Training in Latin America and Weapons Acquisitions Patterns: 1959–1969." Massachusetts Institute of Technology, Center for International Studies, Cambridge, 1970.

Klare, Michael, "The Politics of U.S. Arms Sales to Latin America," *NACLA's Latin American Report* 9 (March 1975): 12–17.

⸻, "How to Trigger an Arms Race," *The Nation*, August 30, 1975, pp. 137–42.

Kozolchyk, Boris, "Legal Aspects of the Acquisition of Major Weapons by Six Latin American Countries," RM-5349-1-ISA, Rand Corporation, Santa Monica, Calif., January 1968.

Lieuwen, Edwin, *Arms and Politics in Latin America* (New York: Praeger, 1961).

Loftus, Joseph E., "Latin American Defense Expenditures, 1938-1965," RM-5310-IR-15A, Rand Corporation, Santa Monica, Calif., January 1968.

Meyer, Charles A., "U.S. Military Assistance Policy Toward Latin America," *U.S. Department of State Bulletin* 61 (1969): 100–102.

North American Congress on Latin America, "U.S. Police Aid—Brazil," *NACLA's Latin America & Empire Report* January 6 (1972): 21–22.

"Peru: More Reports of Soviet Deal," *Defense and Foreign Affairs Daily*, January 26, 1977.

Ronfeldt, David F. and Einaudi, Luigi R., "Internal Security and Military Assistance to Latin America in the 1970's: A First Statement," R-924-ISA, Rand Corporation, Santa Monica, Calif., December 1971.

⸻, and Sereseres, Cesar, "Arms Transfers, Diplomacy, and Security in Latin America and Beyond," P-6005, Rand Corporation, Santa Monica, Calif., October 1977.

Rosenbaum, H. Jon, *Arms and Security in Latin America. Recent Developments*, International Affairs Series 101 (Washington, D.C.: Woodrow Wilson International Center for Scholars, 1971).

Sereseres, Cesar D., "Military Development and the United States Military Assistance Program for Latin America: The Case of Guatemala, 1966-1969," Ph.D. diss., University of California–Riverside, 1972.

Simcox, David E., "United States Military Assistance and Latin American Military Elites," M.A. thesis, American University, School of International Service, 1970.

"The Newest Superstate," *Newsweek*, April 10, 1978. [Deals with Brazil.]

U.S. Department of State, "Inter-American Military Cooperation," *U.S. Department of State Bulletin* 24 (April 9, 1951): 574.

_____, *Military Assistance to Latin America: Background*, 1953.

_____, Bureau of Intelligence and Research, *Arms Sales in Latin America*, Research Study, RAAS-14, June 1973.

U.S. Congress, House, Committee on Foreign Affairs, *Aircraft Sales in Latin America*, 91st Cong., 2d sess., April 29–30, 1970.

U.S. Congress, House, Committee on International Relations, Subcommittee on Inter-American Affairs, *Foreign Assistance Legislation for Fiscal Year 1979. Part 7: Economic and Military Assistance for Latin America*, 95th Cong., 2d sess., 1978.

U.S. Congress, Senate, Committee on Appropriations, *United States Activities in Mexico, Panama, Peru, Chile, Argentina, Brazil, and Venezuela*, 97th Cong., 2d sess., 1962.

U.S. Congress, Senate, Committee on Foreign Relations, *Control and Reduction of Armaments: Disarmament and Security in Latin America*, 85th Cong., 1st sess., January-March 1957.

_____, *Survey of the Alliance for Progress. The Latin American Military*, 90th Cong., 1st sess., 1967.

_____, *United States Military Policies and Programs in Latin America*, 91st Cong., 1st sess., June 24, July 8, 1969.

Weaver, Jerry, "Arms Transfers to Latin America: A Note on the Contagion Effect," *Journal of Peace Research* 11:3 (1974): 213–20.

"Why U.S. Military Assistance Is Given to Argentina: Dictatorship of the U.S. Department of Defense," *Inter-American Economic Affairs* 21 (Autumn 1967): 81–89.

Wolf, Charles, Jr., "The Political Effects of Military Programs: Some Indications from Latin America," Rand Corporation, Santa Monica, Calif., 1963.

Wychoff, Theodore, "The Role of the Military in Latin American Military Politics," *Western Political Quarterly* 13 (September 1960): 745–63.

Zook, Capt. David, Jr., "United States Military Assistance to Latin America," *Air University Review* 14 (September-October 1963): 82–85.

F. Middle East and Persian Gulf

Alexandros, L., "MiG-Affären," *Wehr und Wirtschaft* 10 (October 10, 1966).

_____, "Streifzug durch den Nahen Osten," *Wehr und Wirtschaft* 10 (May 10, 1966): 293–95.

Atherton, Alfred L., 'U.S. Sales of Air Defense Equipment to Jordan," U.S. Department of State, News Release, July 16, 1975.

_____, "Saudi Arabia: Maverick Missiles," U.S. Department of State, News Release, September 27, 1976.

Berman, Bob and Leader, Stefan H., "U.S. Arms to the Persian Gulf: $10 Billion Since 1973," *Defense Monitor* 4 (May 1975): 1–8.

Brown, Neville, "Revolutionary Libya's Arms Potential...Who Will Benefit?" *New Middle East* 13 (October 1969): 11–13.

Cahn, Anne Hessing and Evron, Yair, "The Politics of Arms Transfers: U.S. Arms Sales to Egypt," Program for Science and International Affairs, Harvard University, December 1977.

"Carter's Plane Package," *Newsweek*, February 27, 1978, pp. 32–36.

"Controlling the Middle East Arms Race," *Disarmament* 10 (June 1966): 1–6.

DeVore, Ronald, M., "The Arab-Israeli Military Balance," *Military Review* 53 (November 1973): 65–71.

——, "The Arab-Israeli Arms Race and the Super-powers," *Middle East* 66 (February 1974): 70–73.

Doty, L., "Jordan's Purchase of F-104 Adds to Rumble of Arab Arms Build-up," *Aviation Week & Space Technology* 84 (April 11, 1966): 106.

Duchêne, François, "The Arms Trade in the Middle East," *Political Quarterly* 44 (October-December 1973): 453–65.

Evron, Yair, "French Arms Policy in the Middle East," *World Today* 26 (February 1970): 82–90.

Frederick, Howard H., *The Arms Trade and the Middle East: A Primer* (Philadelphia: American Friends Service Committee, 1977).

Gayner, Jeffrey B., "Limiting Arms Sales and the Iranian AWACs Proposal," Backgrounder no. 36, The Heritage Foundation, Washington, D.C., September 20, 1977.

Gharleb, Edmund, "U.S. Arms Supply to Israel during the War," *Journal of Palestine Studies* 3 (Winter 1974): 114–21.

Government Business Worldwide Reports, "Defense Market Guide to Bahrain," *International Defense Business*, September 1973.

Hoagland, John H. and Teeple, John B., "Regional Stability and Weapons Transfer: The Middle Eastern Case," *Orbis* 9 (Fall 1965): 714–28.

Hurewitz, J. C., *Middle East Politics: The Military Dimension* (New York: Praeger, 1969).

——, "Weapons Acquisition: Israel and Egypt," in Frank B. Horton, Anthony C. Rogerson, and Edward L. Warner, eds., *Comparative Defense Policy*, pp. 482–93 (Baltimore, Md.: Johns Hopkins Press, 1974).

"Iraq: Defense Protocol with USSR," *Defense and Foreign Affairs Daily*, October 13, 1976.

Jabber, Fuad, "The Politics of Arms Transfer and Control: The United States and Egypt's Quest for Arms, 1950–1955," discussion paper, California Arms Control and Foreign Policy Seminar, Santa Monica, Calif., January 1973.

——, "Not by War Alone: Curbing the Arab-Israeli Arms Race," *Middle East Journal* 28 (Summer 1974): 233–47.

——, *The Politics of Arms Transfer and Control: The Case of the Middle East*, Ph.D. diss., University of California, Los Angeles, 1974.

Jeumau, L., "L'Assistance Militaire de Moscou aux Pays Arabes," *Témoignages*, May–June 1964.

Kemp, Geoffrey, *Arms and Security: The Egypt-Israel Case*, Adelphi Papers no. 52 (London: Institute for Strategic Studies, 1968).

——, "The Military Build-Up: Arms Control or Arms Trade?" in *The Middle East and the International System. Part I: The Impact of the 1973 War,* Adelphi Papers no. 114, pp. 31–37 (London: International Institute for Strategic Studies, 1975).

Kennedy, Sen. Edward, "The Persian Gulf: Arms Race or Arms Control?" *Foreign Affairs* 54 (October 1975): 14–35.

Klein, Jean, "Ventes d'Armes et d'Equipements Nucléaires: Les Politiques des Etat-Unis et des Pays d'Europe Occidental Depuis la Guerre d'Octobre 1973," *Politique Etrangère* 40:6 (1975): 603–19.

Kondracke, Morton, "Arms for Oil," *New Republic,* February 25, 1978, pp. 15–18.

Lambelet, John C., "A Dynamic Model of the Arms Race in the Middle East, 1953–1965," *General Systems Yearbook* 16 (1971): 145–70.

"Libya: Soviets Building Up Tobruk," *Defense and Foreign Affairs Daily,* August 25, 1976.

Mallman, Wolfgang, "Waffen nach Nahost: Die Rüstungsexporte der Grossmächte seit dem Junikrieg 1967," *Beitrage zur Konfliktforschung* 4 (1971): 136–86.

————, "Rüstungswettlauf in Nah- und Mittelost: Konfliktherde und Rüstungs potentiale," *Der Bürger im Staat* 25 (1975): 143–48.

Mark, Clyde R., "Assessment of the Middle East Arms Race," D-465A, F-334, Legislative Reference Service, Library of Congress, Washington, D.C., October 29, 1968.

"Massive Egyptian Arms Modernization Launched with Saudi Funds, U.K. Help," *Armed Forces Journal International,* 115 (October 1977): 13.

Meltzer, Ronald M., "The Middle East Arms Race: Suppliers and Recipients," M.A. thesis, San Diego State University, 1970.

"Mid East: New Clashes, New Arms Shipments," *U.S. News & World Report,* February 26, 1968, pp. 58–59.

Mihalka, Michael, "The Measurement and Modelling of Arms Accumulations: The Middle East as a Case Study," Report C/75-8, Massachusetts Institute of Technology Center for International Studies, Cambridge, April 1975.

Milstein, Jeffrey, S., *Soviet and American Influences on the Arab-Israeli Arms Race: A Quantitative Analysis* (New Haven: Yale University Press, 1970).

Morris, Joe A., "Pandora's Ammunition Box," *The Nation,* August 8, 1966, pp. 109–12.

Newcombe, Hanna, "The Case for an Arms Embargo," *War/Peace Report* 11 (March 1971): 17–19.

"Nixon Treds Cautiously in Middle East Arms Race," *Congressional Quarterly Weekly Report,* March 27, 1970, pp. 880–84.

"No Eagles for Arabia," *New Republic,* March 4, 1978, pp. 5–6, 8–9.

O'Ballance, Edgar, "Middle East Arms Race," *Army Quarterly* 88 (July 1964): 210–14.

"Packaging of Fighter Sale Tied to Political Strategy," *Aviation Week & Space Technology* 108 (February 20, 1978): 17–19.

Pearton, Maurice, "The Persian Gulf Has a Deadly Little Arms Race," *New York Times,* December 15, 1974.

Peres, Shimon, *David's Sling* (New York: Random House, 1970).

Pranger, Robert and Tahtinen, Dale R., *Nuclear Threat in the Middle East* (Washington, D.C.: American Enterprise Institute for Public Policy Research, 1975).

Pryor, Leslie M., "Arms and the Shah," *Foreign Policy,* no. 31 (Summer 1978): 56–71.

Remick, Comm. William C., USNR (ret.), "The Case for Foreign Military Sales in American Persian Gulf Strategy," *United States Naval Institute Proceedings* 103

(January 1977): 19–26.

Ropelewski, Robert R., "Arabs Seek Arms Sufficiency," *Aviation Week & Space Technology* 108 (May 15, 1978): 14–16.

Seale, P., "Russia Offers Jordan Arms and Jets," *The Observer*, August 30, 1964.

Smolansky, Oleg M., "The Soviet Setback in the Middle East," *Current History* 64 (January 1973): 17–20.

Soderholm-Difatte, Bryan, "Proposed F-15 Sale to Saudi Arabia: A Pro-Con Analysis," 78-25 F, Congressional Research Service, Library of Congress, Washington, D.C., December 20, 1977.

"Stocking the Arsenals of the Middle East," *Atlas* 17 (January 1969): 42–43.

"Syria-USSR: Soviets Asked to Leave Syrian Naval Port," *Defense and Foreign Affairs Daily*, January 14, 1977.

Tahtinen, Dale R., *Arms in the Persian Gulf* (Washington, D.C.: American Enterprise Institute for Public Policy Research, March-April 1974).

U.S. General Accounting Office, "Issues Related to U.S. Military Sales and Assistance to Iran," B-133258, October 21, 1974.

———, *Perspectives on Military Sales to Saudi Arabia*, ID-77-19 A. October 26, 1977.

U.S. Congress, House, Committee on Foreign Affairs, *The Persian Gulf, 1974: Money, Politics, Arms and Power*, 94th Cong., 1st sess., 1975.

U.S. Congress, House, Committee on International Relations, *United States Arms Sales to the Persian Gulf*. Report of a Study Mission to Iran, Kuwait, and Saudi Arabia, 94th Cong., 1st sess., May 22–31, 1975.

———, Special Subcommittee on Investigations, *The Persian Gulf, 1975: The Continuing Debate on Arms Sales*. 94th Cong., 1st sess., June 10, 18, 24, July 29, 1975.

———, Subcommittee on International Political and Military Affairs, *Military Sales to Saudi Arabia—1975*, 94th Cong., 1st sess., November–December 1975.

———, Subcommittee on International Political and Military Affairs, *Proposed Foreign Military Sales to Middle Eastern Countries—1976*, 94th Cong., 2d sess., February, March, September 1976.

———, Subcommittee on International Political and Military Affairs, *Proposed Sale to Egypt of C-130 Aircraft*, 94th Cong., 2d sess., April 1976.

———, *United States Arms Policies in the Persian Gulf and Red Sea Areas: Past, Present and Future*, Report of a Staff Survey Mission to Ethiopia, Iran, and the Arabian Peninsula, 95th Cong., 1st sess., December 1977.

———, Subcommittee on International Political and Military Affairs, *Proposed Sale to Kuwait of Air-to-Air Missiles*, 94th Cong., 1st sess., October 1975.

U.S. Congress, Senate, Committee on Foreign Relations, Subcommittee on Foreign Assistance, *U.S. Military Sales to Iran*, 94th Cong., 2d sess., July 1976.

U.S. Congress, House, International Relations Committee, statement by Cyrus R. Vance, "Proposed Sale of AWACs to Iran," 95th Cong., 1st sess., July 28, 1977.

Wagner, Charles, "The Impact of Soviet Arms Introduction into the Middle East: A Missed Opportunity,"California Arms Control and Foreign Policy Seminar, Santa Monica, March 1972.

Webster, R. Kenly, *Report for the Secretary of Defense on the Implementation of the United States Foreign Military Sales Program in Iran*, U.S. Department of Defense, September 19, 1977.

Weller, J., "Israeli Arms Production," *Ordnance* 55 (May-June 1971): 540–44.

Wetmore, Warren C., "Egypt Seeks New Soviet Missiles," *Aviation Week & Space Technology* 87 (July 10, 1967): 26.

"Who's Armed Whom," *The Economist*, March 25, 1967.

Wilson, A., "Israel Arms Row Kills Tank Sales," *The Observer*, November 22, 1964.

———, "Why Jeddah Bought Our Planes," *The Observer*, December 19, 1965.

Yodfat, A. Y., "Arms and Influence in Egypt: The Record of Soviet Military Assistance Since June 1967," *New Middle East* 10 (July 1969): 27–32.

IV. ADDITIONAL BIBLIOGRAPHIES

Gillingham, Arthur, *Arms Traffic: An Introduction and Bibliography*, Introduction by Anne Hessing Cahn, Political Issues Series, Vol. 4, No. 2 (Los Angeles: Bibliographic Reference Service, Center for the Study of Armament and Disarmament, California State University, 1976). [Pp. 1–11 should be consulted for works dealing with the pre-1945 period.]

Harkavy, Robert E., "Bibliography," in his *The Arms Trade and International Systems* (Cambridge, Mass.: Ballinger, 1975). [Pp. 281–85 should be consulted for works dealing with the pre-1945 period.]

Johnson, Julia E., comp., *The Government Control of Arms and Munitions* (New York: H. W. Wilson, 1934).

League of Nations, "Supervision of the Trade and Private Manufacture of Arms and Munitions and Implements of War," in *Annotated Bibliography on Disarmament and Military Questions*, pp. 53–57 (Geneva: League of Nations, 1935).

Matthews, Mary A., comp., *Traffic in Arms, Munitions, and Implements of War and Control of their Manufacture* (Washington, D.C.: Carnegie Endowment for International Peace, 1933).

Meeker, Thomas A., *The Military-Industrial Complex: A Source Guide to the Issues of Defense Spending and Policy Control* (Los Angeles: California State University, Center for the Study of Armament and Disarmament, 1973).

U.S. Library of Congress, Legislative Reference Service, *Limitation of International Traffic in Arms and Ammunition: Excerpts from Selected References Chronologically Arranged*, Washington, D.C.: 1946.

INDEX

ABOUT THE EDITORS
AND CONTRIBUTORS

STEPHANIE G. NEUMAN is a Senior Research Associate at Columbia University's Institute of War and Peace Studies. She teaches international relations at the Graduate Faculty of the New School for Social Research. Dr. Neuman has written extensively on international relations, concentrating most recently on linkage issues that relate international affairs to national development. She is the editor of, and contributor to, *Small States and Segmented Societies: National Political Integration in a Global Environment*. Currently, she is working on a research project, supported by the Ford Foundation, which analyzes the impact of arms transfers on the socio-economic development of less industrialized states.

ROBERT E. HARKAVY is Associate Professor of Political Science at Pennsylvania State University. He earlier served with the U.S. Atomic Energy Commission (1966-68) and U.S. Arms Control and Disarmament Agency (1975-77), taught at Kalamazoo College, and was a Senior Research Associate at the Cornell University Center for International Studies. He is the author of *The Arms Trade and International Systems, Spectre of a Middle Eastern Holocaust: The Strategic and Diplomatic Implications of the Israeli Nuclear Weapons Program*, and additional writings on defense and arms control issues.

NICOLE BALL is currently an independent researcher. From 1971 to 1976, she was a research fellow at the Institute for the Study of International Organisation at the University of Sussex in England. She has written about the ecological aspects of Third World development, U.S. arms sales policies, and the relationship between disarmament and development.

RICHARD BURT is presently national security affairs correspondent for the *New York Times* in the Washington bureau. Prior to coming to the *Times* he served as the Assistant Director of the International Institute for Strategic Studies in London where he had been a research associate. Dr. Burt also worked as an advanced research fellow at the U.S. Naval War College, at Newport, Rhode Island, and has been a consultant to several research institutions and organizations.

ANNE HESSING CAHN is the Chief of the Social Impact Staff, Weapons Evaluation and Control Bureau, of the Arms Control and Disarmament Agency. Prior to joining ACDA she held research positions at Harvard University and MIT, was the executive director of the 1973 American Academy of Arts and Science's Summer Study on New Directions in Arms Control, and was a consultant to the U.S. Senate Committee on the Budget. She is the author of books and articles on national security and arms control issues, including *Controlling Future Arms Trade* (New York: McGraw-Hill, 1977).

INGEMAR DÖRFER is currently assistant professor of government at Uppsala University, Sweden, and a consultant to the Swedish Defense Research Institute. His chapter in this volume is an outgrowth of the research for a forthcoming book *Arms Deal* funded by the German Marshall Fund of the United States, and was originally presented as a colloquium paper in July 1978 during his period as guest scholar at the Woodrow Wilson International Center for Scholars in Washington, D.C. He was formerly a special assistant in the Swedish Ministry of Defense and has published books and articles on Scandinavian and Western national security policy, including *System 37 Viggen: Arms, Technology and the Domestication of Glory* (Oslo: Scandinavian University Books, 1973).

EDWARD T. FEI is with the U.S. Arms Control and Disarmament Agency. He has taught at California State University at Chico, and at Colgate University.

CECIL I. HUDSON, JR. is Corporate Vice President and Deputy Manager of the Systems Group, Science Applications, Inc., La Jolla, California. He was formerly a group leader at the University of California Lawrence Livermore Laboratory. He is director of the working group on Implications of New Technology for Arms Control for the California Seminar on Arms Control and Foreign Policy, and is a member of the International Institute for Strategic Studies.

JO L. HUSBANDS is a Senior Research Associate, CACI, Inc.–Federal, and a Visiting Faculty Member, Center for Arms Control and International Security Studies, University of Pittsburgh. She is the author of works on arms transfers, nuclear nonproliferation, and arms control negotiations. Husbands is currently involved in a major study of the interactions between U.S. arms transfers and nuclear nonproliferation policies.

GEOFFREY KEMP is Associate Professor of International Politics at the Fletcher School of Law and Diplomacy, Tufts University, Medford, Mass. He has been a consultant to the Committee on Foreign Relations, U.S. Senate, and the Department of Defense and is the author of many works on arms transfers, defense policy, and strategy in less industrial countries.

EDWARD A. KOLODZIEJ, former head of the Department of Government and Foreign Affairs, University of Virginia, and the Department of Political Science, University of Illinois, is the author of *French International Policy under De Gaulle and Pompidou: The Politics of Grandeur* (Cornell, 1974) and *The Uncommon Defense and Congress: 1945-1963* (Ohio State University, 1966). A specialist in the role of military force in international relations, he is a frequent contributor to professional journals especially in the areas of American and European security and foreign policy and policy making. He is presently working on a study of French arms transfers policy under the Fifth Republic, under the auspices of a Ford Foundation grant provided under terms of its international competition in international security and arms control.

ERNEST W. LEFEVER is the founding director of the Ethics and Public Policy Center and a professorial lecturer, both at Georgetown University in Washington, D.C. For twelve years he was on the senior foreign policy studies staff of the Brookings Institution. He is the author of *Ethics and United States Foreign Policy* (1957), *Uncertain Mandate: Politics of the U.S. Congo Operation* (1967), *Spear and Scepter: Army, Police and Politics in Tropical Africa* (1970), and *Nuclear Arms in the Third World* (1979).

WILLIAM H. LEWIS is Adjunct Professor of Political Science at The George Washington University and a consultant on arms transfer questions with the Arms Control and Disarmament Agency. Prior to his retirement from the U.S. Department of State, he served on the Presidential Task Force on Foreign Aid (1969-70), and subsequently helped to draft legislation reorganizing the military assistance program. In 1973, Dr. Lewis assisted in the creation of a new office, that of the Under Secretary of State for Security Assistance, and thereafter organized the Department's assistance planning and analysis staff. In 1974, he was appointed Senior Fellow at the Brookings Institution where he co-authored a study, *Arms Across the Sea*. Dr. Lewis has lived and worked in the Middle East and Africa, served as Visiting Professor at the University of Michigan, and co-authored a number of books, including *Islam in Africa, The Modern Middle East,* and *French-speaking Africa*. He is a frequent contributor to various professional journals.

MICHAEL MIHALKA is a social science associate at the Rand Corporation, presently on leave from the University of Texas at Austin, where he has taught since 1975. Dr. Mihalka holds an S.B. from the Massachusetts Institute of Technology and a Ph.D. from the University of Michigan.

MICHAEL MOODIE is a Research Fellow at the Center for Strategic and International Studies, Georgetown University. Prior to his present position he has worked at the Foreign Policy Research Institute, Philadelphia and the Institute for Foreign Policy Analysis, Cambridge, Massachusetts.

STEVEN J. ROSEN is presently with the Rand Corporation. Formerly he taught at Brandeis University and the University of Pittsburgh. He did his graduate work at Syracuse University. Dr. Rosen is the author of numerous books and articles on international relations theory and Middle Eastern affairs.

RICHARD H. WILCOX is the special assistant for information systems and former chief of the Arms Transfer Division of the U.S. Arms Control and Disarmament Agency. He has served on a variety of government advisory and study groups both on arms transfers and on information systems, and is the author of numerous papers and co-editor of three books on information systems and on emergency operations.

HERBERT WULF is presently a fellow at the Institute für Friedensforschung und Sicherheitspolitik an der Universität Hamburg (Institute for Peace Research and Security Policy at the University of Hamburg). He has taught at the Universities of Berlin (Free University), Bremen, and Hamburg and served with the German Volunteer Service in India for four years. He is author of several articles on arms transfers and arms production and co-author of *Rüstung und Unterentwicklung* (Armaments and Underdevelopment), Reinbek 1976 and *Arbeitsplätze durch Rüstung?* (Jobs through Arms?), Reinbek 1978.